D1565983

THE
NOTEBOOKS
OF
SOLOGDIN

DIMITRI PANIN

THE NOTEBOOKS OF SOLOGDIN

Translated by John Moore

Harcourt Brace Jovanovich

New York and London

Printed in the United States of America

Library of Congress Cataloging in Publication Data

Panin, Dimitriĭ Mikhaĭlovich, 1911–
   The notebooks of Sologdin.

   Translation of Zapiski Sologdina.
   1. Panin, Dimitriĭ Mikhaĭlovich, 1911–
2. Political prisoners—Russia—Personal narrative
3. Russia—Social conditions—1917–   I. Title.
DK268.P26A3913   365′.45′0924   [B]   75–29051

ISBN 0-15-166995-3

First edition

B C D E

CONTENTS

Introduction   xi

1   Sketches from the Early Past   3

   After the Cataclysm: The Death Blow Falls
     on Holy Russia
   The Thirties

2   The First Year in Prison   17

   Arrest
   The Interrogation
   Lefortovo
   Butyrki

3   The First Transport   33

   How We Greeted the War in Butyrki
   The "Angry *Frayers*"
   How Baron Hildebrand "Fed Propaganda"
     to Minister Yezhoz
   How a Chief Prosecutor for the Republic
     Continued to Climb Over Corpses

The World Behind Prison Bars as a Mirror
    of Soviet Society
The Heathen
Militiaman in Sheep's Clothing

4   Vyatlag: The First Year of the War   46

How Prince Sapieha Met His Quota
Quarantine
The Kuban Cossacks
The Engineers
Those Who "Wear Out" First
White and Blue
How We Fed the Men
How Stalin's Camps Achieved the Same Results
    as Hitler's Gas Chambers

5   Vyatlag: The First Year of the War (Continued) 69

How Our Neighbors Outside Acquired New Clothes
Glory to the Finns!
One Day in the Life of Our Brigade and How It
    Survived the Winter
"You Can Die Today, and I'll Die Tomorrow"
"Captain Borisov's Dacha"
Dancing on the Edge of the Grave
Former Party Members
The Worst Kind of Death
Death's Dwelling Place
Self-Mutilation
How to Keep One's Human Decency in Camp

6   Vyatlag: 1942–1943   88

The Uprising at Ust-Usa
The Red Terror in the Camps
How I Helped to Get the Production of War
    Matériel Under Way

Mistakes in the Conduct of the War
Where Stalin Got the Principles for
    Organizing His Army

7   Vyatlag: 1942–1943 (Continued)   113

Planning an Escape
Some Who Got Away
Dangerous Talk
A Reptile Bites Surreptitiously, a Rat May
    Spring at You
Never Say Die!

8   Vyatlag: 1942–1943 (Continued)   130

The Arrest of the Twenty-Eight
The Camp Interrogation
A Devilish Temptation
Prokhorych's Discovery

9   Lom-Lopata   150

The Holy Terror of Vyatlag
How I Nearly Lost an Eye
The Magic Circle
Mortal Combat
The Secret of the Slavic Soul

10   The Miracle   161

Why We Did Not Die of Hunger in the Camp Jail
Rules for a Starving Man
The Swede's Secret
Death from Loving Hands
A Vow to God
A Miracle on the Fortieth Day
Inspired Goodness

11   The Last Months in Vyatlag   173

     Gifts from Izolda
     A Woman's Heart
     The Question of Caution
     A Nonprejudiced Discussion of Race
     The Leader Who Might Have Been

12   The Transport to Vorkuta   195

     You Cannot Bargain with the Devil
     A Troubled Journey
     A New Year's Toast

13   Vorkuta   213

     Which Camps Were Worse
     "A Trite and Bourgeois Mind"
     The Secret Millionaire

14   Vorkuta (Continued)   222

     The Jugglers
     A Test of My Professional Ability
     "His Lowness"
     On the Wings of Love
     Robin Hoods
     The Prisoner's Code

15   On the Way to Moscow   242

     Execution of Criminals
     A Forerunner of the Dissidents of the Sixties
     Kirov Transit Prison Revisited
     Prince Sviatopolk-Mirski
     Grigori Gryaznoi

My Meeting With Lev Kopelev
The Sailor from Auschwitz

16   At the Sharashka: 1947–1950   262

On Meeting Solzhenitsyn
The Prisoner's Eighth Commandment
"The Language of Maximum Clarity"
The Rehabilitation of Sologdin

17   At the Sharashka (Continued)   275

The Pure in Heart
The Potapovs
The Old and the Young
A Twentieth-Century Faust

18   At the Hard Labor Camp: 1950–1953   286

Stalin's Brand of Hard Labor
Encounters Along the Way
The Blessing
Peschanlag-Steplag
The BUR

19   At the Hard Labor Camp (Continued)   303

A Setback for the Chekist Terrorists
Strength of Spirit
The Storming of the Prison
Reprisals

INTRODUCTION

My decision to write these *Notebooks* rose from a sense of obligation to make the public aware of what my mental activity over many years finally led to and of the conditions that had shaped it. Behind all this lies the fact that it was my generation which fell into the midst of chaos, shattered traditions, and wholesale destruction of the social order. The church was being crushed, the old authorities were being liquidated, and a strenuous effort was in motion to supplant them with idols cast in a new mold.

The crimes and errors of that generation were reflected in my own life, even though by virtue of upbringing—at least until 1917—I had greater protection against them than many of my age, especially those who had entered the world via smoky village shacks, wretched city slums, one-horse towns, whistle stops, or backwaters on the edge of the map.

Like a tiny living cell, each fact holds something striking, mysterious, instructive; frequently we manage to discover just what it is. The bare facts of those frightful years carried impressions of similar force and in themselves may shed as much light on that era as any detailed analysis might. Here they will mainly serve as the basis of my attempt to make sense out of those years—those years which I submit to your judgment.

I am never given to exaggeration. I prefer calling things by their right names. I haven't the nerve to touch up the evidence or keep it under cover as if it didn't exist. In these *Notebooks* I will strive toward the truth and nothing else, with regard to myself. With regard to others, I will do the utmost to avoid inaccuracies.

After I came over to the free world, new friends advised me to delay publication of my manuscript, *The Oscillative World,* which I had written while still in the Soviet Union. Instead, they suggested that I preface it with these notes so the general reader might learn something of what I had lived through and that I describe the lot of ordinary working people in Russia after the 1917 disaster (one of international consequence).

I believe I have earned the right to serve as their spokesman and champion, since for forty years I myself was a working man, sometimes for pay and other times under coercion. I had more than a taste of all forms of Soviet exploitation. Not only did I risk my neck in Stalin's camps; I also watched how thousands around me were dying off. No wonder that I feel compelled to share with you the experience accumulated during the battle for my life and the lives of my friends.

Of my sixteen years in confinement this volume takes in the thirteen spent in jails and forced labor camps.

Even to me it often seems incredible that I was able to survive everything that fate handed out. And yet, in spite of all, the grueling journey could have been worse. In prisons and transports I put in a total of three years. Thanks to my profession as a mechanical engineer, my term at common labor[1] was limited to six months. I did not end up felling timber at the logging grounds; I did not have to go down the shafts of the coal mines. They did not send me out on road construction or to the copper mines or to the legendary and tragic Kolyma. But I must say right now that nobody should get the notion that the camp was in any way a recreational center for engineers or a debating society. A large number of highly trained technicians perished there at common labor. Only a combination of inner strength and good luck could help one pull through. Apart from the rest of the ordeal, the food ration in Stalin's camps and prisons was by itself enough to wreck the health of the sturdiest man over a course of thirteen years.

Although long past, the events of those thirteen years lie deep in the consciousness. I see them as clearly as if they had happened only yesterday. But passing time has produced its blessings. I can now look at things objectively; personal feelings no longer cloud my view; the pain of insult and injury has receded into the past along with the events. At last I am able to draw up a strict account of my conclusions and judgments.

The title of my work, *The Notebooks of Sologdin,* has its origin in

1. Common labor refers to work in lumber camps, mines, building sites, on road construction, etc. The overwhelming majority of prisoners were employed in this way and were expected to meet impossibly high production quotas in intolerable conditions.

Solzhenitsyn's novel *The First Circle,* a vivid and honest record of that era. His leading characters are based on models in real life, and one of them, Sologdin, is my literary double. It is in his name that I pass on to you something from those times.

It has happened to them according to the true proverb,
The dog turns back to his own vomit,
and the sow is washed only to wallow in the mire.
—2 Peter 2 : 22

THE
NOTEBOOKS
OF
SOLOGDIN

1

SKETCHES FROM
THE EARLY PAST

After the Cataclysm: The Death Blow
Falls on Holy Russia

In this chapter I shall touch on the more salient features of my forma-
tive years, but only in outline. Although I am past sixty years of age and
in broken health, it is still my hope, God willing, to elaborate on that
earlier period in a second collection of notes. Right now, I must explain
to you briefly how it happened that a twenty-nine-year-old engineer who
was neither a thief nor a murderer landed in prison. Not until sixteen
years later did I return to Moscow. Thanks to Stalin's death, my sentence
to permanent exile was repealed, and, luckier than the majority of *zeks,*
I was partially rehabilitated in this life rather than the next.

After 1917 most of Russia's dissident intellectuals left with the White
emigration. The country, enslaved by a Communist dictatorship, was
drained of men capable of heading a liberation movement. Many of the
tsarist officers had been killed in the Civil War or finished off by the
Chekists[1] during the purges. Others had gone abroad. Those who had
switched over to the Red Army and come out alive lacked moral fiber
and strength of will. They had become men submissively awaiting their
last hour. The rest of society, the intelligentsia, as they were popularly
termed, were no less docile. All they could do was sputter to no effect

1. Members of the Cheka, as secret police created by Lenin on December 25,
1917. Later called successively, OGPU, NKVD, MVD, MGB, and at the present
time KGB (Committee on State Security).

and giggle up their sleeves. It was in their midst that I spent my childhood and early youth. At first I listened to their talk avidly, but later on I saw them as a generation of bankrupts with neither ideas nor ideals. Nor had they any resolve to stand up and fight.

The so-called "February Revolution" (1917) was stamped on my very young mind as a sudden breakdown of civil order and plain good manners, as a time of foul speech and insolent behavior, of ominous mass meetings. The filthy streets, with husks of sunflower seeds everywhere under foot, remained unswept. Dogs that had been gunned down lay around on snowbanks. Soldiers without a trace of military bearing staggered about in mobs. Youngsters with tense, wolfish faces were toting weapons. The Moscow police were nowhere in sight. And the word *slabóda*[2] echoed and reechoed, justifying all sorts of meanness. These were the tender blossoms; the fruits had yet to come.

The "October Revolution" began with what Muscovites of that time christened the "October Skirmish." Only a handful of cadets stood up against the enemy. Everybody else, after changing to civvies, tried to sit it out at home and protect their own front doors—including my father, an experienced combat officer. My mother and I, by tacit agreement, came to regard him from the depths of our hearts in a different light.

That disgraceful episode released a spate of searches, arrests, and executions. The jails were overflowing. Hunger and disease became widespread. People were dying in the streets. Meat pies made with human flesh were sold in the public markets. Houses went unheated during the cold season. General lawlessness, marked by vandalism and looting, had set in. So had religious persecution. Places of worship were being converted to horse stables. And slave labor was becoming an institution. Common criminals ran riot. Any public discontent with this new order was certain to be quelled, sometimes by foreign mercenaries.

As a ten-year-old boy, I was witness to sights not to be forgotten and heard of tragedy after tragedy. At home I found the conversation of my elders enlightening, and I soaked it up like a sponge. It was keynoted by criticism and derision of the Bolsheviks and their actions. Although the point of it was often beyond my childish grasp, I gained a general notion of Lenin and Trotsky as blind maniacs, brazen liars, ardent atheists, bitter enemies of Russia, amateurs in all matters except violence and oppression.

Our house was a gathering place for Moscow intellectuals (as they

2. An illiterate pronunciation of the Russian word for "freedom."

4

would be called nowadays): engineers, actresses, professors, school-teachers. None of them had ties with revolutionary factions. They were not involved in politics. Even the best informed had only a superficial knowledge of Marxism. These were the same people who had previously heaped abuse on the tsarist government, licked their chops over the Rasputin scandal, indulged in wishful thinking about revolution, sung the praises of leftist orators in the Duma,[3] but after the cataclysm, the fire of their eloquence was directed (this time with complete justice) at the usurpers of power and their crimes. To this day I remember details from their accounts of the atrocities then being committed. I also recall their announcements of the glad tidings that the Bolsheviks were about to flee, that they were going to be evacuated from the Kremlin by plane. Trotsky, they added, was threatening to slam the door behind them by blowing up Moscow as they left. They expected troops to arrive from the Entente, pinned their hopes first on Denikin and then on Wrangel,[4] prophesied the regime's early collapse. With gleeful dilgence they repeated the current rumors that Lenin had syphilis, that it would lead eventually to creeping paralysis and total insanity. I was to see the absurdity behind much of their talk in retrospect just a few years later. For a youngster it had been natural enough to swallow such nonsense, although not everything they said could be called that. Nevertheless, some scraps of worthwhile ideas found their way into my consciousness, and in times ahead I frequently pondered them, turning them over in my mind and fathoming their meaning.

The Western reader may have difficulty imagining to what extent during that period young students in the U.S.S.R. were cut off from the cultural sources of the world. After coming to the West in 1972, I pounced on books that all our lives we had only dreamed of. In Moscow I had succeeded in getting acquainted with a few of them, but only during my last five years there.

What extraordinary privileges my contemporaries among the White émigrés were able to enjoy in the West. They had the heroes of the White Army, bathed in the glory of recent battles, to sustain their spirits. They attended a free church. They were brought up in a highly civilized environment. They were able to read the works of Russia's world-renowned writers and philosophers. They had access to the treasures of libraries and museums. They were reaping the blessings of democratic freedom.

3. The Russian parliament, 1905–1917.
4. Russian generals who headed the struggle against the Bolsheviks in the civil war.

We in Soviet Russia, on the other hand, had to contend with former military officers quite lacking in initiative—time-servers and renegades who had sold out to the enemy. The majority were ashamed of their Red Army service. When asked why they hadn't gone over to the Whites, they either pleaded that they had been "mobilized" or kept silent.

There were still a few intellectuals who had escaped execution right after 1917. In the years immediately following the cataclysm, one still encountered them among small circles of friends and acquaintances and had the benefit of their candid, accurate appraisals of the past events. But since the terror machine was aimed first and foremost at people concerned with the truth, they were soon silenced or disappeared. The younger intellectuals adopted protective covering, and their views had no influence whatsoever on the life of the nation.

Next, there was the brutal uprooting of religion. Horrible persecutions were started against the church. By these means, the authorities encouraged many believers to break away. And then the active propagation of atheism began. Religious literature, as well as philosophical works unpalatable to the regime, were destroyed wholesale. Furnaces burned entire libraries down to ashes. If you were caught with books by the harmless philosopher Vladimir Soloviev in your possession, you were shipped off to Solovki.[5] Even in the major cities we lived like savages, isolated from all the intellectual trends of our time. To fill the vacuum, they pumped us full of political propaganda and other sickening rubbish, all this in an atmosphere of mutual denunciation and constant spying.

In Paris, my White contemporaries were forming various associations: Young Russians, Eurasians, Solidarists. A battle of ideas was raging, and means were being devised to bring relief to our wretched country. But in Moscow, total confusion prevailed among the educated. They were meekly resigned to their fate and gave no thought of offering resistance. The best they could do was grumble under their breath.

The regime, however, took no chances. It lavished billions of rubles on the Chekists, protecting these sinister specialists in their craft.

After graduating from a technical school in 1928, I took a job at a cement works in Podolsk.[6] I came to Moscow only on Sundays. It was a frightful year. Hundreds of churches were being systematically demolished in Moscow. In my old neighborhood, which today includes the American embassy, there were six churches. Only the Church of St. John the Baptist

5. One of the first concentration camps, created by Lenin on an island in the White Sea.
6. A city forty kilometers from Moscow.

in the Presnya district was allowed to continue functioning as a place of worship. The rest were closed, destroyed and desecrated.[7]

The Russian people, deformed by the weight of dictatorship, were being reduced to abject compliance. Never did I so much as hear of a group protest in public, and only once did I see anything remotely like it: an elderly woman was on her knees in front of a demolished cathedral, praying fervently and making the sign of the cross. People said that her husband had been the priest there and that he had died in jail a long time ago. There was also a story about a young fellow who, on seeing a bunch of vandals by the cathedral in Dorogomilov, couldn't restrain himself and hurled a brick at one of them. The youth was seized on the spot and almost certainly executed. Very likely, for this "misdemeanor" all his family was picked up and sent away. As for the famous Chapel of the Holy Mother of Iversk on Red Square, even the Chekists hesitated to put it down in broad daylight. But it made no difference, since no one would have stood up for it anyway, venerated as the chapel was. In 1931 the Cathedral of Christ the Savior, a memorial to the Patriotic War of 1812, was pulled down. It was only in country villages that people showed any opposition to the closing of churches.

In 1931 collectivization got under way in the countryside. As a townsman, I was not there to watch the process. But half the men at the cement works consisted of seasonal laborers who still kept up their rural ties, and from them I heard plenty of tales. Those just coming back from village jobs brought fresh news that made your hair stand on end. Since the days of Attila and Genghis Khan, the world had not been witness to mindless cruelty on such a colossal scale. After the liquidation of the so-called kulaks,[8] a special campaign was organized to wipe out by starvation the inhabitants of certain regions in the Ukraine, in the Kuban, and along the Don. The number who died exceeded sixteen million. The best of the peasantry were driven out of their villages and herded into unheated cattle cars. They were permitted to take almost nothing with them. During the journey they were frequently deprived of food and water. Cries and howls from the trains filled the stations en route and echoed over the surrounding countryside: "Give us something to drink. Something to drink!" As a rule, the men were separated from the rest and dispatched to penal camps. Their families soon perished. The children were the first to die. A few of these people succeeded in clinging to

7. All former churches, chapels, monasteries, and other ecclesiastical buildings became the property of the local authorities, who used them as warehouses, workshops, prisons, cinemas, and clubs.

8. Literally, "a fist": the term for well-to-do peasants, who were the first to be designated for mass destruction.

the soil. They dug out shelters and, by some miracle, rustled up enough food to sustain them until they could cultivate a small patch of ground in the spring. But the Chekists appeared on the scene and moved them farther north. Except for those who either fled or stayed under cover, not many survived. In the districts that Stalin had condemned to death by famine, it was hell on earth. Whole communities were exterminated; mothers ate their children; the men, after dragging themselves to the railroad stations, often got a bullet in the head for "sabotaging collectivization."

But it was the intellectuals who were under closest surveillance and were most subject to intimidation: the destruction of the peasantry and the church had been preceded by the Shakhty trial of "wreckers"[9] in 1928. As part of their primary goal of demolishing the very foundations of Holy Russia, the authorities hammered without letup at the professional people, especially at the strongest in that class—the engineers. The sole purpose of this was to intimidate the intellectual sector of society and to nullify its influence. In such an unnatural atmosphere the average citizen came to regard an engineer or, for that matter, any educated man, as though he were an enemy, a possible saboteur. The constant reign of terror achieved its end: any thought of running counter to the will of the dictatorship now seemed inconceivable, unrealistic, or adolescent.

Despite this prevailing attitude, I considered myself at eighteen mature enough for involvement in the events then taking place. As I fumed and raged, argued and debated, I was convinced of the need to move over to the offensive, to render some kind of help to the peasants and the church. My older companions brushed me aside as a mule-headed kid. Since their minds were bent on graduating from the university, in marrying, on discovering how to live undisturbed through the repressions, they cracked open my arguments like so many sunflower seeds. I heard repeatedly, "Listen, mamma's boy: you don't know what life is all about." They suggested that I take a long, close look at reality and reflect on the line-up of brute force that was confronting us: they were sure that if I did, my wild fantasies would evaporate. But youths of my own age were attracted to my appeals for action.

In those days not all of us could get into the colleges and universities, and even for those who aspired to a higher education labor service to the state was a prerequisite.[10] Around that time a schoolmate of mine and

9. The defendants in the trial were engineers falsely accused of sabotage. This was pure slander, but they were convicted and many were shot.

10. In 1928, there was a secret government directive according to which only members of the party and Komsomol (the Communist Youth League) and workers could be admitted to institutions of higher education.

his two companions were arrested. Since I had my job in Podolsk, I hadn't been seeing much of them. Otherwise, I might very well have been picked up with them.

It became clear to me that young people like ourselves could become a formidable movement if we were guided by a veteran conspirator who knew how to operate. I turned my efforts to locating such a man. I asked my father about it, begged him to help. He shrugged his shoulders; at least he wasn't abusive. Evidently, down deep, he approved of my ardor. It was during that period that my mother died. I thus lost an opportunity to join one of the underground religious groups. She no doubt knew something about them, for she had devoted her last years to the church. My own search ended in failure. All I met with along the way were frightened glances, and all I heard were pleas to reconsider my position and not bring ruin down on the heads of my intimates.

In the spring of 1930 friends reported that a revolt had flared up in the Kuban. I had no idea of where it was centered and was without a single contact in that region. There was nobody I could turn to for advice: it was harebrained even to think about going there. Nonetheless, I did try for a leave of absence from the cement plant, though to tell the truth, I didn't work at it very hard—I was not ready for a sudden leap into the unknown. Finally, in early September, I headed for Novorossisk.

On the train I encountered a young man who, because he didn't have a ticket, had been hiding out among the baggage. He had taken part in the Don Cossack uprising that only recently had been crushed. He informed me that in both the Don and Kuban regions the resistance itself had been smashed by tanks and aircraft. Most of the rebels had been slaughtered; only a small number got away. Red troops were rounding up all suspected parties and shipping them en masse into exile. I split what cash I had with the Cossack youth; then we went off in separate directions.

After returning to Moscow, I ceased speaking out for immediate action. I now understood that without leadership, experience, and knowledge, one could do nothing in such terrible circumstances except to keep oneself in readiness and be on the alert for the signal, which of necessity had to come from abroad.

In the years 1929 and 1930, my generation was growing up and getting considerably smarter. My friends and I frequently talked about a war of liberation led by the West. The need was urgent; we saw that the dictatorship had sunk to the level of cannibalism. We never spoke of the real wrongdoers who had dragged the nation through one tragic disaster after another. We were more inclined to put the blame on those who had left us leaderless, without ideas or moral support. The war with

Poland and the peasant revolts had afforded golden opportunities to carry out plans for an offensive and to correct mistakes the Whites had made in the land question.[11] With youthful straightforwardness, we voiced outrage at the pitiful performance of the tsarist officers who had gone over to the Red Army. But the burden of our recriminations fell on Denikin. Erroneously, we thought that his White forces around Novorossisk had been evacuated to Constantinople instead of the Crimea, where Wrangel, as it seemed to us, had held out with only a part of the White Army. We had been enraptured by Denikin's earlier brilliant victories, thus it was hard for us to understand why he couldn't have made a successful stand, at least in the Crimea. In our opinion, the Crimea should have been retained at any cost. If a region consisting of the Crimea, the Kuban, some of the Don Cossack *stanitsas,*[12] Novorossisk, and the Caucasus could have been kept in White hands, this territory would have become Russia's bastion of freedom. We would have known where to look for refuge and leadership, and White agents could have infiltrated the rest of the country. In such circumstances collectivization might have been averted and with it the systematic decimation of the populace. Forces might have been built up in the countryside which, through a united effort, could have put an end to Stalin's dictatorship. This free Russian territory would have served the West as an effective outpost from which to combat the spread of the Red plague. Our discussions at that time led to these conclusions:

— Through its hirelings (Chekists and party members), the Stalinist regime continually fanned the flames of class hatred. The fact that it was so ingeniously contrived in those years made it all the more loathsome.

— As to whether our nation should revert to capitalism, we had no doubts whatsoever. We would have consented even to its primitive nineteenth-century form. After all, slavery as we now know it did not exist then; labor was voluntary; capitalists could be bargained with; legislative bodies and philanthropists often promoted the welfare of the working man. "The ulcers of capitalism" could in no way compare with the system of "triumphant socialism"[13] unfolding in our midst and begetting forced labor, perpetual famine, cannibalism in the villages, religious persecution, bestiality. How was it possible, we wondered, that men could make such sacrifices, even lay down their lives, in order to

11. The collapse of the White movement was due primarily to their clumsy policy with regard to land distribution.
12. Villages.
13. Two stock phrases of Soviet propaganda.

preserve a system built on fear and repression? To die for a noble idea commands admiration, but to perform a heroic act on behalf of a nightmarish horror is stupid and appalling. We young people could not understand why these willing victims had not listened to the voices of wisdom warning them of everything to come. Instead, they succumbed to the promises of the demagogues and slipped the yoke around everyone's neck, including their own.

— We strongly condemned the attitude of Russia's World War I allies toward the White movement. The Whites had tried to save Russia—and the rest of the world as well—from impending disaster. They held faithfully to the obligations they had assumed. By and large, they were honorable men with whom it would have been possible to conclude treaties and establish relations. The West turned its back on the Whites in the belief that the Red government would be too weak to present any danger. In fact, however, the Red regime became a permanent threat to Western civilization. Thus the Allies gave up a friend in exchange for a ruthless foe; lost an enormous market and their capital investments in Russia, as well as the possibility of the repayment of tsarist debts; and virtually assisted in the formation of the Communist state.

A huge country, basically Christian, had been made over into a nursery for rearing a new breed of men under conditions of widescale terror and atheism. A new society, governed by primitives, began taking shape. Without asking the consent of the peasants or anyone else, the party heads, to achieve their own ends, unleashed their thugs over our vast land and fettered it in slavery. The young Communist state proceeded to mutilate and crush whatever opposed it, secular or sacred, to bury human life under atrocities.

The Thirties

During the 1920's, France and England were still applying verbal pressure on the U.S.S.R. In 1927 Chamberlain issued his famous ultimatum, unique in the annals of history. But none if this was taken very seriously in Russia. Sure of the West's reluctance to start a war with them, the Soviet bosses did not back down. They would hardly have dared undertake the collectivization and liquidation of the peasants had they felt less secure. The West let slip by those years so favorable to the military destruction of Red tyranny. All this at first amazed and then disillusioned us.

11

Meanwhile, the Soviets were telling the people, in order more easily to enslave them, that war was inevitable. People who shared my way of thinking actually wanted war to come; we still had some hope for assistance from White émigré leaders. I continued to envision someone my own age coming over to us secretly with an arsenal of practical instructions and ideas. I imagined that he would remain with us. Probably, he would have to enroll in the Komsomol[14] in order to make his position look legitimate and to gain access to the heart of many events. Such a pipe dream reveals my inexperience and ignorance. My White agent would have lasted no time; fanatical young Reds, drilled in the spirit of class hatred and "vigilance," were always on the lookout for infiltrators.

In 1930 a massive campaign was started in the factories to induct entire shops into the Communist party. Pleading youth and immaturity, I got out of joining the party; but I did enter the Komsomol. I decided that this would be the best way to penetrate into the enemy camp.

Sometime later, I realized I could achieve my aim just as easily outside the ranks of the Komsomol, especially since I was a member in name only. I stayed away from meetings and played no role in serious decision-making. But though I saw I had made a mistake in joining this organization, I could not resign—an open break would have carried the threat of prison. I had to sweat it out until they considered me old enough to be crossed off the rolls officially. All the time I was a member I had a feeling of shameful complicity.

The period that followed seemed like a walk over a tightrope stretched above a horrible, evil-smelling quicksand bog. You try to keep your balance, then you get caught in high wind and driving hail; your legs cramp up; you lose your balance and drop into the mire below. But you keep your grip on the rope. You pull yourself out and continue your way.

A godless dictatorship both sullies and disfigures a man. Only a deep religious faith can provide him with stout armor. When the church is destroyed and people are left on their own, it is easy for them to fall in with evil schemes.

The youth of Paris and Berlin knew the reality behind Hitler's national socialism and Mussolini's fascism. In 1932 articles abusive of the Nazis began appearing in Soviet newspapers. The Nazis' theory of racial superiority and the aggression that it generated naturally provoked our sharp disapproval. I never met a single man in the Soviet Union who made excuses for them. Nonetheless, Hitler's promise of a war against Stalin gave the hope, strength, and patience we needed for enduring a terrible existence while we awaited the hour of our opportunity. Russians in all

14. The Young Communist League.

walks of life expected there would be a war of liberation; it made no difference to them who triggered it off. Our constant dream was that war would start very soon.

Hitler's support of the anticommunist forces in Spain spoke in his favor. Germany and Italy offered the Spanish government help at the very time when the chief Western powers had decided against intervention in the civil war. Communists the world over were obviously in league against anticommunist Spain. Spies, Chekists, and Soviet pilots, as well as weapons and equipment were pouring in from the U.S.S.R. From many countries volunteers flocked into the international brigades. Under these circumstances, nonintervention practically guaranteed handing Spain over piecemeal to the world communists.

The aid given to the Spanish nation by the Germans and Italians was just the kind we had had dire need of in 1918–1920. At the time we were not at all interested in how much the Franco regime differed from the Western democracies—as slaves under a dictatorship, we could not afford the luxury of such fine distinctions; therefore we gave Spain's indomitable anticommunists our approval and support. We were opposed to slavery and oppression, no matter under whose flag.

The Spanish Civil War coincided with the period when Stalinist terror was at its peak. People were so thoroughly scared that conversations in which there was the slightest allusion to politics broke off abruptly. Contacts were broken, acquaintances given up; everybody crawled inside his own shell. But every evening I feasted my soul on the scanty reports in *Izvestia* of events in Spain. Despite the bias and strict censorship that characterized the Soviet news media, reports on the Spanish Army, the Moroccans, and the Foreign Legion aroused my admiration. In daydreams I was with them: my intuition told me what was happening in Spain. The accuracy of my speculations was to be confirmed fifteen years later when I met a prisoner of war from Italy who had been sent to the penal camp because of his Russian origins. He had been a movie cameraman on the Franco side. His account of the Spanish Civil War entirely bore out the conclusions I had reached by myself. He told of the huge role played by the regular army in its all-out defense of Nationalist Spain and by the crack units of staunch Nationalists from the various provinces. These constituted the brain of the army and gave it the will to victory; these men were convinced that their cause was just; they were resolved to drive the Red plague out of Spain or die in the attempt. With rapture the ex-cameraman described the toughness and courage of tiny garrisons surrounded by the numerically superior enemy. He talked about the defenders of the Alcazar—young cadets from the military academies—and told the story of the garrison commander's son, held hostage by the Republicans, who telephoned his father to urge him not to let the garrison fall, even if it cost his life. "I am dying for Spain!" the boy had cried.

The cameraman compared the Moroccans with the Foreign Legion. Even behind the Iron Curtain we were familiar with the Legion's glorious deeds—we had read of them in translation back in the twenties. The Moroccans also had delighted our imaginations. In Spain's civil war they fought in fierce, bloody battles, and served her as a pillar of strength.

In every religion there is something noble, something unique. In the Moslem faith it is a strongly developed sense of loyalty, and during the Spanish Civil War the worthy followers of Mohammed brilliantly demonstrated this strength. Evidently, in the Moroccan encampments was the elite of the Moslem warrior caste.

To the Foreign Legionnaires, also, the Italian gave unstinting praise. Heedless of danger, they had rushed into hand-to-hand combat with the battle cry, "Long live Death!" They once completed a forced march of two hundred kilometers in twenty-four hours, each in only rope sandals and carrying a rifle, a canteen, and a day's ration. Catching the enemy unawares, they swarmed over him.

And so the Italian cameraman corroborated what I had deduced long before: the entire Spanish army was irrevocably on the side of the Nationalist movement. Moroccan and Foreign Legion units, loyal and reliable, had joined with the army and fought right up to the final victory. Franco received only limited aid from Italy and Germany; the Soviet Union gave the Republicans all the help they wanted; yet despite the Red terror organized on orders from Moscow, the Nationalist army was imbued with the courage and will to fight. As a result, they won the victory.

Since that day in 1917 when the Cheka was set up, a campaign of terror has been going on continuously. In their war against the population all the advantages have been on the side of the Chekists.

From 1929 to 1932 the main thrust was aimed at the peasantry; from 1936 to 1939, at the Communist party and its echelons. For sheer violence, the weeding out of party members may be compared with the liquidation of the old social order during the Civil War. The 1937 campaign of terror gained widespread notoriety because it first hit the leadership before spreading downward. This was the most thorough of all the "purges," since almost everybody in the nation was caught up in it one way or another. All the top officials in the hierarchy were sent flying to hell, right on the heels of their department chief. Everyone implicated was pressured into making formal denunciations of his associates. The various reminiscences and memoirs of that era deal in the main with party members; the fact is that millions of victims are left out of these accounts, or appear only vaguely in the background. I consider it extremely important that surviving witnesses leave behind, if only for the historians, a truthful record of their experiences.

The weight of the growing terror meant that even one's closest friends might slam the door in one's face. Knowing my uncompromising position, my acquaintances kept me at a healthy distance. By the end of 1936, I was quite isolated; yet I felt no resentment. I understood that in such terrible times this was the only choice most people had, and yet the future was to confirm more than once my conviction that those who are afraid of rocking the boat, no matter how appalling the situation, are rather puny specimens.

In the summer of 1937 I was married. In the past I had sought out girls with views similar to my own, but to no avail: you cannot tell the heart how to run its business. I chose a wife who was lovely, but she had a Soviet-trained mind. From childhood I had been taught that a beautiful lady was to be waited on, that she was to be spared the savage conflicts of male society, that though the world at large might be a battleground, a man at home could disarm and rest. This universal formula might once have been valid, but in our artificial hell of terror I had stumbled on a booby trap.

As the purges spread, the official disregard for human life worked me into a frenzy. After losing my audience of friends and unable to vent my feelings to the woman then dearest to me, I poured out my fury to the relatives who still kept in touch with me, to casual acquaintances, even to workers I had never previously met. The total dissent that I experienced during this most horrible period was shaping my life in earnest and setting it in a definite direction. I felt that my instinct, sharpened in the extreme, would protect me from mistakes, and, in fact, I was not betrayed at that time but was denounced only later.

The Soviet system was coming to its apogee: the tyrant had been made into a god; cringing servility was universal; mockery and torture had reached their peak; Chekist cellars ran with sacrificial blood; and the purge of the party went on relentlessly. As a consequence, both the army and the industry were leaderless. This meant opportunities for overthrowing the regime during the approaching military conflict. I had no doubt about it; I had thought it over hundreds of times. I awaited my chance with fierce impatience, fearfully aware that for every Communist who was liquidated seven or eight ordinary citizens lost their lives. The value of a man's life had been reduced to a scrap of paper—to informer's reports, often anonymous, sometimes written up by insane people. Anything at all was grist for the mill. In those days prison sentence for some petty crime could prove to be a man's salvation from destruction by terror striking at random. Life was becoming irrational. There were the phrases about vigilance, about "building socialism," about "the intrigues of the class enemy," all of which helped turn people into unthinking, applauding executors of "the will of the party and the government." With such clichés Stalin and his flunkies forced people to inhuman, repulsive behavior. Against this background of a tooth-and-nail power struggle, I perceived the truth of the old principle: the world can advance toward its golden age not through cannibalism, but only through great and tested ideas.

2

THE FIRST YEAR IN PRISON

Arrest

In the autumn of 1939, shortly before the start of the Second World War, I was at a rest resort in the Crimea. There I had an opportunity to see things in the Soviet Union as they actually were. In 1936 I had earned a degree in mechanical engineering and had been immediately offered a graduate studentship. From then on, I had been in triple harness: studying, working for a menial wage, and moonlighting; all this so that I might be able to support a wife. Consequently, I indulged pleasurably in my well-deserved rest down South. I tried not to think about anything. I didn't even seek the company of others. But early one evening while I was sitting alone on a bench outside, another guest of the rest house came over and sat down next to me. I could not help but notice him, probably because of his round, rather comic eyes, which were very expressive. He had the strange surname of Podushko.[1] He was bursting with a desire to pour out his soul, to unburden himself completely. I myself had often experienced the same urge. By showing him that I understood how he felt, I was rewarded with an astonishing tale.

He was an agronomist from Voronezh. The secret police had arrested him in 1938, had held him in a cellar, had beaten him, and allowed him no sleep. After the removal of Yezhov and the appointment of Beria as head of the NKVD (People's Commissariat of Internal Affairs), some of those held for investigation were let out of jail as a public-relations gesture. Most enjoyed only a respite: a year later nearly all of those released

1. I associated it with "pillow" (*podushka*).

were back in jail. Podushko showed me a document by which he had been indicted simultaneously on almost all counts of Article 58[2]: sabotage, espionage, terrorism, treason, counterrevolutionary activity, anti-Soviet propaganda. I had lived by now twenty years under this regime, but this was the first time I had come in contact with the naked fact of monstrous injustice against a man innocent of any crime. He said in a whisper of horror, "Do you really understand what this means? I've been made into an outcast. Nobody will hire me with a document like this." The poor devil! He should have been thinking not about work, but how to get lost in the far-off Siberian taiga and bury himself in some lowly job. But at that time I was unable to give him that only bit of truly helpful advice, since I hadn't yet acquired experience in a Soviet jail. None of us on the outside had access to such wisdom. Even though people were being thrown into the prisons and camps by the millions, the few survivors coming back to the big cities kept their mouths shut, or, worse, spun reassuring yarns.

Shortly afterward, I, too, was in need of the very same advice: a reversal of fortune was awaiting me on my return to Moscow. I was offered a job in an aircraft plant. Everything had been settled, but at the last minute the personnel section[3] stepped in to say they had no work for someone with my particular qualifications. To any inmate of a penal camp the meaning of this would have been perfectly clear, but I did not catch the hint and therefore took no action to try to save myself.

Under the Soviet regime every individual trying to act alone is quite isolated. He is like a fly falling into a spider's web. Everybody around him has only one thought: "Maybe it will all blow over and I will be spared." The Chekists understood very well that only people bound together in association are capable of putting up resistance; therefore they are intent on uprooting religion; therefore their greatest efforts are directed at suppressing organization of all kinds and at isolating the individual. However often the security services themselves may be purged, such objectives remain unaltered and such methods are employed by each successive pastmaster in the art of destroying people.

The person responsible for my arrest in July, 1940, was an engineer, S. D. Klementyev (Avdeyev was his real name). He and I had worked

2. Article of the criminal code of the R.S.F.S.R. (the largest Republic of the U.S.S.R. consisting of Russia proper) which the regime applied indiscriminately to all whom it considered to be its enemies.
3. In every Soviet institution, the personnel department or the section responsible for hiring employees, includes a special section of the secret police which checks recruitment of workers on the basis of records and files.

side by side in '37 and '38. In this terrible period in our country's history I looked on him with complete trust. I am convinced, however, that this informer betrayed me later, after he had been recruited by the KGB in 1939. When he visited our communal apartment, he and I often stepped out into the hallway for a smoke and a chat. Usually my neighbor joined in. He was a middle-aged accountant, a man with a considerable sense of humor. I had recommended Klementyev for a teaching position in the Institute from which I had graduated, and there I had introduced him to a friend called Vladimir. In his denunciations to the secret police Klementyev alleged that Vladimir, my neighbor, and I had formed an anti-Soviet organization. More than thirty years have passed since that time. The accountant was rehabilitated[4]—*posthumously*—and Vladimir has had an outstanding career in science. I purposely omit their surnames in order to spare their relatives needless concern.

At that time I was not expecting any unpleasantness. It is true that I had been feeling deeply depressed every night for several days just before my arrest. Later, seeing the date on the order for my arrest, I understood that my mood had coincided with the time that my fate was being decided. The whole process—arrest, search, and finally incarceration in the inner prison of the Great Lubyanka[5]—went according to an established ritual. Solzhenitsyn in his novel *The First Circle* describes in full detail the similar ordeal of Innokenti. This was all new to me then. I had not been able to read about it anywhere, although bits and pieces of stories had come down to me at second and third hand. At first, I was simply stunned by this disastrous turn of events. After half an hour I started searching through my mind for the person responsible for getting me locked up in a place for political prisoners. I had voiced my opinions and criticisms, along with my indignation, before more people than was wise. Among others, Klementyev flashed through my mind but without leaving a trace of suspicion.

In a tiny cell called a "box," I quieted down and began thinking over my position very carefully. I did not feel like sleeping. When they brought me some bread and a mug of slop that was supposed to be tea, I was still sitting up. After eating, I fell into a kind of daze. I can't clearly remember what happened next: vague shadows flickered past, now and then a door opened, I was led out to the lavatory, they brought me some

4. I.e., cleared of charges after Stalin's death. (Tr.)
5. Name of a street and of a square in Moscow which, since the beginning of the Soviet regime, has been the location of the headquarters of the secret police and its main prison, which looms at least six stories high above the sinister dungeons below it.

food—I did everything robot-fashion. My head buzzed. I was only half-conscious. I don't know how much time went by in this way—perhaps two or three days, perhaps a week. Later, some of the prisoners said that drugs had been added to their food. Possibly that was what had happened to me. As soon as I was transferred to the common cell, my dazed condition wore off.

In the end I found myself in the interrogator's office. At first my mind was dull and my answers beside the point. I strained to focus my attention. Toward morning I began to think more clearly. From the interrogator's statements I made out that they were charging me with spreading anti-Soviet propaganda. Now I understood to whom I was obliged for landing in jail.

There are two opposite kinds of awareness: either things seem to be what the world says they are, or they are known for what they really are. From childhood on I had heard about arrests and tortures, but I didn't see them with my own eyes; I didn't experience them. Nor had I ever witnessed an execution. Knowledge gained secondhand is superficial; it does not determine a man's conduct or outlook. But real experience enters into his very being and shapes his life.

By mistreatment, abusive language, and threatening manner the interrogator soon convinced me that I had fallen into a torture chamber. Though I had not committed any real crime, it was impossible in these circumstances to put up any defense. I had become part of a massive arraignment of people who had fallen vicitm to informer's reports. We were not asked for confessions, but for supporting evidence. Everything had to square with the relevant section of Article 58 under which you had been arrested. Since there were a couple of intelligent, observant men in my cell, I was able to make a few cautious inquiries. On the basis of their various comments, I drew a set of conclusions that had great significance for me:

— Nobody is released as innocent. The Organs[6] impressed on everyone that government agencies don't make mistakes, that they do their jobs to perfection; otherwise there could be serious consequences for the interrogator and his department.

— Those who fail to supply "evidence" and try to demonstrate their innocence are beaten, tortured, and worn down by lack of sleep. The same happens to those who have to be finished off for political reasons. Like parrots, the interrogators kept repeating the words of "the great

6. This is the rather repulsive word that the KGB uses to describe itself.

proletarian humanist"[7] Gorki: "If the enemy does not give in, he will be destroyed."

— After the removal of Yezhov in 1938 the interrogators were allowed to apply physical measures of persuasion only with specific permission. Torture was now administered only in cases regarded by them as being particularly important; in 1937 its use had been much more general. In compensation, they now resorted to mental pressures of a more refined sort, such as the questioning of friends and relatives.

The Interrogation

As a man instinctively opposed to the dictatorship, I could not bring myself to protest my innocence as a loyal supporter of the regime. This would not have helped me in any case: Klementyev had given too many details about me, and his reports could easily be confirmed by the interrogation of my two associates. I thought it would be enough just to corroborate Klementyev's report, to add a few extra details, and thus to enable the interrogator to tie up his case against me without more ado. I would then get my due punishment, and no one else would be put in jeopardy. But this did not satisfy the Chekists. In accordance with their standing instructions, they were expected to show that anyone jailed for any kind of opposition against the authorities must certainly belong to some organization, even if it consisted of a mere handful of members. The Organs thereby proved their vigilance and ability to protect society against enemy activity even before it got off the ground. Thus the line of conduct that I had planned was futile. Politely but unequivocally, I set forth my objections to the regime. When I had finished, the interrogator said:

"Now, tell me, to whom did you say all this?"

"Klementyev."

"Anybody else?"

"No one else. Klementyev took a great interest and said even stronger things himself, always trying to sound out my views. But because of all the arrests, people live very isolated lives and speak to no one except members of their families. I had no conversations with anyone else."

"Don't lie! Didn't you talk to so-and-so (here he gave the names of my two 'accomplices')? You're lying. We know everything."

7. Standard way of referring to Gorki in the Soviet press.

They were determined to make me confess that I had talked with these two people. In spite of this, I held firm through several nights and kept repeating, "Let them speak for themselves." Then they switched tactics. "All right then, we'll go into this with your relatives and acquaintances. They'll tell us a great deal about you."

From the little prison experience I had had up to that time, plus bits of knowledge I had picked up in the cell from others under interrogation, I was able to make some precise mathematical deductions. I saw that I would have to take the interrogation into my own hands. I thought as hard as I could; my instincts were working overtime. Relatives and acquaintances passed in review through my mind. It was all too easy for the authorities to track them down, since all my associations were known to them already. I was by now well aware of the utter ruthlessness of the Chekists, of their freedom to apply any pressures they decided on, of their professional skill when it came to frightening people and forcing them to loosen their tongues.

And I also knew how my various friends and relatives would react. It was clear to me that if the interrogator made good his threat, a score of people would be ruined. Each person he could trick and bully would begin by telling him something about my views. Then they would confirm whatever the investigator seemed to want confirmed. And when he came to worm out of them my scathing opinions of Stalin, he would have no trouble at all in conjuring up a picture of a vast organization of terrorists, saboteurs, and subversives. As a result, five men would be shot and twenty others would get sent up for ten years. (My supposition was, incidentally, fully borne out by something that happened in 1956, at the peak of the rehabilitation program, when the authorities called in to the prosecutor six people who were either relatives or pre-war acquaintances of mine. Even though we were in the "liberal" Khrushchev era when nothing threatened them, five characterized me as a hard-core subversive and an enemy of the Stalinist regime. On that basis I was turned down for rehabilitation. One can imagine what they might have said about me at the height of the terror in the forties.)

After putting up some token resistance, I therefore decided to meet my interrogator halfway by confessing to conversations with my "accomplices." The Chekists kept their stool pigeon and "seksot,"[8] Klementyev,

8. Abbreviation for "secret collaborator."

out of the case, despite my efforts to involve him. They thus got what they were after, and the investigation was over in four months—a fast job for those days. At the time I felt certain of the rightness of my conduct during the interrogation and suffered no pangs of conscience afterward. I only cursed myself for having allowed the situation to arise in the first place. But as time went by, I took a critical view of my behavior, and no matter how often I looked at it, the verdict came out guilty.

My mortal sin did not lie in the fact that I had a burning hatred of our diabolical regime and therefore argued and protested against it, but in the fact that I had not taken into account our unique, ingeniously contrived system and had not restricted my contacts to a small group of intimate friends bound together by unbreakable bonds of loyalty. Instead, I had cast pearls before people who could see no value whatsoever in them. I had been soaring to unrealistic heights, waiting for envoys from the West, while just below me was an underground church that I had never taken the time to look at closely. During the Stalinist era it was only tiny underground cells that held out any promise of genuine struggle, and of the creation of a new Russian elite. In such "microfraternities" we have a reliable means of fighting tyranny. But I did not come to this realization until much later.

Lefortovo

At the end of the fourth month, when the interrogation had been virtually completed, I was suddenly charged with treason against the fatherland, under Article 58, Section 1A. In the pre-war years this was the most terrifying charge of all, comparable only to terrorism and espionage. Anyone convicted on Article 58, Section 1A ended up in the death cell. But strangely enough, in the face of this new accusation my spirit lightened. I said to myself, "Now the battle lines are really drawn. My hands are no longer tied. They can't get anything out of my relatives on this score—this is a very different matter from a charge of spreading anti-Soviet propaganda."

Several nights later, I was out of my cell with my things and driven off in the "Black Maria." I realized immediately that they were transferring me to Lefortovo. This had once been a prison for military offenders, but now investigations of the most serious political charges were carried out there. A great many of those convicted where shot right there in the cellars.

. . .

Lefortovo Prison is of comparatively recent construction. It is shaped like the letter K. At the center of the first floor where the corridors intersect, an attendant stands with a flag and directs the flow of prisoners led to and from interrogation. The jailers here are a coarse, cruel bunch. Instead of simply escorting a man to his interrogation they sometimes drag him there. During the exercise period their evil-looking mugs are always at close range. Many of them take part in executions.

I was placed in a corner cell, Number 196, on the third and last floor; directly beneath was death row. A woman down there was wailing without letup like a wounded animal. I was forbidden to sleep in the daytime and was warned that anyone who disobeyed could wind up in the punishment cell. I soon understood that interrogations were conducted only at night. Even when a man was spared this ordeal, he still slept badly, his senses always on the alert. Each prisoner thought they were coming for him; he listened with strained attention for footsteps, rustlings, the clanging of doors being opened. Screams frequently resounded through the prison. In the early hours of the morning it was not unusual to hear the howling of a man being taken out to be shot. Once in a great while there was a prisoner who, out of weariness and desperation, kicked up a row, vowing that he would not go to another interrogation. But more often to reach our ears were the groans of those being dispatched to Sukhanovka Prison,[9] the ultimate in sadistic, degrading treatment. As soon as you arrived at Sukhanovka, you were told that the authorities there were not bound by any regulations—anyone who landed in that place was outside the protection of the law. And that was the truth. The food ration amounted to almost nothing at all; by order of the investigator's office, a prisoner was not allowed sleep either day or night; the guards could do whatever they wanted with him. As a rule, even a very strong man would break down rapidly in Sukhanovka. One former inmate, though he was never beaten, came away with tuberculosis and a mental disorder. In my cell at Lefortovo was an ex-Red commissar from the Civil War period, Volkov, who had put in his six months at Sukhanovka. He fell completely apart there, gave utterly fantastic testimony against both himself and other people, and was certain that he would be shot. Time and again, he had been beaten with rubber truncheons. He had finally cracked and given evidence. When he suffered a liver attack during one of these sessions, he was naïve enough to mention his illness to the interrogator. Like a vulture, the interrogator tore into his

9. A prison near the railroad station Rastorguyeva, thirty kilometers southeast of Moscow. Its dungeons were formerly the crypts of the St. Katherine Monastery.

24

67624

victim joyfully. Volkov was a man of exceptional erudition. He knew several foreign languages to perfection and had a phenomenal memory. He could recite by heart verses from Baudelaire's *Flowers of Evil,* both in French and in Russian translation.

Another cellmate of mine was the professional thief Varnakov, one of the supposed "murderers" of the actress Zinaida Raikh, wife of the noted theatrical producer Meyerhold, who had died in prison. By the use of rubber truncheons, a confession was forced out of Varnakov and two of his buddies that they had taken part in the crime. It was well known that the Chekists themselves had murdered Raikh—a fact which they scarcely made secret. Nevertheless, they were in a fever of activity to mount an laborate cover-up: in a prison for common criminals[10] they selected suitable types, brought them over to Lefortovo, and beat confessions out of them. To bury the traces of their crime, it would have been enough just to fabricate a single gang of thugs; but as usual they wanted a wide assortment of alternative "murderers"—a reserve to be drawn on in case of need. It was the same thing with Gorki's murder: everybody knows that the Chekists poisoned him, but the number of his "physician-killers" runs into the dozens. I met up with two of them in the penal camps.

Varnakov was gifted by nature; he was good at drawing and had studied at a technical institute. Because of the meager grant he had to live on, he became involved in thievery. Everybody who crossed his path came to grief: his first wife poisoned herself, the second he got sent off to jail; his comrades in theft had now ended up with him on this trumped-up charge of murder and underwent merciless beatings during their interrogation. After the manner of professional criminals, he often went berserk, banging his head against the wall. In a calmer mood, he would give clever imitations of other people's voices. No one could equal him at this, and more than once he threw us into fits of laughter. His tales about his life as a thief were full of imagination. Listening to him made the time shorter.

It is commonly believed that there are many highly talented people among the criminal class. During sixteen years of imprisonment and exile I never met anyone to match Varnakov. Along the way there were, of course, other thieves who were extraordinarily gifted. Some could forge a signature or an official seal; some could pick a pocket without the victim feeling a thing. But they were limited to these professional

10. Common criminals, in Russian *blatnyi* or *blateri,* form a special community with their own rigid code of behavior and language.

talents. It was from Varnakov that I heard real camp swearing for the first time. The vocabulary of the interrogators paled by comparison—a poor, pathetic imitation.

Within a few days I was summoned for interrogation. My interrogator at Lubyanka had been a young man, about thirty, by the name of Tsvetayev. It seems that he had been an engineer before the Chekists had recruited him. Obviously he had only recently completed his course in this new job, and my "case" was in the nature of an exam for him. I felt no ill will toward him, nor do I feel any now. He diligently carried out instructions that his superior had written down for him on a piece of paper. Exactly as they had trained him to do, he conscientiously swore, shouted, and threatened, but without real malice. During my interrogation at Lubyanka he had offered a fresh appearance; he had an attractive face, fair and with a soft rosy hue. There was no sign of brutishness in it. When I saw him again at Lefortovo, I involuntarily thought of Oscar Wilde. Before me was the portrait of Dorian Gray, a face vitiated by evil-doing and depravity. Tsvetayev's face had turned yellow, fat, and flabby, with deep wrinkles and brown pouches under his eyes. He was unrecognizable.

The Soviet Communists call themselves comrades and talk about their humanitarianism. From experience I can say that within their "collectives" there is no magnanimity. There is not the slightest indication that they come to each other's aid. Their organizations consist of packs of trained dogs who snatch at any victim pointed out to them. It is precisely these "collectives" that develop mean, ugly instincts. Throughout my first ten years in the working world, I stewed in this Soviet cauldron, losing hold of the goodness my upbringing had instilled in me and allowing the bad side of my nature to come to the fore. At the end of my first month in prison, a man who was leaving our cell turned over to his cellmates a few provisions he had bought in the prison canteen. And there I was, young and healthy, new to prison life and as yet not debilitated by it—there I was, reaching out for my due share, instead of handing it over to a Pole who had been by now more than a year on prison rations. What an angry look I was rewarded with! I have remembered it ever since.

The interrogation brought home to me once again that the entire Communist system and its central bodies are maintained by terror, suspicion, distrust, and vindictiveness. A story by a Polish officer of

Georgian descent reaffirmed that conviction. An observant man with a soldier's ability to size up a situation quickly, he related how he had thrown a scare into his interrogator. One day there had been some delay as he was being taken back to his cell after an interrogation. When he mentioned this to his interrogator, the latter turned pale. The rule demands that the interrogator must keep a precise record of the times when a session begins and ends, and on returning to his cell the prisoner also signs a special register. Very likely, the interrogators sometimes credited themselves with additional work hours, but they shook in their boots from fear that someone might catch on to such tricks. Also, they are not supposed to leave a prisoner unattended in their office. If they have to go out, they must call in another investigator from a neighboring office to fill in for them. Our Georgian Pole exploited this fact and used it to frighten the wits out of his regular interrogator, saying that on his way back to his cell, he had been stopped by another Chekist for questioning, and that "this other fellow kept shaking his head and cursing under his breath."

A situation calculated to demoralize and dishearten people had the contrary effect of lifting me up. I now adopted an ironclad defense. I made a firm resolve to deny everything, not to give out a single bit of testimony, to be ready for any kind of torture. I told the interrogator in plain words that he was wasting his time—they would get nothing out of me since the charge was sheer fabrication and had no bearing on me whatsoever. From the neighboring offices came frequent sounds of moaning and sobbing, mingled with savage shouts from the interrogator. My Chekist also was loud and abusive at the start; but as time wore on, he grew calmer and quieter. It was clear to me that no new "evidence" was now required to conclude the case against me. My cellmates were of the opinion that the new charge against me would be withdrawn "for lack of evidence."[11] Things dragged on like this for four months, and, sure enough, it ended with my getting a five-year term in the camps only on the original charge of disseminating anti-Soviet propaganda.[12] Naturally there was no trial of any kind. The sentence was passed by the so-called Special Board[13] of the NKVD. My accomplices each got five years also.

11. The standard formula for clearing a person of one or more charges under the criminal code.
12. I was convicted under Paragraph 10 of Article 58.
13. Known by its Russian abbreviation of OSO (*Osoboye Soveshchanie*).

Butyrki

After I was sentenced, they took me, along with others just convicted, to Butyrki Prison. There we were put in separate cells, where we were to wait until they shipped us off to the camps. Large transports went out on the eighth, eighteenth, and twenty-eighth of each month. After such a shipment the cells were almost empty, but in no time they started filling up again. But for four months several young engineers, including myself, who had received short sentences on relatively minor charges, were consistently passed up for the transports. We managed to get an explanation for this: they were holding us in reserve for use in our line of work in the engineering-design office at the prison. Whether this was true or not we were exceptionally lucky. During those four months hundreds of intelligent, educated, experienced, versatile men went out ahead of us. Members of the Communist party from almost every level of the hierarchy filed past: from secretaries of territorial and regional committees down to all sorts of small fry. We even ran into former Chekists who had served under Yezhov. There were White émigrés and ex-White officers among us. Added to these were outstanding Soviet engineers and scientists, workers, and foreign Communists, many of whom had served in the Comintern. The national composition was also extremely diverse: apart from representatives of various Soviet national groups, there were Poles, Latvians, Estonians, Lithuanians, Germans, and many others. Under normal conditions I could never have gone through a teaching academy headed by such an elite. Tremendous resources would have been needed to assemble in one place such a variety of people in such numbers. But even if it had been possible, they would have revealed much less about themselves than in the prison. People who had just suffered great tragedy and the ruin of all their plans, who had undergone the ordeal of interrogation, who were anticipating a speedy death in the camp, became talkative. They now expressed themselves candidly, some perhaps for the only time in their lives. Usually there were several centers of conversation. In groups of sixty or seventy men there were always five or six capable of holding one's attention and interest. As soon as I woke in the morning, I drew up the day's plan for listening in on these discussions. At first I listened in silence; later I began to ask questions; in the final months, my head now buzzing with new knowledge, opinions, and theories, I began taking part in the debates.

In the days of Lenin, the innocent, the gullible, the blindly confident were lured into the party by promises and utopian slogans. In Stalin's time those who joined were nearly all careerists: as a result the party got

0520208

brainier and the proportion of fools decreased. Stalin began throwing into jail the most dangerous ones, those most capable of seeing through his crimes. For this reason, there was a considerably higher percentage of intelligent party members passing through the transport cell[14] than could be found outside the prison. I will refrain from judging them too harshly: the majority paid for their sins and bitter experience redeemed them to some degree, awakening the good instincts they had previously suppressed. They were undergoing penitence of a sort and reaching a higher level of existence. This in itself made contact with them possible. Many aroused sympathy and compassion; some renounced their past altogether. I was greatly impressed by their political knowledge, their observation on party life and on the activity of the Comintern.

We helped them to see clearly; we urged them to stop presenting themselves as the benefactors of mankind and to tell at last the grievous truth about their offenses against the common people; about the elimination of entire social classes, now confined in prisons and behind barbed wire; about the collectivization of the peasants; about the creation of famine. It was a certainty that within two weeks they would be overwhelmed by the barbaric chaos of camp life, and their chances of survival were slim. Most of these Communists damned Stalin, blamed him for all the horrors. Almost no one would talk with those Communists who tried to justify his crimes. They sat apart like people infected with a terrible disease.

It was good to see that some of "the comrades" had now repented— even though this could not bring their victims back to life. We wondered how deep their remorse was, how they would behave if the authorities were to recall them, apologize to them, offer them the opportunity to dedicate themselves again to what they had been doing before. The majority responded to our questions by a "not for anything in the world." Probably most of them were sincere at that time.

What amazed me was the fact that the uneducated clearly saw through the Communist fantasies, while the well-educated for years remained captives of these wretched delusions.

At the start of 1941, before Russia's entry into the war, our discussions ranged over various topics. We discussed, for instance, the religious persecutions. Many considered the religious pogroms as having no ideological basis, as nothing more than outright vandalism. The majority of the Communists agreed, since it was impossible to conceal or falsify the facts.

14. Cell for prisoners awaiting a transport to take them to another prison or camp.

We had frequent talks, in the prison cell, with an old sailor, Izmailov, once chairman of the Central Baltic Committee,[15] about the actions of those who overthrew the state in 1917. At the time he had headed the Communist organization directing the activity of the sailors won over by propaganda. This high-ranking official, who until quite recently had had all the resources of Communist propaganda at his disposal, found himself in no position to defend his conduct and convictions. Understanding how such simple-minded "roughnecks" got stuck in the nets spread by Bolshevik tricksters, we felt no malice against him. In his present situation he was in agreement with all the arguments on the other side. Our conversations went somewhat like this:

"Izmailov, during the war with Germany you sabotaged the offensive operations of the Baltic Fleet. The fact is that you committed outright treason. You handed Russia over to the enemy."

"Yes, that's what it amounts to!"

"You did not try to prevent the murder of naval officers but actually took part in lawless reprisals against them. That was treason!"

"That's what it amounts to."

Though Izmailov agreed with us, his repentance didn't run deep. Somehow he managed to survive imprisonment: in the mid-sixties, as I was watching a newsreel about the Moscow Museum of the Revolution, I saw him being paraded as a "living relic." Pioneers were shown presenting him with a red tie,[16] and a later sequence showed a photo of him back in the Central Baltic Committee days. He was a revolutionary once again, a man in high places. Were I to run across him and remind him of our conversations, he would not even recognize me.

On collectivization opinions varied. A few Communists, never having lived in the countryside, thought that horrible though it was, Stalin's method of collectivization was correct in concept and necessary. Some older and more experienced men pointed out that such a scheme is profitable only to parasites, who themselves are incapable of running a farm and exist by exploiting the actual workers. Only a bloodsucker can hold the peasant by his throat and take away what he harvests. The Russian peasant didn't need the Communists to tell him what he already knew: how to form cooperatives for the working of the land and joint purchasing of machinery. Collectivization is worse than just exploitation. It is downright robbery of the peasants, and it flies in the face of human nature. The most loathsome of all are those who attempt to prove that it was undertaken for the welfare of the peasants. It is impossible to graft

15. Bolshevik organization of Baltic Fleet sailors.
16. I.e., to confer honorary membership of the Pioneers. (Tr.)

a sapling tree on a telegraph pole; it is just as impossible to try to convince people that a disgusting form of slave-holding was created for the well-being of the enslaved. Only through terror could the whole thing be propped up.

It amused us whenever the Communist dogmatists, schooled in Stalin's political lore, endeavored to prove that we live under socialism. With no difficulty we proved to them the contrary: according to all the trademarks of the Stalinist tyranny, it was a cruel variety of enforced state capitalism that was flourishing. Perpetual lies, distortions, and forgeries, implemented by the outrageous imposition of party directives—such was the daily practice of Soviet journalists. The older among us were reminded of the leftist press in tsarist Russia: it had been preoccupied not with truth and justice but with forming the kind of public opinon that would be of advantage to the revolutionary leaders.

When it came to the question of who bore the responsibility for the February Revolution and the October coup d'état in 1917, opinions were divided. A good many placed the blame on the Jews and the Latvians. But the Jewish people, made up of rabbis, scholars, industrialists, merchants, artisans, and workers, were not involved in Russia's upheavals; instead they themselves were victims. The rabble among them made their contribution to the October catastrophe, for they discarded their belief in God and showed only contempt for the cultures of all peoples. The Trotskys, Sverdlovs, and Kaganoviches are no more related to the Jewish nation than the Lenins, Bukharins, Rykovs, and Abakumovs to the Russian; or the Latsises, and Peters to the Latvian; or the Dzhugashvilis (Stalins) and Berias to the Georgian. Every nation, unfortunately, has its moral degenerates with their misshapen souls and perverted minds. And in no way should one regard such people as criteria in judging a nation, for it does not bear any responsibility for them.

The dogmatists among our Communists contended that the revolution had been inevitable, but we took issue with them on that. The fruitful historical development of a society is closely tied to spiritual and economic well being for the vast majority of the populace. As an engineer, I knew that all types of structures must take their initial form in the mind; they must be carefully thought through, and the correct calculations must be made; only then may they be put to the practical test. Not a single part of any machine was ever devised by the knock-down-and-drag-out process; everything efficient and useful is produced by creative forces. Revolutions, on the other hand, are the manifestations of chaotic, destructive forces; as a rule, they turn out to be calamitous for the whole population. Cataclysmic events in public life upset the process of normal

31

development and lead to regression. Gambling on a revolution is justified only in the face of a tyrannical dictatorship, in which case the detonating device must be worked out with great care so that destruction and loss of life will be minimal.

Everybody believed that war with Hitler was sure to come. The majority predicted it would begin on May 20 or June 1, 1941. A few set other dates. Had they known the time of Hitler's invasion of Yugoslavia, they could have predicted the date for the start of the war against the U.S.S.R. even more precisely. Such unanimity of opinion among men who had no previous contact with each other since they were delivered to the prison separately, as it were on a conveyor belt, testified to the level of their intelligence. With few exceptions, they were all to perish during the early years of the war. Besides the date for the start of the war, they also predicted that it would end in a shameful debacle. Almost everyone was certain it would lead to a crushing defeat for the Stalinist despotism. No one then was able to foresee the mindlessness behind Hitler's behavior.

3

THE FIRST TRANSPORT

How We Greeted the War in Butyrki

The war with Germany did not start on June 1, as had been predicted by our Communist cellmates, but twenty-two days later. Jumping from our bunks on the night of June 23 after being wakened by the furious firing of antiaircraft guns, many of us congratulated each other on the outbreak of the war we had been expecting for so long. Others sat in glum silence—the lines were being drawn.

The men who now hoped for the victory of the regime were mainly those who had helped to sabotage operations at the front in 1917; those who had deserted the army, or killed their officers; those who had supported collectivization, the destruction of religion, the liquidation of "antisocial elements"[1]—and those who condoned all these acts.

On the other side were those who now shook each other by the hand, hoping for liberation in the near future. These were men like myself who had regarded the conduct of the propaganda-ridden soldiers and their leaders in 1917 as treason against the fatherland and viewed the ensuing chaos and nightmare as a catastrophe; who were outraged, ashamed, and helpless faced with the enslavement of the rural population and the annihilation of sixteen million peasants; who sympathized wholeheartedly with the victims of the endless campaign to wipe out everybody who was thought to stand in the way; who wanted to save their country, wrest it from the clutches of arbitrary rule, restore liberties that no one had appreciated before they were lost, and put an end to endless mass terror.

1. I.e., people regarded as a hindrance to the new regime. (Tr.)

Along with other like-minded prisoners, I believed in the liberation. We could not tolerate the notion that the Germans would turn out to be conquerors rather than liberators. To come as conquerors would indicate their complete misunderstanding of the actual circumstances in our country.

I won't hide the fact that several *zeks*,[2] having spent time as high officials in Germany in the 'thirties and having read *Mein Kampf*, warned us that Hitler might well be making a bid for conquest. We replied that if the situation were looked at realistically, not everything that he wrote would necessarily come to pass.

In any case, my habit of thinking as an engineer did not permit me to be satisfied with what appeared to be an oversimplification. Since I had ample time, I proceeded to elucidate for myself my view of things, in order to be prepared for any eventuality. These are the conclusions I reached then:

— The real Russia came to an end in October, 1917. The Bolsheviks never made any secret of this. They immediately changed the name of the country to R.S.F.S.R., and later to the U.S.S.R. Anything traditionally Russian was rooted up and destroyed.

— Replacing the real Russia was a gang of political bandits and torturers.

— The new Russia would arise on the bayonet points of liberating armies formed by the peoples of the U.S.S.R.

— A regime characterized by brute force and wholesale criminality divides the population into *oppressors*[3]—the executors of its vile actions —and *victims*. The first are numbered in the millions; the second in tens of millions. The first are the right arm of the regime; the second are put in the army or other enterprises using slave labor indispensable to the regime. If the army is firmly controlled, the victims will bear the yoke and carry out orders in spite of any innate reluctance. If the army is weak, the officers inexperienced, discipline shaken by defeats, the *victims* will show their real feelings toward the slaveholding system. In such a situation the oppressors will still be the mainstay of the army and the regime and will continue to perpetrate inhuman acts—though by now most of them may loathe the system as well. But they are already too closely identified with it and their hands are covered in blood, so that,

2. In Russian, concentration camp prisoners are referred to as *zeks*, derived from the letters *z* and *k* (from *zakliuchónny*—"prisoner").
3. The regime relies for its support on a whole social stratum whose members enjoy special privileges—hence their willingness to serve as oppressors.

in their fear, they will fight on simply to save their hides. The victims on the contrary will surrender to the enemy at the very first chance. From among them, the Germans will form units of volunteers who will fight for the emancipation of Russia.

At that time it did not enter my head that Hitler would begin killing off our prisoners through starvation. As I described earlier, we expected from him rational actions, not madness. When indisputable evidence of this and other crimes of his reached us in the camps as early as the autumn of 1941, in our minds he became Stalin's equal in cannibalism.

We saw that our own struggle would now be more complicated. First, Stalin would have to be overthrown; and after that we would have to come to grips with Hitler.

The "Angry *Frayers*"[4]

After the start of the war, three friends and I were still held in the transit cell for another month and a half. There was a great rush to send men out on the transports, which now were leaving several times a week. Papers of all kinds were being burned in the stoves; prisoners out for their airing in the courtyard got covered with ashes. I realized that in the growing confusion we would not be assigned to the office of special engineering projects. We were much more likely to end up in a late autumn transport that could mean the end of us. We started asking for assignment to a camp, giving as our reason that our sentences were for concentration camps, not for prison. So finally, on August 13, 1941, we were scheduled for a transport and moved to the former prison church[5] that had been converted into a prison ward. Besides our Soviet brethren, there were also a good many Poles and Latvians. Within a very short time a rumor was going about that among the Poles was Prince Sapieha, one of the wealthiest magnates in Poland.

We were packed into a specially fitted "Stolypin" coach. The sleeping compartments had been made over into cages, which had prison-bar doors opening into the corridor. According to the standards applying to the general public at that time, the compartments were supposed to consist of six sleeping berths, including the narrow third baggage rack way at

4. *Frayer* is the slang word for any prisoner who is not a common criminal (*blater*). "Angry *frayers*" refers to those prisoners who offered organized resistance to the common criminals.
5. The building of the Butyrki dates back to the eighteenth century.

the top. By the standards for transporting prisoners (though I doubt whether the word "standard" is appropriate in this context) in an earlier period of relative calm, each of these cages was expected to accommodate fifteen *zeks*. Now that the war was on, they herded twenty-eight of us into each of these moving cells. The entire batch of approximately two hundred men was stowed into a single coach. For the enlightenment of posterity, it is worth describing how so many bodies were packed in. On each of the two top bunks two men lay head by foot. On the two middle ones were seven with their heads toward the door and one crosswise at their feet. Under each of the two bottom bunks there was one man, with fourteen more perched upon the bunks and on the bundles of belongings jammed in the floor space between the bunks and the door. At night all those at the lower levels somehow managed to lie down one alongside the other. Arithmetically, it looked like this: $2 \times 2 + 7 + 1 + 2 \times 1 + 14 = 28$.

Besides the heat, the stuffiness, and congestion, there was a scarcity of water. Once a day water was poured into a dirty pail which all of us had to use. Several men were hit by dysentery. Since they took us out to the lavatory only twice a day, we could all have caught it. I think, however, that this must have been some other kind of diarrhea, brought on by a less virulent germ, for no one on the lower level became ill although an engineer called Smirnov in the bottom berth was tormented by it during the entire journey.

Having heard numerous tales from old-time camp inmates during our four months in the transport wards at the prison, we drew up rules of conduct that were put into practice right away. We resolved:

— to stand together; as the saying goes, all for one, one for all;
— not to provoke the professional criminals by attacking first, but never to give way to them either;
— to help those worthy of help, that is, those who were ready to join the resistance;
— not to get mixed up in quarrels among the common criminals and *"bitches"*;[6]
— to fight unremittingly for one's blessed *crutch*.[7]

On the very first day in the transport, these rules proved their operative force. Three *zeks* (with whom I had been together in Butyrki) and I rushed into the cage assigned to us and pounced on the best bunks, which were the middle ones. At the same time we helped other prisoners close

6. Slang for criminals who had supposedly betrayed their comrades by collaborating with the authorities.
7. Camp jargon for the daily bread ration.

to us in spirit to settle in the best spots near us. Only the bottom section was left for the common criminals. Their attempts to revolt and take over our places ended in humiliating failure. Apparently, they had not expected any such well-coordinated resistance from our group. All the strategic advantages had been wholly on our side. To get to our higher level, they had to climb up one by one. Acting as a team, we grabbed them by the head, slammed them against the bars several times, and threw them into a heap below. Once this was done, the four of us read them a lecture to this effect: the moment they stepped out of line, we would give them a good thrashing; the reign of the criminals was ended; we intended to be in charge of the situation at the camp; if necessary we would form an alliance with the "bitches" . . . and much more in that vein.

Of course, these were rather idle threats, but then the criminals themselves customarily kept the upper hand by the same means—by shouting, by seizing a person by the throat, and by operating as a team. In any case, the vanquished thugs gave us no more trouble for the rest of the trip.

They dubbed us the "angry *frayers*." Over the years, as we continued to keep them in line, our numbers increased substantially.

How Baron Hildebrand "Fed Propaganda" to Minister Yezhov

While we were still in the big transport ward back in the prison, our attention had been attracted to a lean gentleman of Western aspect, who in clipped tones was telling someone a story. Baron Hildebrand, as we came to know him, was a native of the Baltic region. His speech was staccato and precise, his gestures elegant. He had come back from Germany and was full of extremely interesting accounts about her productive might and her organizational ability, her orderliness and discipline. He told how small civilian enterprises could within twenty-four hours be converted to producing essential war material. We were duly impressed. It seems that at the end of 1938 the baron supplied such information in far greater detail to the Soviet high executioner and director of the spy network abroad, Yezhov, who at that time was still a great power in the land. Yezhov got only one thing from Hildebrand's report: in Germany everything was good; in the Soviet Union everything was bad. He began shouting at the baron, "What are you up to, you rascal? Have you come to feed propaganda to me?"

The primitive mind of High Executioner Yezhov should not astonish anyone. What is strange, though, is that a German baron of ancient lineage, an educated European, who was acquainted both with the world outside and our internal problems, would become subservient to Stalin's henchmen, especially in the bloodiest and cruelest period of their rule. It was doubtful that he had been lured by the proverbial thirty pieces of silver or that he had stumbled into a trap; more likely, some intellectual mirage had settled inside his head.

It was never a surprise when a Communist in the West, with little training in these matters and with his head full of propaganda, fell for the lies that the Soviet Union broadcast about itself. But it is unfortunate that instead of giving unquestioning support to this regime, he did not take a more circumspect attitude.

How a Chief Prosecutor for the Republic Continued to Climb Over Corpses

As I was thinking these thoughts, I suddenly heard someone shout hysterically, "Don't listen to him! He's peddling fascist propaganda!"

From our neighbors in the next cage we learned that the shouting came from Roginski, chief prosecuter for the republic in the Yezhov era. His conscience was burdened by the hundreds of thousands of human beings executed by his decree during the Yezhov purges. The incident in the coach was triggered by a story Baron Hildebrand was telling about Germany. It was overheard by Roginski who was sitting in the adjacent cage. A real snake, he calculated that if he could get the baron put away in the isolation prison,[8] he would win favor with the authorities and thus begin his restoration to the good graces of Stalin. The ill-fated baron had already been charged twice with anti-Soviet agitation by the chief executioners of the Stalinist regime. On the very first day after arriving at the camp he disappeared into solitary confinement. We never saw him again. Most certainly he died there.

I had no trouble in picking out Roginski from the others. The psychology of degenerates like him interested me. On the day of his outburst, I immediately recognized him—he stood out as a person always trying to curry favor with the authorities, talking loudly and gesticulating, never missing a chance to boast of his past career.

"You know," he was yelling at someone, "if they give me, a prosecutor,

8. The term for the lock-up in a camp.

the tenth section, it means that they acknowledge my complete innocence, and my rehabilitation will be a matter of no time at all."

Those who ended up in the same camp section as Roginski were to be pitied. Anyone whose bones he could use to get back into the regime's good graces he would throw into the maw of Baal, as happened in eras when human sacrifice was practiced.

Much later, this time in Moscow, I came across Roginski's name alongside that of the general prosecutor of the U.S.S.R., Rudenko, in some newspaper accounts of the Nuremberg trials. Obviously, this monster had managed to extricate himself from among corpses and once again taken his place by the blood-stained altar of human sacrifice.

The World Behind Prison Bars as a Mirror of Soviet Society

Even before the war, I clearly saw that Lenin had simply patterned his famous "party of a new type" after the bandit gangs, which had the following distinctive features:

— unquestioning submission to the decisions of the "boss";[9]

— periodic "purges," with the purpose of eliminating violators of underworld law within their ranks, trials for the offenders and vindictive sentences, antihuman ethics (what is good for the criminals is the only good);

— the drawing of a sharp distinction between themselves, the criminals (or "Men," as they styled themselves) bound together by their own code or behavior, and the *frayers,* the common herd of non-criminals, and *muzhiks,*[10] (or "peasants," as they called them);

— the excommunication and destruction of those renegades ("bitches") who broke ranks and violated their jungle law;

— a special jargon, secretiveness, suspicion toward the rest of the population, which they regarded only as a source of material benefits.

After the first months in the camp, I reached the definite conclusion that the world of prisoners is a mirror of Soviet life in general; much of what goes on behind barbed wire is duplicated outside. More precisely:

— The camp's criminal element corresponds to the ruling Communist

9. In Russian, *pakhan*—the leader of a gang of thieves or bandits.
10. Prisoners who do not belong to the criminal element and who cling to their possessions.

party, just as the Communist party has modeled itself as an underworld gang.

— The most vicious segment among the criminals performs duties comparable to those of the Chekists, while the rest of them act as spies and informers. Their chiefs fulfill the functions of the judges.

— The *frayers,* the *muzhiks,* the *Sidor Polikarpoviches*[11] correspond to the ordinary masses outside the party. These people, like their kind outside, are isolated, timorous, cowardly, mean, easily swayed by rumors, without confidence in their own powers.

The world of the camps, like the one outside, teems with informers, traitors, secret collaborators, and undercover agents. However, among the gangsters this stratum—and this is to their credit—is much smaller than within the Communist party of the Soviet Union.

The prisoners steal everything they can possibly bring back into the camp from their places of work, or consume it on the spot.[12] In exactly the same way, many people in the outside world just take whatever they find lying about unguarded. The word *honesty* has disappeared—a fact for which people living in a society like ours can hardly be blamed.

The majority of intellectuals behind bars behave exactly like most of those who live "in freedom." The strivings of the former for a reduced sentence, a "private cabin of their own"[13] instead of the common barracks, "a bonus,"[14] and similar blessings, duplicate the efforts among those outside to make good in a career, to secure a steady salary, a private apartment,[15] or a higher degree[16] at the university.

And we, "the angry *frayers,*" refusing to compromise with arbitrariness and constantly resisting the assaults of the thugs, bore some likeness to the dissidents of that time on the outside.

11. *Sidor Polikarpovich:* a comic-sounding name and patronymic used in slang to refer to the most passive non-criminal prisoners.

12. Prisoners were taken under guard to work during the day at construction sites, etc. (Tr.)

13. A corner of the barracks with two bunks and partitioned off from the rest.

14. A paltry sum which was given by the camp administration to the prisoners as an incentive every three months.

15. To this day a great many Soviet citizens, even in Moscow, live in shared apartments. When the Bolsheviks seized power, private apartments were subdivided. The only kitchen, the bathroom (where it existed), the toilet were used by all the tenants, with the inconveniences inherent in such unnatural cohabitation with strangers.

16. Such an academic degree entitled the graduate to a raise of not inconsiderable proportions.

The Heathen

Our transport, albeit slowly, was now approaching its destination, the camp for which we were bound.

I was lying in the best place in the cage, on a center bunk next to the wall, with my head toward the bars, that is, toward the window. I was not hungry or sick or exhausted: in my bag I still had some supplies from Butyrki. Below me, on the bottom bunk, sat the engineer Smirnov, tormented by diarrhea. He was obviously a decent man, but we did not recognize him as one of us for he was perpetually silent, expressed no opinions, and offered no assessment of what was happening. I felt I ought to give up my place to him. But here again, the disregard of common standards of ethics in the U.S.S.R. created obstacles. It was not only the conditions in the prisons that brutalized people in the Stalin years; the whole situation was fraught with unpredictable hazards. For that reason, everybody carefully considered and weighed all the undesirable consequences of any action that would have been regarded as mandatory in normal circumstances.

The Christian commandment that we should extend love and hope to those around us in order to atone for our sins through generous acts pleasing to God made it incumbent on us to help the sick man, as did also the following practical reasons:

— We were traveling during a fearful time to a fearful place. To deny help to someone in misfortune meant that one would not have the right to ask others for help or to accept it.

— Why should I demand and fight for a situation that was comparatively better than that of others? If I was better than other men, I did not need privileges. The very fact that I sought them would disprove any assumption that I was better. If, on the other hand, I was worse, then I had absolutely no right to something better.

— It was time to learn the customs and manners of the criminal element, to school oneself in adversity and privation and not to evade them, to learn the camp jargon and profanity, to learn how to get on in the camp.

All these reasons, however, were undermined by the suspicion that Smirnov was holding something back. His attitude toward us champions of free speech seemed ambiguous. However, I thought it necessary to take a risk for our common good. My friends began protesting: "The hell with him! If he's being underhanded about something or just looking out for his own skin, then our conversations are not for his ears."

To that I countered: "For the past four months we have talked so much and heard so many interesting things that we have become much too lax. So it would be as well if all of us learned how to govern our tongues once again before we arrive at the place where the most hostile conditions await us." With the agreement of the others I climbed down and invited the sick man to change places with me.

On the lower level, I found myself in a different environment. For a while I found it wisest to keep quiet until I got my bearings. Of course, I was not afraid of the thugs, and in any case there were only three of them. Once defeated by somebody stronger, the criminals always lie low until the situation changes to their advantage. I thought of how difficult it is in these circumstances for anyone to do an act of kindness, even for a man professing .o be a Christian. How incomparably more difficult it must be for an atheist.

After getting used to the lower berth, where I sat right by the door, and after hearing my fill of the stories being told around me, I myself began entering into conversation with my new neighbors. Next to me was an ill-favored *zek* who several times in discussion mentioned the word "God." Naturally, I became interested and gradually managed to discover what his credo was.

I had often had occasion to hear people, who supposedly believed in God, saying; "I don't recognize the church; I can't stomach priests; I have my own concept of God: God is truth; God is goodness—ritual and dogma have no meaning." People always employ phrases like these to justify their rejection of the church. But by the same token they sever their links with believers and open up their souls to compromise and cowardice. Faith turns into a plaything, into something that imposes no obligations. They reason more or less this way: "As long as I am young, I can get by without it; when I am older, I'll take it up properly." As if man knows when his end will come. . . . On this level of reasoning, self-justification and moral compromise flourish unchecked. Such people cut themselves off from the priests; they no longer listen to sermons and admonitions; they never look at the Holy Scriptures or any other religious books (which in the U.S.S.R. are in any case hard to find); they stop praying and taking communion. And so faith dies out.

At the same time torrents of atheistic propaganda flood their minds. The matrices of the brain cannot help but retain some scraps of the Marxist litany.

The number of people so affected is enormous in our atheistic system, and my neighbor was one of them. The word "heathen" fits them precisely, since their enforced denial of the church, along with their ignorance in matters of religion, leads to primitivism, apostasy, and disunity.

And the way is open wide for atheism, together with totalitarianism of the Stalin or Hitler model.

Militiaman in Sheep's Clothing

My new surroundings brought me into contact with men such as I had never met before. Next to me was a former chief of militia for the Gorki Province. This huge, swarthy, gorilla-like person had no doubt yelled savagely while executing his official duties, used the most abusive kind of language, and resorted to physical violence. Now it was another story. The words from the mouth of the fallen "protector-preceptor" (to use an expression from the bard Aleksandr Galich[17]) flowed gently, he conversed with "benevolence and piety." This was in no way surprising, inasmuch as he was now surrounded by professional criminals. Very likely he was puzzled by the position of dominance that our group had secured since the excellent organization and monolithic solidarity of its friends[18] during these years were well known.

Since he was talkative, I asked him a number of questions. I was particularly interested in finding out how the militia tracks down criminals and whether it investigates the cases of private citizens who have suffered at their hands. At first he cleverly sidestepped the questions. But we had plenty of time. After he became accustomed to my queries, he decided to satisfy my curiosity. The gist of his answer was that the most effective weapon in the hands of the militia is the network of informers who operate among both the general public and the criminal underworld. Without this source of information the militia would be helpless. Scientific methods of crime detection, techniques of a contemporary Sherlock Holmes, are too costly, and the funds allocated for that kind of work go to the secret police (the Chekists). However, in criminal cases where the interest of the state may be involved, the militia does not hesitate to use the same methods as the secret police. Otherwise, when the victims are only ordinary citizens, the militia acts only if it is tipped off by informers. Since I had no sound reasons for doubting what he told me, I could not help feeling extremely indignant. When I asked him how he would handle things if he were appointed head of the kommandatura[19] in a camp, he

17. Soviet dissident who left the U.S.S.R. in 1974. At the present time he lives in Norway.
18. Prisoners referred to the criminals as "friends of the regime."
19. I.e., the internal police in the camp. It consisted mainly of renegade criminals —"bitches."

replied that an efficient network of informers was the only way of policing a camp and of keeping the common criminals under control. Later, the truth behind his words was to be amply demonstrated.

After talking with him for some time, I saw his "benevolence and paternalism" for what they were really worth. There was no doubt in my mind that if he were given a job in the kommandatura he would display his other talents, all directed at obtaining a review of his case or even a cancellation of his sentence. Obviously he had been given a hint of this possibility somewhere along the way, for every now and then a touch of self-assurance slipped into his voice. Once again I ran up against a fundamental baseness: ordinary people are simply dung to be trampled on for the sake of one man's survival—survival at any cost.

The veteran "guardian of the law" was later justified in his hopes. Early in 1942 I caught sight of him among a number of men who had been released from the camp.

As long as the state remains totalitarian, the primary function of its police will be to protect the interests of the state, to crush all dissent with brute force. The needs of the general public will continue to be ignored.

Whenever a "political" prisoner escapes from confinement, a nationwide manhunt is ordered; but when a common criminal breaks out, the police restrict themselves to a local search. The former poses a danger to the state; the latter only to the general public. Whenever a militiaman or a Chekist is murdered, all available forces are thrown into the search. They never fail to find a culprit of some kind—though not necessarily the real one. When an ordinary citizen is murdered, the investigation is half-hearted, a mere formality. The detective in charge is mainly concerned to close the case, not track down the criminal.

When I was living in Moscow after my release, a crime took place about which I cannot be silent. On the morning of January 3, 1966, in the city of Dubno in Moscow Province, a ten-year-old boy who had come there with his mother on a school vacation was hurled from the fourth floor of a hotel to the bottom of a spiral staircase. Without regaining consciousness he died. The circumstances of the murder clearly pointed to a thug who was staying in the hotel after his release from imprisonment. On the evening before the crime, during a drunken orgy, he had threatened the boy's mother in violent underworld language as she attempted to quiet him down.

The police investigation was unconscionably slow in getting under way, and once started, it was conducted in the most lackadaisical fashion. Worried that they might implicate themselves, frightened witnesses told little. After a lapse of three months, the official in charge of the investigation came to the home of the murdered boy's mother to demand her consent to close the case. It appeared that the mother of the suspect had reported to the police that her son had left for a trip across the infinite expanses of the Soviet Union. The public prosecutor's office saw no need to order a nationwide search for the killer. The officials concerned thus acted not as representatives of the state with a duty to find and punish the murderer, but rather as his accomplices, anxious that he go scot free. The contempt that totalitarianism has developed toward the average citizen over the years spoke for itself in this case: obviously no one saw the need to waste time and money on behalf of a murdered boy; just carry out the required formalities and close the affair—that was enough.

4

VYATLAG:* THE FIRST YEAR OF THE WAR

How Prince Sapieha Met His Quota

The day our Moscow transport pulled into Section One of Vyatlag[1]—August 28, 1941—was also marked by the arrival of high officials from the camp administration. Their appearance was linked with the fact that among the prisoners who had been cleared out of the Moscow jails and brought here in our transport were a number of important figures: Prince Sapieha; the former public prosecutor, Roginski; Baron Hildebrand; Kozyrev, a former deputy minister of forestry; the former Latvian minister of internal affairs and several other members of that country's government; many Polish army officers; about twenty engineers, including top ones from the old Putilov works;[2] German and Hungarian aeronautic specialists; high ranking officers of the NKVD[3] and the militia.

Among the camp authorities the chief of the "regime"[4] at Vyatlag, Captain Borisov, stood out in particular; to this day his squat figure and bulldog face sticks in my mind. You cannot deny that Chekists in general have excellent memories of names and faces. To us newcomers the

1. *Lag:* abbreviation of the Russian *lager,* meaning camp. Vyatlag refers to the camp at Vyatka, a town in the north of the U.S.S.R., now called Kirov. The names of other camps are formed in a similar way, e.g., Vorkutlag, Ozerlag, Steplag, etc. (Tr.)

2. Putilov works in Leningrad, now called Kirov works. (Tr.)

3. Name of the KGB in those years.

4. "Regime" is the term for the general conditions under which prisoners are held. Camps are still described at the present day according to their "regime" as "ordinary," "strict," "special," etc.

wealth of information they commanded was staggering. They got it, of course, from the dossiers that were always sent along with us. These also contained our photos. And that was how Captain Borisov recognized Prince Sapieha on the spot and gave him quite a shock by calling out his name.

Tall, strongly built, rawboned, with penetrating eyes and a bold aquiline nose, the prince reminded me of a giant eagle caged and with wings broken but still proud and unyielding. I heard only the last words of his exchange with Borisov. As I came near, Borisov was asking him, "Why did you of all people—a landowner and a prince—remain on your estate rather than make a run for it?"

Sapieha replied, "I simply remained where I had lived all my life. I was not an intruder in a foreign country. It was not up to me to run."

The prince did not speak Russian very correctly; yet the few Polish words he threw in tended to heighten the effect of his reply. The captain reacted with a long tirade in Marxist jargon of the sort everybody in the Soviet Union is brought up on: the invariable clichés about exploitation, expropriation, etc. The prince was not punished for his "impertinence," probably because the camp authorities already knew about the army that Anders[5] was then organizing. As early as September the Poles who arrived with us at the camp, as well as those who had landed here previously, would be dispatched in transports to Central Asia, where the Anders army was taking shape. But until that time the Poles worked as all other *zeks*. Even Prince Sapieha was assigned a daily quota: one hundred and fifty buckets of water to be filled from a deep well and hauled over a considerable distance. However, his fellow Poles did not allow him to lift a finger; they met the quota for him. We later heard rumors that Prince Sapieha left Vyatlag in a special rail car. He was expected to join the émigré Polish government in London.

Among the Poles were five young Western Ukrainians. Of course, they all described themselves as Poles, and nobody betrayed them.

Quarantine

Newcomers to the camp were supposed to be in quarantine for twenty days, but in actual practice this applied only to men who were in no condition to move. As a rule, everybody was driven out to work the very day after arrival. You were under no compulsion to meet your quota,

5. The army of General Anders, formed in 1941, fought against Hitler on the Western front.

though this was expected as soon as you were out of quarantine. For this reason you got the lowest rations and were fed from the so-called first caldron.[6]

They installed us in flimsy structures covered by a pitched roof and walled in by laths plastered over with clay. Inside, two rows of double-decker bunks were aligned neatly along the center.

We had known about bedbugs and mosquitoes from the stories told us by other prisoners, but the reality surpassed anything we had expected. I was lying on the bottom tier, and the damned bedbugs kept falling on me from the upper one. They were crawling out from every crack in the walls. I was constantly throwing off the tiny blanket that I had snatched up at the last minute back home. I tried to fight them off singlehandedly. At the same time, the mosquitoes, buzzing and whining like aircraft, began tormenting me. After two hours of torture I crept under the bunk, hoping that at least the bedbugs would be less numerous there. A vain hope! Within minutes the entire horde descended on me. Scrambling out, I nearly rammed the back of my head against the point of a spike. Since the barracks were not locked up at the time, I dashed out into the yard. There I settled myself on a table, where I finally got to sleep about daybreak. On succeeding nights it was no easier; the torment continued. But exhaustion made its claim. Meanwhile, the parasites were accomplishing their filthy business, sucking out our blood that was becoming increasingly difficult to restore on a diet as insubstantial as ours. During the first year of the war they contributed to the death of most of the 35,000 men in the camp. Then, at long last, the higher-ups gave orders for the extermination of the bedbugs; consequently the prisoners arriving to replace the ones who had starved to death were no longer subjected to this daily torture.

A week after our arrival the camp commissary ran low on supplies; our meals took a sharp turn for the worse. We were served only watery soup and a small portion of kasha.[7] Since the sending of food parcels by relatives had been forbidden from the very start of the war, we all kept going on the bread ration alone.

6. Prisoners were fed by the camp kitchen according to their output. There were generally three "caldrons."
7. Kasha: porridge of buckwheat or other cereal.

48

The Kuban Cossacks[8]

About three days after we were installed, a transport of fifty or so men pulled in from the Kuban. A group of young fellows between twenty and thirty years of age formed the core of it. They stood out sharply from the rest. On their first day in the camp, after they returned from work in the forest, they gathered at nightfall in a tight group just outside their billet and commenced a lively discussion. One of them, somewhat more mature-looking than the others, was in command. His brown eyes seemed to blaze. His speech was rapid and evidently persuasive. The rest listened with close attention, now and then tossing in a comment or a query. It came to me in a lightning flash that they were planning to break out. These were young Cossacks—a breed wholly different from ours. Since infancy they had been victimized by an endless succession of oppressive acts. The older ones might well have taken part in the revolt of the Kuban Cossacks against collectivization back in 1930.[9] No doubt a good many had fled from hellholes in Siberia, where they had been deported. In a camp with only one guard to a work brigade, it is no wonder they viewed escape from the forest as a real possibility early that September.

As yet, I had no experience in the ways of camp life, and in any case it would have been difficult to gain the confidence of these men in a single evening. I might be able to make it out of the barbed-wire zone with their brigade; since the brigades were still of a temporary formation and under quarantine, the camp personnel were not familiar enough with us to recognize anyone on sight. It might make sense, I decided, to wait until the end of their discussion, then walk up to their leaders and say, "I'm with you all the way. Take me along!" And then one of two things would happen: they would either strangle me that same night or give me an okay—the first more likely, for they didn't trust us *"Moskali"*[10] at all. Living among enemies known and unknown had nurtured within them a distrust of everyone and everything around. And even though I have never lacked decisiveness, that evening I simply could not take advantage of the opportunity that had come to me.

It was with extreme anxiety that I walked over to their barracks the next day after work. But the young men were no longer there. I never saw them again. In all probability they had already "blown," the whole brigade at once. It must have been a success; otherwise their mangled bodies

8. Cossacks of the North Caucasian region.
9. See chapter 1, p. 9.
10. A word of contempt among Ukrainians and Cossacks for Russians (literally, "Muscovites").

would have been brought in and thrown down by the guardhouse as a warning to the rest of us.

That was what they did with the smalltime thief Petushkov who had arrived in our transport. It was a well-known fact that "legitimate" criminals did not have to work; so Petushkov goldbricked as much as he pleased—and in every way possible. But the armed guard in charge of the brigade had belonged to the old school of '37.[11] As punishment, he ordered Petushkov to strip naked and then made him perch on a tree stump. Petusshkov, unable to bear the torture inflicted by the swarms of mosquitos, bolted and, like a damned fool, started running. Almost at pointblank range the guard shot him for "attempting to escape."

The Engineers

Our "fraternity" had used its time to good advantage back in the transport cell. We came to the camp with a very clearly defined attitude toward forced labor. We all agreed on the following maxims: a day of shirking[12] guarantees a longer life; don't put in a single day's hard labor if you can help it; work is not a bear—it won't run off to the forest and disappear; even horses will die if they're overworked; "without *tufta* and ammonal you cannot dig a damned canal."[13] We agreed that we would serve out our sentences, but not to end them prematurely along with our lives. . . .

During the period of quarantine the conduct of the other engineers from our transport was the exact opposite. They were all about ten years older than we. When we were all assigned to loading a flatcar, they pitched into it hot and heavy. The rest of us were chatting, enjoying a few laughs, taking it easy, and now and then we would send up a light log, one that wouldn't overtax our strength. But they grabbed hold of the stoutest logs and, puffing and panting furiously, rolled them up the railroad ties that were serving as a ramp.

This absurd behavior was at variance with the camp rules described

11. In the fall of 1941, all the prison guards who had distinguished themselves during the purges of 1937 had been transferred to the garrisons of the penal troops of the NKVD in the regional capitals.

12. In camp slang *kantovka*, which means shirking work without appearing to do so.

13. A common saying among the prisoners who built the White Sea Canal in the early thirties—one of the first major projects on which forced labor was used on a large scale. *Tufta* is a basic word among Soviet workers. It refers to the various ways of deceiving those in charge of them—"going slow" on the job, claiming a higher output than has actually been achieved, etc. Ammonal is a form of TNT used in blasting operations. (Tr.)

above, since they were under no compulsion to meet their quota while in quarantine. But the explanation is simple: they were hoping that a show of "enthusiasm" would get them jobs in the camp workshops. What they were not taking into account was the fact that their work assignment would depend first of all on the length of their prison term, on the article and section under which they were charged. There were a few engineers, like myself, who had been charged under Article 58, Section 10—the most lenient—and given only a five-year sentence; these had some chance of landing in a machine shop or the locomotive shed. But that was not the whole story. The following conditions also had to prevail: need for your kind of training and experience; no opposition from the top *zeks* in the shop, or even better, a little help from them; no "veto by the camp Chekists"; your absolute readiness to take on anything the shop offered you, even if you had only the haziest notion of what the job was all about.

Most of the engineers who came here with us had been convicted of "sabotage" (Article 58, Section 7) and "subversive activity" (Article 58, Section 9) and sentenced to terms of ten, fifteen, and twenty years. These engineers, technicians, and designers, each a veteran in his respective field, were sent off to a lumber camp; all except three were to lose their lives that first winter.

Ten days after arriving, our transport was broken up and distributed among the various sections of the camp. The main body was assigned to felling timber. A few were given indoor jobs—*bytoviks*[14] and ex-NKVD officers got themselves "soft" jobs.[15] The Poles were shipped out of the camp.

The terrible specter of starvation was rapidly approaching. By early September all our food stores would be depleted. The quotas of work output were kept at levels impossible to attain: there was no question of adjusting them to the situation. It was tantamount to deliberate mass murder.

14. *Bytoviks:* prisoners sentenced for minor non-political offenses such as embezzlement. These formed a large category, distinct from the common criminals, and were treated with relative leniency. (Tr.)

15. "Soft jobs: such tasks as working as accountants in the camp administration, as orderlies in the infirmary, and in other such jobs in the camp barracks. Those who landed such assignments were not driven out in the weather under armed escort to do hard manual labor. (Tr.)

Those Who "Wear Out"[16] First

The night before our transport left Moscow, we met an aeronautical engineer who had been brought in from the aircraft design office headed by the renowned Tupolev.[17] Our engineer, Georgi Leimer, was a Russianized German about forty years old. He had first been imprisoned in 1937, when he was sent to one of the death camps. If Tupolev had not got him out by saying that he needed him for his project, he would have perished. But at the start of the war he was transported, together with other Germans and some Hungarians, back to ordinary forced labor. Somehow he withstood the hardships of the camp more easily than other men and was much more adapted to this kind of life. We used to say jokingly that after everybody else kicked off, Georgi would remain as the last living *zek*.

His steady high spirits and self-confidence endeared him to me. His sentence was for ten years under Section 7 of the inevitable Article 58; in short, he was considered a "saboteur." With such qualifications he was a sure candidate for the lumber camp. But the incredible happened. He took advantage of being in quarantine to remain behind in the barracks area while we were taken out to work. This enabled him to strike up an acquaintance with the head of the Second Division, Tkacheya; he persuaded her that he and the other engineers who had arrived in the same transport could set production in motion, step up the output, etc. The camp workshop had fallen into the hands of people who had ingratiated themselves by serving as secret informers; the growing insolence of the project director, the designer, the bookkeeper, and the accountant was beginning to grate even on the camp authorities. For that reason Georgi was able to get the informers thrown out and replaced by himself and short-termers from our transport who seemed right for the jobs. Georgi himself became the project director; a friend of ours, Yuri, took over the designer's position.

From the standpoint of camp ethics it was wrong to encroach upon a

16. In Russian, *dokhodit*—literally, "come to an end"—is camp slang meaning to reach a state of total exhaustion. A person in this state is called *dokhodyaga*—"goner."

17. This was a research institute of the type described by Solzhenitsyn in *The First Circle*. The team headed by Tupolev designed the combat planes for World War II and worked on space rockets in the post-war years. All the scientists and engineers concerned had been arrested during the purges and were confined in these special "prison institutes" (*sharashkas*) to work on projects of major importance. For breeches of discipline or refusal to cooperate they could be sent back to ordinary forced labor camps. The author was later transferred to the same "prison institute" as Solzhenitsyn—see pp. 262. (Tr.)

"live" job, one that somebody else already held. But it was always praise-worthy to oust an informer—a rather dangerous undertaking, I should add.

Yuri's experience in engineering design was considerable. Not only had he worked at it longer than I, but he was also a more gifted designer. I naturally made no claim to this job. Georgi told me that since the camp chief was dissatisfied with the rate-setter,[18] I might take his place. Of course, this job would free me from hard physical labor, but this post was already held by an old mate of mine from Butyrki Prison, Boris R., who had arrived here two months ahead of us. The ways of camp are cruel. If Boris lost the job, he would be thrown out of the brigade[19] and transferred to common labor—which would soon be the end of him. When the chief called me in, I praised Boris extravagantly while pleading my own inability to do the job in question. Then Georgi and Yuri succeeded in changing the chief's hostility toward Boris. And so he remained as rate-setter for the shop. As for me, I had no choice but to work as mechanic in the same shop.

Work in the shop was conducted in two shifts, each lasting twelve hours with a thirty-minute break. I wound up on the night shift. I was required to file the edges of wrench screws down to twenty-two and twenty-seven millimeters at a rate of seventy pieces a shift. Even by trans-forming myself into a robot, I could not manage more than fifty pieces a night. For my failure to meet the quota, they could have placed me on a penalty ration of three hundred grams of bread, but every day Boris brought me six hundred. After twenty days at this job I realized that my strength would not last very long—I was beginning to "wear out."

I should like to share an interesting observation that I made the second or third night. For eleven hours I had performed one and the same operation, pressing down on a file in order to shave off the amount of metal required by my "output quota." As the process went on, I sensed that my nutritive juices were flowing in the direction of my hands and torso. Previously they had flowed into the head, though I had not noticed this until now. The sensation was purely physical, and unpleasant enough to be remembered to this day. It was associated with a feeling of gradually increasing torpor.

Thus, I concluded, in a man doing physical work, the most vital currents are directed mainly to those parts of the body which help him perform his daily labor. This observation could no doubt be verified under

18. The person responsible for establishing or adjusting work quotas.
19. In Soviet factories, farms, etc., workers doing the same job are grouped in teams called "brigades." The same system applied in the forced labor camps. (Tr.)

scientifically controlled conditions in a laboratory; it explains—assuming everything else to be equal—why men whose normal activity is mental usually "wear out" on a manual job sooner than their mates who have always worked with their muscles. In order to come up to match the physical output of a laborer, an intellectual first must reduce his mental effort to a bare minimum; however, to break a habit of long standing demands extraordinary awareness and will power. A man for whom mental activity has become second nature cannot so easily get over the old habit of using his brain. As a consequence he is forced to divide the energy drawn from his submarginal nutriment in two different channels—to put it somewhat crudely. Somebody who theretofore has done only manual labor, on the other hand, uses up only his physical strength.

No wonder people used to working with their minds went swiftly to the grave under the killing conditions of the camps in wartime. From prison and transport a man arrived already on the brink of exhaustion. He was stuck in a job beyond both his experience and strength. At the same time he was given next to nothing to eat. Either from ignorance or inability, he failed to switch completely over to the new "channel." As a result, the energy he expended almost doubled within the first few days. This proved sufficient to put him out of action more quickly than men accustomed to physical labor. The fact that the brain workers reacted more strongly to the effects of their environment also operated against them—feelings and emotions use up their share of energy. A dull, rough type fared better than a sensitive person capable of intense suffering and aware of his situation. The outcome of all this was the frightful decimation of men with education and intellect. In 1945 at Vorkuta,[20] I began a fruitless search for the many men who in a four-month period had gone through our cell in Butyrki. Because of my work as an engineer, I had a pass to a large number of camp points lying within a thirty-kilometer radius of the city of Vorkuta. But in the course of three years I ran across only one of those men—Bril, the former NKVD chief in Tashkent. As for the others, there was not even the trace of a memory.

Naturally, it was the men from the ranks of manual labor who perished in greater numbers, since they were, of course, in the majority. Nevertheless, everything else being equal, they were more adaptable to the horrible conditions of the camp, and they lasted a bit longer. Because of the circumstances prevailing in the winter of 1941–1942, men arrived from the prisons so utterly worn out that a good many of them—whether laborers

20. Notorious camp area in the far north of European Russia, to which the author was later transferred from Vyatlag.

or intellectuals—could take the work at the lumber camps no more than two weeks to a month.

Now I should explain what the camp terms *rabotyaga, pridurok,* and *dokhodyaga* mean.

A *rabotyaga*[21] is a worker doing manual labor in accordance with "production quotas." These quotas were all impractical. The volume of work to be turned out was "set" and never adjusted to circumstances; the member of a "brigade" whose task it was to record the results of the day's work exercised fantastic ingenuity by adding a mass of dummy operations[22] intended to make it look as if the quota were not only fulfilled but exceeded. Whenever the work had some real economic purpose and was not intended to kill off the prisoners, the process came down to establishing a regular rhythm of work actually accomplished and adapting it to the existing norms. In actual practice, there was no difference between piece work and work by hours. The term *rabotyaga* was equally applicable to prisoners engaged on engineering work: we, too, had "quotas" to fulfill.

Pridurok refers to a prisoner working within the camp zone proper and having a supplementary food supply at the expense of the *rabotyagas.* Bookkeepers, clerks, and the commandant's flunkies were fed on rations that were stolen from the kitchen at the expense of the other prisoners.[23]

Dokhodyaga is the term applied to a *rabotyaga* who has gone beyond the limit of his endurance. Having lost more than thirty percent of his body weight, he is incapable of working any further. At the medical checkups given to determine the degree of working aptitude,[24] the *rabotyaga,* after exposing his backside, turns to face the doctor. The triangular hollows running down the middle of his emaciated thighs makes it clear at one glance what stage of dystrophy he has reached.

The *dokhodyagi* are divided into two separate categories: those who have preserved a likeness to human beings, and those who have lost it. Both groups may be equally exhausted, but the first exercise self-control,

21. Literally, "worker." (Tr.)
22. In camp slang, such a "package" of work orders to be executed is termed *tufta*—i.e., "added" work that in actual fact will not be done.
23. *Pridurok* can be translated as "flunky." They were normally recruited from among the "bitches" and the *bytoviks.* Employed as "work supervisors," (*naryad-chiki*) their job was to chase the prisoners out of their barracks in the morning and hand them over to their escort guards at the guardhouse to be taken to work.
24. These checkups could lead to a suspension of the penal confinement for reasons of health. Political prisoners, however, could not be "commissioned," as this process is called.

maintain the will to live, and keep themselves from sinking to the bottom; whereas the others go about in a filthy condition and think only of getting something to eat. They lick all their eating utensils, swarm around the garbage cans, and greedily swallow any muck as long as they can stuff it inside their mouths. The men in the first group have some chance of getting out of the camp alive. Those in the second die off like flies.

It is necessary to say a special word about men with a strong faith in God and a capacity for prayer. The laws which govern physiology and physics are naturally immutable, but the spiritual realm can nevertheless play a role in changing the most hopeless situations—in healing, in bringing wisdom, in rallying strength. This is a vast field awaiting its own researchers.

At the end of my second ten-day shift I asked Georgi to transfer me to the electric shop. But something prevented it, and I was temporarily appointed stockman in a warehouse that supplied spare parts for trucks and tractors. There was little to do there. After a week of boredom I made my mistake. Since I had terribly missed doing things of a technical nature during a year of enforced idleness, I began diligently studying a book on gazogene-generated automobiles; but the project ended just as deplorably as had my job at filing down screws. After a month of laboring over the book, I found myself going further downhill rather than recovering. Thus it finally became clear to me that intense intellectual effort burns energy in amounts quite comparable to those used up by heavy manual labor. Out of this I drew the bitter conclusion that on the food ration I received that winter 1941, I could not engage in both mental and physical activity. It was growing impossible for the mind to operate except when absolutely required. Beyond that minimum it would not perform. In the face of exhausting labor, mental activity would have to cease; any manifestation of feeling would have to be suppressed. To live like a vegetable was the only solution.

This discovery, which I made in my own "laboratory," convinced me that I was absolutely right to believe that anyone who wishes to preserve his intellect must avoid "common labor." However, I was delivered from it almost as quickly as I had been forced into it; for the camp was in need of my skills as a mechanical engineer.

While I continued reading up on gazogene-generated automobiles, I also gave careful thought to a course of action that I might follow. The sinister shadow of the camp prison,[25] where hundreds of the best men

25. I.e., the punishment cells for prisoners who infringed camp discipline, etc. (Tr.)

among us were doomed to waste away to nothing, prompted thoughts of self-preservation. Since I had plenty of spare time in the shop, I soon got acquainted with everyone there. I talked particularly with the old-timers. Their advice was, do not try to excel, hide in some out-of-the-way corner of a work shop, merge in with all the other *rabotyagas,* lie low, stop using your brain, stifle all feeling.

The electric shop proved to be just the kind of refuge I was searching for. Among the workmen were two Finnish-Americans, Albert Loon and Benya Mutroo. Shortly before the war their parents had arrived in Soviet Karelia with all their worldly goods, including cars, tractors, and farm machinery. They had come to take part in building the Communist system. But in 1937 they were all sent off to prison as spies.

Albert and Benya were first-rate young men. Work of any kind came very easily to them. They were competent at everything, despite their lack of theoretical knowledge. At home in America, they had started learning in childhood how to solder, weld, and do other metal work. Except for a few whose fathers had been "Nepmen"[26] with enterprises of their own, Russian boys couldn't even begin to dream about doing anything like this.

By now I was catching on to the ways of the camp. My transfer to the electric shop was arranged directly through my brigade leader after the shop foreman requested it. Very probably I could have sat out my five-year term there provided that I stayed with the job. I might then have spent two or three years as a "free" man, but by 1948 they could certainly have put me away again, this time for at least ten years; for it was then that Stalin began "consolidating the home front." This meant nothing more nor less than reimprisoning everyone who had previously been in the camps. In 1941, however, I was unable to foresee all this. I thought only of how I might survive the terrible winter of 1941–1942. Because they adopted the line of conduct I had designed for myself, three of my fellow prisoners—the student Rusinov, the ship designer Zvenigorodski, and the engineer "Isaak Kogan"—reached the end of their sentences without mishap. "Kogan" had the job of charging storage batteries in our electric shop just as in the *sharashka* immortalized in Solzhenitsyn's *First Circle,* where he appears as a character under this name.

26. In the twenties, during the brief period of New Economic Policy (NEP), small-scale private enterprise was permitted and those engaged in it were called "Nepmen."

White and Blue

No sooner had I put down solid roots in the electric shop than suddenly in mid-November I was summoned to the shed where the designer Yuri and the rate-setter Boris were working. When I came in, Georgi, the production planner, and Vasili, the foreman of the machine-tool shop, were already there—in short, all the "bosses."

"Well, how do you like your setup?" one of them asked me.

"I couldn't ask for anything better. What could be nicer than being a *rabotyaga*?"

"But you're not just any *rabotyaga;* you're a very special one. If they figured your output properly, in accordance with existing quotas, you'd be getting only three-hundred grams a day.[27] Boris is risking his life signing your padded work sheets."

"Boris knows why he's signing," I snapped back. "Somebody else could very well be signing them right now."

"All right, it's nothing to hassle about. But stop slacking. When you were stretched out on your bunk in Butyrki, you sounded mighty brave. But here in the camp you're singing a different tune."

"What is it you want from me?"

"There's no flour in the camp. The mill has broken down. Another week or ten days and the prisoners won't be getting even an ounce of bread. A trainload of barley and rye came in. But since there was no place to store it, they dumped it right on the ground and covered it over in very sloppy fashion. It's starting to rot now. It has to be reground as soon as possible. But first we have to make a couple of millstones and hulling mills. Yuri can't cope with all this by himself. You're a designer, so you must help him work up some drawings for the mill machinery."

By now I understood quite well the meaning of intense mental effort under conditions designed to exhaust a man completely, and I was to understand it even better after the bread supply gave out. Only Yuri could have any real notion of the burden facing me. Any project planning or rate setting is child's play by comparison with the creative work of a designer. The expenditure of phosphorus, which at that time was considered essential for sustaining the activity of the brain, would increase greatly. But what other choice was there? If I refused I would be gnawed by conscience. I would virtually be murdering my fellow-prisoners. It

27. *Three hundred grams a day:* i.e., the lowest ration of bread in the camps. Prisoners were fed according to their output, the most productive getting up to nine-hundred grams of bread a day. Falsifying the quota on the work sheet (record of daily output or work performed) was the commonest form of *tufta.*

was dreadful to think about the men condemned to work in the lumber camp. Working a saw in arctic cold while standing waist deep in snow and with no bread in their bellies would be an unbearable ordeal. I consented, but on one condition: that after finishing, I should be allowed to return to the electric shop.

The next day Yuri and I started working out designs for a millstone and a hulling mill, even though we hadn't the slightest idea of what either was like. The miller, himself a prisoner, had a pass to move to and from the barbed-wire zone without a guard: when he dropped in to see us, he explained the gist of the matter in the simplest terms. After asking him to give us the required measurements, we began to work with a will—in our own fashion, not according to camp regulations. Even under normal conditions a designer's work demands pauses for rest; but when you start feeling lightheaded from hunger, you have no alternative but to take a break. During our respites we talked over a good many things.

A new element came into our conversation thanks to the twenty-five-year-old Boris Kh. He had been given three years for Zionist activities; among the other fantastic trumped-up charges brought against him this particular one at least seemed based on real fact. Eagerly he related how the movement originated and who its founders were. Zhabotinski[28] aroused his special admiration, and for that reason Boris always cleverly managed to add some combination of blue and white to his drab, shabby clothing. He introduced us to the medieval history of the Jewish people. He was proud of his heritage, which he traced back to Spain. The "Hispanioli," as he called them, were in his opinion the most gifted, the most brilliant representatives of the Jewish nation, its spiritual aristocracy, so to speak. It was his dream that the Jews might be reunited, but along purely voluntary lines, and that a national Jewish state might be created. To me all this seemed just and proper.

The viability and firmness of my convictions which originated in my conversation with Boris came home to me during the war between the Arabs and Israelis in 1967. The Egyptians, Syrians, and Palestinians have done me no harm. I have never seen them, I know nothing about them, and I wish them all a just and bloodless settlement of the conflict.

I am aware of the so-called "stiff-necked"[29] quality of the Jews and I have had my enemies among them. In my younger days I used to consider them responsible for the Bolsheviks' success in October, 1917. But when

28. Zhabotinski: One of the founders of Zionism in Russia; influenced the world Zionist movement. White and blue are the Zionist colors.
29. See Exodus 32:9 and 33:3.

I learned of the Six-Day War, I felt their impending troubles as if they were my own.

In the light of all this, I began thinking over a few things:

— I was only a child when Russia and the best of her sons were being destroyed.

— As a youth I was full of energy and good intentions; but since the corrupt environment of that time did not point me in the right direction, I sat on the sidelines while the peasants were being exterminated and the church was being ground into the dust. Moreover, my outward behavior was in no way different from that of the advocates of evil.

— In the prime of life, when I was in captivity, I did not know how to incite revolt among our slaves and so avert their inglorious end.

— In the years that had followed, however, I had gathered insight and experience. Now I saw in my mind's eye the approaching mass murder of a people who had already endured so much and who had lost six million of their number.

— During the Six-Day War I was still unfree, that is, I was still behind the Iron Curtain and therefore unable to act.

Now that I am finally in the free world, I make this vow:

— If the threat of annihilation ever again hangs over Israel and my hand is capable of holding a gun, I will volunteer for service in her army.

How We Fed the Men

At the time the mill broke down, the amount of processed grain still on hand was negligible. The predicted bread famine set in just as our work on the milling equipment got into full swing. Since the breakdown put the mill out of commission for four days, the *zeks* were six days without their bread ration—additional time was needed for grinding the grain, transporting the flour, and baking the bread.

Even the most ruthless boss, if he were guided by sound business sense, would have put only the two designers and the team of repairmen to work during those six days—after making some provisions for feeding them. All the other *rabotyagi* would have been allowed to remain in the barracks. It is hard to conceive of a slaveholder who, besides depriving them of rations for six days, would drive 35,000 exhausted men out to work in blizzards, deep snow, and extreme cold some six to eight miles from shelter. But here in the Kai Forests were mean, worthless little people who actually performed this deed—the kind you might have credited the German SS with. The commandant of the Camp Point,

Portyanov, and the head of the Second Division, Tkacheya, huddling together in the office to keep warm and showing not the slightest sign of pity for the convicts, no doubt discussed the situation in their usual shoddy phrases. One could just imagine it:

"The loss in manpower will rise sharply, and it may show up in production at the lumber camp and the sawmill."

"True, but there's nothing we can do about it, even if we wanted to. Without directives from the administration I simply cannot take it upon myself to halt the work. When I inquired about it at headquarters, they replied that if the camp holds up the delivery of fuel wood for the Perm rail line, the commandant will answer with his head for the whole camp."

If the higher-ups were so abjectly obedient, one could scarcely expect anything better from underlings. The supervisors, the personnel in the commandant's office, the medical staff, the guards, all blindly carried out what they had been ordered to do. The system looked like any normal, everyday routine: men attended to their appointed duties and followed explicit instructions—which were to deliver the fuel wood at all cost. But at the hands of these ordinary little people a monstrous crime was being committed, nothing less than genocide. We were virtually living in an extermination camp. It was a system created by the Devil, with everyone absolving himself of guilt by pointing out that he had been simply following an order; so in the final analysis it was Comrade Stalin who was personally responsible for everything.

It is said that capital punishment in the electric chair is administered by several executioners, each pulling his own separate switch. In this way not one of them knows who it is that pulls the fatal switch, and so not one of them is put in a position of having to consider himself a killer. Our system, as I have described it, has much in common with the team operating an electric chair, but there is also a substantial difference. The massive edifice of the Stalinist hierarchy creates an ever-increasing downward pressure of terror. In addition, there is the vast role played by the army of secret informers, peering into all the nooks and crannies of people's lives. If ever an official is sufficiently moved in his heart to mitigate somewhat the harsh existence of the ordinary citizen, such a generous impulse is abruptly checked by fear of an informer's report.

Yuri and I held up until our job was done, mainly because the miller, fearing for his head and thus more concerned than anyone else that the mill be repaired as quickly as possible, had managed to smuggle in by truck a sizable crate of potatoes to the engineering design office—that is to say, the shed in which we were working. In comradely fashion we split it into five shares, with each of us getting six kilos. Following the example of Jack London, I ate my allotment raw in order to ward off scurvy.

We dared not include more men in our share-out because that would have given the miller away. To make things easier for the *rabotyagi* in our brigade, however, we resolved not to demand any work from them, except for the parts we needed for the mill project. Moreover, we firmly padded their work sheets so that they might receive the maximum ration for those days. Boris was primarily responsible for this, with some assistance from the foreman, Vasili. The former devised favorable quotas, while the latter helped write up details of fictitious jobs. As a consequence, the workshop suffered no human losses. By contrast, the energies of the prisoners at the lumber camp were drained completely, and one after another dropped out of action to swell the number of those dying from starvation.

As my activity as a designer was drawing to a close, I began giving some thought to the tiny burrow in the electric shop that had been promised me. But just at this time a prisoner called Zandrok unexpectedly arrived from the engineering division of the administration. The door flew wide open, and in came a stalwart, manly figure dressed in well-made clothes. His face might have been hewn from marble, the blue eyes were bold and unflinching, and the wiry, gray hair was closely cropped. In Moscow a man such as he had become a great rarity. How shabby, unkempt, and dirty we were alongside him! After removing his hat, he stretched out his hand and introduced himself: "Zandrok."

Urbane and clever, he was an interesting conversationalist. We all found him very likable. He had come to repair a large diesel generator of ancient construction, in which the ignition system had broken down. In the taiga, where there were no models to study, no opportunities for consultation, and hardly any books or manuals, such a job would be no simple matter. I had been quite determined to return at once to the electric shop, but with very little trouble Zandrok was able to change my mind.

"Our comrades at the new Fifteenth Camp Point[30] have to sit in the dark. Besides that, they have no bathhouse, and they're being eaten alive by the lice. We must help them and repair the diesel."

We did not need him to tell us what we already knew, but the phrase "our comrades" sounded unusual in our ears—he meant, of course, "our comrades in misfortune."

Camp life had bred hostility and alienation, mutual distrust and treachery: we retained feelings only for those close to us—relatives and

30. A lumber camp.

old friends. And now unexpectedly we heard this long-forgotten word, conveying at least a sense of human solidarity, if not of brotherhood, in the face of the horrible conditions that bound us all together. A voice spoke within me: These are dreadful days, but we are only at the beginning of them. Let us stop trying to hide. He who has only a short sword must approach closer to danger, as one of the ancient Roman emperors said. And when I learned further that a friend of mine from Butyrki had ended up at the Fifteenth Camp Point, the question as to what I should do was settled once and for all. I started applying my mind to the structure of the diesel engine, and shortly thereafter we had the ignition system back in working order.

But our main problem was how to continue providing food for the men. "All the *tufta* will show up at the first inspection," Boris warned.

Vasili backed him up: "It's too easily discovered. We get caught on two or three doctored work sheets, and they'll ship us off to 'Captain Borisov's dacha' for six months. We'd be lucky to hold out there more than two weeks."

We racked our brains over the matter and then decided to add the signature of the chief inspector to the work sheets, to give them a look of greater authenticity. True, if they caught us on this, three rather than two of us would be sent off to die at the dacha. The choice fell on me, since I was known for my brazen self-assurance in discussions with the authorities. On this occasion I had no hesitation. In this way the three of us were able to feed the men. The *zeks* worked as well as they were able, and got the maximum ration, reaching as much as nine hundred grams of bread daily after the mill reopened. As for our five-man team, we ordinarily received seven hundred grams of bread; often the allotment fell off to six hundred, but sometimes it rose to nine hundred. Because of this system, only a few men on the permanent staff of the machine shop were to die before the spring of 1942.

During the same period at the lumber camp the death rate was so high that few survived. The hopelessness of the situation there was aggravated by detail foremen who, to insure their own survival, imposed murderous extortions on the *rabotyagas,* by forcing them to give up their bread in turn, thus securing for themselves the "liberated" rations. The brigade leaders practiced extortion less frequently; only a few of them resorted to such villainous means. In the machine shops, there was not a single instance of such extortion. It is interesting, by the way, to note that the *rabotyagas* showed not the slightest gratitude for our efforts to save them. They accepted everything as if it were to be taken for granted. Nobody even once said "Thank you" to those of us who had risked our necks for their sake. In 1944 when I came out half-alive from the isolation ward, not one of the *rabotyagas* (who by now were being fed reasonably well) offered me as much as a hunk of bread.

The reason for such behavior lies in the brutalization that takes hold of a man whose intellectual development is at a rudimentary stage, who has been deprived of the light found in Christian precepts. Under the influence of a bestial environment, the basic goodness and humaneness within his heart become atrophied; gradually his compassionate feelings shrivel up and disappear altogether. He justifies his actions with standard sayings made up of the vilest underworld speech. His assessment of people and events reverts to the law of the jungle: "You die today, and I'll die tomorrow." The *zek* was acquiring the habits of a jackal—wagging his tail in the presence of the mighty, preying on the weak, and taking anything he found lying around unattended.

I have no intention whatsoever of passing judgment on any working man at the end of his tether. He should not be held responsible. Those who have created this regime of universal corruption and mass extermination are the ones to blame.

In order to fill in the picture, I should also relate how we were fed in the spring of 1942. The grinding stones and hulling mills that we installed went to work at processing the grain that had simply been dumped on the ground. Since there were no facilities for storing a large quantity of flour— and in view of the fact that production had been severly impaired by the horrifying death rate—the administration voiced no objection to our feeding the starving prisoners with the surplus. From the ground barley dough-like kasha was made, as well as thick gruel and baked puddings. The bread ration was also increased.

But instead of falling off, the mortality rate continued to climb. The *zeks* who had managed to survive were in a thoroughly weakened condition, for their diet had been not only devoid of carbohydrates and proteins, but of fats and vitamins as well. The grim reaper cut a broad swath through our ranks. Because they could not assimilate the large amounts of barley, the men became covered with sores. Dystrophy, pellagra, and night blindness raged among us.

It was clear that only those who could get hold of green onions, which in this part of the world didn't appear until June, would endure. My American friend in the electric shop, Ben Murtoo, died of scurvy, even though I had brought him the one onion I was able to obtain. But that was only a drop in the bucket compared to what he needed.

For many of the other camps during the war, grain deliveries came too late. Vyatlag was simply very lucky. After the partial evacuation of the camp serving the White Sea–Baltic Canal, we received, in addition to equipment and sick inmates, its unused grain. Vyatlag was chosen probably because it was less than two hundred miles from a main rail route. The other camps, by and large, were situated in the middle of nowhere, at remote distances from centers of supply. Imagine the conditions in those places!

Hunger begot certain other consequences at our camp. There were hordes of rats, which occasionally fed on the bodies of dead *zeks*. The authorities were faced with the problem of burying thousands of corpses: large heaps accumulated while awaiting burial. In spite of terrible hunger, very few of our men resorted to eating rats. In all that time I ran into only one. If there had been more instances of this, we surely would have learned of them.

Nor did we hear of cannibalism, except for a single case. A man on a loading detail fell beneath a freight car and had his chest crushed by the wheels. As a result, his lungs became exposed and wound themselves around a wheel. They were consumed on the spot by another *zek,* who wasted no time getting at them.

Instances of corpse-eating were also rare. In 1943 we had a corpse-eater in the isolation cell because of his proclivities. His pale, slobbery mug, thick-lipped and moon-shaped, always appeared just before feeding time, when he would rise from his bottom bunk, lean against the one above while rocking on his heels, and inevitably launch a discussion on the joys of stuffing the belly. He presented such a sickening spectacle that on one occasion even an underworld character, lying in the bunk opposite his, could not refrain from kicking him with a bare foot. Not long afterward, the corpse-eater was taken away for a psychiatric examination, which at that time could lead to his being set free, especially since he had not been convicted as an enemy of the regime.

It is difficult to explain why incidents of the kinds just described were not far more numerous, particularly when viewed against the background of mass cannibalism that occurred during the famine in the Volga region—especially in 1923—or during the government-planned starvation of the peasants that was part of the collectivization process in the Ukraine and other areas. In those days it was not uncommon for a mother, driven to desperation, to devour her own child behind the closed shutters of her hut. Such unspeakable acts were certainly made easier by a sense of impunity induced by isolation from people who might have been able to lift the fallen spirit and direct it toward God, or at least toward humaneness. Even when the average human being reaches the point of total exhaustion, the temptation to commit heinous crimes and indulge in loathsome vices will meet with moral resistance so long as he feels some pressure from everyday society and public opinion, from fear of disgrace and punishment. Since a *zek*'s life was constantly in plain sight of all his fellow inmates, it was nearly impossible for him to perform vile acts in secret or to cover them up afterward. Another restraining factor was that there were always enough men convicted under Article 58 who had not lost their human attributes, even in the most frightful times.

How Stalin's Camps Achieved the Same Results as Hitler's Gas Chambers

By now you are more than ready to learn how the Stalinist camps, particularly in 1941–1942, fulfilled the function of the gas chamber. The majority of men in the lumber camps were so worn down by their earlier experiences in prison and transport that the work of felling trees killed them off within a month. Here the role of the gas chamber was played by these factors:

— a starvation diet, which by itself could kill a man, whether he worked or not;

— no issue of camp clothing, everyone continued wearing what he arrived in;

— production quotas that were wholly unrealistic under the prevailing conditions;

— a cross-country trek of five or ten kilometers between barracks and work area, which had to be made twice a day, often in deep snow;

— the dreadful arctic winter of 1941–1942, when the air temperature never rose above minus-thirty-five degrees centigrade; but no matter how cold it got, the men were still driven out to work;

— no day of rest—the only respite came when, instead of being marched off to the woods, the *zeks* were taken just outside the barbed-wire zone to undergo a body search while they stood in the snow;

— hordes of bedbugs, and frequently of lice as well;

— the cold in the unheated barracks.

I repeat: a month—or even two weeks—of backbreaking labor was quite sufficient to put a man permanently out of action. By the end of that time what little strength he had preserved was gone. He could no longer make the hike to the logging area or even stand upright while the flunkies assembled the men for work; he began dying a slow death.

Such was the method of extermination in the camps—a method made worse by agonies that could stretch out over months. Death from a bullet would have been bliss compared with what many millions had to endure while dying of hunger. The kind of death to which they were condemned has nothing to equal it in treachery and sadism.

Monstrous as it is at heart, the Soviet regime always tries to put on a pharisaical air of being quite normal, just like any other system. Since famine and death from hunger are recurrent features of it, it has to attempt to explain them away—and it made special efforts to do so during the period I have been describing: "We are at war. Men are being killed at the front. Citizens behind the combat zone are also going hungry. If we make conditions in the camp better than they are outside, then it will no longer scare anybody."

Imagine the following dialogue, if such a thing had been possible, between an adversary of the Soviet system and one of its champions:

"Let me ask you this. What's the good of forced labor if mass murder is the result?"

"Well, you see, the country is hard pressed for manpower. If we had to turn the army into lumberjacks, we would certainly lose the war."

"But how come England and the U.S.A. don't have a single labor camp? How come they don't drive men to death?"

"You know as well as I do that we're surrounded by the capitalist world[31]—we must defend ourselves. . . ."

Note how convenient this was: a man is handed the cruelest of death penalties in the form of an interminably slow agony, but since no clear-cut order for instant execution (by firing squad, for example) has been issued, nobody in particular is to blame. People are easily lulled into acceptance as long as you use the right semantic tricks. It should not be forgotten, however, that millions of people became involved in this murderous enterprise and, therefore, morally are accomplices.

I cannot find the slightest justification for the slaughter of millions by hunger. The fact is that the regime applied it on a wide scale, not only during the war but before and after as well.[32] Let me simply say that a government that boasted of its preparedness for war in actual fact had exhausted its supplies by the second month. Not only the camp inmates

31. A favorite propaganda slogan. The people knew that the capitalist world sends its spies and that the camps are needed to keep them imprisoned.

32. Of all the many organized mass famines, it suffices to mention the two worst ones that affected the whole country. The first was during the Civil War and resulted from the grain requisitions, when special detachments roamed the villages, stripping them bare. Particularly affected was the Volga Region in 1921–1923.

The second big famine, in 1931–1933, afflicted the whole country. The Ukraine suffered in particular. The authorities confiscated all the grain reserves and thereby condemned the population to starvation.

but military and civilian populations as well were condemned to famine; such a government has no legitimate claim to regard itself as representing the people and protecting the interests of the country.

How can anyone who is aware of the tremendous burden of crime that our leaders have perpetrated continue to support them!

5

VYATLAG: THE FIRST
YEAR OF THE WAR
(Continued)

How Our Neighbors Outside Acquired New Clothes

There were a great many Latvians in the camp. Those who arrived in our transport were, by and large, men who had held important posts. They were Latvia's elite—not only by virtue of position and education, but also by their understanding of their nation's way of life. The majority were brought into the camp without having undergone the preliminaries of interrogation and prison; consequently, they had managed at the last moment to stuff their traveling bags with clothing, pork fat, cigarettes, etc. At first, the supervisors, since they had all this to be offered by way of bribes, let them loaf. The Latvians shunned the mess hall altogether. They passed the time smoking long cigarettes and chatting among themselves.

After all the pork fat was gone, the supervisors started calling them out to work, but at the same time they cast a meaningful eye in the direction of their luggage. In due time the contents were emptied—suits, jackets, and fur coats, all of Western quality and cut. We had never seen the likes of them. Some of the stock went to the supervisors as payment for days of idleness, but the bulk of it was exchanged for bread and pork fat. It wasn't long before even the folks dwelling in the villages of the Kai Forests were going about in the most elegant finery—all obtained at the price of a little fat or plain black bread.

But eventually the suitcases yielded the last of their treasures; the last of the tobacco went up in smoke; the food supplies had been consumed long ago. The supervisors no longer smiled when they entered the barracks. With a menacing swirl of their sticks they now summoned the Latvians out to work. The poor devils were finding out for the first time in their lives the meaning of hunger. They were being initiated in the daily ritual of output quotas, of the meager bread ration and the watery soup. Very shortly they would gain first-hand knowledge of the "penalty ration"[1] at mess and the truncheon. As early as November they began presenting a horrible sight. Wearing whatever remained of their splendid wardrobes, these work-spent Latvians would file past like animated corpses, their faces a sickly blue. Along with other men whom a lack of nourishment had reduced to helpless bags of bones, they were soon crowding into the "death" barracks.

How this diet affected a man is illustrated by the example of Turmanis. Once a soldier in the foreign legion of either France or Spain, Turmanis was a powerful giant of a Latvian, who stood at a height of six and a half feet. Now he lay nearly motionless, except to take a slight stir when his bread ration was brought around. After nibbling on it a brief while, he would sink back into his stupor.

For prolonging this agonizing death from starvation, it might have been Satan himself who had measured out the exact dose in the form of the prisoner's daily bread allowance: 375 grams, of which only forty percent, or less, consisted of genuine flour. It virtually amounted to nothing more than a soggy clay-textured lump. I should add that during the baking process husks and other substitute ingredients less definable were mixed in with the rye and barley flours, thereby lessening the already negligible calorie content of our so-called bread. It is no wonder that under such murderous conditions only two or three man from a transport of a hundred *zeks* would still be alive after a year in the camp.

As Westerners, the Latvians were used to a free exchange of opinions. But even within their circle the camp authorities managed to recruit stool pigeons. Consequently, more than a few Latvians landed in the camp punishment cells; in general they were the best from their group—very outspoken fellows who voiced their indignation pointedly and fearlessly. During the first year of the war the only way anyone could expect to come out of the punishment block was with his toes pointed skyward. Dysentery, scurvy, and pellagra were just as rife there as anywhere else in the camp.

A *zek* named Maslov, who had gone through six months there in the

1. Three hundred grams of bread.

winter and spring of '42, told us the following. From time to time a professional thug was thrown into the cells for committing robbery within the camp. These people, tormented by hunger, would occasionally under cover of night strangle some debilitated Latvian lying on a bottom bunk. To give the corpse a live appearance, they would prop it up in a sitting position—all this to get the man's tiny bread ration. Since decomposition was slow to set in in a body so wasted, they were able to sustain the fraud for two or three days. But when the stench became unbearable, they would yell out to the turnkey, "Hey, chief, let's get this carrion out of here!"

Glory to the Finns!

We were witness to the destruction of some of Latvia's finest men. Their wretched end might have been averted. I had already come to the firm conviction that men are destroyed because they do not know how to help each other—or, rather, are unwilling to do so. Thus it was that I began analyzing, at first in a desultory way, then with passion, the question of what the conduct of the Latvians, Estonians, and Lithuanians ought to have been at the time of the Russo-Finnish War.

In 1939 the heroism of the Finns awoke the world's admiration. They truly won eternal glory as Baron Mannerheim led his nation of three million against Stalin, who was backed by a population of two hundred million. Like the ancient Spartans at Thermopylae, the Finns waged a fierce struggle to retain their freedom. Generations to come should be made aware of how the Mannerheim Line crushed one clumsily mounted Soviet attack after another; how hunters and small farmers, equipped with rifles, skis, and keen eyesight, defended a frontier that stretched nearly a thousand miles; how they strapped themselves to the upper branches of trees to pick off the enemy with sniper fire; how wounded Finns ripped off their bandages when they were taken prisoner. Ordinary people behaved like heros, since they had genuine faith in their military and political leaders. They were battling to save their independence and their countrymen. They were battling against the threat of enslavement and annihilation. Their conduct should be for us an object of study, and in many respects it should be emulated.

The three small Baltic countries ought to have allied themselves with Finland against Stalin's naked aggression; for after Poland had been partitioned—by then an old story for her—in 1939, the fate of the Balts was foreordained. To any thinking person it was clear that the division of

Poland between the two aggressors was, in effect, a division of their spheres of influence. This should have been understood by the Baltic governments immediately after the partition; any illusions they might still have cherished should have evaporated the moment that Stalin attacked Finland. Knowing perfectly well what their fate would inevitably be if they simply sat back and waited, they should have united in mobilizing their forces and in issuing a joint protest to Stalin with the demand that he cease military operations against the Finns. Most probably Stalin would have then moved troops into the Baltic region, but a few months later that was going to happen anyway. If they had immediately taken the initiative, without waiting for the aggressors to strike, these nations might not have been so completely crushed by Stalin and Hitler. Or, if they had responded with joint resistance once the invasion was launched, they might have preserved something of their independence and thereby won glory and true greatness for themselves. Such a resolute stand should have had an enormous moral effect. Hitler, no doubt, would have urged Stalin to end his war with the Balts just as he had previously asked the Red dictator to wind up his conflict with the Finns. Undoubtedly, Stalin would have gone ahead anyway and sliced off half of the Balts' territory; but the losses might have been only temporary. Perhaps a war fought by partisans in their native forests would have made it possible for the prisoners in Stalin's camps to revolt. But in 1939 it was out of the question for either the Finns or the Balts to translate any such idea into practice, for they had neither the means nor the forces to implement it. Had the Western allies contributed some much needed direction and support, the Finns, together with the Balts, might have carried out a trial raid against a Soviet camp near the Finnish border. But that was the most they could have done at the time. Under the conditions then prevailing, it would have proved to be a fatal mistake for the Soviet prisoners to respond with an uprising: Stalin would have wasted no time putting such dangerous men to death. An uprising in the camps would have been possible only in the course of a major war and on condition that all would have been coordinated well in advance and use made of the element of surprise.

One Day in the Life of Our Brigade and How It Survived the Winter

In our central camp[2] during the winter of 1941, there were two other work brigades besides ours in the machine shop that were considered fairly lucky: those assigned to the locomotive repair shop and, even better, the freight depot. Here life was just possible, and the men had some hope of getting through the winter.

A normal day for the machine-shop brigade began at four A.M. We were aroused by the clanging of an iron rail that hung from a post. One-third of our seventy men were sent out to fetch the bread, for which task we had constructed a sturdy box with handles and a lid that could be locked. While the bread was being handed out, eight men guarded the box from attacks by the criminal element; then they carried it to the barracks in order to distribute the bread among the *zeks*. The other fifteen armed with sticks provided additional protection. The law of the thugs—"You can die today, and I'll die tomorrow"—held savage sway. This saying was the motivating principle behind the behavior of every criminal. They had no desire to work, nor did they know how. Since the very beginning of the war we had not been allowed to receive packages from home, so there was nobody to shake down. Since the kitchen was low on supplies, it could give extra handouts only to the administrative staff and their most loyal flunkies. Meanwhile the petty thieves were virtually as famished as the ordinary *zek*.

Because our brigade was indispensable to the camp and because it had sound leadership, it was fed better than the others. Consequently we were the strongest group in the camp. Like moths to a flame, the criminal element was drawn toward us in their relentless urge to survive at the expense of everybody else. But our "brain trust" worked out appropriate defensive measures. Therefore, after the first attack on our bread carriers, we had made a box and had organized a rotating escort of twenty to twenty-five men. After that incident subsequent attacks by the desperate thugs were fended off without any loss to us. Similar assaults upon the logging brigades often succeeded. The authorities were deaf to complaints and simply shrugged them off, thus letting it be known that there was no objection to the victimized *zeks* settling accounts with the thieves on their own—this was essential if the brigade was to meet its output. Every successful attack by the thugs undermined a brigade's strength, and the

2. Vyatlag consisted of a whole network of camps under the same administration. (Tr.)

work suffered as a result. But the administration lacked effective means of suppressing the depredations by the starving thieves.

Whenever a *rabotyaga* was deprived of his "staff of life," his bit of bread earned by superhuman effort under horrible conditions, he went wild, and so did his comrades. In no time lynch law became rife, or to be more exact, primitive vigilante law, Russian style. An offender caught in the act of stealing bread would be tossed in the air by other prisoners and allowed to crash to the ground; this was repeated several times, damaging his kidneys. Then they would heave him out of the barracks like so much carrion.

As early as the end of September 1941, our "brain trust" made it a rule among us that bread was not to be left. It was either to be eaten at once or taken along to work and finished off on the job. In this way we avoided brawls and mob justice.

But once in December, the leanest time of year, I had a pain in my stomach, and I made the inexcusable error of leaving half of my bread ration in the barracks. No sooner was I on my way to work than I became absolutely certain that it would be stolen. All day long I could not shake off a sense of guilt. My only consolation was the thought that one of the orderlies[3] left behind on barracks duty might take it. If this proved to be so, then as long as I kept quiet about it, nobody would suffer on account of my mistake. When we returned to camp that evening, I walked at the head of the column of prisoners in order to be one of the first to rush into the barracks. There the orderlies, looking pleased with themselves, immediately showed me a captive whom they had driven into the corner by the stove. He was a fourteen-year-old thief of small stature. His little eyes, filled with mortal terror, darted from side to side. He fully realized what was coming to him. If he had been an adult, my intervention could not have prevented his being punished on the spot, since hostility toward the thieves had reached its peak. The orderlies confirmed his theft out of self-preservation, since otherwise the blame might easily have fallen on them. Their testimony should normally have sealed the fate of this youngster, but on seeing him, I said in a tone that allowed for no contradiction that we could not put children on trial. A few cuffs would be sufficient punishment. The others consented to this, and the frightened little animal, thoroughly relieved at getting off so cheaply, bolted out the door.

Let us get back to the daily routine of the brigade. After receiving our bread ration and thin soup, shortly after five A.M., we prisoners

3. I.e. prisoners assigned to look after the barracks.

were driven outside, lined up by brigades, and were then sent unit by unit through the gate and past the sentries. Around six A.M. we were already at our stations in the machine shop and at work. First of all, we took care of jobs that had to be expedited immediately. The whole machine shop was subject to penalties for delays and for failure to complete orders. We all were quite aware of this and worked as hard as we could. The *rabotyagas* knew their fates rested with us, just as ours depended on getting the most urgent projects done.

Jobs of secondary importance were done whenever we could get to them. As I have explained earlier, the system of output quotas existed only on paper, since we simply "dressed up" our actual daily output to make it look as though we had fulfilled them. Otherwise we would have been worked to death and ended up in the mass graves where dead prisoners were dumped with numbered tags on their right legs. To work twelve hours non-stop was impossible and nobody badgered us too much as long as the priority orders got done.

We spent a good deal of time drying out our heavy wadded-cotton stockings, which had been issued for winter wear. Because the stockings retained a great deal of moisture, our feet could easily become freezing cold.

At six P.M. our shift finished work, but we could not head back to the barbed-wire zone until the new shift arrived. This could mean a delay of a half-hour to two hours. Lights-out came at ten. As soon as they had eaten their evening soup[4] the work-spent men wasted no time crawling into their bunks to seek the oblivion of sleep. It was not always possible to sleep peacefully. Within each ten-day period we were roused two or three times in the middle of the night, either for a body search, a head count, or a visit to the bathhouse.[5]

"You Can Die Today, and I'll Die Tomorrow"

In the camp there was a constant war between the "regular" thieves who lived according to their code and the renegade thugs, known as "bitches," who did not. The latter were either put in charge of barracks or detailed as supervisors. Actually, though not very numerous, they held a frightening amount of power; after the top brass went home, they

4. *Balanda:* thin watery soup—the main nourishment for the camp prisoners, apart from bread.
5. As a rule, prisoners were taken out to the bathouse only at night; during the day they were expected to work.

remained in sole charge of the camp during the long winter nights. During our project of designing the mill equipment, our camp commander, who was ultimately responsible for seeing that such urgent work orders were filled, took it into his head to create "better conditions"[6] for us by moving us from the barracks into separate quarters. This consisted of a small room intended for six people and containing double-decker bunks; it was next to the Kommandatura, separated from it by a thin partition. It was impossible to get to sleep before two o'clock: we could hear the "regular" criminals being tortured by their renegade brethren in the administration. It made no sense for the renegades to use their fists, since this was a waste of energy and was hard on the knuckles, so the chief executioner, "Uncle Sasha," had introduced a refinement. Instead of his fists, he employed a small sledgehammer, which he applied with carefully measured blows. The torments of his victims sometimes began even before we returned from the shop. But more often they took place only after lights-out. Through the wall we could hear, "Uncle Sasha, I won't do it again! Uncle Sasha, I don't know anything!" Then Sasha's voice, "Speak up, you scum. Who did him in?[7] Speak up, you snake!" Then another blow followed by a scream. "Oy, stop Uncle Sasha! I don't know!" There was a sound of water being splashed on the man to revive him, then more blows; and again we could hear, "I don't know anything, Uncle Sasha!"

I had seen too much of the criminals' vile behavior to have any sympathy for them, but in fairness I must say that some who were dragged into Uncle Sasha's torture chamber comported themselves like heroes and did not betray their comrades even on the point of death. Two of them failed to break during the one week that we managed to endure in our "special quarters." Georgi, who stayed on longer, told us of later instances when Uncle Sasha's sledgehammer was ineffective against the recalcitrance of his victims. I give these due credit, though in the end most of the others squealed on their accomplices.

The persecution of the regular criminals was ruthless; but it helped us to get through that terrible winter with almost no casualties. Naturally the "bitches" who ganged up against them were concerned only with saving their own necks as they settled scores with the regular thieves. But had the regulars not been subjected to such cruel punishment, it would

6. A ritual Soviet term endlessly repeated by the camp commanders as an incentive to workers to fulfill quotas.
7. Evidently it is a case of the "regular" criminals having killed off an informer, or a "bitch." (Tr.)

have been much more difficult for us to devise methods for defending ourselves, and many of us would have been killed in fights with them. It would have needed at least half our numbers to guard our bread ration, and to avert the eventuality of an attack we would have required ten or fifteen men to be on watch every night. Since the regular crooks were well organized and quite numerous, they could easily have intimidated certain members of our brigade and overpowered anyone caught alone in the dark, since they were in complete control of the camp at night.

"Captain Borisov's Dacha"

The punishment detachment at Camp Number Six was known to the prisoners as "Captain Borisov's dacha." If you landed there, you were sure to die. A prisoner was usually condemned to the punishment detachment for no less than six months. During the war this period was purely nominal, since in the best of circumstances almost no one could have held out there any longer than in the average lumber camp— approximately a month. The regular criminals were the lords of the punishment detachment, and any "bitch" who was brought there could expect his life to end almost instantly. The ordinary prisoners—that is, the non-criminals—got a different kind of treatment at the hands of the criminals.

It should first be explained that under wartime conditions open defiance of the established order might be regarded by the authorities as "counter-revolutionary sabotage" (Article 58, Section 14), punishable by a ten-year sentence or sometimes by the death sentence—*vychka*.[8] Consequently, the "orthodox" criminals, having previously considered themselves immune from any obligation to work, began altering their mode of behavior—at least outwardly. One after another, they started to make some pretense at working. Although it was the non-criminals who were actually performing all the labor, the criminals would claim credit for achievement to themselves. As long as they could get away with this, wide-scale slaughter of the non-criminals would not serve their best interests. Only for that reason was a *rabotyaga* able to keep himself alive for any length of time. But the moment he fell ill and landed in the barracks for people who were dying, the criminals did not hesitate to take away his bread ration.

8. In camp slang, the term *vychka* means capital punishment, i.e., execution by bullet—in Russian, *vyschaia méra nakazania* (hence the abbreviation *vychka*).

Terrible hunger, together with other brutalizing conditions, drove the criminals into attempting to deprive the non-criminals of their bread. One result of all this was that many non-criminals exhausted by work and malnutrition were finally finished off by the guards who treated them as malingerers. Since the number of prisoners doing any work was hence rapidly diminishing, the camp authorities put a new rule in force: the bread ration was to be issued to each man at roll call, just before leaving the barbed-wire zone for work. Thus catastrophic mortality was averted for the time being. However, the criminals, finding it no laughing matter to have to go out into the forest every day, invented ways of getting around the new regulation.

Dancing on the Edge of the Grave

In the autumn of 1941, after arriving in the camp we got to know a *zek* who had been arrested at the height of the Stalin purges in 1937. He was quite young looking, although he was already almost fifty. His beautiful black eyes harmonized with his fresh complexion. His name was Feigin; he was a Jew from Odessa and a professional clown who always enlivened whatever company he was in. At that time he was in charge of the bathhouse and had a privileged position; he lived in a small room next to the bathhouse, not in the barracks with everybody else. Feigin realized that his job was bound to be given to some informer who had been a Party member with a history of good service to the regime, and he was therefore already trying to find another job for the coming winter. He was very glad at having made our acquaintance since this would help him to get work in the shop. Apart from this, however, he liked us because we were good listeners and appreciated the comic acts that he put on for us when he was in a good mood. I particularly remember the songs of Odessan Chekists sung before going out to execute people at night. To the accompaniment of a sad Jewish tune, he would clink his empty glass against an empty bottle on the table. The picture was completed by his melancholy, slightly bent figure, the glum expression of his face, the gestures and intonation. For a long time he would go on singing mournfully and appearing to get drunk before our eyes until finally he became the very image of an executioner in his cups.

Winter came early that year and it was a very severe one. We found Feigin a job in our shop. The work required no special skill—he simply had to look after the premises. But one day, unfortunately for him, the little shed which he occupied in the yard next to the diesel generator burned down—a spark from the generator had flown into a crack in the wall and the inflammable material of its inside lining had burst into flames. Nobody was to blame, but in the camps the Chekists regarded any such accident as the work of hostile agencies. The "criminal" or, even better, the entire "anti-Soviet organization" would be called to account and receive the punishment they deserved. Since Feigin was responsible for anything that happened in the yard, the chief of the shop was forced to give Feigin's name to the authorities, otherwise many innocent people would have perished in the overcrowded camp prisons. It was hoped that Feigin might somehow be spared since he was well known to the camp authorities. This was, of course, a slender hope, but he was in fact saved by a stroke of luck. On New Year's Eve, the camp hierarchs decided to have a party and gave orders for a "concert" (as they used to call it) to be arranged. The *zeks* all said as one man that it could only be done by Feigin. When the show took place under Feigin's efficient direction, the hungry, exhausted *zeks* at first looked on apathetically. But suddenly, toward the end, they all livened up. They saw before them an Odessan bootblack, a representative of the special breed of that southern town noted for gaiety, wit, and resourcefulness. Feigin held two brushes in his hands and had a box dangling at his side. The dance he performed bore some resemblance to modern rock-and-roll; clown and dancer had become one. With his brushes he described circles in the air and from his lips issued incoherent English phrases and snatches of tunes. The only incongruity in this gay dance came from the clown's large black eyes which seemed to be begging for mercy. I have never seen such an emotional performance. Dumfounded, everybody broke into applause. The agony that could be read in Feigin's eyes must have touched even the wolf's conscience of the head of the camp, for the order for his transfer to a penal camp was rescinded. The mute language of the soul had proved stronger than any logical arguments or verbal pleas. This was how Feigin saved his life.

Former Party Members

In our midst there were prisoners who had been sentenced during the purge of 1937. Every purge carried out by the regime had its own particular objective. In the early years of Soviet power, those who were liquidated included military officers, noblemen, workers, peasants, clergymen, Cossacks, merchants, house owners, and bureaucrats. During the collectivization period the regime once more hounded the peasantry, as well as the clergy and surviving members of the former commercial class; and for the first time the boom was lowered on the engineers. In a later period it was the turn of officials of the party itself.

When people speak about those purged in 1937–1938, they generally have in mind party bosses and all sorts of lesser functionaries, people who had always adhered rigidly to the "general"[9] line. But in fact many others were also rounded up at that time under an order listing no less than forty-eight different categories of persons liable to arrest, which affected all sections of the population, beginning with those "former people"[10] who still survived. Obviously, this left very few who were not grist for the exterminating machine. Within our little group of five, for instance, neither Georgi nor Vasili had ever been affiliated with the party but they had nonetheless been arrested. Georgi was a brilliant aeronautical engineer, formerly a colleague of the aircraft designer Tupolev. Vasili was a first-class technician who had worked with the cold-metal process in a major Kharkov plant. These excellent men had lost whatever illusions they might have had in respect to the realities of Soviet life.

Back in the transport wards of Butyrki in Moscow we saw a great number of former Communists file past us during our four-month wait there. They could be divided into two groups: those who evoked our sympathy—these were the majority—and those who aroused deep disgust. The former cursed Stalin, and a few even admitted their crimes against the nation. The latter proclaimed themselves as Stalinists and spun outrageous lies. Most of the first group did not live to reach the camps: I met only very few of them there. All the others I met belonged to the second category of ex-party workers.

A great many camp inmates who had worked in the party until they were rounded up in '37 or '38 remained loyal to its ideals; at least they professed as much. They regarded those outside the party with contempt and hatred. They lived in an atmosphere of treachery which they had created themselves. It was dangerous to get into conversation with any of them; the majority had close connections with the secret police. Every one of them regarded himself as an innocent victim of circumstances. They were sure that everything had been done according to law, that the party was never wrong—"When you cut down a forest, a few chips

9. This expression is used by the party to describe its program and aims and constantly occurs in the Soviet press.
10. Members of the privileged classes under the tsar.

must fly."[11] If any one of these men had been summoned by the camp commandant and told, "It was all a mistake. The authorities have reviewed your case and found you innocent. You will be released and your rights restored, but the party asks you to serve as an interrogator or a secret agent," he would certainly have eagerly agreed and taken up his duties with zealous self-righteousness.

I do not wish to say that all imprisoned party leaders were cowards and traitors. Those who in prison refused to sign their interrogators' spurious indictments and to name "accomplices" were tortured beyond endurance and ended up with a bullet in the back of their heads. Only those whose resistance had been completely broken and who had confessed to crimes they had never committed survived to serve sentences in the camps. And it was this scum who set the tone in the camps from 1937 to 1941. When we first arrived at our camp, we ran into a number of them. The picture began to change in the first months of the war as new contingents arrived from the army and the "veterans" of '37–'38 died off.

Anyone who has survived his first year in a camp knows how easy it is to behave well as long as everything is sunshine and roses, and how difficult it is under conditions designed to debase and destroy a man, when it is a struggle even to preserve human dignity. Concomitantly, a doctrine that purports to define a man's relationship toward the world at large is truly tested only under extremely trying circumstances rather than when life is going relatively smoothly. The Communist doctrine, dedicated only to the oppression of ordinary people, transforms many of its followers into traitors, informers, slaves of outworn formulas, and hypocrites forever fearful for their own hides and incapable of either individual protest or united action.

The Worst Kind of Death

In September, 1941, military men who had been charged with crimes at the front began arriving in the camp. In the army at that time "justice" was meted out swiftly: very little time was wasted on an investigation, and as a rule military tribunals passed the death sentence. However, some offenders received a ten-year sentence instead, and it was those who began swelling the numbers in the camps. The mood of these new arrivals was at first very cheerful. During their quarantine, many of them

11. The Russian equivalent of "You can't make an omelet without breaking eggs." (Tr.)

were cock-a-hoop that their lives had apparently been spared. In the evening they would drop into the barracks which served as the club-house,[12] and would break out into a merry *yablochko*,[13] a dance very popular with Soviet sailors in the early post-revolutionary years. But after tasting the sweetness of labor in the lumber camp through several days of unremitting rain just to earn a bit of bread, their mood took a sober turn and they no longer felt like visiting the club. They now sensed that death in the winter just ahead would be inevitable—and they were right. When a military officer showed up in the camp some time later for the purpose of recruiting for service at the front prisoners, such as them-selves, who had not been sentenced for political offenses, the ex-army men groveled at his feet and begged to be returned to the combat zone, even to a penal battalion.[14] Evidently they had divined the truth that death from a bullet or shrapnel was instant and certain, and thus preferable to dying by degrees from extreme overwork.

In our first contacts with these military prisoners we were taken aback when we saw how incompetent military commanders or, as they were again called, Soviet army officers were as leaders of men. Long ex-perience had shown that a prisoner is capable of commanding a work brigade only as long as he holds the respect of those under him. To be successful, he must have perfect mastery of the foul speech used by the criminal element, and in bad situations he should be able to restore law and order to his brigade through personal intervention, applying strong-arm methods whenever necessary. He must also see to it that his brigade is clothed and fed. If he himself is short on knowledge and experience in these matters, then it is his responsibility to pick a right-hand man with the necessary know-how to help him along. As a brigade leader, he is in duty bound to fight for better working conditions and reduced output quotas, to talk the supervisors and foremen into accepting falsi-fied work sheets, to pay out bribes, etc. In addition, he has the duty of insuring his brigade against performing anything that is not strictly re-quired or that can possibly be avoided.

A former submarine officer named Peterson badgered us endlessly to be appointed brigadier. He told us that all his life he had worked with men and that as a consequence he thoroughly understood the problems of leadership. Then one day he was ordered to replace our brigadier (an

12. The camps had a "Cultural-Educational Section" which in theory provided certain recreational facilities for the prisoners. As in the world outside, the premises set aside for such "cultural" activities were referred to officially as the "club." (Tr.)
13. Literally, "a little apple."
14. Units used for particularly dangerous tasks, such as clearing mine-fields. (Tr.)

old-timer in the camps, jailed as a kulak[15] back in the early 'thirties) who had fallen foul of the camp authorities. The main problems of feeding the men and keeping the work assignments down were out of Peterson's hands, since they continued to be handled by three of our fraternity. Nor did he have to worry about supplying clothes; except for the wadded-cotton stockings, there was nothing available. But even so he was unable to cope with his responsibilities.

As soon as he took over, members of the brigade began to growl in discontent. Factions hostile to him formed. Soon his orders were no longer obeyed. He appealed to the men, begging and pleading in lamentable fashion, but he didn't know how to use camp language forcefully. And when he used his talents for command, it was for the wrong cause. In the days before Peterson was put in charge, the supervisor would walk into the barracks after working hours and order the men to clean up the grounds outside. But our old tried-and-true brigadier, knowing very well that they were not required to carry out such an order, would engage in a fierce verbal duel; in the end, the brigade was left inside to sleep. As for Peterson, the moment the supervisor made a similar outrageous demand of him he would burst into a roar—God knows where he suddenly acquired such a stentorian voice—and rouse the men from their sleep. With a great show of earnestness, he would then drive everybody outside.

And the brigade had other reasons to be displeased with him. Complaints were heaped on him from all directions. He should have been removed outright, but we (that is, the members of our fraternity) did no more than lecture him. Although a rumor was circulating that Peterson was trying to turn the men against us, we ignored it—much to our cost shortly afterward.

It was Peterson who sent a comrade of ours to the grave. We had just managed to rescue him from the logging brigade. Badly frostbitten as he was, he had a strong will to stay alive; and in our opinion, he would have pulled through. But then one night the bathhouse attendant came stomping into the barracks, whereupon Peterson, true to form, began chasing the men out for a bath. Despite the fact that our comrade, who had a high temperature, begged the brigadier to let him lie in peace, the overzealous ass still ordered him off to the bathhouse. Several days later our friend was dead of pneumonia. We most certainly would have intervened on his behalf that night if we had been on hand; but as luck would have it, we were quartered at that time in the barracks next door. Unfortunately, it never entered the poor devil's head to come to us.

15. A well-to-do peasant in the early years of the Soviet state.

But Peterson had overplayed his hand this time. He was fired, and to everybody's satisfaction our old brigade leader was restored to his position.[16]

The incompetence of regular Soviet army officers as leaders, even as heads of lowly work brigades, was to be underscored by many future incidents. As a result, we could not help believing that the "conscious sense of discipline" which before the war had been much publicized as a feature of the Red Army was simply another lie turned out by the propaganda mill. In actuality, everything in the military was based on terror and brute force. An officer was not respected by his men for his personal merits. He was respected and obeyed only because all the instruments of oppression stood in support of him, and the lot of his subordinates was a hard one: constant assignments outside the line of duty, the guardhouse, the penal battalion, suicide missions, courts-martial.

Death's Dwelling Place

That first winter, as the men in the logging brigades rapidly lost their strength and, in due time, their ability to work or even to move, the camp barracks, one after another, were converted into houses of death. Whenever these men were taken off to the bathhouse, they resembled a procession of animated corpses. It was becoming unbearable to walk through the camp area at night and glance through the dully lighted windows of those sepulchral barracks: men in the prime of life were stretched out half-frozen and totally exhausted on their bunks, capable only of scratching flea bites and fighting off bedbugs. By the spring of 1942, the death rate in this camp of a thousand men had climbed to a rate of eighteen a day. Thousands of excellent men had gone to their graves. I will never forget how they were carried out of the barbed-wire zone in specially-made crates with lids, and how at the sentry post a bayonet was run through their heads—just to make sure that none of them was merely feigning death with the intention of trying to escape once they were outside.

Neither these lines nor the book itself are being written out of any desire for vengeance, since there is no longer anyone or anything to avenge. But it would be absolutely unforgivable of me to ignore or consign to oblivion these frightful episodes, for I feel a special re-

16. Peterson was eventually sent to the battlefront, even though he had been convicted under Article 58. As far as I know, this was a unique case.

sponsibility for the fate of millions of today's ordinary citizens, who themselves could be thrown into slavery at some future time and exterminated in the same way.

Self-Mutilation

I should like to pass on my observations concerning the absence of suicides under the extremely severe conditions of our concentration camps. The more that life became desperate, the more a prisoner seemed determined to hold onto it. For some prisoners, however, this resolve showed itself in an ugly form: survival at any price. Such people were quite willing, if needs be to walk over the dead bodies of others in order to save their own skins.

At the other end of the spectrum were men who strove both to survive and maintain their human dignity. They were the stoics. They held to a Christian viewpoint; thus they gained strength from prayer and set their hopes in the Divine Creator. Mean behavior was alien to their natures. They were always making an effort on behalf of others, either with a kind, meaningful word or by the example of their indomitable courage. As for suicide, they never gave it a thought.

The "self-mutilators" formed a somewhat odd category, which lay about mid-way between the two groups just described. As their name more than suggests, these prisoners, driven to the limits of endurance, sliced off their fingers; sometimes they amputated the whole hand. Punishment for such an act was harsh; they were charged with Article 58, Section 14.[17] In 1941–1942 they were sentenced to be shot; later they were given a ten-year prison term instead. The "self-mutilators" counted on their amputations to deliver them from the rigors of common labor, but the camp authorities were not of course deceived as to their motive, and often went so far as to deny them medical aid even when they were bleeding profusely. In years ahead, I ran across "self-mutilators" who had managed to come out from the camps alive. Evidently their plan had not entirely misfired. But to me, their scars served as a symbol of the horrors that were unleashed on millions of us in those terrible years.

How to Keep One's Human Decency in Camp

In the winter of 1941–1942 the underworld precept "You die today and I'll die tomorrow" was in operation not only among both the regular

17. Sabotage in time of war.

and renegade criminals, but also among the camp flunkies, the non-criminals convicted under Article 58, and a great many others. In the feverish effort at mere survival, many prisoners peddled information to the authorities and denounced each other. Everybody hated and feared his neighbors and thought nothing of sending someone else to the grave.

Standing in opposition to this general philosophy was our fraternity of five, bound together in misfortune and close friendship. Three of us voluntarily risked our necks every day by signing padded work sheets so that the rest of our men might eat. No one outside our group could be allowed to hear about this because of the ever-present danger of betrayal—since we were all classed as "counterrevolutionaries" and enemies of the regime, we would be tolerated by the camp administration only until the moment when we could be replaced by others with similar specialized skills.

Because we stood up for one another, furthermore, we had been able to resist the assaults of the criminal element, which was tightly knit together by its own bloody code of discipline, accepted as an ally of the regime, experienced in the arts of oppression, and skillful in taking advantage of any disunity among the rank-and-file workers.

By winter's end, however, only a pathetic handful of the criminal element remained alive; at the outset there had been about three hundred.[18] Of the seventy ordinary prisoners, on the other hand, who formed the mainstay of the machine-tool shop, not more than three had died. This discrepancy was not due to the fact that our men were essential to the camp because of their professional skills, but to the fact that the thieves' code was based on false premises. Our brigade had been properly fed during the winter because it was led by people who rejected this code. If any of the previous stool pigeons had stayed on in a supervisory capacity at the machine shop, I am sure that by spring we would have lost nearly half the work force but, fortunately, Georgi had succeeded in getting them kicked out. In the nearby locomotive repair shop where everything was controlled by secret informers the casualties were almost as high as those among the criminal element.

The deadly feud between regular and renegade criminals had sprung from the same ruthless code to which both sides adhered, namely, that you can put off your own death till tomorrow by killing your enemies today.

The contrast I am drawing here is between the tremendous strength of good and the self-destructiveness of evil. To be sure, one must be strict in defining the good. A man who embodies good must be capable of

18. Of these, fifty were sent to the war front.

loving those around him, of sacrificing his well-being, or, if necessary, even life itself—his own, not someone else's. And such sacrifices must be made not in the name of putting into effect some grotesque vision of the future but for the sake of principles which the common man holds dear, which touch on his daily life, which he can understand.

Is it possible for anyone to live honorably under dictatorship that rejects God, that is based on human enslavement? Atheism denies the existence of God; it denies the divine origin of the commandments passed down from Moses. Consequently, commandments are devised by mere mortals, with only limited validity. Ethical standards designed for an atheistic society, advantageous as they may be to the ruling class, run counter to the vital interests of the rank-and-file citizens enslaved by that class. And so we have two diametrically opposed ethical codes in our land. When the godless masters demand the truth from us, their slaves, we will not give it. When the masters forbid us to poach on their sacred preserves, we will poach. For such is our ethical code—the code of slaves in an atheistic state.

6

VYATLAG: 1942–1943

The Uprising at Ust-Usa

Back in 1927 our biology teacher read in class a brief item from a Moscow newspaper on an expedition in Siberia that had discovered in the Sayan Mountains a new range, extending over more than seven hundred miles. And with a smile, he explained to his young pupils that in our era such an event is possible only in the Soviet Union and in the region of the South Pole. Our teacher backed up his statement by pointing out to us the incredible vastness and potential resources of our land. It is not by chance that I recall this incident. It is also "only in the Soviet Union" that one may find young underground writers, talented and with something to say, but still—perforce—awaiting discovery by the world at large.

Not long before my departure for the West, one such writer allowed me to read a chapter from a story that he had devoted to the extraordinary events connected with the prisoners' revolt at Ust-Usa[1] at the end of 1942. He had himself been an eyewitness. As long as I was in the camps, not even the faintest of rumors about that episode came our way. It is my hope that one day Western readers will have an opportunity to read this man's book in full, and for this reason I will take the liberty of presenting here only a bare summary[2] of the episode, omitting names, statistics, and a good deal of other detail.

1. Ust-Usa was the administration center for the Pechora camps in the northeast part of European Russia.
2. A few inaccuracies may occur, since regrettably I did not have his manuscript at the time I wrote this outline.

Distinguished by starvation and overwork, the first year of the war left an indelible mark on all who survived it. For the camps in the region of the Pechora River, the second year was no easier; terror and despair continued to reign. The revolt there was organized by the commandant of a small camp stuck in the middle of nowhere. He himself had served a sentence on a non-political charge, and his "general staff" by and large also consisted of former prisoners, all of whom had been sentenced under Article 58.

From personal experience I know that when a man reaches the limit of physical endurance, he becomes thoroughly indifferent. The most he can manage is to reply with a firm no to any demand made on him. He no longer has the energy for even the slightest exertion; therefore, no one should doubt the statement in this eyewitness account that the prisoners by themselves would not have had the strength to start a revolt at that time without help from outside.

The "general staff"[3] established contact with the prisoners through the supervisors. At the same time the commandant ordered that they be given the maximum bread ration and did his best to improve their diet. On the day set for the uprising, the bathhouse, situated inside the barbed-wire zone was heated for the camp's armed security guards. After they had entered, undressed, and begun washing, the bathhouse was locked from the outside by the insurrectionists. After changing into guard uniforms, the commandant and his aides went to disarm the other security men—those who had remained in their barracks, or were doing sentry duty in the watchtowers. Then they distributed what they had seized— rifles, ammunition, sheepskin jackets, and *valenki*[4]—among the prisoners who were considered most trustworthy. Up to this point, there had been no casualties.

Shortly afterward, a patrol of rebels was sent marching in the direction of Ust-Usa, where the central headquarters of all the camps in the Pechora area was located. They made swift forays into several small camps lying along their route, where their guard uniforms enabled them to capture weapons and provisions without a struggle. Some of the prisoners from these other camps joined the rebel force. The next morning they moved in on the central headquarters and broke into the barracks of the security guard there. For the first time they now met real resistance. Since the prisoners knew they would be shown no mercy, they fought like lions. The authorities did not lose their heads, but began to

3. I.e., those responsible for arranging work details, etc. (Tr.)
4. Woolen felt boots, mainly produced by peasant home industry and now, also, in factories. In the Russian winter, this form of foot protection is indispensable, particularly in rural regions; there is, however, a constant shortage of felt boots.

draw in forces from elsewhere, threatening to cut off the small group of insurgents from their line of retreat. The rebels' commandant then decided to take his men to the north right through the heart of the main camp area, freeing all the prisoners as they went. Then they would descend like an avalanche on all the camps along the Kozhva River. Although they succeeded in liberating a few small camps, the price they paid was far too high, and the number of reinforcements they collected along the way was negligible. Hunger and exhaustion still served as the Soviet regime's allies. It was the same old tale of despair: men who are demoralized and physically worn out have no interest in becoming actively involved in a struggle. It would take more than one powerful appeal to arouse the multitudes in the camps.

The insurgents now took up the best strategic position they could find, laid in supplies of ammunition and food, and prepared for a last-ditch stand. For two weeks the prisoners valiantly held off the district militia as well as reinforcements from regular army units. The authorities were seriously concerned that a "Northern Front" might be forming against them, and very soon U-2[5] aircraft were also thrown in against the rebels. The rumble of gunfire could be heard as far away as Ust-Usa. Freezing weather was by now setting in with a vengeance. The insurgents had to be extremely cautious about lighting fires in order not to attract enemy fire. Still they continued to beat off the attacks. Even though they killed many soldiers, they themselves were almost down to the last man. When their ammunition gave out, the outcome was no longer in doubt. The handful of heroes still alive decided on suicide. The commandant was the last of his band to put a bullet through his head.

I call them heroes advisedly because they demonstrated that some men refuse to be changed into cattle and show themselves capable of rebellion.

In the first year of the war more than seven million zeks[6] were killed off. The survivors of this tragedy have no country[7] to call their own. Such a country must still be fought for.

5. A Soviet make, not to be confused with the American U-2. (Tr.)

6. I do not know exactly how the historians arrive at the figures for those killed in war, but I imagine that they use the evidence of official reports. No doubt they sometimes question participants or eyewitnesses, apart from consulting memoirs and diaries. Nothing will be found in the archives about the Stalin camps, since all evidence has been carefully destroyed by the central administration of the camps (Gulag of the NKVD) in Moscow during periodic purges and on the special orders of Stalin. Also destroyed were the people who had handled this evidence and hence knew too much. Perhaps, by a lucky chance, one may some day discover lists that have survived in some provincial NKVD headquarters or department of Gulag—

The Red Terror in the Camps

After the uprising at Ust-Usa had been suppressed, Moscow issued a directive to the effect that the Chekists must launch a new wave of terror against the inmates of the camps. I learned that the secret police had everywhere fabricated major cases charging prisoners with attempts to prepare an armed rebellion. Under Section 2 of Article 58,[8] their "crime" was punishable by death by a firing squad. If there were "mitigating circumstances," the sentence might be reduced to ten years.

Intimidation and repression—in other words, the Red terror—were achieved by the usual devices of propaganda and a massive deployment of secret agents, both official and unofficial. Then there were endless arrests of the nation's finest and most valuable citizens; investigations and interrogations, conducted in the most brutal manner; convictions that allowed for no appeal, and the wide-scale handing out of extrajudicial sentences based on the decisions of a "special tribunal"—the so-called "troika."[9] Vast numbers of people were thus condemned to death by execution, or were sent to the forced labor camps where they were killed off by exhaustion, hunger, and disease.

In the early period, there was a carefully fostered myth to the effect that terrorism is an inevitable consequence of the struggle for power and a valid means of retaining power in a time of fierce opposition. Then the creator of our system, Lenin, not long before he completely lost his sanity, went further by proclaiming the virtues of terror as "a method of persuasion." This raving lunacy was accepted as gospel truth though it must be said that Lenin was right in a certain sense: a government that is abhorrent to the great majority of citizens can be upheld only by constant terror. Terrorism by itself, of course, "persuaded" no one. But it

from these it could be possible to extrapolate figures for the whole country. Another approach would be to carry out a special census in some one part of the country in order to find which families have disappeared in part or in whole.

But those of us who lived through it all and were victims of it did not want to

---

7. In Russian, the author distinguishes between two diametrically opposed words for "country": a) *rodina* (native land) is used in the sense of a person's place of birth from a formal legal point of view; b) *otechestvo* (fatherland) refers to the whole complex of traditional and moral concepts which bind a man to the place where he was born. It is the second word that the author uses here.

8. Article of the penal code: ten years in camp or death by shooting is the penalty for insurrection.

9. So-called because it consisted of a committee of three high officials representing the KGB, the Prosecutor's office, and the Party.

did intimidate, coerce, corrupt, and break the spirit. During their reign of terror the Chekists sought to destoy anyone of marked capability, for such a man is always potentially dangerous. The jealousy and resentment of subordinates was a contributing factor.

How I Helped to Get the Production of War Matériel Under Way

It may seem strange that in view of all I had by now lived through, I still held to my old principle "Work with a will, but think as you please." Only after serving time in the punishment cells would I be moved to abandon this formula and refuse to play a role in finding solutions to major problems—by which I only helped to strengthen the regime. But at Vyatlag in the first winter of the war I was still not fully conscious of this and engaged in activities that, in effect, lent support to the Stalinist system: I worked conscientiously and gave no thought as to where my efforts were leading.

My regular duties in the machine shop—which took up about three hours a day—consisted of checking on the results of our work. As I have

---

wait for the historians and felt obliged to make our own estimate of the numbers involved. This we did by the following means:

—by questioning Chekhists who served under Yezhov and were arrested and imprisoned after his fall between 1939 and 1941;

—by questioning *zeks* in the transit prisons about the average numbers in their camps and about the death rate there (we were thus able to estimate the general figure for those who perished in each camp area);

—by collecting evidence from *zeks* who had worked in the administration offices of the large camps;

—by doing our own rough count of the number of people in the camps, based on information gathered in the transports.

The most difficult thing was to decide which of those figures were reliable; here we relied on our intuition. In this way we arrived at our estimates for this gigantic destruction of people.

After arriving in the West, I saw the map published by Isaac Don Levine (*"Gulag"-Slavery*, 1951). It shows about 310 camp administrations which accounted for fourteen million *zeks*, which an average annual mortality rate equivalent to 12%. The author rightly adds that he has not taken account of many other places of detention such as labor colonies, prisons, the detention cells of police stations, and colonies for juvenile delinquents. I am absolutely certain that future historians, having made all due corrections, will arrive at a larger total of those destroyed than was possible by our rough-and-ready method.

Meanwhile, it is safe to say that the number of *zeks* in camps between 1939–1941 was about twenty million. After 1942, it was about fourteen million. This already explained, I exploited my position in the interests of our men by countersigning work sheets which showed a greater rate of output than was in fact the case. But when it came to inspecting work that really had been done, particularly when priority orders were involved, I was extremely scrupulous indeed. I saw to it that accurate measurements by micrometers and other precision instruments had been taken and that all the various specifications had been met down to the tiniest detail. This, too, was necessary for the protection of my workmates; otherwise we should have got into very hot water as a result of the spot inspections that were made from time to time with no advance warning. Complaints about faulty workmanship were sometimes passed on to the security officers of the camp, who might easily use them to trump up charges of *sabotage*.

Even in early childhood I had a great enthusiasm for things connected with engineering. Later I chose it as my natural vocation. Through all the years since, my love for it has not diminished. So it was not surprising that early in 1942, after getting a substantial increase in my daily diet, I gradually became absorbed in engineering projects that caught my interest.

At first I helped Yuri in the designing department. But it was not long before the camp authorities issued a priority order (at that time orders

---

number was constantly replenished by an endless flow of new arrivals.

The following table gives the approximate numbers of civilians in the U.S.S.R. who perished at various periods.

Years	Cause of Death	Numbers of victims (in millions)
1917–21	Shootings, tortures	6–12
1922–23	Famine in the Volga region and other areas	7½–13
1922–28	Destruction of the old social classes, the clergy, and believers	2–3
1929–33	Liquidation of kulaks; organized famine	16
1934–41 (up to the outbreak of the war)	Mass executions in prisons and camps; starvation in camps; artificially created epidemics	7
1941 (from the start of the war) to 1942	Destruction of *zeks* through hunger and overwork	7½
1943–45	Death in Stalin's wartime camps	5
1946–53 (the year of Stalin's death)	Death in Stalin's camps after the war	6

Altogether (at the lowest estimate) approximately sixty million died. Other authors in the West give figures ranging from forty-five to eighty million.

were always priority orders) calling for the immediate reconditioning of the equipment in the machine shop. The assignment naturally fell to me, since as the person responsible for checking the quality of our output, I was inevitably concerned that our machine tools should be in top working order. Thus it was that I was appointed engineer in charge of equipment—corresponding to chief mechanical engineer in an ordinary factory. After picking the two best fitters to help me, I started determining the degree of wear and tear in the various lathes. Then we got down to the job of cleaning, scraping, and repairing them. I even began to lend a hand with some of the donkeywork myself. But at this my friends took me aside for a little chat and strongly advised me against helping the fitters with their job. This, they said, might set an unfortunate precedent. A great effort had been made to convince the authorities that an engineer's knowledge and experience were indispensable to the work of the camp. As the mediocrities they were, the authorities hated every educated person,[10] particularly someone who had been convicted under Article 58. They would be only too glad to bring all engineers down to the level of ordinary laborers—attempts to do so had been made more than once: engineers had been transferred to ordinary hard labor and replaced by criminals, etc. But usually within a short time boilers had blown up, "repaired" trucks and tractors had stopped dead in their tracks, generating plants had power failures, production came to a standstill—and the engineers were promptly restored to their proper jobs.

Boris, who occasionally stood in for Georgi, quite often came to me when the lathes were idle, and I provided him with the necessary drawings and samples to enable our toolmakers to turn out machine parts that we needed for refitting our equipment—things like shafts, gears, spindles, pulleys, etc. For a full six months we were busy getting our machines back into good shape, including some that had originally seen service in the machine shops of the White Sea-Baltic Canal project[11]—and we did a good job. But without realizing at all what my efforts might lead to, I had made it possible for our machine shop to change directly over to war production.

Another engineer, Lindberg by name, was no less guilty than I in this respect; thanks to his ability, our shop was now ready to manufacture such essential machine accessories as drills, cutters, reamers, braces, etc.

10. "Educated" had become a term of opprobrium, and was used by the people to designate intellectuals, also referred to, with sneering emphasis, as "members of the intelligentsia."
11. The White Sea-Baltic Canal was built by forced labor in the early thirties. (Tr.)

94

Despite the conditions we lived under, we achieved our results because, in addition to excellent engineers, we had first-class fitters and toolmakers from the leading industrial plants of Leningrad, Kharkov, and other cities. My fitter Kondrat, for example, had been with an electro-mechanical works in Kharkov. Savitski, a veteran inmate of wide experience, had been employed in a similar plant in the Baltic works.[12] Among Lindberg's crew were two lathe operators from the famous Putilov works. One of them, Zverev, had been imprisoned repeatedly. He had once served a term for supporting Shlyapnikov and his "Workers' Opposition"[13] back in 1921.

It is an outright lie when the Soviet regime advertises itself as a "Workers' and Peasants' State." In the jails and camps I rubbed shoulders with hundreds of veteran workers. All of them were united in their hatred for a regime which, not content with robbing them of everything and making virtual slaves of them, had also humiliated them by performing all its crimes in their name.

If Lindberg had not ensured the smooth production of machine tools and if I had not refitted our machinery, then it would have been impossible for us to fill a government order received shortly afterward asking us to make casings for antipersonnel mines—or rather it would have been held up for at least a year.

A special wooden-frame building where this war matériel could be turned out was hastily erected in Section Five of the camp. I arranged for the transfer of the equipment so expeditiously that a machine tool was ready for operation in the new premises twenty-four hours after its removal from the old machine shop. Soviet inefficiency being what it is, production had never before been resumed at such speed. Everybody was astounded and predicted my early liberation. Against my wish and expectation, I found myself suddenly an important person, for though I continued as the chief mechanical engineer, I was acting also as head of technical supervision.

To insure greater efficiency in carrying out our work, several engineers, including myself, were issued passes that enabled us to move from one area to another without a guard escort. The administrative chief of the camp, Major Levinson, dropped in to see me almost daily. Invariably he would ask: "How's the production schedule doing, Panin?" For everything intended for the army had to be given a final check by a military representative and could only be passed after he had personally

12. An important factory in Leningrad.
13. One of the first opposition groups within the Bolshevik party; later, under Stalin, there were others.

put his stamp on each piece. Levinson was interested only in the quantity of finished production. If we exceeded the quota, he would leave without a word. If not, he demanded explanations. Always in a hurry, he seldom summoned the other shop supervisors, who were quite content to remain out of his sight altogether.

Having become an important cog in the local Soviet mechanism, I would be held answerable for anything that went wrong. I knew that my days were numbered. Meanwhile, I at least used my position to good advantage and extricated more than ten prisoners from the lumber camp, all of them with technical qualifications like those of the other members of our fraternity, whose general views they also shared. One of them was even rescued from the punishment section. But there was another one, Shcherba by name, whom I should have done better not to have extricated from a distant camp just on someone's recommendation. Not long afterward I received word from his old camp that he was an inveterate informer. The others began reproaching me. At first I lost my temper: "Look, you're only here because of me, and I have to answer for all of you. I have far more to say grace to than you could ever imagine, but none of you could even bother to check on the recommendation we were given." But it was no good making a fuss. The plain fact was that I had taken on a stool pigeon, and it would be up to me to get rid of him, especially since he was in my department.

I had to apply to Levinson for the transfer of prisoners from the logging camp into my department to serve as supervisors and inspectors, but I noticed that he seemed somewhat uneasy about exercising his authority. He would sign without hesitation for one man's transfer, while for the next one I would have to repeat my request several times. Later we found out that our administrative chief was in some way dependent on Sharov, the NKVD officer in charge of security at the camp. To put it in camp parlance, Sharov had Levinson "on the hook." It seems that the Chekist had accumulated a file on the numerous relatives for whom Levinson had found jobs inside his little empire. If Levinson was not exactly sympathetic toward me, he trusted me, at least on an official plane. But I knew that if an informer's report against me were ever to get into Sharov's hands, the administrative chief could do nothing to protect my position, nor would he have any desire to do so. I did not have to wait long to learn the truth of this.

There were no shearing machines in the shop; therefore the half-finished casings for the mines had to be cut on a lathe of the Leman system. In this operation a clean slice was cut simultaneously with the central core. The lathe did this automatically. But, not satisfied with this, the technical director of the camp administration, Yevko, a former Chekist and an extremely stupid man, ordered that a large handpress be hauled over to the shop yard. It had been inherited along with the other leftover equipment from the White Sea-Baltic Canal camp, and Yevko proposed that the cutting operation on the half-finished parts be transferred from the lathe to this press. The shop supervisor and his assistant feared Yevko like the plague; they made no objection to this "rationalization proposal"[14]—they were banking on me to take action. They knew that by virtue of my position I would be obliged to intervene should there be any danger to our production process. The idiocy behind Yevko's plan was apparent enough, but I decided to bide my time, feeling reasonably certain that his innovation would flop during the tests that would have to be made—these were no concern of mine. He had put eight men to work on the press—four were needed on each side to operate the machine handle and bring the press down with a loud crunch on to the casings. On the lathe they could be cut off neatly with a minimum loss of metal, but the press simply butchered them, producing ragged edges which had to be evened up on another lathe. When I saw with my own eyes what was happening, I felt bound to exercise my authority and stop this stupid operation at the outset.

When our production process was working smoothly again, I took pleasure in reflecting that we might even be able to take on some civilian orders over and above our military ones. I was examining a design for a welded plowshare when suddenly someone's contorted features appeared in front of me like the face of an enraged animal.

"Did you know there's a saboteur named Panin in this shop?" Yevko snarled. Being so engrossed in my work, it took me moments to realize that this creature was addressing me; but my instinct for self-preservation prompted a quick reply: "You're right. We do have a saboteur in the shop. But his name happens to be Yevko. Your 'rationalization proposal' and that idiotic press were sabotage pure and simple. I can prove it to any board of experts. What's more, you have tampered with technical operations connected with a defense project in time of war. That cannot be regarded as anything but sabotage. Our production plan has been approved and authorized by the director of administration, Major Levinson. As head of the checking department, I will make a report to the administrative office. I will also forward a copy of it to the State Defense Committee."

Although it looked as though the honors were mine, I was left with a

14. This was the term for any proposal aimed at improving technological production.

bad taste in my mouth. Even during and after a talk I had with Levinson the next morning, the sensation persisted. With a resoluteness that in those days characterized my interviews with persons in authority, I demanded of him that all interference from outside should cease. On an earlier occasion, after first getting the whole process underway, I had persuaded Levinson to sign an authorization for the technological procedures we were to follow in turning out the mine casings. In view of that, everything should now be in my favor. But Levinson looked as if he were tired of the whole business. Even though he appeared to be in full agreement with me, he said that the situation would be better if there had not been the episode with Yevko. It became perfectly clear to me that Levinson would not back me if I were ever hauled before the security officers.

The hopelessness of my position was plain enough for anyone to see, and inwardly I began to feel quite desperate. Shaky as it was, the ground under my feet might still not give way as long as I could keep the job running smoothly. But it would open up wide at any time the Chekists from the security department decided it would be to their advantage to arrest me on some trumped-up political charge. Once that happened, they would write off all my achievements in getting our defense production under way as a front for my real motives, or "camouflage,"[15] as they called it.

Mistakes in the Conduct of the War

Beginning with the winter of 1941 and up to early 1942, a railroad engine was kept standing idle on a siding in the yards by the First Camp Detachment. Constantly blowing off steam, it was in full readiness to move out at the first sign of danger, evacuating the top administrators and the secret police. For us it symbolized the possibility that one day these captains of our fate might take to their heels and flee. Its departure would have brought the end of our subjugation to cannibals and the beginning of freedom.

But we waited in vain. The Germans had occupied Kiev, but had not set up a Russian provisional government. It was now clear to us that Hitler was a predator and not a liberator. When reliable eyewitness reports began reaching us that Hitler was killing off Russian prisoners of war by starvation, even though the majority had shown no desire to resist his troops, and that he was committing atrocities against the un-

15. A term frequently used in the U.S.S.R. as ground for numerous accusations.

armed populace, we realized that he, too, like Stalin, was a cannibal. Our hopes fell; the task of reclaiming Russia was growing more and more complicated. We debated among ourselves in search of new ideas.

Military science is based on the study of past battles and operations. These are carefully analyzed to see what lessons they may yield for the future. Errors are exposed; successful tactical and strategic plans are scrutinized.

The horrors of World War II are long forgotten; since then, another generation has reached maturity: but in that distant time, we were slaves under a dictatorship, trying to throw off our chains. We saw the war as an opportunity not only for emancipating our country, but also for freeing the rest of the world from the terrible dangers lurking within the Communist regime of the U.S.S.R.

I crave your indulgence as I share with you some of the thoughts which occupied the minds of many of us in those days. We did not believe ourselves to be building castles in the air. Neither I nor others who shared my fate doubted the feasibility of the alternatives that I will now attempt to set forth.

The "balance of power" between nations was now an outmoded principle, no longer effective in safeguarding the peace against the forces of destruction. However, the statesmen of the world failed to learn anything practical from that fact. The political realists, as they then called themselves, had demonstrated their attitude toward the Bolshevik regime during the Civil War of 1918–1920 in Russia. Wedded to outworn ideas, they allowed the White movement to fall apart. They believed that by doing so they would weaken Russia while strengthening their own position.

The Western powers had two excellent opportunities as early as 1918 for putting an end to the Communist regime:

— They could have allowed the German forces to go ahead and crush it at birth.

— They could have furnished the White Army with all the military supplies it needed, and then simply allowed it to get on with the job free of interference.

At that time one might have put a stop to this anti-human regime. Initially, perhaps, the West might have misjudged the situation, but more than a million persons had fled from Russia of whom the majority were educated and knowledgeable. Their experience should not have been ignored. But not only did the West turn a deaf ear to them; it also tried to ease its own conscience by reviling them for the truth and counsel they brought with them.

Westerners gave their attention to John Reed's[16] superficial book, which described the Bolsheviks' triumphant parades and mass meetings. But they placed no credence in the courageous Sidney Reilly,[17] who plumbed the very depths of the inferno and thus really knew what it was like from first-hand experience.

The concepts of Western statesmen were colored by their fears of parliamentary opposition, violent criticism from the leftist press, or defeat in future elections. Parliamentary prevarications are legitimate enough when dealing with ordinary day-to-day problems, but they are inadmissible when the survival of the human race is at stake. When it is a question of averting a calamity that threatens to bring world-wide destruction, it is essential that—with due respect for democratic safeguards—the debate should rise above partisan squabbles, electoral rivalries, and pressures from the masses; for the average voter does not have a clear grasp of the situation, misjudges it, and therefore cannot measure correctly the danger threatening him.

The leaders of Europe's democracies began seeing the menace posed by the Red dictatorship only after its network of agents had become systematically engaged in subversive activity right under their noses. Yet they could not reach any joint decision to take action; all they did was to play down the importance of the problem, thus making it possible for the godless and ruthless dictatorship to establish itself. It now indulged in endless human slaughter and sharpened its knife for an attack on the rest of the world. The democracies drifted complacently along, even though each one of them may not have been averse, in its heart of hearts, to strangling the new regime. They took no action, when, with a small-scale war, they might have crushed the Stalinist tyranny. I have in mind the years 1929–1933, during which collectivization was under way and the peasants were being murdered en masse.

Measures the Western powers could have taken at that moment:

— issued an ultimatum demanding that the U.S.S.R. open its frontiers so that they might go in unhindered and rescue the peasants who were dying of hunger. If the Soviet government had refused to comply, the West would have then engaged Stalin's Black Sea fleet in battle and destroyed it. At the same time, Western forces would have landed at Odessa, Sevastopol, Novorossisk, and Batum.

— announced to the world that this war was being waged for the purpose of freeing a nation from the regime.

16. American journalist, author of *Ten Days That Shook the World* which caused a great stir at the time.
17. Agent of the British Intelligence Service.

— provided air cover to support its advancing tank and infantry columns.

— launched a propaganda campaign, also from the air, with pamphlets directed at Red Army men, peasants, workers, and other elements of the population.

— organized liaison with insurgent strongholds and eventually supplied both them and their partisan units with weapons, ammunition, and food.

Civil war would undoubtedly have flared up over the entire country, and the Red Army, consisting mainly of peasants, would have begun disintegrating. Within a year and a half, Stalin's despotic reign would have ended.

True, these were no longer the times of the Civil War, when the Allies need not have committed a single of their soldiers. Now it would have been necessary at the very outset to commit large forces and count on substantial losses. However, this particular time for undertaking such a war was exceptionally favorable for the West for yet another reason: the terrible economic depression of 1929–1931, a result of overproduction. The very idea of the war would have been popular, since it would have served to bring that crisis quickly to an end. Just as if they had been purposely designed for this war, hordes of jobless men and a huge stockpile of excess matériel were available.

And the West would have delivered the peoples of Russia from slavery and slaughter. History would have recorded the war as one of the world's most generous ones, a war of liberation of a Christian people subjugated by criminals, a war that would have destroyed a focus of international contagion which by its existence favored the counter-development of Nazism. With deep gratitude the new Russia would have paid its debt to the democracies. Last but not least, the West would have gained a large market for its goods. A new climate in Europe would have averted a second World War.

Except for the advent of Nazism and the atomic age, the shape of things to come was perfectly clear even to us who were still youths back in the 'thirties. It amazed us that the chiefs of staff in the West did not see the advantage of a military offensive against Communism. We young people were well acquainted with conditions in our own country, and we thought that the West must surely be united in its view of what was going on here. Alas, the only voice that reached us then—like a lone voice crying in the wilderness—was that of the Pope calling for a crusade of prayer.

Much was being written in the West about the desirability of a show-down between Hitler and Stalin. Naturally we too would have welcomed one. It was very evident that for the sake of it the West was making a great many concessions, even going so far as handing Czechoslovakia over to Hitler through the Munich Pact. But for a head-on conflict to materialize between the two dictators, a common frontier was needed. For that reason, the West's decision to sacrifice Czechoslovakia was to us incomprehensible. But when a common border arose as a result of Hitler's invasion of Poland, a good many of us were certain that his war with the Soviet Union was no longer far away—our people were convinced of its inevitability.

Finally came the day when Hitler attacked Stalin. And now Churchill, who more than once during his long lifetime had declared himself an implacable enemy of Communism, rushed to conclude a treaty with Stalin. Then he, along with Roosevelt, proceeded to save the life of this regime. Because the Allies continued to have faith in an outmoded concept of coalition between powers, they forgot that the two dictators had only recently shown the whole world what utter contempt they had for formal agreements.

The West realized that Hitler was bent on conquest and not on liberation, and that consequently he was bound to make war on the Russian people. But captive to obsolete principles, the West chose to make an alliance with a despot, a slaveholding monster, rather than to seize the opportunity of supporting the peoples of such an enormous country, which once liberated would be capable of a spectacular recovery. One would think that Western statesmen had been brought up on books from the time when soldiers wore powdered wigs and advanced to attack in close order. By a wise, bold decision the West could have disposed of both tyrants and delivered mankind from the horrors of the most terrible dictatorship.

In return for their faith in him, Stalin now subjected the Allied leaders to fraud and blackmail. He extorted from them everything he needed, seizing European border lands in the process and opening the way for Communist regimes in China and several other Asian countries. After their so-called victory in 1945, the Western leaders wasted no time in scrupulously carrying out all the provisions of Yalta and other such conferences, to which they had subscribed without any clear idea of the consequences. Stalin insinuated into the terms of these agreements anything that best served his purpose, while his Western partners, busily pursuing their interests, automatically put their stamp of approval on all points that had no direct bearing on them. One shameful result of the

Allies' lack of concern was the handover to Stalin of Soviet war prisoners, as well as of men who had served in General Vlasov's army and other such military units. Nothing could better demonstrate how ill-informed the Allies were about the attitude of the peoples of Russia toward Stalin's rule, and how little the West thought in those days of a future struggle against him. In the light of all this, I believe readers will now be in a better position to understand the real position of the Russian people in those years.

The German offensive of 1941–1942 was directed toward the south, the northern fronts having become stabilized. Hitler was incapable of understanding the immense force that the inmates of Soviet camps could provide in the effort to destroy the Stalinist dictatorship. He had only to land guns and provisions by parachute—and revolt would have spread like wildfire. But nothing of the sort! He doublecrossed the Benderists[18] whom he had supported before the war, and he failed to recognize the huge anti-Stalinist reserve among the Soviet prisoners of war.

All thinking people under the Soviet regime pondered the same question: what should be the strategy of a Russian "Provisional Government" if one were formed in 1941. Events were developing rapidly, and I put all my energies into the search for the right solution. It was clear to me that our only possible course of action was to work toward a future Russian government. Such a government would not come down to us from the heavens. It would have to be created by men who were ready and able to redeem the land of their fathers.

But there was no point in counting on disinterested behavior on the part of Hitler. Even if he had attacked Stalin under the banner of "Freedom for Russia," he would have done it for ulterior motives, as part of a master plan to smash Stalin with the assistance of Russian liberation forces, but then to subjugate the new, still fragile Russian state and thus proceed quite openly to the conquest of the country as such.

Hitler's plan, sound as it might have seemed by the standards of twentieth-century thinking, would have eventually come to nothing. Twenty years of continuous Chekist terror had made us suspicious, endowing a great many of us with a heightened sense of caution—at times to an extreme degree. Thanks to this, we would certainly have been able to sniff out any dirty business even before it started. Without delay the new Russian government would have established diplomatic ties with England and the United States; and in the event of any military action

18. Ukrainian Nationalists of the western Ukraine, led by Stepan Bendera. (In Western literature on the subject I have seen this name spelled Bandera. I prefer to keep to the spelling Bendera.)

by Hitler against the Russian army, we would not have been caught napping. The enemies of Germany would have gained in Russia a loyal ally, one in the process of being reborn, of mobilizing its tremendous spiritual strength in this burst of genuine freedom. Hitler would have ended up with a broken neck.

But everything turned out very differently: Hitler chose invasion, and since no provisional Russian government was proclaimed, we camp inmates dreamed up our own strategy for the country's liberation.

Our primary objective was an unremitting struggle against the Stalinist dictatorship until its complete overthrow in all parts of the country. We realized how grossly England and America had miscalculated; by not destroying *both* dictatorships, they had actually reinforced the surviving one.

Our aim could have been accomplished by the formidable army of 20,000 prisoners held in the Soviet camps. But to set things in motion, the United States would have had to assume the responsibility of landing aid in the vast camp areas of the Soviet Far East, Kolyma, and Siberia.[19] American assistance would also have been needed for the British fleet, which by itself and without support bases in Northern Europe would have had some difficulty in coping alone with the task of getting supplies to the camps in the White Sea and Ural regions. The whole operation should have been carried out without any warning—a sort of surprise attack such as was favored by Hitler and Stalin and used by them to such good effect. Under the protection of a strong naval force operating somewhere near Narvik, carried-based aircraft would have been sent on two successive days over the centers of the main camp areas to drop paratroop units, along with stores of light arms, ammunition, and enough provisions for several days. Immediately on landing, the invaders would have announced that Stalin's regime had been overthrown, and that they were taking all labor camp prisoners under their command as soldiers of a provisional Russian government.

Detachments of prisoners would then have placed all secret police units under arrest and taken over the camps. Once the inmates were no longer in danger of liquidation, air transports would begin to fly in supplies on a massive scale. Units of the Red Army in the Far East and in Siberia would have been immobilized; and as the struggle progressed, a large part of them would doubtless have joined the rebels. Moscow

19. Such a bold decision on the part of the U.S.A. might also have had the effect of averting Japan's entry into the war, or, at least, of making it much easier to prepare for it.

could receive no outside support and, as a consequence, would fall in October. Siberia, the Urals and all of northern Russia would be in our hands within the first few months. Hard-pressed from the west, east, north and south, the Stalinist regime would have collapsed in 1942. The armies of camp prisoners, with their ranks swollen by soldiers from Soviet units, would then direct their blows at the Nazis, concentrating everything now on the battle of Russia. And American aid would be going to friends instead of to enemies pretending to be friends. Hitler would have been completely crushed.

Everything that I have written here in respect to what we prisoners might have done at that juncture is quite realistic and practicable. In 1941 we had not yet been exhausted by starvation. Millions of us were ready to give our lives in battle rather than die ignominiously in the camps during that first year of the war. From the Allies we needed a minimum of material aid and a good plan of operations, both of which they would have been well able to provide. But events moved in a different direction, and we had to look for other solutions.

Roosevelt and Churchill hardly experienced any feelings of warmth toward Stalin, in spite of their ties with him during their joint war against Hitler. Similarly, we could have nothing in common with Hitler, except for the objective that we would have shared only temporarily: victory over Stalinist tyranny. But even more important was complete freedom, and once Hitler tried to enslave the peoples of Russia, we would have fought him to the last man.

But in the upshot neither the Allies nor Hitler provided the prisoners in the labor camps with weapons. Thus the colossal force pent up inside them was gradually undermined by hunger, cold, and backbreaking labor.

Large numbers of Russia's peoples lived, as we did, in a constant daydream of a war that would set off the impulse toward liberation. This thought helped them to bear their torments. It was also the reason why nearly five million soldiers gave themselves up to the Germans during the early months of the war. In the first days of it, the camp inmates lived in the hope: to join a Russian liberation army that had yet to be born, and, together with other Soviet nationals, carry on the battle for the deliverance of the rest of the country. By that time we understood, viscerally, that there was no point in hesitating and wondering what would happen to our families. Only by liberating the nation as a whole could we save those close to us and snatch them from their tormentors.

In blind savagery Hitler smashed this hope of ours and made us into his fiercest enemies. There were those who began to fight him in earnest;

in so doing, they were reinforcing Stalin's dictatorship. Others, after their capture, believing that they could help bring about the fall of the regime rather than rot behind barbed wire, joined Russian units of the Wehrmacht and later went in Vlasov's army. Stalinist propaganda has presented these heroes as traitors to their native land. But before the tribunal of history they stand as men who, despite the mistakes made by the powerful and mighty of this world, were able to salvage some of our military strength, which might have influenced the course of events.

It is necessary here to define the concept "fatherland," since the country of which we are natives is a purely geographical notion. The various peoples of the U.S.S.R. did not have a fatherland, they merely lived in the lands of their birth. That land had become the booty of an usurper. Hence, there was no fatherland we could betray.

As soon as I arrived in the West, I listened to the apprehensions expressed by my friends as to the consequences of a possible victory of Hitler over the U.S.S.R. They sketched a most gloomy picture—a worse one you could hardly imagine: by the end of the war against Stalin, the Vlasov army would have been totally destroyed since Hitler would have thrown it, as a part of the Wehrmacht, into the costliest battles. In the end, a pitifully ravaged Russia would have lain at Hitler's feet, defenseless and bled dry. He would immediately have put into effect his racist laws, according to which the Slavs were not much above the level of the Jews. Gas chambers and crematory furnaces would have been constructed in Siberia, and then the extermination of all who were recalcitrant or in any other way objectionable would have proceeded on a vast scale. As a conqueror, Hitler would have had the full support of his fellow Germans; his supremacy would have been unshakable. The Russians, inured to Stalinist tyranny, would have meekly submitted to the new dictatorship. Furthermore, Hitler would have detached all of Russia's outlying regions and their inhabitants and made them his allies and satellites. There would have been an influx of Germans, who as the new lords of the land would have brought their industries and enterprises into Russia, employing native labor at rock-bottom wages.

This dire picture was drawn by people lacking personal experience of life in the Soviet Union. In making such predictions my Western friends do not always proceed from the realities of the situation, which are as follows:

— In the liberated regions millions of volunteers would have joined the Free Russian colors to replace the warriors who had fallen. Free Russian troops in those areas would have done away with the collective farms, turned the factories over to the workers, opened the churches, allowed private enterprise, dissolved the Communist Party, put an end to Chekist activity.

— In the West the war would have gone on: Hitler would have sustained defeat at the hands of the English, Americans, French, and other allies. He would have been forced to move his divisions fighting in Russia to the West. The war against Stalin on territory still under Soviet rule would have been conducted mainly by the armies of Free Russia.

— In view of the insane race theories of Hitler and his clique, it is quite possible that units of the SS and Gestapo would have begun persecuting the populace in localities under their control. But they would thereby only have been digging their own graves. For after finishing off Stalin, the Free Russian forces, already active participants in the popular renaissance, would fall on the Nazis like an avalanche. Caught within the iron grip of the Western Allies and the Russian national forces, Hitler would have been crushed.

— If for one reason or another the liberation movement against Hitler had stretched over several years in the occupied zones, and the Nazis had set up there the kind of rule that prevailed in Poland during World War II, they would have met with massive partisan retaliation, sabotage, and terrorism. We know what a volcano both Hitler and Stalin were sitting on in the territories seized by them. One can imagine what would have happened after Stalin's fall in the course of a war of liberation waged by the peoples of Russia.

— The system of both cannibals were basically identical, but in some respects there were differences: with their mendacious propaganda and their inexhaustible fund of semantic tricks, the Stalinists were particularly dangerous. In the war years, for instance, they made use of all kinds of traditional phraseology to delude the public. They started using such expressions as "the Russian nation," "the homeland," "the land of our fathers"—even "God."[20] They promised to abolish the collective farms, open the churches, become more liberal, grant an amnesty . . . There were some who became hypnotized by these high-sounding phrases and held on to some of their illusions.

The phraseology of Hitler, on the other hand, overwhelmed the hearer by its primitiveness. His program was obvious enough, and it left not a glimmer of hope.

— The chief horror of Stalin's brand of terror was its furtiveness, its

20. Although they continued to write "god" with a small letter, as had been decreed right at the beginning of the atheist regime.

spiritual and intellectual corruption. Hitler condemned himself out of his own mouth, and his propaganda was so obvious and crude that it did not need to be exposed. If anything, it would have induced the peoples of Russia to rally their forces against him.

— Under Stalin's terrorist regime, slavery and corruption continually increased. But Hitler's terrorism would have generated among Russians a national consciousness, a sense of civic duty, a capacity for struggle, and solidarity.

And so, if the downfall of Stalin had been brought about, then Hitler too would have been finished off—and without the need of an American atomic bomb.

Where Stalin Got the Principles for Organizing His Army

According to the historians, Frederick the Second of Prussia once quipped that his soldiers went enthusiastically into an attack because they had a deadly fear of their corporals. Stalin, who all his life pilfered the ideas of his more intellectually advanced colleagues, in all likelihood took this jest seriously and made it the foundation of his own military concepts. Having no originality whatsoever, he merely followed the policy originated by Lenin and Trotsky: that of keeping the army under rigid control through the use of "commissars," who escorted every troop commander and who set up a network of informers inside the ranks of the Red Army. As early as 1921 the Red general, Tukhachevski, based his plan for crushing the poorly armed peasants in Tambov Province during the famous Antonov[21] uprising, on joint operations by regular units, tanks, and Chekists (known as "blood-suckers").[22] Going back to ancient times, we find that the army of the Persian despot, Cyrus, in many of its features anticipates Stalin's military organization. Everybody knows that the Persian hordes who battled against the free men of the Greek forces went down in history as an army of slaves. But the Emperor Cyrus may be excused, for in that far distant era the whole structure of life was based on slaveholding.

Stalin's idea of controlling an army amounted to instilling in every

21. Anarchist peasant leader. (Tr.)
22. At the height of his military career, in 1921, Tukhachevski had described the Cheka troups put under his command as "blood-suckers." In 1937, Tukhachevski was himself liquidated by them.

soldier and every officer the unshakable certainty that the very worst would await them if they failed to carry out an order from a superior. For this purpose:

— The regulation manual plainly stated that an officer should be merciless and in case of serious disobedience from one of his men was bound by duty to shoot him.

— It was categorically prohibited to become a prisoner of war. Soldiers and officers had rather to commit suicide. Whoever allowed himself to be captured was officially considered a traitor to the fatherland, with all this implied as consequences for his family.

— Troops thrown into battle were backed by punitive units[23] who forced the soldiers to advance.

— The party and Komsomol elements within the army were expected to enforce all decisions and orders. They also had to make reports on everything they saw and heard, on everything that happened around them.

— A network of informers and secret agents, recruited from within the army itself, operated within the ranks and had a demoralizing effect on the soldiers.

— So-called Political Sections were organized in order to provide an extra eye and antenna to the octopus. Their task was to watch for the slightest sign of discontent, to inculcate the precepts laid down by the regime, to play upon the men's baser instincts. Every soldier was strictly accounted for; everyone was classified according to the degree to which he could be trusted. The names and addresses of his relatives were also kept on record: it was constantly pounded into his head that if he should be found guilty of wrongdoing, the members of his family would be punished as well. The laws applying to a "traitor" would also apply to them.

— A terroristic system of administration was another menace hanging over the head of the common soldier. For the slightest violation he could be immediately turned over for court-martial. He could be executed by firing squad or sent to die by degrees in a camp—or, if he were lucky, placed in a penal battalion[24]—not on the basis of common law, but by emergency decree. The large number of his comrades who had already suffered one or other of these fates served as a constant object lesson.

23. It is noteworthy that these NKVD special troops were never committed in battle during the war, but were reserved strictly for their function of carrying out reprisals against regular combat troops, and the civilian population (e.g., for alleged collaboration with the Germans in the occupied territories).

24. A battalion recruited mainly from among the criminals which was literally used as cannon fodder at the front.

— During the war, a new agency known as SMERSH[25] was established, amounting to an open Chekist dictatorship over the regular military personnel.

— Military tribunals were organized on a scale larger than that found in any other army. They included military police units responsible for looking after condemned soldiers and carrying out executions.

— With the exception of some idealists, Soviet officers bore only an outward resemblance to officers of a normally constituted army. Concepts of honor, human dignity, and true comradeship did not exist for the majority of them. An officer held his rank mainly because of his political reliability. His mind was largely dominated by party directives, political orientation, intrigues, and obligatory atheism.

It is legitimate to ask: Can the unquestioning adherents of such an ideology, who have imbibed the poison of a dictatorship and who have no restraints on their authority over the men in the ranks, rightfully be considered military officers? Of course not. Such a so-called officer is simply a grotesque hybrid—at once a military leader, a party functionary, a secret-police agent, and a political flunky—who worries about saving only his own skin and is capable of doing anything for the sake of his own well-being. Such a man is not an officer but a direct descendant of the ancient Persian satraps, with a mind cast in the Stalinist mold. Our ingenious Generalissimo would have been very well satisfied if all his commanders conformed to this model. But under conditions of war, when the number of men subject to call-up stood at twenty million, they inevitably included a substantial group of mobilized officers who still had the qualities associated with the best military traditions of Europe. But under the oppressve system I have described, they could not possibly change anything for the better. Anyone who, in the tradition of the old tsarist army, showed any sign of trying to be a "father to his men," would very quickly have been blacklisted as "unreliable," as someone attempting, for sinister motives, to gain "cheap popularity" with his men by currying favor with them.

And a second question: Is a man in the lower ranks of the Red Army (or, as it is now called, the Soviet Army) truly a soldier? Indeed not. He is the product of a system of terrorism, a serf who is summoned to bear arms in wartime. His conditioning is so effective that even when he is no longer under the system's direct control, automatic conformism and other implanted patterns of behavior continue to operate in him like conditioned reflexes. This explains why there were so many cases of

25. Counterespionage corps, whose name in Russian is an abbreviation of "Death to Spies."

ostensibly patriotic (but in fact pro-Stalinist) behavior among people who were captured or encircled by the Germans.

Stalin's methods of conducting warfare, seen from the standpoint of European military science, appear to be a revival and a refinement of the principles applied by the warrior despots of the ancient East. In today's parlance, Stalin's military establishment could be described as Chekist terrorism dressed up in an army uniform. The basis of Stalin's strategy consisted of driving the enslaved masses off to the front with satanic cruelty; of totally disregarding casualty figures; of crushing the enemy, not by superior military skill, but by waves of doomed cannon fodder.

But we should make allowances for the following:

— the idealists, who with patriotic fervor shrugged off anything that might otherwise have offended their preconceived ideas and sensibilities;

— those who served in the army because they had no other choice;

— those who carried out evil acts of repression out of blindness or under threat of execution.

As for the others, who wittingly supported Stalin's version of an ancient Eastern army, disgrace should be their reward.

It even looks as though Stalin considered it an advantage to his position as dictator that there were abnormally high casualties in his army—many returning veterans, after all the grim experiences of war, might eventually have got out of hand and started making trouble. The statistics seem to bear this out: the number of Germans killed on all fronts in World War II totaled 3,250,000, whereas Soviet military losses came to 20,000,000. This means that, roughly speaking, for every slain German soldier, five Red Army men died. Actually the ratio was even greater, since while Germany was at war with much of the world, the U.S.S.R., on the other hand fought only against Germany and the small armies of Italy, Hungary, and Rumania. This staggering ratio could in no way be blamed on the usual scapegoats of the Red propagandists: the ineptitude of the tsarist government, etc.

During World War I the casualties had been nearly equal: one dead German soldier for each Russian killed. Our losses exceed the German ones only in 1915, when the Russian army fell short of ammunition for the artillery, a failure resulting from a general belief among all the governments involved in the war that the conflict would be over within six months. However, with assistance from patriotic circles, the tsarist government corrected the situation with extraordinary energy and enterprise. Thanks to these efforts the eastern front held up until the overthrow of the tsar; the Germans made no great progress there. The operations of the Russian armies under General Samsonov[26] made it possible for the French to defend Paris. Furthermore, the Russians occupied Galicia, took Erzurum from the Turks, mounted a successful offensive under General Brusilov, and by 1917 were poised for a decisive breakthrough on their front with Germany and Austria. If it had not been for treason at the front and in the rear, Russia would have carried off one of the greatest victories in her history.

26. In East Prussia in 1914; the Russians suffered a severe defeat here, but the argument is that only the diversion of German forces to the East saved the French from a debacle at the beginning of the war. (Tr.)

7

VYATLAG: 1942–1943
(Continued)

Planning an Escape

As it became evident that none of the belligerents was interested in enlisting our help for the overthrow of the Stalinist regime, I began to suffer keenly from the hopelessness of our situation. The vast majority of my fellow engineers, filling less conspicuous positions in the camp but also responsible for some part of the work, were in a similar mood. We felt rather like captives tied to trees, with cannibals prancing all around and from time to time taking another victim to be served up at their feast.

It was no wonder I began thinking about escape. Opinions were divided. Yuri and Boris were against the idea. Georgi was no longer with us; he had stayed behind in the shop at Camp One. I was supported by our friend Vasili, who was foreman of the lathe section, and Vladimir, an engineer who at that time was working on a farm run by prison labor. By descent Vasili was a Zaporozhian[1] Cossack. In his dashing manner, he was the living prototype of Ostap in Gogol's famous tale *Taras Bulba*. He was vigorous, steadfast, dependable, decisive, courageous—I could find no fault at all with him and loved him like a brother.

If you are under the impression that I idealize people or even make them seem larger than life, then I should like to dissipate it once and for all. If anything, I often fail to do justice to their qualities in my necessarily brief descriptions. The fact is that it was the best people—the most brilliant and courageous—who fell foul of the terror machine. As a general

1. Ukrainian-speaking Cossacks from the Dnieper region.

rule, they were the ones to suffer most, and, for the most part, it was only the rabble who sold themselves out to the Chekists. No wonder then that there was such a high proportion of estimable people in the camps and so few on the other side of the barbed wire.

I placed all my hope and trust in Vasili. We had passes that allowed us to go out of the barbed-wire zone at any time of day or night without an armed guard, but we had only three days off—the tenth, twentieth and thirtieth of each month. We had been so busy getting production of the mine casings underway that we had no time even to think of our own plans until August, 1942. Both of us were very conspicuous: although I was able to get extra supplies of bread through our civilian supervisors, we would immediately have fallen under suspicion if we had started hoarding it. But we did succeed in making a compass: we magnetized an indicator needle on a device used in repairing automobile ignition systems and suspended it from a thread inside a small bottle. During the night shift we fashioned out and sharpened some blades, and patched up our clothing, especially our footwear.

That summer Vladimir, also a pass-holder,[2] frequently came over from the camp farm to our shop on production matters. We were well acquainted with him. He had come out with me in the same "cage" on the transport from Moscow. He was an amusing fellow and reminded me somehow of a trained dolphin. Having a phenomenal thirst for knowledge, he was able—so it seemed to me—to master anything he wanted to, and with his extremely well-stocked mind, he was also capable of logical reasoning, sometimes arriving at deductions that smacked of brilliance. But he lacked the most important element—intuition. If his career had developed along normal lines, he might well have become a classical Soviet academician. However, in circumstances where he had to act on his own and come up quickly with just the right solution, he would get confused and make the most glaring mistakes. Although he had been convicted on a minor charge and given only five years, he had somehow managed to land in the logging camp; and if we had not managed to get him transferred to the camp farm, he would not have lasted through the first winter. When he asked me one day how he might get hold of a magnetic needle, I saw that he was making on the same lines as us, so I let him in on our plans. I did not exactly like the idea of his coming with us. He had the faults of a man who has always lived in the city and they were not offset by his good qualities. But he won us over with a promise to start immediately gathering provisions and hiding them at some secret

2. *Zek* who received a permit allowing him to move freely outside the camp without a guard.

spot in the woods near the camp farm. When he managed to steal a detailed map of Vyatlag off the wall in one of the offices of the administration—something vital to our purpose—we were even more impressed. Even so, Vasili disliked him intensely. But despite strong misgivings of my own, I insisted that we take him along; for it was clear that for Vasili and me alone to make a break, with only two days' bread ration tucked inside our shirts and without knowing the location of all the checkpoints, would be to invite disaster at the start.

The escape was set for eight o'clock on the morning of August 30. Vasili would be getting off the night shift just before that time. Our absence would not cause any alarm in the machine shop before ten o'clock on the night of August 31, giving us thirty-eight hours to make our getaway. For this purpose I had secured a mission to a woodworking plant which was doing a job for our shop. Vladimir was supposed to arrange a similar pretext for his absence that day.

On the evening before the break was to be made, Vladimir paid me a sudden, hurried visit. Pale, shifty-eyed, and with trembling hands, he said that he had been ordered to go that night and carry out an inspection somewhere. I did not like this at all and sensed that he was lying. But what could we do? We were at his mercy, since only he knew where the provisions were hidden.

"I tell you what. Let's take a walk in the woods," I said.

"Let's go."

And so we went. Sure enough, everything was there: map, compass, flour, dry bread. There was also a small can of lime chloride that we would sprinkle on our shoes in order to throw the dogs off our scent. Apparently, everything was in order.

We reset the date for September 10. But again something went wrong: we learned that an army consultant was coming over that same day from Kirov to check on our measuring instruments and other matters. This meant that I would have to be on the job.

We moved the date up to September 20. By now the weather was not so good and there were heavy rains. But our escape plans remained as before. Around nine o'clock we arrived at the cache. Vladimir was already there. He looked terrible. His general state was worse than the first time. In a stuttering voice, he told us that some camp thugs had discovered the cache and taken the lot.

Vasili let out a roar and grabbed the doubledealer by the scruff of his neck. I was tempted to finish him off there and then. But we would then have had to make our getaway without so much as a crust of bread between us—counting on Vladimir's supplies, we had brought nothing with us. For city-bred men unused to dealing with nature in the raw, it would have been madness to trek for several days through the felled trees of the rain-sodden taiga with neither food nor compass. In the end we would be caught by the security guards who, along with their specially trained watchdogs, were stationed along all the forest trails leading from the camp. As it was, we would need all our wits about us, for we were proposing to break out of the central part of the camp located near the administrative residential area that was very heavily guarded. If an escape was to succeed in such conditions, there could be no last-minute hitches.

I had only myself to blame for the failure of our plan. Knowing Vladimir as well as I did, I certainly should have foreseen that things might turn out this way. I might have moved the supplies to another hiding place, and then Vasili and I could have broken out by ourselves. If I had had fewer responsibilities in the machine shop, I most likely would have thought of this in good time. I could have left a third of the stores in the first hiding place for Vladimir, making a new compass and a copy of the map for us. Then Vasili and I would have been perfectly justified in taking off without giving Vladimir any advance notice. Later, at the shop, Vladimir would have found out about our escape. It was my fault that our plan failed ignominiously.

I had reached the conclusion that escape was imperative because terror in the camp had been steadily on the rise. Vasili also had his reasons. In 1938 he had received a sentence of three years[3] (what is called a "baby's sentence") and damaged kidneys as a memento of his interrogation. He ought to have been released in July, 1941; but like many others who had been serving similar terms, he was simply "held over,"[4] because of the war that had begun a month earlier, and now had no other prospect than to sit it out in the camp until the end of the war. During this time it would be all too easy to pick up another sentence or starve to death. It is just possible that in view of his position as a shift foreman he might have avoided this fate. But his love of freedom, of a life of open contest, outside barbed wires was so strong that he preferred to take a chance on trying to escape. As for Vladimir, there is nothing to say—

3. Boris and Dick also had three-year sentences, like most of the people accepted for work in the shop. In general, however, such short sentences were exceptional in those years. The overwhelming majority of the prisoners had ten-year sentences. After these came those with eight or five years. There were also a few leftovers from 1938 who had been sentenced to twenty years—these were people whose death sentences had been commuted, as occasionally happened.

4. *Zeks* whose sentences happened to end at the moment when war began were in fact kept in the camps until well after it was over, until 1946–47.

vacillation, cowardice, and treachery proved stronger than his original intentions.

I believe that with some effort of imagination the Western reader can understand the reasons that impelled us to attempt an escape. To men who have never experienced it, the fantastic power of Chekist terrorism must seem beyond credibility, and the actions that issue from it must appear without rhyme or reason. To make this statement clear, let me give an example, quite usual in the climate of those times.

In the spring of 1942 two prisoners were desperately craving a smoke. For a whole month, they hadn't had as much as a single drag. When a man has reached a certain stage of acute exhaustion, the traces of nicotine in his bloodstream produce tormenting effects for months afterward, just as terrible as those produced by hunger, or even worse. After all else failed, there was only one last resort: bolstering themselves with the criminals' principle of survival at all costs, they went off to see the camp "godfather" (as the security officer is known in camp slang). They knocked and walked in. The godfather received them cordially. "Have a seat," he said. On his desk was an open cigarette case with cigarettes made of real golden *makhorka*.[5] But he didn't offer them one. He simply waited to hear what they had to say—these hand-rolled cigarettes had their price. . . .

"Chief, our tongues are hanging out. How about a smoke?"

"What is all this? Did you drop in just for a smoke?" he asked mockingly. "Or do you have some business?"

"You know we wouldn't dare walk in here just for nothing, don't you? We want to tell you about a *kontrik*[6] who is spreading propaganda and denouncing the system."

"Who is he?"

They gave his name.

"Very good! First of all, let's write down all the details. Then we'll have a smoke."

All the while, he blew smoke practically into their faces. A formal statement was drawn up and signed. After receiving their blood money— a hand-rolled cigarette apiece—the two nicotine addicts left the "godfather's" office, almost reeling as they took puffs.

The possibility of being denounced in this way kept us in a constant state of terror.

Furthermore, although by autumn of 1942, prisoners were no longer

5. Home-grown coarse tobacco of a type favored by Russians. (Tr.)
6. Slang abbreviation of "counter-revolutionary." (Tr.)

dying like flies, the monstrous work quotas still remained, and to fulfill them was quite impossible. Unless the work sheets were "padded," members of brigades did not get a daily bread ration sufficient to keep them alive. But to fake a man's production record requires a certain skill and experience. In the course of my years in the camps I came to excell in the art of feeding the men in my brigade despite crippling output quotas and very limited allotments of rations. I have explained earlier how this was done.

But the average brigade leader rarely possessed this kind of ability, and unless he had the assistance of such an "organizer," he was entirely at the mercy of the supervisors. A brigade as unlucky as that could have trouble even in relatively good times. In every brigade there were always a few men who were reluctant to work. They were either the physically weak or the good-for-nothings or the common criminals who brazenly claimed the maximum bread ration though they went out to work only because they were frightened by the prospect of getting a ten-year term for an "act of sabotage" in time of war. A brigade leader could easily disappear into the punishment cells simply for trying to impose some discipline on such people—all they had to do was to tell some lying tale about him to the camp authorities. Murderous episodes of this kind were part of the ordinary background of camp life.

What our eventual fate would be was rather uncertain even to us. The rational was separated from the irrational by a very thin line. What chance did we have, Vasili and I, two young men, one of whom had stepped right out of Repin's painting *The Zaporozhians*[7] and the other who had suffered all his life from being too conspicuous? In a country where spy mania had taken on dimensions previously unknown in history, two young fellows in suspicious dress—and right in the middle of a war— would have been easy game for the well-indoctrinated people who lived in the vicinity of the camp.

Escape to the north and the east was out of the question because there were extensive camp networks in those directions. Also, the local population had been corrupted by the regime's payment of a fixed bounty for the capture of a fugitive convict: several packs of *makhorka,* thirty-six pounds of flour, some codfish, and a few quarts of kerosene. I am not likening this reward to "thirty pieces of silver." The regional population—often consisting of Siberian minorities or amalgamated with them—had been

7. Repin, Ilya: Russian realist painter. His famous painting of the Zaporozhian Cossacks shows them writing a defiant letter to the Turkish Sultan. (Tr.)

transformed into bloodhounds by terror, and their cruelty had become second nature.

We had heard stories about a few successful escapes by criminals from one of the remoter camps in the Ivdel[8] group. But they were recaptured one after another by inhabitants of the same local village. Even before the war, the apprehending of fugitives had become a means of livelihood for these people—just like hunting. I imagine that the authorities can scarcely have relished the idea of stationing security forces, as well as the normal camp guards in these remote places, so they made a special arrangement whereby the local people took on the job of policing the whole area. Then one day a band of escaping criminals, instead of giving it a wide berth, headed straight for the village, butchered some of the inhabitants and burned down their houses—most of the male villagers had gone off to the army. The incident became widely known and a temporary halt was called to this kind of head-hunting; for the next two or three years the local people behaved themselves fairly well. But after the war everything went on as before.

Anyone who managed to escape to the south would have to find some accommodating young widow to hide him in her cellar and wait for the end of the war (or some radical change in the system) in her embraces—but this solution did not suit temperaments like ours, even though it was the most practical. It was hardly worthwhile to escape one prison in order to enter, voluntarily, another one.

This left only the way to the war front. It was the most dangerous, but it offered a promise of a total change in our situation. We thought of obtaining military uniforms and the right kind of identity papers and then making for the combat zone. Once there, we would either cross the front-line straight away or first join some unit or another until we could get over to the other side and organize a detachment of Russian freedom-fighters. I was convinced that my ultimate objective was the right one, for I clearly understood the mood of our people and their attitude toward Stalin's rule: they would not deliver us up to the authorities. But to make our way from Vyatka to Stalingrad or the Finnish border would be far from being simple—we would be very conspicuous. This thought undermined our confidence in our plan and explains our lack of determination to go ahead with it.

8. Ivdel: a camp complex farther east in the Ural region.

Some Who Got Away

A year later, I was to meet in the punishment cells a recaptured escapee whose experience warrants special mention. In the summer of 1943 he had fled along the route that Vasili and I had considered. He had started not from our main camp but from a small outlying one. He was not so well prepared as we and had no inter-camp pass. But he got all the way to the Vyatka River and then followed it downstream to the Volga. From there he went on to Stalingrad. A good part of the journey he made alone in a small boat. He got most of his food from buoy keepers and from vegetable gardens that he raided. At Stalingrad he joined an army unit and made himself completely at home until one day the chief of the political section noticed something amiss in his papers. He was interrogated at SMERSH, then locked up, and finally returned to the labor camp—where he was put straight in the punishment cells—with an additional ten-year sentence. Apparently he had once been a forest ranger, for he was very much at home in the natural world. Besides being tall, wiry, and tough, he had a priceless advantage over us: a plain Russian face in no way distinctive from other plain Russian faces. I am sorry I cannot record his name in these pages, but regrettably I do not remember it.

In 1943–1944 I spent eleven months in the punishment cells, and there came in close contact with other would-be escapees. Their relatively large numbers in that period, and their desire to profit even from their failure, hoping to be sent to Kirov Prison on recapture and thence to some other camp, all reflect the relentless Chekist terror in the camps and the murderous conditions there. *Zeks* much preferred to escape at whatever cost. Nearly all these escapees were recaptured on their first day, simply because they were so thoroughly unprepared. From the very outset they did hardly anything right. For example, one of them, "Aleksei, Man of God" (as he often styled himself for some peculiar reason), ran straight out of some woods and smack into a sentry post in another section of the camp. They seemed to be unaware that moving through the taiga without a compass meant dying of starvation. In the summer of 1942, a couple of fifteen-year-old boys (their parents were free workers from a nearby residential area[9]) got lost there. A search was undertaken, but it came up with nothing. So that no one would have a bad conscience about not making every effort, the authorities then ordered a lumbermill to turn on its steam whistle. It shrilled steadily for more than two weeks. Still the

---

9. Many Soviet forced-labor camps were situated near industrial zones, and prisoners were often used on jobs that also employed salaried labor.

youngsters were not found. It was apparent that they had failed to stumble onto any of the trails that might have led them back home, to a checkpoint or to a camp, Most likely, weakened by hunger, they either drowned in a swamp or were sucked down in a bog. The taiga is a terrifying environment, not to be entered lightly. To succeed in an escape, one must have the benefit of three preconditions: careful planning, a highly developed sense for survival in the wilds, and extensive experience of the woodlands.

In the camp there was a persistent story, regarded by many as a legend, that whole bands of prisoners—in fact an entire brigade—who, after disarming their guards, had broken out and were still roaming the forest. Everyone said they were Latvians. But I kept wondering whether they might not be those prisoners from the Kuban who must by now have become quite at home in the Siberian taiga. In peacetime such a band undoubtedly would have been rounded up, but under wartime conditions the Chekists obviously did not have the necessary manpower.

One of the escapees I met had failed through an unlucky chance because his trail had been quickly picked up by a dog. His fitness for life in the forest was most exceptional. He was a "wolf man" in his attitude toward life, in his powers of endurance, and in the keenness of his instincts—even his eyes were yellow, like a wolf's. He regarded his unsuccessful attempt with ironic humor, and was dead certain that in the spring he would have more luck; the "green attorney"[10] would secure him liberty, as the saying went. He considered it as good as done, and made no secret of his plans. I could not help sharing his confidence.

In full contrast to him was a former store manager, a city-bred man, frightfully garrulous and extremely nervous. His escape was so eccentric that the Chekist patrols searching for him were thrown off the scent. Instead of making for the woods, he went tramping straight down a road leading to a village. There no one showed the slightest interest in him. In those days everybody was very badly dressed. Even in the towns, not to mention the outlying villages, many civilians went about in quilted jackets and pea jackets of the type worn in the camps. He continued walking quite openly from village to village, past one camp after another. This went on for a week or so. But since he was clearly of military age, he was finally stopped and asked to show his papers, after which he was back in the camp in no time.

I also recall an engineer from a munitions plant who had been sentenced in the winter of 1942–1943. He corresponded exactly to my idea of a cadet officer in the White Army—tall, solidly built, and unusually broad-shouldered. His face, with its regular features, was straightforward;

10. This name was given by the prisoners to the forest.

he was blue-eyed and fair-haired. I sensed that our views were somewhat similar. But he was in our cell only for a very short time. In any case, I could not have talked with him in an open manner, because there was a stool pigeon in the cell who was carefully noting every word I uttered—I was under interrogation—at the time. All the odds were against the engineer's escape to freedom, despite his courage and determination. He was a living reproach to me, an avowed enemy of the dictatorship, who by force of circumstances had contributed to its war effort by making possible the production of a vital part for tens of thousands of anti-personnel mines.

Dangerous Talk

In my hatred of the regime I was fairly determined not to give up. My escape plans having fallen through, I began making written requests for transfer to a penal battalion. This would have been a good way of getting through the lines, since these units were generally thrown straight into battle. I was also convinced that death from a piece of hot lead would be more merciful than what was awaiting us at the camp. In a six-month period I wrote five letters of request, but none of them was answered. I felt more and more heavy-hearted.

It was more than ever clear in my mind by now that the vast army of prisoners could play no part in events unless it received some impetus from outside. All I could do in the meantime—and this at least helped to raise and sustain my spirits—was to check on our readiness for future action.

By this time I had also fully realized that it is always a few individuals who lead the way. In the first year of the war the example of our small fraternity of five had convinced me of that. We had behaved very un-obtrusively, showing our hand only in emergencies and then almost always only in connection with our jobs in the machine shop. Each of us had his own close associates among the workers, but we never tried to "indoc-trinate" them, knowing very well that when the moment for direct action arose, they would fall in behind us. In some strange way this was known not only by the *zeks* but also by the "free" workers who were in close contact with us, the security guards and our immediate supervisors. This showed in their faintly ingratiating manner toward us, in their vague hints that, despite their official positions, they felt some sympathy for the prisoners. It was amusing to watch the fluctuations in their attitudes depending on the situation at the front. But there also was an element of grave danger in this, since they saw in us future leaders, men who would seize power at the earliest opportunity.

For the time being it would have been unwise to make any specific plans of action. At this particular stage it was enough to keep an eye on the mood of those prisoners who would be of key importance in our cause. More than once people said that deeds were more important than words. This is true enough in respect to very simple matters where the outcome is clear-cut. But for more complicated matters for which you are compelled to work out a clear line of action in your own mind first, you have no choice but to discuss your ideas by word of mouth, especially in a situation where written communication is impossible. For this reason, there was a great deal of talk among us in the summer of '42—much more than was necessary.

Pavel Salmin was a man of no mean talents. He had been a boxer and a chess player of tournament standard. He advocated the most extreme measures, even an immediate armed uprising. At first I tried to make him understand, talking as one engineer to another, that the camp in the present circumstances was a system in a state of equilibrium which could only be upset by the action of some external force. An uprising would have some chance of success only, say, in the event of a parachute landing from abroad, followed by an announcement that Stalin had been deposed and a provisional Russian government had taken over. A detachment of armed prisoners from another camp could also conceivably set the ball rolling. This last idea was much to Salmin's liking, and he began elaborating on it and advocating it to all and sundry. He had a vision of breaking into the camp's guardroom and passing out arms to prisoners. Then we would hijack a locomotive and move in it from camp to camp along the railroad line, urging the inmates to revolt as we went. All this would have been nothing less than another version of the Ust-Usa insurrection which I have already described.

I believe that during the summer months in the taiga such a plan could have been carried out. But there was one serious stumbling block: the disruption of rail traffic along the branch line that ran through the camp area would have cut off the supply of fuel wood[11] for the Moscow-Perm railroad, the only line that at that time linked the capital with the East. This meant that troops would have been rushed in at once and the revolt swiftly put down. Thus it would have been a mistake to organize an

11. During the war many Soviet trains were fueled by wood, which was largely supplied by the forced labor camps. Vyatlag was situated on a branch line which joined the main line from Moscow (via Perm) to the Soviet Far East at the town of Kirov, the administrative center for the whole area and a major rail junction. (Tr.)

isolated revolt at Vyatlag at that time. This objection occurred to us only much later, and it was not the factor that decided us against the idea at the time, since there were many other snags. The basic one was the lack of a man who could have provided us with the necessary leadership. As I eventually realized, all we really needed was a seasoned company commander. From 1943 on, especially after the war, I met a great many officers of this type. But at the time of our particular need, there was not a single one among us. Another problem was that atheism and terror were having their usual deadly influence, so that our ranks were no longer all that united. When it came to taking action, we did not entirely trust each other: our initiative was throttled by a long habit of thought that any joining of forces was a risky business.

In those days neither Salmin nor I could have persuaded the prisoners in our camp to stand up against the regime. But if a detachment of rebel prisoners from elsewhere, armed to the teeth and bearing scars from their latest skirmish, had come on the scene to announce the overthrow of Stalin, the impact on the other inmates would have been tremendous. But as long as the inmates knew that no provisional government had actually come into being and that everything still remained in the hands of the old authorities, we would require a man of extraordinary caliber to get a revolt under way.

Without question, Salmin had been talking too much. I am not accusing him of provocation, though now and then it did occur to me that he might be getting everybody stirred up with the deliberate aim of getting better rations out of fellow *zeks* for himself. The dreadful fact is, however, that he involved a lot of people with his loose talk—and then upon his arrest named every one of them during his subsequent interrogation.

A Reptile Bites Surreptitiously, A Rat May Spring at You

Once set in motion, production in our machine shop went full speed ahead. We had only to keep it on an even keel. I now had time to devote to lesser matters. I had been hearing stories that some of the *zek* inspectors were forcing the free employees in our department to bring them extra food. I paid no attention, figuring that if the half-starved *zeks* we had rescued from the logging grounds were trying to get food supplements, this was hardly a punishable offense in concentration-camp conditions.

The manager of the shop, the technical chief engineer, the man in charge of the plan, and myself, were all supposed to make an occasional

124

tour of inspection at the end of the second and during the third shifts. On my regular round one night in December, at about ten o'clock, I went into the lathe section and caught sight of Shcherba, one of the inspectors, sitting near the machine and enjoying a snack: a teaspoon in one hand, an egg in the other, and on his lap some white bread and a piece of salt pork—a Lucullan repast in those days. We on the supervisory staff couldn't begin to dream of having a meal like that. The most that any of us could hope for was to scrounge a few potatoes and a little black bread from the free workers. Such delicacies as Shcherba had could only have been obtained by extortion. A single glance told me the whole story: he was clearly a stool pigeon who got people to bring him food by threatening to inform on them otherwise. But it would have been against camp ethics to voice my suspicions there and then—and, in any case, what proof had I that he was not just fending for himself as best he could, like everybody else? When I walked over to him, he jumped up obsequiously. I went to the bin where he put the things he was supposed to have inspected. I picked up a pair of calipers and began checking everything he had deposited there. I saw that he had not put his inspector's mark on a single item, and also that he had let a number of defective ones pass—plainly a dereliction of duty. I had him just where I wanted him. I called the shift foreman over and ordered him to record the details of these violations. Then I cursed Shcherba roundly, camp-style, making a great point of the fact that war production was suffering because of him. Only then did I come to the question of his blackmailing the free employees. I told him outright that I knew exactly what he was up to and that I would get further details by questioning some of his victims. Finally, I pointed out to him that now we knew what his game was, he was about as much use to the camp Security Section as a used contraceptive.

I already knew from my conversations on the subject with old hands in the camp that once the moment for a showdown with an informer arrived, he had to be put on the spot in public, fearlessly. Whatever harm he might still be able to do would thus be minimized; the more spectacular the unmasking, the more rapidly all harm would be eliminated. Of course, informers almost always gave themselves away in any case, and the prisoners knew very well who they were. In this sense a public showdown with one of them revealed nothing new, but it always had an important psychological effect: it left the security officers who employed him with a sense of failure.

The next morning I sent in the foreman's report on the incident, and Shcherba received a severe reprimand and a warning from the administration.

The mortality among *zek*s who worked in the lumber camps was rising again and there was a constant shortage of labor. In January, during the severest frosts, they on two occasions even took everybody out of the machine shop and made them saw wood in the forest for the railroad. Five blacksmiths, used to working in the warmth of their forge, died of pneumonia. But Shcherba was kept on in the machine shop where the atmosphere was now very strained because of increased work quotas. The head foreman, whom I had instructed to keep close watch on him, caught him in yet another serious lapse of duty. On the basis of a further report, he was removed from the shop. But he was not transferred to hard labor as I had insisted. Instead, he went to a brigade which made charcoal for the smithies' forges.

The work of a charcoal burner was far easier than a logger's and the output quota was more reasonable. But it was nevertheless much harder than being an inspector in a warm shop. The charcoal-burning brigade was quartered in the same barracks as the machine-shop workers. After a month or so, my friends there told me with some relish that Shcherba was going downhill, that he sat around for hours, gnawing on old horse's bones[12] without a shred of meat left on them. He asked the boys to tell me that he wanted nothing more than to be taken back in the machine shop.

One of the roads leading from the camp to the shop went past the field where the charcoal burners worked. One day in February, as I was passing by, I ran into a wreck of a man whom I did not even recognize at first.

"Dimitri Mikhailovich, forgive me. Take me back to the shop."

The gist of my reply was as follows:

"Shcherba, you've not hurt me, nor could you. I struck first. Ask forgiveness of those you destroyed this winter, even though it's too late to do anything about it. You have the deaths of seven men on your conscience, as we now know from talking to witnesses. I can pardon a Chekist who openly interrogates me—that is his job; I can pardon the henchman who carries out orders; but not a traitor who betrays a trust, who lies and destroys his fellow workers. It's informers like you who do most harm to the prisoners. It is the duty of everyone here to fight against people like you as a lesson to others. If we don't, you will destroy us all."

"But you're wearing a mask, too," he replied. "You detest the Security

12. In the summer of 1942, the camp began to receive the hooves and innards of horses killed at the front. This supplied us with fats and helped to stem the catastrophic death rate in the camps, which reached its height in the spring of that year. Eighteen months later American lend-lease supplies began to arrive and this saved the lives of those who had survived so far, as well as the many new prisoners.

Section and the administration, but I have heard about your polite chats with Levinson. . . ."

"Shcherba, you see how the coal burner going into that hut over there ducks his head low? That's because the doorway is not high enough to allow him to go through standing up straight. It's the same with our whole behavior here. But that's not our fault—we didn't invent the system. You're right—we do wear masks of politeness. But when the situation demands it, I am quite capable of speaking my mind. All this should be well known to you—after all, you were spying on me. The difference between us is that people like me are forced to put on a disguise to protect ourselves and the other prisoners, but without harming anyone; whereas you are only out to destroy people. I've driven you into a corner. You'd dearly love to get your own back, if you could. But you're finished. You're not dangerous anymore. As long as I'm in the machine shop, you won't set foot there again. Vermin like you have to be judged on earth as well as in heaven."

That spring, word came to me that Shcherba had finally—to use the camp expression—"put on his wooden jacket."[13]

Never Say Die!

Just before New Year the deadly monotony of our diet caused me to make an awful blunder. One of my neighbors in what I called "the barracks of the doomed"[14] invited me to have a "drink" with them. Ordinarily I wouldn't have been tempted, but suddenly a strong urge overcame me. The fellows had laid their hands on a little raw alcohol—that wouldn't have been so bad, but we were unable to stop and went on to drink a dissolvent that tasted strongly of pears. It was obviously this that brought on the diarrhea from which I began to suffer soon afterward. Since it was not pellagra, I was not too alarmed. Nevertheless, I was in agony for two weeks, the second of which I could not even work.

While I was ill, a man called Paul Marcel came to keep me company. His real name was Rusanov. Before his imprisonment he had been a composer, and he was in charge of musical activities in the C.E.C.[15] We knew each other only slightly. He had lived abroad as a White émigré and ought

13. In camp slang, this means burying somebody.
14. This was the name I gave to the barracks where we engineers lived, since I knew that sooner or later Chekists would put us all in the camp jail and fabricate new cases against us.
15. The "Cultural-Educational Sector" of the kind that existed in every camp.

to have been aware of the situation, but his artistic temperament kept him from evaluating events correctly. We had innocent chats in French. I was glad to have somebody to talk with, since otherwise I should just have lain there brooding. I had still not forgotten my French, and we conversed hour after hour. Except for two elderly barracks orderlies, no one was around to mistake us for foreigners engaged in hatching subversive plots.

My guest offered to introduce me to a *zemstvo*[16] doctor from the camp infirmary: "Your illness is still holding on. You shouldn't neglect it. I'll ask my friend to have a look at you. He is the only one at the camp who can help you."

He was fervent in his insistence. And sure enough, fate smiled on me for once and sent me help.

That evening I went to the doctor, a white-haired, wizened old fellow. He did not bother to examine me. After asking me a few questions, he thought for a while and then got up quietly, walked over to a cabinet, poured water into a small glass, added something from a bottle, and told me to drink it. It was a solution of hydrochloric acid. Its effect was like fire racing through my veins, but I immediately felt my strength coming back. On returning to the barracks, I was as hungry as a wolf. I continued going to the old man another month, and with his unfailing, gentle smile he gave me medicine from his little vial.

To think of all the kind and learned men like him who have perished! There was no field, indeed, in which many of the best people have not been wiped out. In medicine the consequences have been catastrophic, leading to an irreparable decline in standards of treatment. In just the same way the wholesale destruction of those devoted to the cure of souls led to the rapid decline of moral standards, the brutalization of ordinary men and women, a horrifying spread of nervous and mental illness.

It is interesting to note that when the editors of the *Large Soviet Encyclopedia* were working over the article on the word "love," they suddenly got into a panic. The matter was passed "all the way up to Comrade Stalin personally" (as they used to say in those days). Our great scientist was true to himself: he decreed that love "is a concept alien to the Soviet people." And so in that edition of the encyclopedia the word "love" was omitted.

In tsarist Russia executioners were often hard to find, but under Stalin's rule there was no limit to their supply. Even the recruiting process was a highly simplified one. You were summoned by your local Party committee and asked, "Are you a Soviet citizen?"

16. *Zemstvo:* provincial assembly in tsarist Russia. A *zemstvo* doctor signifies a doctor from the provinces.

"Yes, of course!"

"The party and the state are offering you an assignment of extreme importance—a job in the security forces."

If you tried to decline, you were berated as a pariah, an enemy. Then they started bullying and intimidating you. By these methods they got eight out of every ten to comply.

8

VYATLAG: 1942–1943 (Continued)

The Arrest of the Twenty-Eight

The Stalinist dictatorship resembled a great ant heap where hordes of ant-policemen, by a process of continual terrorism, forced the others to perform jobs alien to their instincts and inclinations. Discipline was maintained through oppression and deceit. Columns of slaves meekly moved along the designated track. The system could also be likened to a cyclotron, where accelerated particles move in one direction, because it is impossible for them either to stop moving or to change direction. To predict the movement either of ants or of accelerated particles is equally simple. Hence my certainty that my arrest was only a matter of time. Moreover, I could observe certain portents.

At Camp One there was a young prisoner, a *bytovik,*[1] who was in the Supply Section and therefore had a camp pass. But he had been caught in a theft and thrown out; and now he requested a transfer to my department. According to the inquiries I made, there was no particular objection to him. A pass-holder with larcenous abilities could even be useful to us, and after consulting with my associates I arranged for his transfer. We planned to use him for stealing potatoes from the gardens of Chekists and other camp dignitaries. I also thought he would be a good person to send to collect the small quantities of buckwheat meal which the miller

1. The Soviet penal code does not distinguish between the three types of criminals. Life itself has categorized them into *common criminals, bytoviki,* and *politicals.*

130

still regularly set aside for us since the time when we had repaired his machinery.

For the Western reader the term *bytovik* demands explanation. Apart from swindlers, embezzlers, and persons guilty of other kinds of fraud, that is, offenses that are indictable not only in the Soviet Union but the world over, this category includes many whose only crime consisted in showing private initiative, thereby in some way encroaching on the monopoly of the ruthless state capitalism that in the Soviet Union goes by the name of "socialism." In general, we were sympathetic toward the *bytoviks,* and with certain ones we had excellent relations. Nonetheless, we kept ourselves somewhat aloof from them, for the reason that they were particularly liable to be recruited for all kinds of dirty work, in the manner I have described earlier. The line of approach was very simple: "We know you're one of us, a Soviet man. We can make things easier for you by reducing your sentence. But first you must help the security services to uncover subversives, who go on plotting even here in the camps. If you are unwilling, then obviously you're not a real Soviet man. We will have to deal with you in a special way. Perhaps you, too, are subversive? You could even get a new sentence if you are not willing to help us." In this way a good many of them accepted and became stool pigeons, and some promised to report whatever of interest they saw or heard.

Soon after the young man from the Supply Section was transferred to us, I noticed that he displayed a particular interest in me, attempting to eavesdrop on my conversations. True, he did it all somewhat clumsily. After I had caught onto his game, I waited for two weeks—until he had lifted all the potatoes from the vegetable gardens belonging to camp officials. Then I put him on the night shift as an inspector, which made it impossible for him to keep me under effective surveillance. This was the first clear intimation that the camp Security Section was taking a great interest in me.

The second intimation came from a man called Adolf Dick. In the autumn of 1941, on starting to work in the machine shop, we new arrivals were very struck by this Russified German. He was a splendid specimen of the Nordic race, of a type much talked and written about in those days, as we knew even in the camps. I admit to a weakness: I was always partial to handsome people; thus I was immediately drawn to this blond with blue-gray eyes, the steely glint of which is difficult to describe. I also recall his regular aquiline nose, firm mouth, strong jutting jaw. He was tall, with well-proportioned arms, broad shoulders, and long, slender legs. His pleasant voice was tinged with irony. He wore a frayed uniform of the tank corps. Forage cap, trousers, and field shirt, all covered with black oil, bespoke an excellent mechanic as well as a first-class engineer. He had completed the armored corps school, then he joined the party, and in 1938 he received only a three-year sentence. These facts had made him rather cautious. He had no desire to work as an engineer and, in fact refused to—evidently because of his German origin. In general, we liked him. But other prisoners in the machine shop told us that a year and a half previously he had appeared as a witness for the prosecution in some trial or other, and they said that this should be borne in mind.

His life was in our hands: it depended on us whether he would stay or be sent off to do common labor in the forest, which would be the end of him. But since he had not been caught red-handed as an informer, we decided to give him a chance to continue repairing tractors—the heaviest work in the shop. At the beginning of his life in the camp, before the war, his mother had sent him parcels from some town on the Volga. He had a natural inclination toward physical labor. But in the autumn and winter of 1941, the increased expenditure of energy caused by hunger, cold, and hard work began to tell, despite the fact that we were managing to get the maximum bread ration for all the men. Dick began to wear down. There were no complaints, threats, or pleas from him, but it became a little frightening to look at him—the bluish, haggard face, the terrible transparency of his eyes. One day I went after hours to the camp infirmary to see a nurse I knew there, Anechka, and I saw Dick naked to his waist in a wooden chair. He was half-lying rather than sitting. His long legs were stretched out and propped against the wall. His arms were draped limply over the back of the chair. At first glance it seemed that his armpits were open sores, but actually it was a cluster of boils of the type known in the camps as "bitch's teats." His head drooped weakly against his chest. He looked exactly like a wounded condor. I stood in silence by the entrance to the office. Anechka was not around. She had gone to the pharmacy. Suddenly he came to; our eyes met. He did not look away, but his head lolled helplessly toward his right shoulder. And then something cut sharply into my heart; I suddenly saw him smile. His smile was sad, but it was in no way pitiful; and I read in it a mute supplication. I could not be wrong about that. I fixed my eyes on his face, feeling very distressed. The silence lasted two minutes. Anechka returned. I went outdoors. She merely confirmed the camp physician's diagnosis. Even without my being told, it was clear that he had dystrophy of the severest kind.

The next morning I told all I knew about Dick's condition to the other men in the shop and proposed they decide what to do with him. If he had been a genuine *seksot,* he would long ago have begun to raise a stink; instead he had suffered in silence. His evidence at the trial had been given quite openly, but this was not by itself the act of an informer, so that there were mitigating circumstances. I therefore recommended transferring him from the tractors, which he obviously could no longer cope with, to lighter repair work; I would give him a horizontal drilling machine to recondition and not bother him until he had finished the job in his own good time. My proposal was accepted and Dick started work on the machine, sitting on a trestle he rigged up next to it, and looking every inch the mechanic he was.

As early as the thirties, people of our generation, in the brutal conditions of Soviet life, began to undergo a process of natural selection— or rather, artificially "unnatural" selection. All who were less able to endure the constant shortages, hunger, and other hardships perished. But those who survived developed a remarkable capacity for putting up with it all, provided, of course, they did not exceed certain limits. Dick was of this case-hardened breed; with each passing day his strength and energy noticeably increased. By the end of two months he had put the machine in excellent working order and was then given the job of operating it. All the while we kept our distance.

When the machine shop was split up and our group was transferred to the new building at Central Camp Five, Dick remained behind at Camp One. At the beginning of December 1942, he took the place of Georgi, who had died. In February 1943 I went over to the shop at Camp One to pick up some drawings for a new tool we needed. Dick greeted me cordially, talked, and joked about the work, and recalled all sorts of trivialities. While we were looking over the designs, his smile suddenly vanished, his eyes took on the gleam of a steel blade, and with only a slight change of intonation he said, "They're interested in you!" And in a second his face resumed its former expression; in the next sentence he was talking again about a new drilling process.

It is essential that the reader (not only in the West but under the Soviet regime today) should understand the enormous effect of this incident on us and the debilitating strain that it put on us. These words of warning, spoken by Dick under the conditions of that time, marked the extreme limit to which many men of good will could go to warn a friend of approaching trouble. He had said all that was necessary. If I had demanded further explanations, I would have been met with a cold, vacant stare. I saw I had been right from the first: Dick was no traitor, but it was obvious that he had recently been summoned by the Security Section in connection with their attempts to gather material against us.

Yet a third warning signal was the arrival of a new engineer who turned up—quite out of the blue it seemed—in our midst in November.

In those years, even though totally stripped of rights, prisoners with special knowledge or qualifications nevertheless yielded certain power, despite their general situation, simply by virtue of the fact that they had been put in charge of vital jobs. From time to time, however, we were reminded of the strict limits of our power. The new arrival, with a purely Russian name and a solid appearance, was smooth-tongued and plausible; but we took an intense dislike to him at the start. His patriotic jingoism smacked of the stool pigeon. Everybody stoutly spoke against having him in our shop. In the camps men were chosen not only for their usefulness on the job, but first and foremost for their acceptability to their fellow prisoners; any other criterion could lead to disaster, as we knew only too well. In any case, our production line was by now working so efficiently that we had absolutely no need for another technician. But despite our opposition, he was enrolled in the machine-shop brigade; the technical director had to create a special job for him, since at that time the distribution of the camp personnel was not yet ordered by the central administration.

Nobody could deny that he was well qualified, although since production was already set up and in motion, he had no real chance to prove his worth. But as a man with a trouble-making character and a desire to survive at the expense of others, he concentrated on pointing out small defects or suggesting minor improvements which could only be carried out by using machines badly needed for more important purposes. All his proposals were backed up by demagogic slogans: at every opportunity he would repeat, "Everything for the Front! Everything for Victory!"[2]

He and I clashed constantly. And, of course, he wrote informer's reports about me and everybody else. Eventually, I managed to get him assigned to the job of repairing rejects. He was able to cope with it, although he shrewdly drew on our experience and knowledge whenever any really hard problem cropped up. We were unable to kick him out of the shop. This was a sure sign that the Chekists were getting ready to pounce on us.

There was one final sign. In early March, 1943, a young Estonian by

2. During the war, these slogans were spread by all the means of Soviet propaganda.

134

the name of Kilk was installed in our barracks. Another Estonian had been put in with us the previous spring, an elderly man who worked in our shop. The older Estonian now began to beg us to take on his young compatriot who had no experience of metal work or mechanics. He pleaded with us as if the boy were his own son and promised to teach him everything. In general, our relations with Estonians had been excellent: they were very loyal, and we had heard of no informers among them. The old man was as good as his word and within three months had taught the boy to operate a planing tool—one of the simplest jobs on a lathe.

And then sometime in July Kilk made a mess of an important job that had required handling by the shop as a whole. There was an inquiry by all the foremen, and it was soon apparent Kilk must have done it deliberately. Such outrageous behavior could only mean that he acted under orders from the Chekists of the Security Section. I happened to be ill just at that time; otherwise, I would have thrown him out of the shop without more ado. But the others were afraid to take action without me, and they lacked the necessary authority. When they put him, an ordinary manual laborer, in our barracks—which was for engineers—they virtually exposed him as an informer. We now went for the elderly Estonian: "What the hell did you mean by bringing that snake in here?" The old man was beside himself. Trembling, he cursed the boy for all he was worth. Later on, we learned that they had planted the boy in our midst to find out where we might have hidden arms. In fact, the only hidden object he succeeded in discovering in a locker between two bunks was an old saucepan, which we used to boil our illicit supplies of buckwheat. When they came to arrest us, one of the officers in charge swooped down on it unerringly. Of Kilk's ultimate fate I know nothing, but I am almost certain that he cannot have survived the war. Someone so stupid and brazen was a danger to everyone around him and it is most likely that the Estonians themselves killed him off.

The basic weakness in our position, as we carried on our struggle at great risk to ourselves, was that a sense of honor of the traditional kind could no longer be counted on: the old steadfastness and loyalty were simply lacking. As I had discovered early on, back in the Moscow prison, the chief commandments, if a man wanted to keep his self-respect, was to become neither an informer nor a thief, and to keep iron control on his tongue.

In the most terrible conditions of the wartime camps the members of our group satisfied the first two of those conditions, but not, alas, the third—particularly after we had been arrested and put in the camp interrogation cells.

The blow fell on March 19, 1943. In one night the Chekists swooped on all the main camps and arrested twenty-eight prisoners. I was among them. The operation was carried out in the classical style of 1937: the preliminary compilation of blacklists, the same suddenness and coordination, the same ratio of four or five agents to one unarmed, unprepared prisoner.

The Camp Interrogation

In mounting their wholly fabricated cases, the Chekists used all the techniques devised by Beria and Vyshinski[3] to force their victims to provide "irrefutable evidence" and sign "full and sincere" confessions. They worked with a will, since the successful completion of every such case meant bonuses, awards, and new apartments.

All of us arrested that night of March 19, 1943 were charged under Article 58, Section 2: armed insurrection in time of war. Either execution or a ten-year term was in store for us. Most of us had had no previous contact with each other since we had been held in different camps of the Vyatlag area. How could we possibly have engaged in a joint conspiracy?

As it now appeared, an experienced informer called Knebel, in Camp One, had diligently reported all the indiscretions of Salmin. It was said of this little hunchback in a leather coat, who had been arrested in 1938, that the inventory taken of the goods confiscated from him at that time covered almost thirty pages. He came from the very rich family of a former publisher. He had a comfortable indoor job in the camp administration, which, since he had been convicted under Article 58, was only possible with special permission from a pal among the security people. We had taken little interest in him. But on the basis of Salmin's stories and his own imagination, Knebel had written a series of reports that implicated us all.

We were held in cells at quite some distance from the place to which we were taken for interrogation. Every time we were summoned, it meant a trek of five miles there and back. In the second and third months this became something of an ordeal—our strength was steadily diminishing as a result of the meager jail ration.

In the first month of the investigation they bothered me very little, except to call me out once and charge me formally under Article 58, Sec-

3. The first was chief public prosecutor under Stalin; the second, head of the KGB.

136

tion 2. I simply refused to give testimony, hoping that the others would adopt the same line of conduct. But the Chekists, who were old hands at frame-ups of this sort, deliberately left the more uncompromising among us in peace and for the time being concentrated all their energies on the pliable ones. The "fiction" rapidly mushroomed. The principal "fiction maker" was Salmin, but our friend Vladimir ran a close second. Within a short time they were echoed by a couple of young *bytoviks*. And six weeks later, their damning testimony against me was produced at an interrogation.

At first, whenever the interrogators wanted to see those of us who refused to compromise, they had us picked up by the armed escort early in the morning, before the bread ration was handed out in the cells, and then brought over to the Chekist department where we were kept in a separate cell until we were summoned for several hours of questioning. Afterward, we were locked up again before finally being taken back to our cells. The Chekist strategy was easy to see through: our starving cell-mates who had been left behind would yield to temptation and wolf down our share of the ration. But we quickly caught onto the Chekists' game and found ways of foiling them. I, for example, flatly refused to go off to an interrogation without first receiving my morning ration. Furthermore, I demanded that it not be left behind in the cell but turned over to our guards for safekeeping.

A threat to complain to the prosecutor would have had no effect whatsoever. But a blank refusal to move (they had no transport in which to take us) and a promise to shout at the top of my lungs while going through the residential area for the families of camp personnel, then overflowing with civilian évacuées, made some impression. If ever they happened to see a prisoner on his way to interrogation, people were always very horrified at the spectacle of a debilitated man, scarcely able to move his legs, being urged on with shouts and curses by a strapping young guard who must sometimes himself have felt ashamed. Often I have observed the extent to which tyrants and evildoers fear public exposure! An effective weapon for us to seize and use. Passing citizens always hurried by as quickly as they could, but they naturally took everything in. Once, while I was being escorted through the residential area, my eyes met those of a boy of about sixteen, the son of a high-ranking Chekist, and I thought I saw a momentary look of sympathy in his face.

Generally, during my interrogation, I merely refused to answer questions. But on a couple of occasions, having nothing to lose, I adopted an aggressive attitude toward the officer in charge of my case, Assistant Divisional Chief Romanenkov. Once, after sitting at some length in silence while he was assiduously writing at his desk—his usual practice —I suddenly spoke up and named several prominent interrogators under Yezhov, all of whom had been shot within the first year after Beria succeeded him. I had heard of them from tales told at Butyrki Prison. "What were they executed for, do you suppose?" I challenged Romanenkov, then answered the question myself: "For sabotage. For the destruction of innocent people, including top civilian specialists and military men. The war has demonstrated the tragic consequences of this crime."

Then I began speaking of myself. "Everybody here knows that I got our defense production underway and that I've achieved excellent results. But all of a sudden I'm locked up, production starts to lag, and a wild accusation is made against me. It begins to look as though somebody is deliberately depriving the production line of its best men. My cousin is a combat pilot. If I am murdered here, he will not rest until he finds out who the guilty parties are. This whole farce will cost you dearly."

The interrogator had not cut me short, and his rather handsome face started to twitch convulsively. His reply was polite and restrained.

"The purpose of the investigation is to get at the facts, to establish who is guilty. And the evidence we have gathered already shows that you are guilty of subversive activity."

At this I threw off all restraint and let him have it.

"That may be true, Citizen Chief.[4] We all know that the Security Service never makes mistakes. But what ever became of all the Chekists who served under Dzerzhinski, Menzhinski, Yagoda, and Yezhov?[5] I suppose they never made mistakes either? So why have I met so many of them in prison?"

On another occasion I made use of my brief glimpse of the sixteen-year-old boy of one of the Chekist's children to good effect:

"The other day I saw one of your youngsters—he is still only a child, but compassion was written all over his face. It is not hard to guess what he must think of your methods. Can it be that no responsible officials have been alarmed by this sabotage of production during the war? Surely somebody must be upset by these arrests of engineers, which are bound to slow down the rate of output. Even a child would see that."

Later on I could see that I had been right to take the offensive. Romanenkov did not put me in the punishment cell. Shortly afteward, I was handed over to another interrogator, and I am fairly sure that it was

4. This was the way in which camp prisoners were required to address camp officials.
5. Heads of the secret police at different periods.

because of my outburst that I was not made into Salmin's main accomplice. Obviously Romanenkov must have had some difficulties in the past. Not knowing what the war might bring, he had become cautious and avoided going to extremes. In truth, the future was as uncertain for our jailors as it was for us prisoners; that's why it was possible for me to say such things. My interrogators did no more than shout at me for the sake of appearance and then quickly calmed down.

These two outbursts were the only ones I allowed myself during the whole course of my interrogation. At all other times I tried to display supreme indifference, saying nothing at all.

In 1935–1937, a massive recruitment of Chekists was undertaken, rather along the lines of mobilization for the army: refusal to comply was regarded as sabotage. The new recruits were then inducted into the police system, in which mutual surveillance and denunciation were all-pervading; then they were indoctrinated with the ideology and made to fear for their lives. Thus was a man transformed in the shortest possible time into a state-employed assassin. Of course, he had long ago been weaned from the civilizing truths of religion. But these fledgling agents had delicate nerves. Many showed up at interrogations pumped full of morphine or after sniffing cocaine; it was the only way some could hold down the job at all. Others were struck off the rolls because of "ill health," which meant they were either on the verge of insanity or were literally twitching as the result of a severe neurosis. The rest complacently followed the daily routine until the next purge came along. In the Soviet Gestapo it was customary to shoot all those who knew too much about the crimes that had been perpetrated by it. Many were sent off to special camps; still others landed in run-of-the-mill ones. The lucky few were retired on pensions or sent to remote parts of the country where they continued to operate as Chekists. These last knew better than anyone else how things stood in the land; consequently they tried to moderate their professional zeal and pathological tendencies and to cloak their activities in correct procedural forms just to avoid "complications," lest there should suddenly be a review of the cases they had handled. They were in mortal dread of being sent to the front, so they busily tried to justify their privileged position far behind the front lines by fabricating one case after another in the camps.

A few of the interrogators were outright sadists, though they were kept in check by their more responsible superiors. Among these was a young one called Nechayev. The mere sight of the prisoners drove him so wild that he foamed at the mouth. He took it upon himself to carry out surprise raids on the mill in the hope of catching prisoners red-handed as they made tasteless patties of meal for themselves. He then accused them of sabotage and mounted cases against them. Once, while I was having one of my sessions with Romanenkov, I was witness to the following little episode.

Nechayev came running into the office. Squirming like a grass snake, he reported to Romanenkov that his wife—Nechayev's, that is—along with a female neighbor had been caught with forged bread-ration cards while they were shopping. Swallowing nervously, he punctuated every sentence with "Are you going to order an arrest?" They had both either forgotten my presence or regarded it as of no importance. In telling his story, Nechayev put all the blame on the neighbor and represented his wife as an innocent victim of deceit.

It was quite clear that Nechayev's wife had been involved in these little dealings not out of need but from a profiteering motive. But obviously the arrest of her neighbor would cast a shadow on Nechayev's wife as well as on the Security Section as a whole; therefore Romanenkov did not order it.

The chief of the Interrogation Section, Kurbatov, was a terrifying personality. A corpulent man around forty, the distinctive feature of his rather handsome face was the eyes, dark as two ripe cherries. On the surface, he was quiet, even-tempered, even ponderous. He seldom swore. He spoke of our fate with the assurance of a clairvoyant. But on two occasions I saw how in a split second his face could become ugly and distorted, as though the Devil were peering out of it. I then understood that this was Vyatlag's Number One Chekist. It was he who was preparing our doom (though leaving the actual dirty work to his minions); it was he who held me for eleven whole months together with common criminals and insisted on prolonging the interrogations even after sentencing. And it was he who sent off to their death in other camps those whom he disliked most. But an executioner does not go undetected by the keen eyes and ears of his victims, who may be men of unusual quality: he always leaves a discernible trail. We eventually heard rumors that after the war Kurbatov was transferred to the Western Ukraine. There he was killed, ostensibly by Bendera partisans.

Among all the testimony produced against me, I had no great trouble in picking out the reports written by Shcherba, the young potato thief, and the jingoistic engineer who had been foisted on us. With some sarcasm I remarked to Kurbatov that despite the vast number of stool pigeons who had been planted among the prisoners, he had no really effective network of agents in the camp; the agents had all been exposed;

we knew who the informers were; nobody talked with them; they were forced to invent lying tales which they then palmed off on him. I said to him:

"Everybody is in honor bound to do his work as best he can. I am only a prisoner, but I nevertheless set up our war production line and got it moving. (I realized that my good performance had been noted; otherwise I should not have been kept on at the camp despite my five applications to go to the front.) "You and your colleagues have misguided notions about people and trample on their work."

Once more I got away with my impudence, but I saw how his face was distorted with rage.

The point I have been leading up to is this: we had to be on constant lookout for the enemy's weaknesses, to lay them bare, to hammer at them. By so doing, we undermined our executioners' self-confidence and exploded the myth that they could do what they liked with impunity. Those of us who went on the offensive and kept it up were never caught off balance. But anybody who viewed this organization of butchers as a solid, unbreachable monolith was, in effect, surrendering his weapons to them. The secret police, like all other agencies of the totalitarian state, consisted of human beings with flaws and vices—cowardice, for example. For that reason, it was best to adopt a militant attitude against our interrogators.

Among the people accused with us was a man called Ratmanov who had been a lighthouse keeper. He had worked with us in the machine shop in the autumn of 1941. He was serving his sentence for spreading anti-Soviet propaganda, though in his lonely job it is hard to see how he could have peddled propaganda to anybody except the seals. To all questions from the interrogator he invariably replied with either "No" or "I don't know." He also kept pointing to his working-class origin and was particularly contemptuous in dismissing the charges against him. Nor was he shy about resorting to the earthiest of language. But in spite of all this—or rather because of it—he got off with only five years. On the other hand, workers who gave in to the interrogators and denounced each other received ten.

Since the days of Yezhov, the Chekist methods of conducting an interrogation had undergone great changes. Interrogators were no longer willing to lose sleep, overtax their nerves, or knock themselves out in any other way. Since they constituted the highest authority in the camps, they were not obliged to demonstrate their zeal. In any case—most important of all—experience had shown them that hunger, disease, and foul air bring a man to the breaking point more surely than do endless hours of interrogations, beatings, and tortures, for which, moreover, they hadn't enough guards, warders, or other aides to assist them. There was also the problem that the screams of any torture victim would no doubt have carried from the wooden quarters of the security services to the ears of the people in the residential area. There was a war on, and one had to simplify. Therefore, they did their "work" in the daytime and finished around six P.M. Their wives brought them hot homemade lunches, packed neatly and covered over with white cloth napkins. For a starving prisoner the smell of good cooking was a cruel mockery. Obviously this, too, was a part of the Chekists' refined program.

But the most refined instrument of torture was tobacco. By holding out the promise of a few handmade cigarettes, or even of a drag or two, they could destroy a man's capacity for resistance, especially if he was already thoroughly worn out. In a situation like ours, smoking was not simply a nasty habit; it was an evil for the sake of which a man could sell himself to the Devil. This fact was confirmed time and time again in the concentration camps. But the majority of people could not overcome their habit. A man is always destroyed by his unnatural addictions. Traces of nicotine in the bloodstream create unbearable craving in a man suffering from acute dystrophy, and he loses all resemblance to a human being. Tobacco hastened the deaths of millions of prisoners, because the urge to smoke often overrode a starving man's need for food. For a matchbox full of tobacco grown in somebody's back garden, a walking bag of bones would surrender his meager bread ration— his only chance for survival. I saw with my own eyes how a vast number of men prematurely brought on their own deaths, just because they were unable to conquer this addiction. This is the reason why I changed from a heavy smoker to a sworn enemy of nicotine. Ever since then, I have always sternly warned the uninitiated against the terrible danger that smoking can expose them to.

My refusal to answer at the interrogations led to a series of open confrontations with my accusers. These human apparitions proceeded to implicate me in criminal actions invented by the Chekists. I felt as if I were watching Chinese shadow plays—shadows of men, shadows of crimes. In one way or another, one gradually became entangled in a web of lies—at least on paper—in spite of all one's protestations. This kind of frame-up was patently unconvincing; yet if such an accusation had been leveled in 1937, a whole section of the camp could have been executed on the strength of the "evidence" gathered in support of it— even in the first year of the war, it would have been more than enough for all twenty-eight of us so accused to go before the firing squad. Fortunately, executions had ceased over the previous six months; for some time now, no lists of condemned men had been read out to the prisoners when they were paraded for work in the morning. But since the war was still by no means over, the interrogators were clearly concerned to show —at our expense—that they were worth their salt. At the grilling sessions I openly spoke my mind. I knew that if we were executed, I would at least die with the thought that even though my life had amounted to nothing and had been filled with mistakes and failures, some future historian, as he slogged through mountains of documents containing nothing but stupid inventions and lies, might be grateful for a few honest words spoken by a man of the time. I was also aware that the outcome would not be affected by an open expression of my views, unless the prosecutors felt quite sure the false evidence was strong enough to make a case for shooting us.

During the confrontations with the informers, I attempted in the interest of self-defense to bring up my plan to escape and fight at the front. But this single real piece of evidence the interrogator chose to ignore. The Chekists were interested not in facts, but only in the lies that people told about each other. In the end they found that, despite all their efforts and all the false testimony provided by their stool pigeons, we were too experienced for them, and they were unable to extract from us what they needed to construct a plausible picture of a mutinous group plot. It was all too clumsy and stupid for words. We later learned that the "special assembly" had sentenced us to only five years apiece.[6] Our interrogators took these light sentences as a personal insult and immediately set about getting us stiffer ones. This also we only realized later, since we were not called out for further interrogation; the Chekists concentrated entirely on getting additional testimony from those who had already "cooperated." The end result was that we all had our sentences increased to ten years, and the only ones to get off with five years were the traitor Vladimir, my friends Yuri and Boris, who had taken no part whatsoever in our conversations, and a few others.

If we had been put on trial simply for striving to make sense of our situation and to find a way out of it, I should have been the principal culprit to be convicted.

6. Sentences were passed by a three-man Special Board (OSO) in the absence of the accused. (Tr.)

If we had been on trial for wishing to throw off the chains of slavery and escape the forces bent on destroying us, then every prisoner in the camp would rightly have been judged guilty.

A Devilish Temptation

Several days before his death a starving man loses all desire to eat. I have observed this peculiarity more than once. As a man begins to go steadily downhill, his craving for food grows. But it reaches a peak, then starts to subside. I don't know whether physiologists will agree with this, but it is an indisputable fact. For me the desire for food became especially strong in the autumn; I had been nearly six months in the cells. The trouble came one day when I violated a very strict rule: I allowed myself to daydream about eating, and it only aggravated the hunger pangs. To make matters worse, an hour before our *balanda* was distributed, I started gnawing on a bone which I had been keeping in reserve for the time I could no longer stand the hunger. Right away I broke two molars —they had become abnormally brittle from lack of calcium. At the same moment I had a nasty hallucination, a sort of waking nightmare, in which I asked for some paper and then sat down to write a formal letter to the Chekists, telling them that the "wolf man" (whom I have described earlier) was preparing to escape and that I knew what route he had chosen. As a reward, I got a full pot of *balanda* and a chunk of bread— the very things I would get in a short while but could not bear to wait for any longer. All this, of course, was just a sick man's fantasy, but it showed that hunger had already proved too much for me and that I had succumbed to the point of indulging in a dream of filling my belly at any price. It is characteristic of a man who is wasting away from hunger to daydream not of gourmet dishes—nor even of a hunk of bread with salt pork and garlic—but only of the thin daily diet that was slowly wasting him, rather than nourishing him. Through earnest, intensive prayer I got rid of the obsession; then I threw away the bone. That month was exceptionally hard—the relentless pains of hunger had brought me to the end of my tether. Later on, they eased up. I clearly recall that in my tenth month in the cells I was worried not about how thin the *balanda* was, but about how cold it was; for my emaciated body now needed heat.

One day, two of the prisoners broke into a fierce quarrel. Suddenly one of them, a well-educated young man, went down on all fours like a dog. He darted nimbly toward the other man, bit him in the leg, and

144

just as quickly sprang back. Everybody, including the victim, was so taken aback that they were rooted to the spot until the whole pantomime was over—then they all burst out laughing.

In that gloomy extremity when one is near death, when death has already started creeping into all the cells of one's body, some savage force within the spirit suddenly asserts its control and impels one to some monstrously absurd or irrational act.

Prokhorych's Discovery

Back in 1928 I had been fortunate in having at school an excellent teacher of literature, F. Berezhkov, an expert on Goncharov and Dostoyevski. The latter he positively raved over. Dostoyevski had already then long been excluded from the curriculum, but Berezhkov devoted half a term to him and frequently referred to him later. To this day, however, the great power of Dostoyevski as a psychologist, seer, and prophet of the Russian revolution remains utterly mysterious to me.

Yet even a genius is not immune to error. Dostoyevski spent four years at hard labor as a convict and served in the army as a common soldier. Consequently he could not help coming into direct contact with the Russian peasantry. Yet this did not prevent him from fostering the myth of "the God-bearing people."[7] Unfortunately, his good, pious, kindly, broad-shouldered peasants with magnificent long beards turned out to be a small minority. In times of ordeal, it was not they who set the standards of behavior for the peasant class as a whole.

Another writer who fell into the pitfall of idealizing the peasants was Lev Tolstoy, even though he had passed nearly all his life among them. Most probably, Platon Karatayev in *War and Peace* was derived from his observations of the type of peasant who played "God's fool," who knew how to please his master.

Solzhenitsyn gives us a detailed portrait of a peasant in *The First Circle*. But his Spiridon is no Karatayev. A man forged of iron, Spiridon is convincing, astonishing, awesome. I knew him in the flesh at the *sharashka,* where I used to borrow a saw from him; I had imposed on myself, as physical training, a daily chore of sawing wood and sometimes I had a row with him. I have met other Russian peasants in my life and all of them bear out the deep truth of what Solzhenitsyn manages to convey in his portrait of our Spiridon at the *sharashka.*

7. The name given to the Russian people by the Slavophiles and by Dostoyevski. They made the mistake of attributing the fine spiritual qualities of a few peasants to the general populace.

Among my Spiridons, I particularly recall one who had been a soldier in the First World War. He was less moody than Solzhenitsyn's character and I liked him better. During my lifetime I have met many veterans of the First World War. Most of them had fallen for revolutionary propaganda, had stopped fighting, and had fraternized with the enemy, abandoning their front-line positions to him, deserting, and murdering their officers. But conscious, no doubt, of how shameful and stupid their behavior was, they were never very anxious to talk about it.

I met my Spiridon—whom I shall refer to by his middle name, Prokhorych—in the large common cell where I was held for six months while undergoing interrogation. A great many people passed through during this time, including *bytoviks,* ordinary criminals, "politicals," and prisoners who had attempted to escape. Prokhorych, a peasant about fifty-five years of age, was one of the latter. During his service in World War I, he had risen to the rank of a noncommissioned officer. He showed all the signs of having been a good soldier. Quite an intelligent man, he had obviously had his share of troubles and had grown deeply suspicious of his fellow men during all the years of the Soviet regime. But even so, his inherent talkativeness often got the better of him, and his booming voice could be heard throughout the cell. In everything he said there seemed to be some hidden meaning, though an informer would have difficulty in pinning it down. Whenever I wanted to ask him any questions, I tried to do so out of earshot of the others, either in the lavatory or during exercise. Or I would go over to him in the cell and talk to him as he sat on one of the lower bunks. Since time hung on our hands, I was able to draw him out and get the gist of his views, even though he often spoke in riddles.

I was sure that he had no doubt whatsoever that the peasants were far better off in tsarist days, when his family had benefited greatly from Stolypin's[8] reforms. After he finally came to trust me, he would recall tsarist Russia as if it were an enchanted realm that had vanished forever. "Anyone who didn't drink and wasn't lazy," he said, "could get everything he needed. Our sovereign was a plain man, and he felt for his people."

He had been certain that Russia would be victorious over Germany in the First World War. He had been with his battery during the Russian offensive in the summer of 1917. As everyone knows, the units that spearheaded the breakthrough had been forced to pull back because they

8. Stolypin, Peter (1862–1911): Minister of the Interior who encouraged the growth of a class of independent smallholders in Russia by distributing land to the peasants. He was assassinated in 1911. (Tr.)

had no support from the reserve troops—these were too busy attending political rallies. If it hadn't been for their blackhearted betrayal, the June offensive could have ended the war. As we sat on his bunk in the darkness, he would roar with indignation whenever he got to this part of his story.

His accounts of the Civil War period were fragmentary and inconsistent, and I could not get him to say plainly whether he had been on the side of the Whites or the Greens.[9] It seemed unlikely to me that he would have spent his time aimlessly with the Greens. One thing was sure: he was not with the Reds. He had too much intelligence not to perceive at the very beginning the antipopular nature of the new state. Furthermore, his later actions revealed him as a man who had learned from watching how the well-to-do peasants were plundered, how their "surplus" goods were confiscated. He also remembered the food-requisitioning units, the way they shot people or beat them up with ramrods when they came to get the harvest.

When he saw that the regime was out primarily to oppress the peasantry, his first step was to leave the small farm he owned and move with his family to a distant village where nobody knew him. His memory of "war communism" was still fresh, and he was too smart to fall for the new policy of encouraging the peasants to enrich themselves. He therefore took no loans from the state and tried hard to keep himself at the level of a "middling" peasant. In this way he saved himself and his family from sharing the fate of the kulaks in 1929.[10] He even went on to attain the rank of collective-farm chairman, which he still held when the

9. Greens: independent peasant partisans who defended their villages and opposed both the Bolsheviks and the Whites.

10. During the Civil War, the Bolsheviks pursued a harsh requisitioning policy ("war communism") toward the peasants and provoked "class warfare" among them by setting up the "committees of poor peasants." After the war, a laissez-faire policy was adopted as part of Lenin's New Economy Policy (NEP), which allowed restricted private enterprise and even encouraged the peasants to "enrich" themselves through the grant of loans to the more enterprising ones, etc. This temporary halt in the process of communization was forced on Lenin by the economic prostration of the country after years of war, particularly after the mutiny of the Red sailors in the naval base of Kronstadt (1921) and the simultaneous peasant uprisings such as the one in the province of Tambov mentioned by the author on p. 108. During NEP, wide economic divergencies developed among the peasantry, peasants were officially classified into three groups: "rich" (popularly known as kulaks, "tight-fisted ones"), "middling," and "poor." When Stalin decided to wind up NEP at the end of the twenties and to embark on a policy of rapid industrialization and enforced collectivization of agriculture, these class differences were exploited to speed the liquidation of the kulaks, who were killed or deported by the millions. The "middling" peasants were treated more leniently, as long as they joined the collective farms (kolkhozes). (Tr.)

Germans arrived in his village in 1941. It was just outside Volokolamsk, not far from Moscow. He flatly denied having had any part in the expropriation of the kulaks. Very likely his claim was true. His appointment as chairman probably came only after a long string of predecessors had failed at the job. Somehow he managed to cope with his responsibilities. The kolkhoz was in wretched shape, and the peasants were paid nothing for their work days, but he was able to keep the mortality low. Just before the German army came, he had distributed supplies of seeds among them. The Nazis burned half his village, including his own house. It was not long, however, before Soviet troops retook the locality. Prokhorych was again named the farm chairman. But someone with a grudge against him reported to the authorities that he had earlier handed out all the seeds, and now there was nothing to put in the soil. He was immediately arrested, tried, and sentenced.

The life of this man was nothing extraordinary, and perhaps I have given it more space than it deserves. But he came up with one idea that struck me by its originality. He believed that it was bad for people to have more land than they could properly cultivate, that under current conditions a half-acre plot was the most that a small family could possibly care for with manual labor, and that what counted most was the quality of their work. I had never heard this idea so well expressed and so well backed up with experience as by this former kolkhoz chairman. Having realized the advantages, in his earlier days, of being a "middling" peasant, he had gone on to apply the lesson on the private plots of his collective farm. Many kolkhoz peasants were forced by dire necessity to reach the same conclusion as Prokhorych, and they cultivated their individual plots much more intensively than the vast areas belonging to the kolkhoz as a whole.

Just before the end of my detention in the common cell, Prokhorych fell ill with dysentery. He was put into an isolation cell, allegedly for an attempt to escape. Together with other unsuccessful escapees he was transferred to the Sixth Punishment Camp, where he soon died.

Subsequently, I often tried Prokhorych's views out on other peasants, especially ones whose father had owned rather extensive farms until collectivization, during which they were liquidated as kulaks. They all laughed bitterly as they told me how their fathers wore out their horses— and themselves in the process—as they struggled to plow up their oversized fields, all the time casting envious eyes on those neighbors who had more land than they. These peasants' sons were entirely in agreement with Prokhorych.

Much has been written about the "land-hunger" of the peasants in the name of which they constantly have been incited against their landlords or each other. My conversations with Prokhorych encouraged me to believe that the land question could be resolved not by appeals to envy or malice, but by the efficient use of labor, sound working methods, and the adoption of advanced agricultural techniques. The practicality of this viewpoint has been shown by the example of India, where starvation and death as a result of crop failures used to be chronic until the English improved the situation through irrigation projects. But the final conquest of famine in India—and in China as well—can only be brought about by means of a "green revolution" of the type made possible by the research of the American plant breeder Norman Borlang, who has offered the world new high-yield varieties of rice and wheat.[11]

11. Thirty years earlier, similar research was conducted by our plant geneticist, Academician Nikolai Ivanovich Vavilov. But the regime concealed his discoveries from the world. In 1943 Vavilov himself died of starvation in Saratov Prison.

9

LOM-LOPATA[1]

The Holy Terror of Vyatlag

After my interrogation had ended, I perceived that the Chekists were determined to settle accounts with me one way or the other. By now, of course, they could have no doubts as to my opinions and attitudes, and they saw that I was totally uncompromising. Frustrated in their attempts to get me sentenced to death—thanks to their own ham-handedness—they evidently decided to try and finish me off in the cells of the camp prison. Of this I am quite convinced because for eleven months I was left in that prison together with the worst of the common criminals, including some who were brought into my cell right after they had been arrested for murder. During those months, I had to endure the company of the most vicious brigands in the camp. On one occasion two men were shoved into my cell who were still covered with the blood of their victims.

But all of them paled in comparison with a legendary figure of evil known as Lom-Lopata. In 1930 Lom-Lopata's parents had been deported as kulaks, and the whole family perished in Siberia—except for Lom. He survived, though still a child, only because he had managed to run away from home just in time and get to a railroad station where he hopped a train for the nearest city. Of course, the only possible way for him to exist was by stealing, and this eventually became his profession. Then came prison, a series of attempted escapes, and additional sentences to serve as a result. At the start of the war, in order to avoid landing in a front-line penal battalion, he deliberately picked a quarrel with another bandit at

1. The bandit's nickname, consisting of the Russian words for "crowbar" and "shovel."

the prison and killed him. For this he received ten years under Article 58, Section 14: sabotage in time of war. In gambling games with other common criminals he beat them by using marked cards—which exposed him as transgressor of their code.[2] He was marked out as a "bitch." Soon he got embroiled in a succession of brawls and slayings. After committing a number of further murders, he was pronounced mentally unfit and therefore not responsible for his actions—which meant that he did just what he pleased. For each new murder committed in the camp he got an additional ten-year sentence, to go into effect the moment he finished serving the previous one. Consequently, he found himself in the camp with a perpetual ten-year stretch ahead of him. He never had to stay long in the camp prison, since the evidence against him for his latest crime was virtually the same as for the previous one, and the necessary report could be drawn up after the briefest of interrogations. Shortly before my encounter with him, Lom had murdered a fellow prisoner simply in order to get put in the cells—he figured it would be more prudent to spend the winter there in view of the large number of "regular" criminals out for his blood. The case was not as clear-cut as his previous ones and he was able to drag out the investigation by demanding psychiatric examinations. After undergoing the first one, Lom was installed in my cell, which was intended for several prisoners but where I was now held alone with him. For quite some time we both lay on the top bunks where one might see a bit of the sky and get a breath of air—on the lower bunks you always felt as if you were suffocating inside a sack.

There was nothing particularly savage about Lom's appearance. He looked rather like a drayman of the kind I remembered from my child-hood. He had a broad, clean-cut face with a firm, thin mouth. When his stomach was full, he could chat, listen, and ask questions, all in quite normal fashion. When he was hungry, the beast inside him awoke. Obviously this was the Chekists' calculation: they reckoned on my clashing with him sooner or later—and they were right.

In the camp he had always lived at the expense of the non-criminal prisoners, and while they were emaciated and exhausted, he, not sur-prisingly, was in excellent shape when he arrived in the cells. Con-sequently, during his first weeks there, he suffered no pangs of hunger, even though our ration was a starvation one.

I had no choice but to pass my time in conversation with him. I listened to his tales of adventures and escape, of the horrible conditions in the camps of the Pechora River region back in 1937 and 1938, when

2. The criminal who loses at cards and does not pay his debts, or who plays with his own people (fellow criminals) using marked cards.

"counterrevolutionaries" were executed for failing to meet their work quotas, and where there was a deliberate ban on the boiling of water, so that the prisoners were forced to drink it straight from the marshes. As a result, dysentery mowed them down right and left. He sang songs from the underworld, and some of the lyrics still linger in my memory: *Clouds black as coal fly overhead!* . . . In return I often told him tales from O. Henry I remembered from my reading. He followed the stories with considerable understanding, laughed at them, and even caught the point at the end. He certainly could not have been taken for a half-wit. He was, after all, a professional criminal with all the quick intelligence of his kind.

Almost a month passed without any trouble between us. Then he demanded another psychiatric examination, after refusing to sign the report drawn up at the close of his interrogation. Since the Chekists regarded habitual criminals as kindred spirits, amenable to reeducation, they more often than not made concessions to them. Lom was sent to a psychiatric ward at Camp Four. There he proceeded to gorge himself on the food intended for the genuine patients, cheating them out of it by every possible means. After six weeks he returned to our cell in fine condition.

When the interrogation of our group of twenty-eight was completed, the materials in the case were sent to a Special Board of the NKVD: henceforth our fate would be decided by it. The camp interrogators no longer had the power of life and death over us. The vulnerability of the Chekists lay in their fear of each other, in the constant interdepartmental intrigues. During an interrogation those conducting it could order the Medical Section not to allow special rations for a sick prisoner in the cells, and their word was law. Similarly, an interrogator had the right to order confinement in a punishment cell with rations of only three hundred grams of bread per day for as long as he specified, and the authorities at the camp jail would have to carry his instructions out to the letter. But as soon as the interrogation was over, a mere verbal order no longer sufficed to deny a sick prisoner the ration to which he was entitled; the chief of the Medical Section, fearing possible repercussions in the future, would demand written instructions which he could produce in the event he were ever called to account for obeying an illegal order. The Chekists, by the same token, naturally hesitated to commit themselves to paper in such matters.

This was the reason why I—together with other badly undernourished prisoners—now began to receive a special "sick ration" consisting of an extra 150 grams of bread, a cube of sugar, and a piece of fish. The difference between our rations was too much for Lom-Lopata and he grew frantic with envy. He began badgering me to play cards with him. I had never had much to do with cards and I knew that to play with him would have been to court disaster—since he and his kind always used marked cards in games with non-criminals, I would certainly have lost my ration to him.

How I Nearly Lost an Eye

Just at this time, as my relations with Lom-Lopata were going sour, three more professional criminals were thrown into our cell. Until then, we had slept on the top bunks, he on one side of the cell and I on the other. As soon as these new criminals joined us, I gathered up my belongings and climbed below. There would scarcely have been room for us all up there, and having nothing in common with them anyway, I thought it best not to wait until I was invited to get down.

After an hour or so, curses and screams rang out, and Lom-Lopata suddenly hit the floor with a thud. The three new men were "regular" criminals and Lom a "bitch"—that is, they belonged to opposite factions in the endless feud now going on in the camps. The three "regulars" had therefore thrown Lom off the top bunk as a traitor who could not be tolerated in their immediate vicinity. I looked up to see a head hanging over the side. It was indicating with beckoning jerks that I should climb up. The proposal was extremely insistent. I did not consider it feasible to refuse, for I was too debilitated to offer resistance. Besides, whenever I thought something was inconsequential, I forebore putting up a fight.

But the fact that I was now on the upper bunk in the company of his enemies had a terrible effect on Lom and aroused all the malice within him. To think that he, a seasoned veteran of the criminal world, should be banished to the darkness of a lower bunk, while I, a mere *frayer,* should lie *above* him! I could tell from his manner and certain remarks that his attitude toward me had changed. He regarded me as a much worse enemy than the fellow-thugs who had heaved him out.

The guards always came round to check us off and give us our gruel at about six in the morning. After nine months in the cells, I looked forward impatiently to this moment, as did everybody else. In anticipation of it I would get down from the top bunk and take a little exercise—

three steps in one direction and three in the other. There was not room for more. One morning I was feeling weaker than usual; so I just sat on one of the lower bunks and waited in apathy. Several days before, the small electric bulb that lighted the cell and even a bit of the adjacent corridor had burned out, and the bottom bunks were therefor · in complete darkness; the upper ones were almost as dark, except for dim patches of light reflected from the corridor. Lom-Lopata, who ordinarily sat without stirring, suddenly got up. He walked closely up to me several times and stopped in front of me. I paid no attention to him.

Then the check on the prisoners began. As a rule, the cell door was opened only halfway; the warder would stick his head inside and count off the prisoners. That morning he was going through this daily routine, when all of a sudden, like a released spring, Lom rushed at him, holding a small wooden rod into which he had inserted a long, stout sewing needle of the kind used for stitching together bags from sackcloth. He had clearly intended it as a weapon of cruel revenge to be used against me. But in a fit of blind savagery—apparently it was one of those times when he lost his reason altogether—he went for the guard instead. Lom had aimed the needle at the man's eyes, but it struck the bridge of his nose. The guard reeled backward and set up a fearful howl. The three bandits jumped down from the top bunks, grabbed Lom-Lopata, and gave him a savage beating before other guards ran up to take him off to the punishment cell. It was only the darkness that had saved me. If it had not been for a blown-out light bulb, I might have lost an eye—or possibly both of them.

Not long afterward, Lom was sent back to our cell. For some strange reason, this dreadful murderer continued to direct his animal ferocity and hatred against me instead of the three other men who had beaten him almost senseless and helped the guards to disarm him. Because of some loose screw in his brain, he was evidently quite haphazard in his choice of scapegoats for his wrath. Before long, the other three criminals were removed from the cell on the conclusion of their interrogation—they had confessed to everything out of eagerness to get back to the camp and resume living off the other prisoners.

The Magic Circle

I was thus left all alone with Lom—and a grim experience it was! The presence of other criminals had kept him in check, but as soon as they left, he clearly felt free to settle accounts with me once and for all.

154

Addressing me as "Engineer" (a word he could not pronounce), he kept saying ominously:

"Well, Engineer, you won't get out of the camp alive."

I invariably replied, "I'm sure I will," and tried not to enter into further conversation. What evidently saved me was that I showed no sign of being scared even though I had good cause to tremble. After all, I was caged up with a wild beast. Indeed, my situation was even worse than that, since Lom combined brute force with the superior cunning of a human being. He was, needless to say, much stronger than I—after ten months in the cells I was in poor shape, while he was still fresh from his "outing" to the psychiatric ward, where he had fattened off the other patients. However, I was not afraid of him. Later on, as I tried to make sense out of the whole episode, I came to realize that the spirit is always fearless. Only the flesh trembles. And since my body was so wasted, my center of perception had shifted toward the spiritual sphere. Sitting quietly on my bunk, I devoted myself to what was most important: silent prayer. The average well-fed man is less likely to attain a state of heightened spirituality than one hypersensitized by starvation. In this condition the mind becomes wonderfully clear, perceiving things which would otherwise escape its attention.

I could see that Lom was constantly on the point of doing something such as hitting me or snatching away my bread. But he could not. In Gogol's story *"Viy,"* one of the seminarists draws a circle on the ground around himself in order to fend off an evil spirit. I had certainly not done anything like this, or even thought of it, yet my prayers and clear consicence threw a kind of invisible cloak of protection around me. It is the only explanation I can offer as to why this wild animal never struck me or shoved me off the bunk, even though he was seething with rage against me all the time. Such a strange, incomprehensible phenomenon I can explain only by the astral protective zone around me.

Mortal Combat

But then something happened that broke down the protective barrier around me. Lom was by now suffering terribly from hunger. He had no source of supply other than his meager daily ration, and he was unable to make me give up mine.

He then decided to resort to an old prison trick in which he would need my assistance; but unfortunately I refused to play my part. Lom had with him a nail and a stone, which he must have obtained during a visit to the bathhouse, although after the incident with the sewing needle he had undergone a very thorough body search. What he now did, however spectacular it might seem to a newcomer, was nothing out of the ordinary to the hardened prison guards who usually treated it as a joke. Lom took a rusty nail and drove it through his scrotum into the edge of the bunk with the stone, thus impaling himself there. At this point, I was supposed to start yelling at the top of my voice. But I refused to play the game—though it would have cost me nothing, and I was later to regret it. I was so weak that my reactions had become very slow. After a few minutes, he started howling himself. The guards came running in, pulled out the nail, gave him a few cuffs on the back of the neck, and left it at that. The authorities took a fairly lenient view of this kind of thing as a traditional practice among the criminals, who were always faking illness and performing little stunts like the one just described, usually as a way of getting themselves out of a jam, of getting shipped out to another camp. In this case Lom had pulled off his trick simply in order to get a second helping of *balanda*. To heighten the effect that he wished to achieve, it was necessary that someone other than himself should call the guards.

As a general rule a second helping of *balanda* went only to prisoners in a more privileged category. Now, however, for the first time in my ten months there, "seconds" were brought to our cell as well. It was at this point that I made a further mistake—a very big one. Since I had not played my expected role in Lom's bloody and horrible stunt, I had no claim whatsoever on this bonus which had been earned entirely by his efforts. But I was so famished that when the guard banged on the lock and said in a half-whisper, "Seconds! Bring your bowls," I darted from my bunk before Lom could move, and it was all poured into my bowl. In righteous indignation Lom roared that it all belonged to him. But I didn't listen and greedily wolfed down the lot—the stuff was a little thicker than usual. At this Lom flew into a rage, feeling for once that right was entirely on his side. He declared that if I took any the next day, he would finish me off. I replied in his own criminal jargon that he had no special privileges here, that I had already spent ten months in the cell, whereas he had been there only six weeks; therefore my claim was greater than his. Nonetheless, I knew inwardly that I was making a terrible mistake. The next day, he managed to get the lion's share—enough to fill three bowls—but not before I had filled mine, too. This was quite enough for him to decide that I had once more encroached on his rights. Later I understood myself that I had indeed acted unjustly—and thus forfeited my right to "astral" protection.

I began greedily eating, at the same time casting glances in his direction. He set out his three bowls in a row—a good supply of them was always to be found in the cell since it was designed to hold eight men—and with an ominous look on his face, he raised his right fist above his head and then slowly lowered it as he advanced toward me. It was the fist of a butcher, or of a man used to wielding a sledge-hammer. His muscles were still in excellent trim, and with his powerful arm he clearly intended to drive his fist straight into my stomach, making mincemeat of my guts, which had grown very tender over the last ten months. Instead of thrusting my arms out to fend off the impending blow, I drew them in close to my abdomen. I knew I was no match for him, but I was keyed up and ready, and the moment the great fist began to descend, I immediately went into a crouch. As a result, the fist landed not on my abdomen, but on the ribs and chest, with only a glancing blow to the midriff. The impact of it, along with the excruciating pain, completely took my breath away. Gasping for air, I bent forward as far as I could go. This movement saved me from death. By instinct I had adopted a position that made it impossible for him to hit me a second time in the same spot. It was a long time before my body was free of throbbing pain, but at least he had not killed me, as he might well have done. I was also saved by the fact that he was not quite right in the head: once he had vented his rage by delivering this one savage blow, he simply went back to his food and began gorging himself.

After catching my breath, I also finished off my portion of the *balanda*. Then he asked me. "Well, will you try it again tomorrow?" "Yes, I will," I replied without hesitation. I now felt spiritually renewed, having made up for my error by the fearful pain endured because of it. My "armor" had returned, and I was henceforth invulnerable. My adamant stand, as well as my lack of visible fear or hesitation, were too much for him. He was crushed by his own inability to make me submit to his demands.

The next day I heard him thrashing around on the bunk below. Later, quite beside himself, he paced the cell like a caged animal. I could see that my stubborn behavior was getting him down. It was even interesting to watch the process.

I now took a share of the extra *balanda* for the third day running, telling him once again in no uncertain language that I had more right to it than he. It is true, of course, that to some extent I was driven to assert myself like this by sheer hunger, but I also felt that it was wrong in principle to yield to him. By now I had won a decisive moral victory and I saw how he squirmed, muttering to himself: "What kind of a fellow am I, if I can't knock off this pigeon? . . . Not worth a damn!"

Fortunately, three days later, they stopped giving us extra *balanda,* so there was nothing to fight about any more. But it was obvious that he could no longer stand being in the same cell with me. His sense of humiliation and defeat, his frustration at not being able to deal with me were just too much for him. After two more days had passed, he said to me: "Tell the guard to have one of us moved out of here. Otherwise I really will do you in."

I could see that he was working himself up into an uncontrollable frenzy, and that he really meant it this time. During the morning inspection I asked to see the chief warden, repeating my demand again in the evening when our *balanda* was brought. I told the guard that if I were not taken out of the cell, all my friends would conclude that the Chekists were deliberately trying to arrange my murder. After a half-hour or so I was summoned. The chief warden was a young man who had recently come from the front. His hand still showed traces of a wound. I explained the situation to him: "You have me locked up with a monster. Everybody knows that he is not responsible for his actions, which means that he can literally get away with murder. Things have now come to a head between us, and I cannot stand up to him anymore. Today he will finish me off. He has the strength of an ox, and despite all the murders he has committed already, he is deliberately put in with other prisoners as a way to kill them. Bear in mind that you are a young man with lots to lose, whereas I have nothing to lose at all. If one of us is not moved by tonight's inspection, I'll shout out for the whole jail to hear that you personally are responsible for my murder."

My threat may not seem very terrible, but it was scarcely music to the ears of a man who was well aware that his subordinates were watching him closely. At any rate, I got results. That evening the order rang out: "Lom-Lopata, get your things and come along!" I knew that I would live another day.

Lom-Lopata was moved to a cell for *bytoviks* and common criminals who had already undergone interrogation and were now waiting to be sentenced and then sent off to various camps. Meanwhile, they were taken out to work at the sawmill. The very first day Lom-Lopata, for no apparent reason at all, split the back of another prisoner's skull with an ax. It was evidently his way of relieving his feelings—since he hadn't been able to kill me, he vented his wrath on the first man unlucky enough to cross his path. He was given ten more years, but that meant absolutely nothing to him. Men like him were never shot—they were too useful to the authorities in dealing with "politicals."

158

The Secret of the Slavic Soul

By a curious twist of fate, Lom-Lopata and I were to run into each other again. Three years later, in 1946 at Vorkuta, I was working as a factory engineer—a position of some privilege. Lom-Lopata was sent there with a new batch. As a criminal considered a "bitch" by his fellows, he was eligible for posts of minor responsibility, and on his arrival in Vorkuta he was appointed brigadier of the disciplinary work gang[3] in the camp where I too was now being held. One day I caught sight of him in the distance, and we had a brief exchange in camp jargon, which in normal parlance would sound something like this:

"Well, Lom, your prediction didn't come true, did it?"

"I guess not. You're certainly a tough one."

Not long afterward, a draftsman of ours was about to go into the disciplinary brigade for some misdeed or other. Deciding to take advantage of our old acquaintanceship, I went over to see Lom in the evening after work.

"Lom, one of our boys is being sent to work with you. See to it that he doesn't come to any harm. Make sure he's treated right."

"Well, of course. What do you think?" Lom replied.

On a table close by him was a mess tin of kasha, and he invited me to share it. The most extraordinary thing was that I felt not the slightest resentment or malice toward him. We chatted a little while about something or other and even had a few laughs. Then I left.

Not long after this, Lom left Vorkuta after playing a trick which was then very common in the camps: he got a "goner"[4] to impersonate him at a medical examination and thus had himself declared unfit for heavy work. In those years men who were in an extremely weakened condition were not kept at Vorkuta. Even though he probably had more meat on his bones than any other prisoner at Vorkuta,[5] Lom was transferred to Karaganda.[6] Before his departure, I asked him how he was.

"Not bad," he replied. "When my belly's full, nothing bothers me. I don't need anything else."

3. I.e., a brigade composed of particularly hardened offenders or of prisoners who had infringed camp regulations. For the role of the brigadier—a kind of overseer always appointed from among the prisoners themselves—see note on p. 82. (Tr.)

4. Camp slang for prisoners already too worn out to work. See note on p. 52. (Tr.)

5. *Vorkuta:* Coal-mining and industrial area in the far north of European Russia. Both the mines and factories were manned largely by forced labor.

6. *Karaganda:* city in Kazakhstan, in Soviet Central Asia; the center of one of the largest labor camp areas. (Tr.)

The reason why this second encounter was so good-natured and un-marred by any ill feeling dawned on me only when I later went over the whole episode in my mind. I detest false and pernicious ideas, together with the fanatics who peddle them, but I seldom feel hatred or vindictive-ness toward people with whom I have had direct contact, however dis-agreeable it may have been. At the most they have inspired only revulsion or contempt.

The many criminals whom I have encountered in my life have been clearly divided into two opposite types: at one end of the scale are the degenerate mugs, with all the universal hallmarks of total viciousness and criminality; at the other are those with normal, everyday faces. If you dressed anyone from the second group in ordinary clothes, he would look no different from the average man in the street. The only signs that might betray him are the shifty eyes and the downward lines at the corners of the mouth which always mark a man who has been in prison for murder. With respect to this second category, which in those days predominated in the camps, I can say with assurance that they were victims of an in-human regime. In their lucid moments the majority of them understood who the guilty ones were. The sharp antagonism between them and the "political" prisoners arose almost wholly out of the appalling conditions of hunger that the regime had so ingeniously devised. In periods when all the prisoners were getting enough to eat, ill feeling vanished almost entirely. If any lingered, it was mainly because it was deliberately kept alive by the Chekists.

I think that now you will better understand why my second encounter with Lom was so different from the first. When we both were decently fed and clothed, and were not being worked to death, we had no good reason to be enemies. Our relations then took on a wholly human aspect. We might still have harbored grudges, but by and large rancor is not a feature of the Slavic soul—hence our final meeting was entirely amicable.

In a normal society, the theory that criminals are products of their en-vironment is basically false and erroneous. Dostoyevski dealt it a crushing blow in his day. But a regime that is propped up by towering horrors and crimes fully justifies the proposition; we need only substitute the word *regime* for *environment*.

10

THE MIRACLE

Why We Did Not Die of Hunger in the Camp Jail

Our group of twenty-eight, accused of "attempting armed insurrection," was detained in the camp jail at Vyatlag for eleven months from March 19, 1943 until February 19, 1944.

In 1941–1942 the cells had been filled to overflowing by prisoners held on charges of a similar nature. They had died of scurvy, dystrophy, and pellagra. And some were taken out and shot.[1] By 1942–1943 the wave of such fabricated cases had subsided a little: the mortality rate had also fallen.

Out of our twenty-eight, only one died. This was due to food supplies that were starting to arrive as part of American aid. Without it most of us would have perished—to last through eleven months on the customary camp-jail ration would have been impossible, especially for people like ourselves who were already in an acutely emaciated condition. Naturally, these American supplies played no direct part in our diet, but the mere fact that some were arriving at the camp in general meant that we were able to sustain ourselves thanks to the hospital rations now coming to us from the camp kitchen. Because of America's generous help, many millions of lives were spared. Our heartfelt thanks to the people of the United States. This was not the first time that America had aided Russia;

1. In the winter of 1941–1942, a transport of a hundred men would be reduced to two or three. It was the same, and even worse, in the punishment cells. During this period my comrades and I never once met a "political" who had come out alive.

in the years from 1918 to 1923, American famine relief (ARA) had also rescued our hungry people. In Moscow during the Civil War, bowls of buttered noodles were distributed daily among us starving children. Such assistance had saved millions of Russian lives in that earlier period.

Rules for a Starving Man

Man does not live by bread alone. But when he has too little to eat, he lacks the strength to function in any sense. It is then that he must rely on sheer will power and force himself to observe certain basic rules. However exhausted and apathetic you may feel—and however cold the weather —never refuse to go out during the exercise period, as most prisoners do. Even if your legs are giving way under you from weakness, get additional exercise by walking round your cell—for hours on end! When you want to lie, sit instead, even though your backside is so shrunken—almost to the bare bone—that it hurts to sit upright.

You will want to think only about food, to dream about it, to talk about it—nothing but food. But you must not—not for anything in the world! Otherwise, you will die.

When you get your ration, you have an overwhelming desire to stretch out the pleasure of eating it, cutting your bread up evenly into tiny pieces, rolling the crumbs into little balls. From sticks and string you improvise a pair of scales and weigh every piece. In such ways you try to prolong the business of eating by three hours or more. But this is tantamount to suicide!

Never on any account take more than a half-hour to consume your ration. Every bite of bread should be chewed thoroughly, to enable the stomach to digest it as easily as possible so that it gives up to one's organism a maximum amount of the energy (prana) contained in it. Of course, you may know nothing of yoga, but in your desperate fight for life you may unwittingly stumble across its secrets. If not, you will surely perish.

If you always split your ration and put aside part of it for the evening, you are finished. Eat it all at one sitting; if, on the other hand, you gobble it down too quickly, as famished people often do in normal circumstances, you will also shorten your days.

Worst of all is to smoke. Only men of quite exceptional will power can give it up when they are in a state of complete exhaustion. I have never come across such people. You have to give up smoking while you still have flesh on your bones. Otherwise your chances of going under multiply sharply.

162

Finally: anything that leads to the unnecessary secretion of the digestive juices can be harmful, since they have a ruinous effect on the lining of an empty stomach. Anything that increases the amount of vital energy is beneficial.

The Swede's Secret

Since I have alluded to yoga, I should like to tell of one phenomenon for which to this day I have not found a satisfactory explanation. I never missed a single exercise period—we were entitled to it, and I always insisted on going out, though this scarcely endeared me to the guards. It was usually after a snowfall, just as the cold was intensifying again, that I noticed how the snow along our exercise path was flattened in places, as if by the body of some animal. It was only in the transport to Vorkuta at the end of 1944, that I learned that these impressions on the snow had been made by Lev K., one of my "co-conspirators" (whom I had never met before). He told me the story on the way to Vorkuta. A Russianized Swede, he was by training a historian. During his exercise periods he had stripped to the skin and then rolled about in the snow. It is easy to describe—and easier yet to read about—but it seemed absolutely incredible that anyone living under our conditions could have actually done something like that.

Much later, in the winter of 1962, when as a free man I took up swimming in the Moscow River, I sometimes watched "walruses"[2] from our neighborhood rolling about naked in the snow just to show off. I also attempted it a couple of times, but only on warmer days when the air temperature stood at ten or twelve degrees below zero centigrade. On one occasion, when two of our hardy Moscow swimmers rolled about naked in the snow in minus twenty-four degrees centigrade, one of them got frostbite in his ear—and that was all! But these "walruses" were well fed and in excellent shape, while Lev K. was just skin and bones. And the "walruses" could run back to their heated quarters immediately afterward. Lev K., returning from his exercise, had to wait until the guard opened the cell door and let him inside. Most astounding of all was the fact that he inflicted this torture on himself at a time when he was on a prison ration, barely enough to sustain life.

During one period at the camp, when I was in much better condition, I tried a few times to bathe in water up to my waist in an enclosed

2. Winter swimming has always been customary in Moscow and Leningrad and people who indulge in it are known as "walruses." (Tr.)

building; but I was soon forced to give up such attempts. The expenditure of calories rose, and a sharp loss in weight followed. Thus I find it very hard to understand how Lev K. got away with it. Perhaps he held the yogi's secret of utilizing the energy that accumulates in the gonads and the solar plexus? Yogis in the Himalayas are known to dry out damp bed sheets with their own body heat, even when an icy wind is blowing. These snow baths certainly helped Lev to become physically tougher than his cellmates, which bears out my theory that he was able to tap hidden sources of energy, indeed that he was a yogi.

Lev's example illustrated the tremendous potentialities of the human body and spirit. We tear at others' throats and covet what does not belong to us, all the time ignoring our own inner wealth. We have the potential of becoming godlike, but we prefer to sink to the level of pithecanthropes.

Death from Loving Hands

Illness held off long enough to enable me to leave the camp jail on my own two legs. However, along with my "accomplices," I was by now classifiable as a *dokhodyaga*,[3] and we were all taken straight from the cells to the camp hospital, which was hardly distinguishable from our barracks. The only difference was that in the hospital the upper tier of bunks formed a single, undivided platform, while on the lower deck some of the slats had been removed at regular intervals to make a semblance of separate cots. The upper section was for the patients still strong enough to climb up. there; the dying lay down below. As soon as a man contracted pellagra,[4] his strength began to decline rapidly, and he could no longer make it to the upper level. He would be placed on the lower bunks, in the space vacated by a corpse. The disease progressed with considerable intensity. The victim might last fifteen days, or in rare instances, twenty.

Except that we were stripped of our clothing and left in our underwear, life in the camp hospital was essentially the same as in the jail. And because for the whole ward there was only a single pair of worn-out shoes, and a nondescript pile of rags, we had to give up our outdoor exercise for the rest of the winter. On the other hand, we didn't have bars on the windows and anybody could drop in for a visit, occasionally bringing

3. See note on p. 55. (Tr.)
4. A wasting disease caused by diet deficiency; one of the main symptoms is bleeding from the bowels and diarrhea. (Tr.)

a little something with him. Once in a while the radio was switched on. On one occasion, as if from another world, we heard the Vakhatangov Theater[5] company doing a broadcast performance of *Cyrano de Bergerac*. All of Cyrano's emotions came flooding over the airwaves. Out there, the limelight, applause, actors taking their bows in triumph; here, in the shadow of death on the lower bunks, foul air and foul language.

Every day the hospital issued us its measly ration. We were allowed to add to it, provided that we could lay our hands on something extra. This, however, could land you in terrible trouble. One day, shortly after settling down to our new routine, I dressed myself in that collection of rags and went wandering off toward the camp accounting office. Along the way I ran into several old acquaintances. Some pretended they didn't recognize me; the rest looked in another direction. It was obvious that the idea of contact with a person who had been charged with taking part in an "attempted uprising" terrified them. I could well understand their behavior and considered it justifiable.

Behind the counter in the accounting office sat a middle-aged woman.[6] When she raised her head in response to my inquiry as to whether I had any money[7] left in my camp account, I caught a view of an aquiline nose, light blue eyes, and dark brown hair, with a narrow ribbon over it at the top of her brow. That is how I have always remembered Marika. I repeated my question. She looked up. Then she got up and walked over toward me. After asking some questions of her own, she found my account and told me I had a hundred roubles[8] for which, as she suggested, I could buy myself an extra bread ration. From that time on, she visited me two or three times each day. She always brought me something to smoke, either a butt or a whole handmade cigarette. She often presented me with a hard biscuit or a crust of bread. In a word, she treated me with extraordinary kindness and confided that when I first appeared before her in my rags, she was struck by the expression of great suffering in my eyes.

Marika was a German from Riga. Her husband had been a Latvian in a high position. Together they were seized by the Soviets during the purge of 1941. Their two adolescent sons were able to get away and, as she believed, later joined with some Latvians who were hiding in the forests. In those days one could still find people who refused to sit meekly by and await their fate. Marika's husband, of course, died in camp; but

5. A Moscow theater.
6. Until 1948, mixed camps were the general rule.
7. Every three months, prisoners received a bonus which was sufficient to buy one ration of bread.
8. This money was in currency until 1947. It was later revaluated by ten.

thanks to her vitality and unshakable will, she had survived the worst. Having a truly Christian heart, Marika was unstinting in her love. Her globular blue eyes radiated tenderness and compassion. It was her vocation in life to do good. She was forever putting herself out for someone— making requests on someone's behalf, or collecting warm clothing for men being shipped out on transport. Charitable contributions flowed into her hands and were then passed on to the dying and to those still struggling at the edge of the grave. She kept nothing for herself.

I held a high place in her affections and she wanted very much to help me. And what I wanted most was to get more to eat. One day she brought me a voucher entitling me to a meal from the camp kitchen. She ought not to have done this; unable to resist the temptation and throwing caution to the winds, I gulped down two quarts of watery *balanda*. This upset some kind of balance in my metabolism. Long accustomed to meager amounts of food, my system was unable to assimilate the nutritive elements contained in that huge quantity of slop. I soon developed diarrhea.

In the prevailing conditions, diarrhea could only mean certain death. There were no drugs, no medicinal herbs, no vitamins. Nothing to stop the diarrhea, neither boiled rice, blackberries, or *Kagor*.[9] As for a special diet, it was useless even to mention it. There was nothing but the hospital ration! The doctors, naturally, could do nothing. Neither I nor my companions knew of anyone who had recovered[10]—even if one asked for bread that had been dried hard—but a drowning man will clutch at a straw. My friends obtained charcoal from the charcoal-burners in exchange for bread. They ground up the charcoal, and I ate it in the fond hope that it would absorb water and thus stop the diarrhea. But it was foolish to hope for anything like that. In pellagric diarrhea, the walls of the gastro-intestinal tract become extremely thin. Along the walls are cilia which induce spasmodic motions that enable the walls to absorb nutrients from the food being digested. But the disease almost completely destroys the cilia, and those that remain flatten themselves against the walls. Food passing through a smooth-surfaced canal cannot be held long enough to be digested properly. This condition rapidly worsens day by day. Before death sets in, the victim loses his appetite and smokers even lose their

9. A wine recommended by doctors for stomach complaints, the name derived from the French wine, Cahors. (Tr.)

10. We learned from one of our fellow prisoners about an experiment carried out at the beginning of 1942 by two "free" doctors. They isolated a young man suffering from pellagra and started to feed him on butter, honey, and milk from a special food reserve intended for the camp Chekists. (This was possible because a woman doctor involved in the experiment was the wife of one of the Chekists.) It appears that the result was positive.

craving for nicotine. This form of diarrhea usually occurs only after all the body's most essential organs have become totally impaired. The Creator in his great wisdom has seen to it that the body retains the use of its most vital parts until the very final stage of its resistance to the ravages of hunger. The end comes when the brain is attacked—memory, being the last important part of it, is the first to go; the neurons, which control the thinking process, are destroyed at a later stage. Then pellagric insanity sets in, and the destruction of the cortex finally brings death.[11]

A Vow to God

Nearly all this I realized very well at the time; so with cold objectivity I began estimating the span of life still left to me. But my heart and spirit positively refused to submit to a death sentence. I was even borne up by something akin to joy: it was a unique opportunity to engage in a duel with death on the most unequal terms. Such a feeling came as a result of fervent prayer, during which I promised God to help carry out His sacred will, and thereby to bring aid to all men who had been deceived, to protect them against liars and murderers. In some way not understood by me, I had long been prepared to make such a vow. At the moment of self-dedication I experienced a feeling of confidence which has not abandoned me to this present day. I knew with certainty and conviction that God would save my life, that I would have the ability and resolve to move mountains. Although I did not see what directly lay ahead, I felt quite sure that my lofty goal could be attained. In the very near future it would take on a definite form.

A Miracle on the Fortieth Day

But meanwhile there was the business of fighting for life, of wrenching myself from the icy clutches of death. The only means at my disposal were prayer and meditation. I had been in the habit of praying since childhood. As for meditation, I knew nothing about it—until I began my struggle with illness. I chose the Lord's Prayer, the noblest of all prayers, given to us by the Savior himself. I began reflecting on each word of it. Even though my brain had grown sluggish, I was still able to reach the conclusion that nearly all the principal ideas of Christianity are contained within this prayer.

11. In the final phase of the illness, under unsanitary conditions, there is for some reason an extraordinary increase in the number of lice on the dying man's body, and they literally bite him to death. In our hospital this horror did not occur.

The first several days I entertained the hope that it was not pellagric diarrhea, but a simple stomach disorder. For approximately five days I kept my condition secret from anyone else, thus clinging to my right to stay on an upper bunk. But it was becoming increasingly difficult to climb up. Besides, the hospital staff was beginning to suspect what was wrong with me. Finally, they suggested that I move to the lower level—the "hold" as everybody called it—and occupy the cot of someone who had just died . . . The days passed. Marika dropped in twice daily and always brought me something to smoke. Hunger had already ceased its torments. I frequently gave away my *balanda* and limited myself to dried bread. Even that I ate unwillingly. Fifteen days passed, but the diarrhea showed no signs of abating. How long the illness would last and what its outcome would be were no secret. Every morning I read in Marika's horror-struck eyes the unspoken question and the timid hope.

I spent my time in prayer. My strength steadily declined. Twenty days passed by—twenty-five—thirty. Through my willed resistance to death, I had lasted almost twice the time that a dying man usually occupied a cot. Everybody regarded me as a unique case.

Another five days went by; the diarrhea continued. Thirty-six—thirty-seven. I prayed to God with the intensity of a candle burning before His altar. But it made no difference—the diarrhea continued and I had lost all desire to eat. Even smoking repelled me now.

Thirty-eight days—thirty-nine. I was dreadfully weak, but when Marika appeared in the doorway I raised myself up and dragged my feet toward her. All the consoling words had been spoken long ago. I was such a sight that she could not bear to stay long. She wanted to cry. Cutting short her visit with some excuse or other, she left, and I made my way to the cot.

I prayed. I meditated. I prayed again.

On the fortieth day I woke up with a new sense of being. I crawled out of the cot. No diarrhea! I felt an upsurge of strength. I could have sung from joy. The sun had never seemed so beautiful. I got back into the cot and turned toward the wall. Tears of rapture and gratitude streamed from my eyes. I praised Almighty God. He had taken notice of me! From that day on, I was a soldier of the Church. Filled with the spritual energy that comes from prayer, I walked toward the door with youthful lightness of step. There waiting for me, and looking her usual radiant self, was Marika. Immediately she read in my eyes that I had been saved. A miracle! A splendid miracle that God had worked for me, a sinner!

I have told a great many people about this miracle that saved my life. The skeptics, of course, put it down to autosuggestion. But both modern science and yoga, which has a much broader base of experience than all our techniques of psychotherapy, has the following to say in respect to a case like mine:

Functional disorders may be cured by suggestion, including autosuggestion. But certain physical changes within the body are irreversible. The leading practitioners of yoga in its higher forms can restore ravaged tissue in the liver, lungs, and other organs. However, this requires many years of training under the guidance of a veteran teacher. Also indispensable are light, fresh air, and an abundance of food. Finally, one must perform the proper ablutions and have a complete mastery of the yogi's methods of breathing.

None of those prerequisites figured in my particular case. And even if I had accidentally stumbled upon the correct form of mental discipline, without the necessary nutrients the damaged tissue could not have been restored. So, in my case, the miracle could not be explained by autosuggestion. Another important consideration is that in order for the diarrhea to end, millions of cilia would have to be produced overnight.

Highly significant is the fact that recovery began immediately after my memory blacked out. If a few more hours had been allowed to elapse, the substratum of the brain which controls mental processes would have started to deteriorate. God's role in my case is evident. The malady had run its course under the direction of the Divine Intelligence, which had preordained that it be halted at the most critical stage.

It was not until five years later, when I began in earnest to fulfill my sacred vow, that I understood the logic behind this. Constantly burdened with the business of surviving from day to day, I had been forced, almost without the benefit of books, to seek an understanding of the world all by myself, pondering in my own mind all the most important aspects of human existence and rejecting one hypothesis after another in the process of speculating about them. And if it had not been for the impairment of my memory during my illness, I would never have made any progress. In order for me to succeed, it was essential that my mind become *tabula rasa*. Only thus was I able to arrive at totally new conclusions uncontaminated by the lingering traces of dubious propositions that I had previously rejected.

As the beneficiary of an undoubted miracle, I have naturally often considered how phenomena of this type may be explained and can only say that for me they constitute absolute proof of that view of the universe which presupposes the possibility of their occurrence.[12]

12. My hypothesis on the nature of miracles is set forth in my book *Le Monde oscillatoire* (ed. Regain; Monaco, 1974, p. 375).

Inspired Goodness

Life without elements of goodness withers and dies. Wherever naked evil holds sway, destruction and death also prevail.

If men condemned to exist under a system of brutality designed expressly for their annihilation manage somehow to come out unscathed, if over years of imprisonment they have not lost their hold on life, we may safely assume that at one time or another they must have run into someone in whom the spirit of goodness was not extinguished. Despite all their faults, medical personnel in the camps—even the meanest among them—had not totally lost their capacity for mercy. One or two such people on the staff were enough to turn it into a veritable haven, where a prisoner might be given a job as an orderly, certified as unfit for work—permanently, if possible—or prescribed a "sick" ration. Still, it should be borne in mind that the activities of the medics were always under close surveillance from the Security Section, as well as from the other camp authorities and their stool pigeons. It took great courage for a *zek* doctor—even for a free man like the staff director—to carry out his duties humanely, in spite of all the obstacles. Of course, most of the time, the medics knuckled under to the camp authorities, with the result that death took a heavy toll among the prisoners. But even the most complacent medical staff, however limited its possibilities, occasionally made life more bearable for some of us and thus earned a warm place in our memory.

The transfer of our group of twenty-eight to "sick" rations immediately after the interrogation ended was an example of how the medics could sometimes display a certain independence in taking decisions. The woman in charge of the camp infirmary did not, in this instance, leave us to starve in the cells until we were too weak to move—though I must qualify my praise of her by mentioning that after the dreadful winter of 1941–1942, when so many prisoners died of hunger, the camp administration had been instructed by Moscow to reduce the mortality rate.

What I have been saying about the medics applies equally well to other categories of camp personnel on which a prisoner's life might depend.

There was Rimma Rabinovich, a free civilian employee in the administration office. It was her responsibility to set up quotas for non-priority projects undertaken by the machine shop, the farm, and other departments of the camp. Being a courageous, amiable, sympathetic girl, she did a world of good for the prisoners. With her assistance two engineers who luckily had not been charged with political offenses got medical releases from their jobs. She was not shy about dropping into the machine shop and sharing in our candid discussions. By the same taken, those of us who had passes to move freely from zone to zone often visited her at the administration office. The authorities were quick to remind her of this after we had been arrested and put in the cells. Nonetheless, she came through unscathed.

At the end of 1942, someone pointed out to me one day a vicious-looking prisoner, who was all dressed up in foreign clothes, and said, "There goes the murderer of practically every Latvian who ever came to Vyatlag." It seems that he had held the job of establishing production quotas for several camps in our area where Latvians predominated. These quotas, along with the assignments he gave, decimated the Latvians just as efficiently as a machine gun would have done. He had refused to allow any padding of their work sheets with dummy entries. His shifty, green-flecked eyes filled me with indescribable loathing. Our group put him on our list of "snakes."[13] The camp was full of such monsters.

After my miraculous recovery I was ravenously hungry. It was obvious that the weight I had lost urgently needed restoring.[14] The long period of lying idle, the lack of outdoor exercise, together with my overall debilitation, had affected my heart. My face and legs had become swollen. I needed all my strength just to walk up one step on the stairs. Engels's phrase about man having evolved from the ape through labor now seemed the height of absurdity and could only have been made by someone lacking in experience. Armed with intelligence, determination, and faith in my own strength as well as in a Higher Power, I learned, through tremendous effort, to stand upright once more—otherwise I knew I would die. And Engels expected an ape, endowed with neither intellect nor will, to achieve a feat a thousand times more strenuous!

I constantly forced myself to walk around the camp zone in order to overcome my physical weakness. It was a good thing that the weather continued mild. About that time I and my "accomplices" were given our sentences—ten years apiece. At least this had the effect of putting us back on a par with the other inmates. They were no longer terrified by chance encounters with us.

Shortly after sentence was passed, I encountered a prisoner called Zaitsev. Before my arrest we had lived in the same engineers' barracks,

13." Snake": common term of abuse in the camps, used particularly of prisoners who betrayed their fellows. (Tr.)

14. My normal weight of seventy-eight kgs. had gone down to forty-eight kgs. A loss of thirty-eight percent is a catastrophe for the human organism. One should not lose more than twenty to twenty-five percent of one's normal weight. To recover it is no simple matter, even under medical supervision, let alone when one is starving and suffering from pellagra.

although I do not recall that we had ever engaged in conversation. But now he joined me as I was walking about the camp one day. No doubt I presented such a pitiful sight that he was quite overcome. He asked me to come inside. I replied that the five steps up were too much for me and suggested that if he had something to show me, I would be better off waiting for him on the bench outside. A minute later he came back out, holding a small package that turned out to contain bread. The compassion of this virtual stranger so impressed me that, in my weakened condition, my eyes filled with tears. I whispered, "What marvelous people there are in this world." With perfect clarity I saw how the power of goodness was uniting the two of us in that single moment of time, how it ignited the spark of love. This is what holds the world together.

11

THE LAST MONTHS
IN VYATLAG

Gifts from Izolda

With the new ten-year sentence lying ahead, I felt it best that my family should remain ignorant of all that was happening to me. Eventually my wife would conclude that I had perished, and she would then be free to marry someone more suited than I for life under a dictatorship. But the pain in my heart was not easily stilled, and I particularly wanted some news about my little son whom I had never seen. I could not, therefore, refrain from writing to my wife, even though under the circumstances I had no moral right to do so. I should have thought over more carefully what effects the letter might produce, but my brain was not working very well in those days. After my illness I had sunk into a torpid state of mind; it was the most I could do to force myself to go for walks, to climb steps, to make all the other efforts necessary to keep on my feet and overcome my physical weakness. At the same time, I never ceased to feel ravenously hungry.

Evidently my letter had a shattering effect. My wife went to the black market and spent everything she had on food supplies from America. Because the mailing of parcels had been suspended at the start of the war, she had to make an arrangement through an acquaintance of hers, a cashier. For a sizable payoff, the provisions were to be shipped by rail as ordinary passenger baggage. Of course, this meant that the labels could not be stamped with any official seal. For that reason, the railway people warned that the shipment could not be guaranteed a safe journey.

Until 1917, in Russia, the concept of honesty was drilled into the children of families professing to be Christian and was reinforced by church, school, and good literature. After the disaster of 1917 and the opening of the new Bolshevist era, this traditional process went into a sharp decline. For no other reason than ingrained habit, the words *honesty, truth,* and *honor* still remained in use, but the new regime encouraged people to behave in despicable and devious ways and threatened with destruction all those who did not conform. As the campaign to wipe out religion got under way, large numbers of people in all walks of life began losing their integrity. The very word *honesty* became unfashionable and was used only in a tone of cynicism or mockery. However, among the generations who had come to maturity before the national cataclysm, one still encountered decent behavior within the family or between friends. This no doubt explains why the railway workers kept their bargain with my wife.

As soon as I found out from Marika that the shipment had arrived, she herself went directly to the supply officer of a labor detachment made up of Germans. Since they were acquaintances, she told him of my critical condition and implored him to obtain all of the shipment. The next day a man showed up in the camp zone with a pint bottle which had been filled with melted butter and some scraps of dried bread. His face looked as though it had been smeared by grease. My pitiful appearance must have affected him somewhat, since he became embarrassed and launched into a tale about how he had opened the box and found, besides what he had brought me, only some stones and paper. It was a barefaced lie, of course. The pint bottle gave him away—if a genuine thief had done the job, he would have cleaned out the entire contents. Naturally, the supply officer and those who shared the spoils with him had reckoned on my defenseless position; they were well aware that my only prospect was either death or transfer to another camp. But his conscience had troubled the supply officer to the extent that he felt compelled to bring me at least a small part of all that my long-suffering wife—my Izolda with her clear blue eyes and curly brown hair—had gone to such heroic lengths to send me. I was too weary to resort to threats or abuse; I just stared at him. And I refused to sign the receipt which he shoved in front of me, and on which he had not even taken the trouble to note that most of the contents of the package had been lost. He went off as fast as he could go.

As time went on, I began to understand that when it comes to leaving a permanent scar on another's soul and consciousness, words of truth, combined with an outraged look that suggests the victim's sense of what is right and just, are more effective than a bullet. A bullet hole may heal and close up, but a wound inflicted on the conscience remains forever open and causes lifelong pain.

I could not stand the hospital any more, and Marika, despite the risk to herself, gave me a job in the accounts department. I had to add columns of figures on an abacus. Sitting opposite me, Marika watched anxiously over me like a mother hen, ever ready to come to my assistance. Since my brain was still foggy, I was forced to go over the same column many times, and the totals kept coming out differently. It always ended with Marika herself making a quick check.

My condition was worsening. My legs were stiff as fence posts, and I found it a great effort to move from one place to another. Like it or not, I was obliged to go back to the hospital for a couple more weeks. Again, Marika visited me every day. Even though the food was inadequate, my health improved little by little.

By the summer of 1944, American aid resulted in a qualitative improvement of our food supply. Genuine flour began to appear, along with vegetable oil and powdered eggs. Prisoners fed from the third caldron[1] were even served *ponchiki*.[2] Because the regular cooks had more than they could handle, women were asked to help in the kitchen after putting in their normal hours of work. Solely for my sake, Marika hired herself out on two occasions. She became friendly with the woman in charge of the mess, a free employee who had been evacuated here at the beginning of the war and who had previously worked in the retail trade system. Highly proficient at needlework, Marika knitted a blouse for her. In return, the woman gave me a night watchman's job. It was simple enough. My main task was to sit by the kitchen entrance and stop anyone who might try to take out food. The rest of the time I could devote to the business of getting enough to eat myself. At night the *balanda* was prepared for distribution the next morning. After boiling cauldrons of water, the cooks would pour in flour and salt. Then they would add some vegetable oil. Whenever I walked over to one of the cooks, he would ladle out a bowlful right from the top, where the stuff was thickest and most nourishing, and hand it to me. I must have put down twelve pints or so during the course of a night. Previously I had listened to similar tales from other men with wry amusement, but now I discovered for myself that the capacity of the stomach and intestinal tract is indeed quite enormous. The night watch offered me nothing else quite so valuable and satisfying as this revelation.

Two weeks after I began the job, the woman in charge of the kitchen

1. A bonus ration for good work.
2. *Ponchiki:* dumplings with some filling or other. (Tr.)

was called in by the head of Security, and I was fired. It seems that someone had reported on me. Despite this reverse, the groundwork for my recovery had been laid. My skin had lost its grey scaliness and was taking on a smooth, satiny finish, pleasant to the touch. The bloated condition of my face and legs had vanished, and I was steadily gaining strength.

At about this time we were given permission to receive packages from home. I asked my wife to send me only tobacco. When it arrived there was enough for me to reward the people who had been so kind to me and also to exchange for bread. From the tailors and shoemakers who were employed in the camp and who earned what by our standards was very good money, it was possible to get not only extra food but also cash in exchange for tobacco; the money so obtained I was able to send back home through a trusted intermediary and thereby pay for the tobacco and the cost of sending it.

Even when suffering from extreme exhaustion and hunger, we still held to certain ethical principles, one of which was that this tobacco trade could only be carried on with those "affluent" prisoners who could afford to have their minds on more luxurious things than bread. I would never have thought of offering tobacco to an ordinary working prisoner in exchange for his vital bread ration.

My two-week stint in the kitchen filled me with shame. It was bad enough to have to do such a demeaning job, but even worse was the realization that I was stealing food intended for other prisoners. I tried to gain comfort from the thought that when a man has been reduced to the condition I was then in, he doesn't fret over niceties; but it did not lighten my sense of wrongdoing, and when they kicked me out of the kitchen, I was actually glad. The burden of guilt was made even heavier by the fact that, while in the cells, I had carefully thought out my attitude to the whole question of how we were fed, and I could not therefore plead in my defence that I was unclear in my own mind as to what I was doing.

A slave may normally expect to be amply fed and clothed, to be provided with shelter fit for human habitation. If a slaveowner lacks the proper means for maintaining his slaves, then he is under an obligation to let them go free. Any slaveowner who subjects his slaves to starvation and man-killing labor becomes no less than a criminal. However, it is not up to the slaves to resolve the moral dilemmas of their keepers. Since the slave has been deprived of any right to protest, the slaveholders must bear full responsibility for all the consequences of the system—it is up to those who have created the system to answer for it.

The wretched camp rations were devised by cannibals. The prisoners were fed not on the basis of their physical needs, but according to the amount of work they could turn out in a day; the whole point of the system was to squeeze as much work as possible out of everybody. A prisoner who did menial jobs within the camp was entitled to be adequately fed like any other prisoner. If he stole food he needed from the central camp commissary, he was within his rights from the standpoint of our ethics. But as soon as he pilfered anything from the kitchen where the day's ration was prepared for his fellow prisoners, he was in effect robbing them and became a thief.

My legs were still refusing to function properly, and there was no question of my going out to work. I was therefore assigned to the Communal Services Section, where I did some relatively simple jobs as a draftsman. By this time I was reconciled to the hard fact of an additional ten-year stretch; so I sat down and wrote my wife a letter, urging her to forget about me and take her freedom, since my life was no longer my own and I was clearly not destined to be a family man. I was trying to do what I thought was the only decent thing. But at the same time a hope of some kind lingered within me. Therefore, when the obstinate dreamer flatly rejected my suggestion and even reproached me for wanting to be rid of her, I felt reassured that no course was open to me except to do as she wished. Nonetheless, for a long time I tormented my Izolda with pleas to reconsider her decision; but she was adamant in her insistence on remaining my wife.

I knew that for her the ideal of marriage consisted of motherhood, family, and home. Everything else seemed to her alien, remote, unappealing, and, as a consequence, hardly comprehensible. What right did I have to ruin her lofty dream and push her into a life of wretchedness when like the wife of a medieval crusader, she was prepared to spend the rest of her days waiting for me? Therefore, I said to myself, better that she become a martyr than be forced to abandon her ideals and make shameful compromises. It was our duty to support each other in the struggle for truth and justice; we are all too easily led astray by the temptations of the flesh, by our human weakness.

Many times I asked myself which was worse; to know that your wife had started a new life and was bringing up your son in total ignorance of his father; or to bind her to you, depriving her of her freedom, demanding faithfulness without the same in return, wasting her youth, fostering vain hopes within her heart? Naturally the first course was the easier one to follow: you simply cut her out of your life and ceased being responsible for her. You no longer worried or thought about her. But in making this choice, you forfeited the experience of a great spiritual struggle, while at the same time you cast the one dearest to you adrift. That being the case, I decided that it must be the second alternative which carries God's benediction. Whatever setbacks we might have to endure, our spirits would burn in a white dazzling flame, and defeat would turn to victory.

A Woman's Heart

Women under interrogation, in prison, or behind barbed wire are a shattering subject.

Until 1948 the camps contained both men and women; thus I saw a great many female prisoners pass through. As soon as my daily diet improved, I began suffering a great deal from the loneliness inherent in my situation. But as a rule, I did not indulge in intimate relations, since under existing conditions they would have been much too degrading.

If on some other planet they were to tell me that according to the laws of the land women had the same rights as men, and enjoyed complete social equality, and were hence perfectly contented with their lot, then I would most insistently request permission to look into various aspects of life for myself and in my own way, instead of being taken on guided tours through carefully selected areas. Upon getting consent, I would investigate the most demanding, dirtiest occupations. I would want to see who repaired the railroad tracks in temperatures of thirty degrees below zero, who was joisted up on ropes to a height of twenty or thirty meters in order to plaster by hand the walls of industrial buildings, who was employed in chemical works with their stinking, poisonous fumes that sterilize all hopes for maternity, who was doing the most backbreaking chores on the collective farms. Next, I would visit the prisons, the interrogation cells, and the places where tortures and executions were carried out; then the camps where the undernourished inmates were required to do hard labor far beyond their physical capacity. If in any of those places I came across just one woman and learned further that a working woman had also to run a home, stand for hours in long lines to buy essential provisions, travel on official trips to other cities leaving her family abandoned, attend endless meetings, and was subject to mobilization in time of war, then I would put a curse on such a planet and all its "achievements," its bombs, rockets, and space ships. Such a system would be intolerable; for it is nothing more or less than a shameful form of ill-disguised slavery. To treat women like this is incompatible with the nature of a civilized man.

The fact is, in the Soviet camps during the war, men nearly always did their best to help the women whenever they had the slightest chance. In spite of terrible hunger, of the inhuman Stalinist policy of deliberate extermination, the women were protected whenever possible and were thus the last to die. The opinion exists that the female is better adapted to hunger, thanks to the larger reserves within her system; the blockade of Leningrad during the war is cited as proof. I don't dispute this. But in conditions where it is necessary to meet an exhausting work quota, this natural advantage rapidly disappears; having less strength, a woman is soon exhausted by too much hard labor. During the war at Vyatlag, for some reason, a special women's detachment was organized at Camp Seven. The results were horrible: everyone died. It was quite different when women were put in a brigade of men who were in fairly sound condition; here they survived throughout those years in which so many male prisoners perished. In our machine shop we protected the women like sisters and did not allow them to do any heavy work. They carried out secretarial duties, made copies of records, etc. Among them were Olya, a Russian, and Zoya, an Ossetian,[3] who was the widow of a prominent party leader. Zoya had loved her husband dearly, had been happy with him; after the destruction of her family, she had become consumed by a hatred for the regime, especially for Stalin. When Olya came down with pellagric diarrhea, those of us with passes to move outside the camp performed the near miracle of getting rice for her. In return, the two women gave us their love and devotion.

All my life I have worshipped beauty, and this is no doubt why I have often idealized the attractive women who crossed my path. But in all my passing affairs the main thing was always lacking—love. And therefore, though having no desire to harm them and even sincerely endeavoring to bring happiness to my female companions, I usually caused them only grief and suffering in the end.

This was so in the case of my affair with a nurse called Anechka in the hospital at Camp One in Vyatlag. My relationship with Anechka was purely platonic. A pretty, fair-haired girl, she had been imprisoned before the war when she was still a student, at the time when Stalin ("the student's best friend"!) made things ever harder for our already impoverished citizenry by suddenly introducing fees for university education. The specialists in fabricated cases chose to present the natural grumbling of some young people as anti-Soviet plotting, and a Special Board gave most of them eight-year sentences. But because she was so obviously harmless, Anechka got a lesser sentence of five years and was given a job in the

3. *Ossetians:* a small people in the North Caucasus.

179

camp's medical section. For this reason—and also because she worked very near the camp's main food distribution center—she avoided the fate of the others and survived. I knew that she got enough to eat and did not have to worry about her on this score. In that horrible winter I dropped in fairly often at the dispensary to chat with her and to drink a small glass of pine syrup, which we were sure had medicinal properties effective against scurvy.

In the spring things got a little better for us—the working day was shortened. In the evenings, after finishing her work at the dispensary, she joined me for walks around the camp zone—walks which I also believed helped to ward off the scurvy. Those walks could easily have gotten us into trouble as a breach of camp discipline, but since at that time there was a raging epidemic of scurvy, and as many as eighteen people were dying in one day, there were more important things for the authorities to worry about. At that season of the year, in those latitudes, it was still bright daylight at ten in the evening; thus we were able to make out very clearly the death cart going out loaded with corpses. We always got as far away as we could from the guardhouse so as not to see how bayonets were thrust into the heads of the corpses.

In May the main body of our shop was transferred to Camp Five; Anechka and I became separated. Apart from the fact that I was extremely busy and did not have the time to keep up the relationship, it would have been wrong for me to associate with her when I was so preoccupied with our plans for escape. When I visited Camp One the following winter, she was no longer there. If I had tried hard enough, I could undoubtedly have found out where she had been transported; but it was the very ominous time when I already sensed that I was going to be arrested, and I did not want her name to be linked with mine during the coming interrogation. After the arrest of our group a short time later, the memory of this charming companion gradually slipped from my mind.

Not until two years later did I learn that my association with Anechka had served her as a kind of shield and that shortly after I left she had become the object of dreadful pressures—if she refused to go to bed with some trustee or other, he would threaten her with common labor. She had tried to inform me of all this, but her letter hadn't reached me. If I had known in time, I could have arranged her transfer to my department as an inspector. Because she did not understand the reason for my silence, she decided as much in sorrow as in anger that I had deserted her. As the trustees continued pressing her, she began seeking counsel and comfort among her own people in the medical section. On special duty there just at that time was a pharmacist from Camp Four, who had been fond of

Anechka for quite a while. He not only took on himself the role of her deliverer from evil, but he also asked her to live with him. Since there seemed to be no other way out of her predicament, she consented; and so she became one of the most prosperous female prisoners in Vyatlag. Drugs for the prisoners were practically nonexistent, and whatever was available at the central pharmacy was worth its weight in gold. In addition, Anechka's pharmacist controlled the camp's supply of alcohol. By virtue of these positions, he had the entire camp leadership eating out of his hands. Anechka was thus living very well indeed, yet the letter I got from her while I was in the hospital in 1944 was that of an unhappy, abandoned woman. All the same I believe that if it had not been for our parting, she would have been the twenty-ninth person to be convicted in the fabricated case of the anti-Soviet uprising—her association with me had been very conspicuous.

During my life I have encountered a number of amazing women. Marika was one who came to me as if from heaven. Her care, her concern, her advice and attention were like divine gifts for me. She made one think of those saintly Catholic nuns who, animated by Christian charity, help the forsaken, nurse the sick, sacrifice themselves, and go into the gas chambers for the sake of others.

Occasionally, the head of the day-to-day administration service was visited by his wife. She was pale, emaciated. Her loyalty caused her so many sufferings that I shudder even thinking of them. In much more horrible cricumstances, she was spiritual heir to Maria Volkonski, who, in the early nineteenth century, had joined her husband, an exiled Decembrist, in Siberia.

Ever since my arrival in the free world, I have encountered a number of women who discreetly, virtually imperceptibly, dispense help to those who need it.

The Soviet woman, in her humane instincts, does not occupy a place inferior to that of her sisters in the West, but mass atheism in its bestiality has crippled her soul. Her existence, harsh and brutal beyond measure, makes it next to impossible for her to reveal spiritual strength outside the microfraternity[4] so parsimoniously allotted to her within her home. Nevertheless there are those who, in spite of the obstacles that have been deliberately thrown into their paths, find God and the will to do genuine good. Thanks to their inner strength, they are capable of attaining true majesty.

4. I call the small groups of people who totally trust each other "microfraternities" (see *Le Monde oscillatoire*, p. 145).

The Question of Caution

I would like to tell about one of my "accomplices," Boris Rozhdesdven-ski, and add a few observations about the question of caution. One evening in the autumn of 1942, I was returning from the machine shop with my friend Yuri. Because it had been a long and difficult day, we decided to take a short walk to get some fresh air. Just before reaching the camp, we turned into a road that led us up to the bridge over the river Nyrmoch. We stood looking down at the dark, icy waters below and chatted quietly. Suddenly we heard a shout, "Hands up!" and saw the head of the camp jail pointing a pistol at us. We obeyed his order and calmly explained what we were doing. He knew very well who we were, but he nevertheless marched us over to the guardhouse, putting on a great show of pseudo-vigilance—after all, it was wartime and you never could tell . . . Yuri was none the worse for this ridiculous episode; yet some time afterward he lit into me for having suggested that we stop for a while on that bridge. And he also took me to task for engaging in talk about escape plans. On the whole, he was a courageous man, tough and dependable. But his sense of caution went beyond acceptable bounds.

I am touching here on an extremely complex matter. If you play with fire and cast all caution to the winds, you will simply be destroyed and die to no purpose. If, on the other hand, you carry prudence to extremes, you may save your skin, but it is doubtful whether you will contribute anything to the cause of liberation. If you play an endless waiting game, all that can possibly happen is that the Chekists will seize you before your hour strikes and throw you in jail—the astronomical number of fabricated "cases" made it a virtual certainty. I am not saying that caution was not necessary, but you also had to take action of some kind. Caution should serve as a warrior's shield, but not as a funk-hole.

Shortly after the shop at Camp One went into operation, a magnificent figure from a bygone era suddenly appeared in our midst on horseback. It was during our work break that he rode in. Since the weather that day was exceptionally fine, we were resting outdoors. Thus we watched as he sprang down from the saddle, tied up the horse, smoothed out his drab field shirt, struck the leg of his top-boot with a riding crop, and then strode into the barbed-wire zone. What a sight for our eyes he was, this man who looked as though he could have been an officer of His Imperial Majesty's Guards: stately, well-proportioned, virile, handsome. His bearing and manners were faultless; his voice had great charm. The lift of his head reminded me of the heroes of the ancient Russian epic songs. He had brown hair and smartly trimmed mustaches. His eyes were as blue as the waters of the Black Sea. He greeted us courteously, his immaculate, manly person radiating health and vigor, and asked where headquarters was located.

This man who looked like a Guards officer and epic hero proved in fact to be an Estonian Communist, once a member of the Central Committee of the party. By origin, however, he was a Russian. An engineer by profession, Boris Rozhdestvenski was also a poet, an expert in seven languages, a man who was good at anything he undertook. If his parents had chosen to remain in the vicinity of Leningrad, his appearance and manners by themselves would have landed him behind barbed wire years earlier. But a hundred miles away, across the frontier, in Estonia which had become independent after the catastrophe of 1917 in Russia, he and others like him who had left home as children became possessed with the desire to return to the Soviet Union and help to build Communism there. Their blindness and ignorance, their rejection of trustworthy information about the Soviet Union as so much reactionary propaganda, led to his crossing the tightly guarded Soviet border in 1938, bringing along his wife, in order to serve the objectives in which they believed. But they had arrived just as the terror, aimed primarily at the Communists themselves, was at its height. Naturally, they were picked up right away and given terms of three years. They were lucky not to be charged with espionage but only with unlawful crossing of the frontier. Boris had been released before the war began in 1941 and had remained as a free employee in Vyatlag, working in the technological department of the camp administration. I got to know him because he came with orders for our shop. My acquaintance with him grew into friendship after we ran into each other again on the transport to Vorkuta.

He had also been arrested during the operation against our group of twenty-eight, even though he had absolutely no connection with the whole affair. The history of his arrest is simple: the wife of a high-ranking official had fallen madly in love with him. She even deserted her husband, who, of course, was glad to find an excuse to settle accounts with the two of them. I must say to the woman's credit that, despite all threats and the grave danger to herself, she did not return to her husband, nor did she cease giving Boris aid and comfort while he was in jail, sending him food parcels, so that, unlike us, he did not suffer from hunger at this period.

Besides being a first-class raconteur, Boris composed verse in Estonian, English, and Russian. He brought color to the gray life of our transport. By this time he had shed, like an old, unwanted skin, all the rot and nonsense of Communist idealism. He resembled Yakonov, a character in Solzhenitsyn's *The First Circle,* for whom world politics were a sort of chess game. Boris now regarded life as if it were a hockey match, with himself in the role of a referee. He had no intention of himself getting caught up in the melee; he had already had enough. He preferred to write poetry. I feel sure that except for telling the usual lies—which few can avoid under our kind of system—he had in no way compromised himself. But it is not for me to sit in judgment on him. The example of this excellent man does show, however, that even the most idealistic service of the Communist doctrine, followed by disillusionment with it and finally rejection, ravages a man's soul and makes him indifferent to the sufferings of those around him and keeps him from regaining religious belief.

My last meeting with Boris took place in the company of a mutual friend, a university professor, some twenty years after the events I have just been describing. By this time he and his beautiful wife had long been reunited. As the parents of a lovely little girl, their family happiness was complete, and they had worked hard to make it so. But it is too bad that such remarkable people should withdraw so completely into their own shell. As far as they were concerned the hockey match was nearly over, and the main thing was to sit quietly as mere onlookers—otherwise somebody could still slice off their heads with a hockey stick. Yet all around we see young people, immature and gauche as they may be, who with courage and enthusiasm are trying to save our civilization.

That evening I said to him, "I have decided to leave the Soviet Union and go to the West in order to have the opportunity of helping my people from there. But you must help the young people here. Our experience combined with their energy is bound to produce results." But once the fire of the spirit has burned out, it is easy to think up excuses for not getting involved.

That same evening we talked about his long-time acquaintance and fellow townsman, A. Osipov, formerly a professor at a theological seminary and later an unfrocked priest and a renegade. In 1959 an article of his, directed against the church, appeared in *Pravda.* It had interested me how a theologian could base his renunciation of God on Biblical texts; and I made a close study of Osipov's writings. In the face of the hard facts I gave him, Boris could produce no convincing defense of Osipov, yet he persisted in his opinion that he was nevertheless a man of principle and a searcher for truth, with whom he exchanged letters. I felt shame for Boris, an intelligent and subtle man with good intention.

Earlier in our conversation, Boris had told me that he had recently read

184

in the newspaper something about Vasili Lukich Panyushkin, from which it appeared that he was not dead but was alive and flourishing. A screenplay had been written about him and made into a fairly decent film (*Midshipman Panin*)[5] about the Revolution. In it Panyushkin was shown inciting the sailors, organizing Bolshevik cells, distributing propaganda leaflets. I could not believe my own ears as Boris told me all this.

Together with Misha Dyachkov, Panyushkin had worked as a coppersmith in Camp One. He stood out sharply among us with his thick, old-style Russian beard and deeply lined peasant's neck. Since he and Misha were well liked by everyone, our fraternity of five was on very good terms with them. We often dropped into the coppersmith shop to hear Panyuskhin's tales about the way of life of workers and peasants in tsarist days. He denounced the Bolsheviks and all other revolutionaries as scoundrels and told us how well the people had lived before the 1914 War. Those good old days had been the beginning of prosperity. Workers no longer demanded payment in gold coin but accepted paper money instead. It cost little to eat well; for five kopecks you could go to the food stalls in any marketplace and buy enough to last you the whole day. He would also quote the prices of various food items. But he complained about the high cost of housing in those days, though workers with regular employment would be put in inexpensive company houses.

And now, all of a sudden, I learned to my amazement that this man of whom we had been so fond, who had so often cursed the seditious intellectuals, now turned out to have been no better himself—indeed much worse, because he had not been a mere windbag like them, but had participated actively in the destruction of Russia's power between 1914 and 1917, helping to undermine the very foundations of the empire. I was certain of his sincerity in those days when we had been together in the camp, with death staring us in the face. Since our sixth sense was so highly developed, he could only have been putting it all on if he had been a phenomenal actor, a Chaliapin, Mikhail Chekhov, Kean, and Garrick all rolled into one. But these were on the stage only four hours at a time, while he would have had to keep it up for sixteen hours every day, and eventually he would certainly have given himself away.

But, as I now learned from Boris, his circumstances had changed dramatically. He had been rehabilitated and, upon returning to Moscow as a Communist who had suffered for the sake of the party, was given an apartment and a personal pension. Once a year he was entitled to a state-paid vacation in a health resort. He had become eligible for admission to an exclusive polyclinic that catered to Old Bolsheviks. Whenever he was

5. In the film, Lukich appears as "Midshipman Panin."

laid up with an illness, he could expect a supplementary benefit. I felt absolutely sure that he was just as sincere in his reversal to the anti-human values of the party as he had previously been in his rejection of them. Still, I wanted to make certain for myself; so I sent a letter off to him, addressing him as "Lukich," as we had always called him in the camp. I did not use my own name, since my die-hard point of view was well known to him and might easily have put him off at the outset, so I got his old friend, Misha Dyachkov, to sign the letter. Misha was a marvelous Russian jack-of-all-trades whose soul had remained as pure as his honest blue eyes were clear. He and Lukich had been inseparable buddies back in the camp. Like brothers, they had shared every crumb of bread between them. The letter was friendly enough, with expressions of pleasure at his success, but I got no reply.

A leopard does not change his spots.

A Nonprejudiced Discussion of Race

After joining the Communal Services Section, I was able to restore my health, thanks to the thriving trade in tobacco I carried on there. It was extremely important for me to obtain some of the vegetable oil and powdered eggs now showing up—even in the camps—thanks to generous aid from America. These delicacies were issued to the main categories of prisoners engaged in manual work. But it was the flunkies, of course, who were first in line for them. As a working convalescent who had been taken off the hospital diet, I was receiving only second-class rations, in which these new American products scarcely figured at all. There were day and night shifts in the kitchen, but the same cooks were always on duty at night; I had therefore not been able to strike up an acquaintance with those on the day shift. Soon, however, I thought up a plan for getting to know a Chinese chef whose particular job on the day shift was to make *ponchiki* and baked puddings. I did not realize how difficult it would be to carry out my plan.

In the years of the New Economic Policy, that is, until 1929, the Soviet government tolerated the existence of small private enterprises, which included Moscow's many Chinese laundries. I still remember looking through shopwindows and seeing people in white shirts and trousers busily washing and ironing. Eventually these establishments were shut down and most Chinese were arrested under suspicion of espionage. During the nationwide purge of 1937, the Chinese and Koreans living in the Soviet Far East were shipped to Kazakhstan in Central Asia, and a large number of these were also arrested as spies. In the camps they were all kept together in their own work brigades, but always with a non-Chinese *bytovik* in charge of them. Nearly all of them were worked to death in the pre-war years. These exceptionally conscientious workmen were hardy to an unusual degree, but without an understanding of our language, they were in a particularly defenseless position. In 1938, when prisoners were being deliberately killed off to reduce overcrowding in the camps, the foremen were specially instructed to give the Chinese brigades the most backbreaking jobs on excavation projects. Work that they had done was credited to other brigades of non-Chinese *bytoviks*. For failing to meet quotas, the Chinese were punished with shorter rations and thus were brought to a state of complete exhaustion. Later, they were caught up in the great wave of executions that swept over the camps. In consequence, the only Chinese who survived the pre-war period were those lucky enough to get a foothold inside a camp laundry.

The representatives of this ancient race were far removed from Russian and Western culture, and among themselves they kept up their traditional customs, which though inevitably somewhat modified were still very distinctive; as a result the Chinese stood out sharply from the rest of us. This was all the more interesting since the general pattern of life among the prisoners in those years rarely preserved any original features deriving from national peculiarities.

The Chinese I saw in the infirmary were a case in point. Like us, they were frightfully debilitated; nevertheless, their behavior set them markedly apart. They communicated only among themselves; by way of reply to any question of ours, they simply put on a look of incomprehension. In the daytime they either slept or lay motionless with closed eyes, often in strange or improbable positions. I could not help thinking of the opium smokers I had once seen many years previously in a silent movie from abroad. When our food was brought in, they would wake up—or snap out of their stupor—just long enough to receive their rations and stow them inside the small chests that they had next to the lower bunks on which they always slept. They came to life only at night, about an hour after the lights had gone out and when almost everybody else had fallen asleep. They would move about, their homemade slippers quietly shuffling, and exchange words in soft tones. And finally they would begin eating, a kind of sacred ritual that lasted for hours. Since they were none the worse for this odd method of feeding themselves, it would seem that they possessed some secret knowledge that was unknown even to the yogis.

I had the most honest intentions in respect to the Chinese cook. My first move was to find out when there would be no other people by the little hatch through which he handed out third rations, which were superior to the others. The best time for me to do my business with him would be an hour afterward—by this time the flunkies, the barracks orderlies, and the other prisoners who worked inside the camp proper would already have been fed, while the production brigades had yet to return to the barbed-wire zone. Finally one day, with an air of aplomb, I handed him my second-class ration ticket and almost simultaneously I stretched out my right hand, on the palm of which lay some tobacco wrapped in a rag. As an inveterate smoker, he could see at a glance that I was offering him at least enough to fill three matchboxes—which meant a three-day supply. There were not many around who could make that kind of offer. But he jumped back and waved his hands at me in refusal. I was quite amazed—after all, my home-grown tobacco was famed throughout the camp for its quality and was in great demand among the flunkies. The boys used to say that it was heady as alcohol. I went over to the next hatch and picked up the bowl of *balanda* that my ticket entitled me to and went back to my quarters.

On the way the reason for my failure suddenly dawned on me. The system in the camps was such that each cook found himself forced to feed a good many people on whom his job in the kitchen—and, indeed, his personal safety—depended. This meant that he had to pass out the best food, in excess of the amount they were entitled to, to a number of people without the proper meal tickets. Supervisors, for example, would have their mess cans filled with *ponchiki,* or pudding, and sometimes even meat, with a generous helping of butter on top—this was then covered over with a thin layer of buckwheat *kasha* to disguise it. The other flunkies lower down in the hierarchy were fed according to their rank and the degree of influence they had in the kitchen. Besides these, the criminals also had to be well taken care of—their leaders expected to be fed on the same scale as the supervisors, and the lesser ones got at least an extra portion of *kasha.* In all the camps of the Soviet Union the situation was the same. Only in rare cases were effective curbs on all this thievery applied with any success. But nowhere was it stopped completely. The authorities, as a rule, did not take measures against it except when someone was caught red-handed. Usually such a thing happened only when an offender was denounced to them for reasons of personal vengeance. Then an order would go out for the culprit's arrest, and he would be thrown into the punishment cell. This, of course, offered great scope for blackmail and those who worked in the kitchen could be forced to hand over extra food under threat of exposure. The orderly in the

Communal Services Section, of whom we were all afraid, was notorious among the kitchen staff for this type of blackmail, and since I worked in the same section, the Chinese had put the worst possible construction on my approach. Realizing this, I was amused rather than upset, and I decided to make further advances to the cook—but now more for my own enlightenment than for material gain.

Shortly afterward, I discovered that Vanya, as the cook was called in Russian, lived in the same barracks as the rest of the Chinese prisoners. I dropped in there a couple of times in an attempt to see him. The barracks orderlies met me with extreme hostility, but I stood my ground and explained that I urgently needed to speak with him on an important matter. After a consultation among themselves they decided that I was evidently not simply to be brushed off and told me to come back just before Lights Out. That evening when I reappeared, I heard someone say, "Vanya's in," and I was led to a remote corner that had been partitioned off from the rest of the barracks. In a logging camp such an odd arrangement would not have been surprising, since the barracks there were constantly being rebuilt or extended, often to provide space for workshops.

I walked into a spotlessly clean room measuring approximately fifteen by eighteen feet and with an opening in the floor, under which Vanya probably kept the food supplies he used for barter as well as the goods he received in exchange. In case of a search, anything lying in sight on the floor could be quickly hidden below and covered over with boards that were stacked up in the corner. The barracks orderly pointed to the hole in the floor and as I approached it, I caught sight of someone getting up and thrusting his head out. But I could not immediately make out who it was, although there was light enough coming from the lamp. This setup was so fantastic and so out of keeping with the din and congestion common to the other barracks that I momentarily lost my bearings. Vanya had certainly taken full advantage of his favored position.

In all probability, this private apartment had been put at his disposal by my chief in the Communal Service Section. Surveillance at that time was extremely lax, since the guards responsible for checking on the barracks were men who had been invalided out of the army. They made a cursory inspection of the barracks only once a day and never interfered with what went on there—and the officers in charge of them, by time-honored custom in the camps, were among those who got special treatment from the kitchen.

Squatting down on the floor, I saw the upper half of Vanya's torso as he emerged. He stared at me unblinkingly. Then for the second time I went through the same routine: I held out my hand with palm upward and displayed the same old rag containing a quantity of tobacco. A gleam came into the Chinaman's slanting black eyes. Leaning forward with his arms propped against the floor, he brought his face up close to mine and hissed, "Vanya honest Chinaman. He no take tobacco. Vanya honest Chinaman." As he drew himself back, I replied, "You are an honest Chinese, and I am an honest *lagernik*."[6] Perceiving that he would not understand the little speech I had prepared, I restricted myself to a few broken phrases in underworld jargon. In essence, I said: "I nearly died recently, and now, through honest barter, I want to get the food needed to build up my strength. A number of the flunkies are doing business with me. You can, too. Why don't you say something? Are you afraid? . . . Look, to go on this way won't do us any good. So long!"

Afterward it occurred to me why Vanya had chosen to receive me standing under the floor: a trap had been set for me, just in case I became aggressive and threatened to expose the Chinese barracks. Most likely, a couple of witnesses to our conversation had been hiding down below next to Vanya and would have come to his defense. It would have been no trouble for him to find fellow Chinese with a good knowledge of Russian. I have no doubt that eventually we could have begun to do business. However, my problem was soon solved in another way: I was transferred to work at the lumber mill, where the food was somewhat better.

After the failure of my attempts to enter into negotiations with the Chinese cook, I came to a conclusion that stayed with me all the remaining eight years of my confinement: only a man capable of extracting everything necessary to sustain life from the wretched bread ration and *balanda* supplied by the camp kitchen can expect to pull through. When you constantly have to fight in order to obtain something better, the toll on your nerves and stamina is far greater than any hoped-for good results. Fervent prayer nourishes the soul, and in turn the soul helps to support the body. Trust in God and a calm spirit enable a man to endure deprivation and draw the last atom of nourishment from the miserly rations of the camp. One should only accept help in the form of food parcels from home in the very last resort, in case of serious illness—if one comes to rely on such parcels, there is always a danger of being subjected to Chekist blackmail.

6. *Lagernik:* camp prisoner. (Tr.)

The Leader Who Might Have Been

The chief of the Communal Services Section was a former tsarist officer named Nikolayevski. He resembled a huge bear. For his years he was still in pretty sound condition. His head was already balding, and he kept his hair cropped close to the skull. The muscles of his face were strong and mobile, although his markedly snubbed nose somewhat spoiled his appearance. Life had tamed his cheerful prankish nature and made him bitterly ironical, but although he knew exactly what he could say and when he could say it, he was nevertheless sparing with his words and jests. Since our rations at that time were too meager for a man of his dimensions, he was always hungry despite his civilian status; and so he frequently assigned himself to night-watch duty in the kitchen. Toward me he was amiably inclined, yet he had already told everything about himself that he was going to tell. What I heard instead of conversation were disjointed exclamations accompanied by gestures and grimaces. In the office he commented readily about the sort of things his section was concerned with: cesspools, sanitation carts, the repair of ladders. He also talked, in line of duty, about the digging of mass graves, the making of the numbered tags that were attached to the big toes of dead prisoners before burial, and the preparation of markers with special code numbers to be placed over the mass graves. . . .

Using the method of the great Cuvier, who could restore the likeness of a prehistoric monster from a single bone, it is possible to reconstruct with considerable verisimilitude the salient features of this man's life on the basis of the principal events of a recent past we all knew so well.

As a young officer he took part in the First World War, and received the Cross of Saint George for military valor. About this phase of his life he sometimes allowed himself to talk—now that we were again at war with Germany, his heroic deeds in the First World War were officially regarded as patriotic, even though until 1936 all who had given military service to the tsarist government were viewed as reactionaries by the Soviet state and hence were subject to every kind of denunciation.

During the period of the Provisional Government in 1917, he came home on leave. When he stepped out into the square next to the Aleksandrovski Station[7] in Moscow, some soldiers jumped him with the intention of tearing off his epaulettes, but within a matter of seconds after testing his bear-like strength, his assailants were rolling along the sidewalk. In America he undoubtedly would have become a boxing champion. He told us about this incident one day in the barracks while

7. Now called the Byelo-Russian Station.

the duty officer was out. He mentioned it apropos of a run-in he had had with the administration chief, Levinson, in 1943 when old-style officers' epaulettes were adopted by the Chekists.[8] He had muttered something to the effect that the insignia which had been taken away from him twenty-five years ago were being restored to the shoulders of a very different breed of men. . . .

While serving in Kolchak's White Army, he was wounded and taken prisoner; but since he agreed to train Red Army men, he was not executed. In 1920 he fought in the ranks of the Red Army against the Poles. Afterward came years of ordeals, persecutions, prison, and camps—the only place where he could exist, nominally as a free employee; but he was under constant threat of being arrested again.

Nikolayevski, of course, was not cast in the mold of the heroes of classical antiquity; neither was he a crusader inspired with great religious fervor nor a soldier of the Swiss Guard ready to die in the name of sacred duty. He was not among the mutineers at Ust-Usa; he would not have been a proud defender of Alcazar. Nevertheless, I looked on him with much respect. He had abandoned the White cause only after it had been totally defeated, but until then he had served it with loyalty and honor. Under the Soviet regime he now dragged out a pitiful existence as a camp employee, while other ex-tsarist officers, after helping the Red Army to victory, had later taught in the military academies and were once again giving their active support to the Red regime in World War II. If the war had been fought differently and if landing parties had been dropped in the camps, Nikolayevski is one of those who would have immediately come forth as a military leader, and he would have been followed by legions of prisoners. This would have been his moment of destiny. But we can expect ordinary mortals to behave like heroes and saints only if the policies of both great and small nations conform to clear ethical standards. The mistakes of the great ones of this world cannot be shifted to the shoulders of the common people, who may be excellently adapted to carrying out their own tasks but are incapable of setting right the massive blunders of their era.

The accountant in the maintenance section was a very nice fellow with long mustaches—a former Cossack captain. I found his company agreeable, and I have no doubt that we would have found much in common had it not been for the presence of the barracks orderly, who was always

8. Tsarist-type insignia, uniforms, and the old names of military ranks were reintroduced at this time by Stalin as part of his strategy of enlisting traditional Russian patriotism in the struggle with the Nazis. (Tr.)

running errands for the head of the camp Chekists and was one of their chief sources of information. This personage was a gloomy Ukrainian with an owlish scowl, an altogether dangerous individual. It was he of whom the Chinese cook was so afraid. Whenever he showed up in the barracks, we all knew at once that he had come to fetch someone for an interrogation. He had had quite a few men sent off to the cells, not only in his capacity as a Chekist collaborator but also on his own personal initiative. And whenever it might suit him, he could pass on some scurrilous lie about me as well, though the fact that I had just undergone a long series of interrogations and had been resentenced insured me against another arrest for some time to come. The Chekists lost sleep mainly over prisoners who held some position of authority and influence. I was already at rock bottom and could sink no further; therefore, I went quietly about my trifling duties in the office and completely ignored the master informant from the Ukraine. My new job was very convenient, for it enabled me to ply the tobacco trade and, with the earnings, buy provisions to supplement my diet. Everything went on very well for about a month, until Nikolayevski was transferred to another job outside the camp. He was replaced by an Ossetian named Debirov, an incorrigible stool pigeon and a former inmate of the camp. This alliance of two of the Chekists' top informants bode no good at all. The atmosphere took a sharp turn for the worse; there were sidelong glances, veiled hints. It was obvious that my presence was not welcome to them. I had no choice except to get out of this situation as soon as possible. The only thing that protected me for the time being was the fact that I had been certified by the medical commission as an invalid—otherwise I would certainly have been sent off to do common labor. Suddenly I had a stroke of luck: an engineer at the saw mill was being shipped out to another camp, and I was asked to fill his place. By now my legs had regained their strength, so it was with considerable rejoicing that I accepted the offer. But two months later, just as I was getting fully adjusted to the mill and was beginning to make myself again indispensable, I was suddenly called out for transport.

I got some intimation of this drastic shift of fate in the following circumstances. At the end of working hours I was standing near the guardhouse at the entrance of the mill from which there was a clear view of the place where *zeks* were lined up before being taken back to the camp. Overhead was a lamp that lit up the area surrounding me. My profile was quite visible from the roadway that ran through the area where the work brigades were lined up. This stretch of road served as a short cut between the offices of the Security Section and the jail at Camp Five. All at once

I caught sight of Kurbatov, the chief of the interrogation division, walking along the road. He was wearing a beaverskin cap with earflaps, a white mackinaw, and elegant felt boots. I watched him as he passed by. All of a sudden his coal-black eyes darted sharply in my direction; his mouth curled into an ugly sneer, a dreadful grimace that quite contorted his fleshy, rather handsome face. This was the second time I had seen this man momentarily transformed into the Devil, and I now prepared myself for something horrible to happen in the near future. Sure enough, a few days later we learned that Kurbatov intended to send a group of us to a death camp for prisoners building the Kotlas-Vorkuta rail line. Fortunately for us, it turned out that the line had just been completed. Because the whole project was surrounded by secrecy, Kurbatov had not known this. It would have been a good way of getting rid of us—the building of that particular railway had cost a tremendous number of lives. Thanks to this fortunate error, we were despatched instead along the already completed railroad—to Vorkuta.

12

THE TRANSPORT TO VORKUTA

You Cannot Bargain With the Devil

Since the authorities seldom stood on ceremony with the prisoners, they did not hesitate to call us out for a transport without a moment's advance notice. Any morning the supervisor could walk into the barracks and announce that such-and-such a prisoner need not present himself for work that day. Whenever the authorities had reason to think that a prisoner, getting wind of his impending transfer, might try to hide out somewhere within the camp, they hauled him off to the cells and from there direct to the transport.

Everyone loved Marika for her kind, sympathetic nature. A good many prisoners, as well as some of the civilian employees, were gratefully indebted to her. As soon as the list of men to be transported from Vyatlag to Vorkuta had been completed, someone passed the details on to Marika. So for several days before we were shipped out, I knew what was coming. At least I was able to prepare for it and warn my friends.

Out of our fraternity of five I was the only one to be put on this transport. Vorkuta at that time was reputed to be a hellhole. After my silent encounter with Kurbatov, I was ready for the worst. It had been only six weeks since I received my additional sentence. And even though I was still classified as an invalid and had not fully recovered, I was being sent to the far north with its cruel winter, to work there, as I thought, on the railroad. By comparison with this horror, the lumber mill where I was now working as an engineer seemed like a vacation resort. Though it was hard to swallow the thought that I had no choice except to knuckle under and put up with more humiliation, this fresh disaster did not cloud my spirits.

In thought I have always sided with those who had the opportunity of rebelling, weapons in hand, against the terrorist yoke. I consider it my duty to tell the reader how many people were exterminated in the bolshevist holocaust. Having examined my conscience, I feel entitled to give at least one example of terrorism for every hundred that I saw happen —as one whose own life has been threatened by the terror machine for a quarter century and who has himself barely escaped being crushed to death under its wheels. Those lucky enough to have been spared such sufferings would do well, for the sake of themselves and their loved ones, to make an effort of the imagination, to try to understand what it was like, and to heed the warnings of survivors. Otherwise it will be too late. History is always repeating itself. It was quite foreseeable that the new regime established in 1917 would lead to terror and would be accompanied by grandiose hecatombs.

And yet even of those who realized what a terrible nightmare was in store only a handful were ready to risk their lives in defense of the nation, of freedom, and human rights. Such a man was one of my fellow prisoners by the name of Zandrok, a born hero if there ever was one. In the spring of 1942, he was summoned by special order to a labor camp in Kirov where he was needed to organize the production of land mines in the shortest possible time. But there was some delay in providing him with a guard escort, and he was not able to leave Vyatlag for about ten days or so after receiving his instructions. He whiled away the time by visiting us in the machine shop, where he kept up a steady conversation. I tried hard to finish up all my jobs in the morning so that I would not be interrupted later on while listening to this marvelous storyteller. He had not been old enough for service against the Germans during the First World War. However, in 1917 this splendid, pure-hearted youth with noble ideals was already a cadet officer somewhere well to the east of Moscow—in Kazan, I believe. His entire academy had gone over to the White Guards and become one of Kolchak's[1] most reliable units. His descriptions of the actions he had taken part in were quite original and absorbing, and we were deeply impressed by his staunch devotion to the

_____

1. Admiral Alexander Kolchak (1874–1920), commander of anti-Bolshevik armies in Siberia and the far East. He was captured and executed by the Bolsheviks, after troops of the Czechoslovak Legion (consisting of former POW's of the Austrian army) had become disaffected. (Tr.)

whole idea of the White movement. Wherever sacrifice and heroism were required, he and his comrades were sent into the fray.

After the Czechs had betrayed Kolchak and handed him over to the Reds for execution, Zandrok remained with one of the few units that were still fit for combat. They managed to make it into Mongolia. He described his years as an émigré: a reception given by Chiang Kai-shek, for instance, where he was treated to such gourmet delights as brains from a live monkey; and his stay in Japan, where hospitality was un-believable—at least from the standpoint of European customs. Eventu-ally he settled in Shanghai—or perhaps it was Manchuria—but he con-stantly felt homesick. He returned voluntarily to the U.S.S.R. where he paid for his naïveté with many years of imprisonment. His ancestors had come from Scotland, and he reminded me of the heather, a plant with the hardiness to endure savage winds and all weathers.

In 1952, at the end of my twelfth year as a prisoner, I got to know yet another man who had fought for the White cause. He had been, in his own way, as representative of it as Zandrok. At that time, after a series of vicissitudes, I had finally succeeded in getting assigned to a part of the camp where conditions were relatively easy and had been given work in the machine shop there. Although the job was not without its perils, it at least involved no manual labor, since my task was the old and practiced one of "dressing up" the brigade's work sheets. In this capacity I had already considerably improved its situation—until then, it had been hard put to meet its quota. Under my direction it moved to the forefront and exceeded—on paper, at least—the production plan. The number of men working for it went up from ten to twenty and they began to get first-category rations, as well as a hundred rubles in cash, which enabled them to buy bread, sugar, and margarine from the camp commissary. I was beginning to feel like Odysseus after his years of wandering—it was a return to relative peace, and I again found myself among good friends, as so often in the past. One evening a huge giant of a man walked up to my bunk and sat down beside me. I had noticed him previously in an-other section of the barracks. Putting out his hand, which was the size of a gardener's spade, he introduced himself: "Nechkin, horse-rider." By this, I soon gathered he meant that before his arrest he had performed at a hippodrome and, in his youth, had served in the cavalry.

From the lips of this ex-officer from Tiflis, a rather rakish and cynical man, I heard innumerable tales about tsarist Russia, all with the same refrain. In the years just before World War I the country was flourishing as never before. He and his fellow-officers in the Caucasus had lived a very gay life indeed. Wine flowed in an endless stream. Then in 1914 came the war. A first-rate commanding officer, he fought in scores of engagements, assisted in the capture of Erzerum, was awarded the Cross of Saint George several times, and finally was witness to the collapse of the Army of the Caucasus and its shameful evacuation. Because of his natural skepticism, he was unsparing in his comments on Rasputin and Protopopov,[2] while Rodzyanko[3] and Milyukov[4] he denounced as traitors and windbags. Seeing executions of field officers and garrison commanders take place before his eyes, he decided to escape—which he managed due to his courage and physical strength as well as to the respect he enjoyed with his men. He got as far as Rostov and, along with some of his remaining subordinates, joined Denikin's army. Though he had no illusions as to the outcome, he stayed to the bitter end, through all the ups and downs of the Civil War. But he was not averse to helping himself along the way. In Kremenchug he even took part in a jewelry store robbery, and he went frequently on drunken sprees after getting leave from the front. Once, when he and his cronies hadn't the money to pay their bill in a night club, they found a portrait of Denikin on the wall, touched it up with grotesque mustaches, put a cigarette in the corner of the mouth, and then called for the owner, shouting, "What do you mean by this? You ought to be shot, like a dog!" Of course, the night club owner was only too glad to let his guests off free of charge.

But in spite of this and other such escapades that could only give the White movement a bad name, he continued to put his heart into it— even, for example, getting indignant because the horses in his regiment were not as well shod as those in Budyonny's[5] Red Cavalry. He remained a soldier until the very end and, without a murmur of protest, carried out the last order given to him: to cover the evacuation of the White Army by engaging his troops in rear-guard actions. As the last ships were about to pull out into the Black Sea and many of the Whites were still left on shore, in a characteristic gesture, he sold a pair of the diamonds he had stolen in order to get a place on the hospital ship. As a result of this deal, a wounded man had to be put ashore.

Memories of the camp at Gallipoli provoked him to bitter laughter. Once out of there, he made his way to Alexandria, where, after a drunken orgy at the British garrison, he ended up in the guardhouse. There, on

2. *Protopopov*, A. D. (1866–1918): last tsarist minister of the interior.

3. *Rodzyanko*, M. V. (1859–1924): president of the Duma (Russian parliament), 1905–1917.

4. *Milyukov*, P. N. (1859–1943): leader of Cadet party and Minister of Foreign Affairs in the Provisional Government. (Tr.)

5. Commander of the Red Cavalry during the Civil War.

the ground that he was a guest of King George V, he refused to observe the regulation under which prisoners were required to carry out their night slops. As Nechkin told it, later in London he was invited by the king to attend the royal palace, because he had so impressed the Englishmen with his appearance and conversational brilliance. Before long, however, he came to the end of his diamonds and had to take a job in a horse-riding show. Just at that time the New Economic Policy was announced in the U.S.S.R., and an amnesty was declared for all who wished to return home. Though a little skeptical, he nevertheless thought he might get by with his native wits and find a modest job as a circus rider, so he followed the example of others who returned to the Land of Bolshevism at that time.

These two former White officers, Zandrok and Nechkin, had been men of great courage, but for their different reasons they had eventually thrown themselves on the mercy of the victors. Zandrok, the idealist, had hoped that things might genuinely improve; Nechkin, the cynic, had simply miscalculated. For both men the end was the same: prison bars and barbed wire. The "statistics" that I collected during my years of imprisonment demonstrated that all the White officers and soldiers who had put their trust in the Soviet government came to a bad end in prisons and camps. You cannot bargain with the Devil!

The night before our transport was due to leave for Vorkuta, my envy of those men who had attempted an armed defense of their nation's right to freedom was especially acute. Yet I also felt grief over their inglorious capitulation to the regime just at a time when resistance against it was each day becoming more and more urgent. What great blessings they might have brought our country!

A Troubled Journey

Saying good-by is always tiresome. So it was with a feeling of relief, notwithstanding the menace of the future, that we settled in a railroad car of strange design. It was not partitioned into the usual compartments but was lined with bunks along the whole length of it. These were separated from the corridor by a steel grille. We came to know each other and tried to find out what our ultimate destination was. Were they simply trying, as usual, to get rid of "goners," invalids, and criminals with whom they could no longer cope? The composition of this transport left no doubt in my mind that the Chekists had punitive ends in mind.

Besides myself were Pavel Salmin, Boris Rozhdestvenski, Misha Dyachkov, and Lev K.—all of us had received an additional ten-year term.

Salmin was the one alleged to have planned an armed uprising. He had been the chief prosecution witness against the rest of us. But, by virtue of his cooperation, he was now very well versed in the Chekist techniques and knew all their weaknesses; he thus represented a potential danger to them in the event of changes at the end of the war. They would all breathe more easily if he were shipped off to die in another camp. Boris was being punished for stealing the wife of a Chekist; and Misha Dyachkov, a young man from the working class, for endlessly telling the interrogators to their faces what he thought of them. Among other things, he called them fascists and saboteurs. Lev K., like myself, was picked out because of his inflexible hostility toward the regime, which he expressed even more openly than I.

Without any prearranged agreement among the rest of us, a boycott was placed on Salmin right at the start of the journey. It was repeatedly driven home to me over the years that victims of the Chekists had little desire to take revenge on their tormentors but thought only in terms of putting them out of action, if the opportunity ever arose. However, a conciliatory attitude toward a collaborator or stool pigeon was rare among us. Even then, it was shown only by craven cowards or by a man who had been completely broken. Normally we all stuck to the principle: "Death to stool pigeons!" Salmin was not a real stool pigeon—he was simply a man of weak nerves who had quickly been broken by his interrogators. All the same, Salmin thought it best to keep out of sight and he crawled into a dark corner, as far away as possible from the rest of us.

In the two days it took us to reach Kirov the prisoners had already formed new friendships and alliances. An engineer named Ruchkin attached himself like a hungry orphan to Boris who had been furnished for the journey by the Chekist's wife with stout winter clothing and a substantial supply of food. Now, at last, I was able to get to know the Swedish-Russian historian, Lev. K., who proved to be very interesting. My old friend Misha Dyachkov continued to stick along with me. And two other men of working-class origin joined us, partly because they were lured by what remained of my tobacco supply—whenever we made a cigarette it was passed around in brotherly fashion.

A criminal with the nickname "Red Sava" also tried to latch on to us. He was almost as much of a legend as Lom-Lopata, though he was scarcely in the same class, and the Vyatlag authorities had been just as anxious to get rid of him. Keeping to themselves were a pair of *bytoviks* who had been employed in one of the camp commissaries and were hence regarded by the rest of us as plutocrats. Most of us were undernourished, and there was no way for us to pick up any extra food along the route—consequently, we could not help casting covetous glances at the parcels so jealously guarded by the *bytoviks*. Since they would get no farther with the stuff than the first transit prison, the most sensible thing would have been for them to turn over a reasonable share to us and keep the rest for themselves. But when we proposed this, they replied, "We'd rather stay with the criminals!"

"Red Sava" went over and squatted down next to them. They produced some bread and salted fish for him. Sava wolfed it down and smoked a cigarette as thick as a finger. The two *bytoviks* seemed happy. If that's the way they wanted it . . .

Late in the evening we arrived in Kirov. It was bitter cold. The old transit prison was located on the river bank. To reach it, we had to be taken on foot to the other side of the city. En route we passed another vast prison—the main one in Kirov—where executions were carried out. One of the executioners employed there had been a security guard at Vyatlag, a Ukrainian by the name of Getman. He had held the same office there. Whenever a sizable number of condemned prisoners had accumulated at the prison, Getman was sent over on special assignment. After doing his job, he would return to his duties as armed sentry on one of the watchtowers near the camp. As a reward for his "services" at the Kirov prison he naturally enjoyed certain privileges. For one thing, he was never required to go out to the forests as a work-brigade guard. He was endowed with no talents whatsoever, except for those needed in a killer. It was enough to look at his low-browed, brutish mug to give full credence to the horrific stories circulated about him. One day he played an extraordinary trick on his wife when she came to the watchtower with his lunch, something she did every day, though strictly speaking it was against the rules for anyone except the corporal of the guard to approach a sentry at his post. On this occasion, his wife had no sooner reached the foot of the watchtower than Getman bellowed out in Ukrainian, "Lie down flat and don't move!" Knowing her husband's character only too well, the good woman carried out his order to the letter. It was an hour before he allowed her to pick herself out of the dirt.

It was cold, and our guards forced the pace. Lev K. found it hard to keep up. Besides what he had on his back, all his worldly goods consisted of nothing more than a ragged cotton blanket, which he had draped over his shoulders. Because the man behind kept treading on the end of it, he decided to move to the rear of the column, but now he fell back even more, still trailing his blanket along after him. One of the guards set a vicious dog on him, and it snapped at his legs. The fact that we were just then walking through the town saved the situation. The guard commander halted the column. We took Lev by the arms and helped him along—not forgetting his blanket, too.

Finally we reached the transit prison, but the guard did not let us in immediately. As usual, there was some kind of hold-up. We stood in the cold for forty minutes, nearly freezing to death. Our only wish was to get into the warmth. After another delay in the corridor, we finally made it to the big common cell. Looking round, we saw that other prisoners had settled in earlier, but there were still vacancies on the upper tiers of bunks and we staked our claim to them. We then found out that half of the prisoners who had arrived before us had been sent off to the baths, so we remained dressed and waited for them. Our little group had decided to make a stand as one man. All of a sudden the doors were flung open, and a band of criminals burst in and began storming the bunks we were sitting on. Apparently they had been tipped off about our arrival. From our vantage point on the top bunks, we were able to hold them off, kicking at them with our feet as they tried to climb up. But some of them managed to clamber up at the end of the row of bunks and were trying to attack us from the flank. Then as if on command we started jumping down on the heads of the howling mob below. Dressed in heavy winter clothing and with packs strapped to our backs, each of us came crashing down like a ton of bricks. Ruchkin and I were the last to join the fray, and I thought I heard somebody's bones crunch under my weight.

The cell door was very close to where we were, and we made it our target, jumping in that direction, thus blocking it with the solid mass of our bodies, and simultaneously lashing out at the criminals like savages. Since many of us could still be classified as invalids, it would have taken only another two minutes for our strength to give out. A natural-born soldier, Ruchkin in particular distinguished himself in the fray. Unencumbered by extra gear and being in fairly good physical shape, he was at a better advantage than the rest of us. The din inside the cell now became twice as loud, as we began hammering at the door with our feet. The jailer, at the end of his patience, flung it wide open, thus enabling us to make a break for the corridor. In the relative silence that now ensued, we heard Lev's voice behind us: "Hey, boys, don't leave me! I'm still with you!" We insisted that he be allowed out to join us. Pushing through the mob and looking as red as a crab, he got through to us, still with his inseparable blanket.

Our group was intact—all ten of us. We refused to go back among those bandits and were led away to another cell so cold that there was even frost inside it. But after our narrow escape we were only too glad to be there. Our gear evidently had suffered no damage, and Boris passed out all the bread he had.

The jailers, who were clearly in partnership with the criminals, now announced that they would transfer us into a cell that they described as "quiet." We didn't believe them. Boris advised us to sit tight, demanding to see the head of the prison. It was all very well for him to stay here, since he was dressed in a fur coat and felt boots. Glancing around at the others with faces blue from the cold, I could not share Boris's view. Still, we should have stayed. We could easily have held out another hour or even until morning, lying in a huddle on the bunks with Lev's blanket to cover our legs and feet, and putting Boris, as well as another man in a heavy coat on each side of us. After a while the head would have appeared, or the guards would have given up their designs on us and put us in a cell that really was quiet.

But we took the promises of the guards at face value. They were reckoning on other criminals taking the things they wanted and later giving them their share. The cell we were now taken to proved to be an even worse trap than the first. During the transfer the guard kept casting greedy eyes on such conspicuous items as Boris's fur coat, somebody else's mackinaw, and several bundles of personal belongings that looked as though they might yield more than the others. Again, half of the prisoners who were already installed in the cell had been taken out for baths. But those who had remained behind gave us a reception entirely different from that we had received in the first cell. There were welcoming smiles, and some of the men even offered to give up their places to us. Just by the entrance was a technician with whom I had been on friendly terms at Vyatlag. Although a Soviet citizen, he was of Czech origin.

"Rzhehak, greetings." I shouted, "What's it like here? Do they take the whole of your stuff, or leave you half?"

"It's not such a bad setup. Make yourself at home." I couldn't help noticing, however, that he seemed very rigid in his manner, as though he had crapped in his pants. But his reply was sufficient to allay suspicions, and we all began to settle down in the new cell. At the invitation of our new friends we took off our outer clothing and began to relax, chatting quietly. Then all of a sudden the door clanged open to admit the others returning from the baths. The scene now changed dramatically. Each of us was approached by criminals intent upon getting what they could from us. Standing before me was quite an educated-looking fellow, who started talking to me in a language that showed he had not always been a criminal. But the moment he made a deft grab for my ditty bag, I realized that here was somebody who had gone over to the criminals. So I gave him a belting blow to the face. I felt a hairy paw gripping me by the neck, and two other criminals grabbed hold of me on either side. The first one swiftly recovered and caught me on the nose with a backhand blow. The blood spurted out and trickled down over my white undershirt. Then they let go of me and started digging out of my bag everything that looked of value to them. Because of the pain and the bleeding, I was in no condition to resist. But at that moment a man in uniform with blue shoulder epaulettes[6] suddenly appeared at the entrance to the cell and yelled, "Listen here, all you engineers who just arrived—come out of the cell!"

It was Ruchkin who had saved us. A quick-witted fellow who, unlike us, had no possessions to defend, he had quickly sized up our situation, and with a pencil stub he had managed to preserve through all the searches had dashed off a message to the head of the prison saying that a group of engineers en route to Vorkuta on a special assignment were being robbed and beaten in his domain. Upon arrival at Vorkuta, surely a complaint would be registered with the authorities there. As luck would have it, the guard outside our new cell was annoyed with the criminals for cheating him of what he considered his share of the loot. So when Ruchkin handed him the note, he wasted no time in getting it to the head of the prison. But even without this stroke of luck, being of one mind and one purpose, we would have won out in the end. If the cell guard had received the treatment that he expected from the bandits, he would not have lifted a finger on our behalf, and we should then have been forced to get our way by going on a hunger strike.

Standing before the head of the prison, we made a sorry-looking sight. My shirt was smeared with blood, and my companions were all completely disheveled. Therefore, Ruchkin who had come out unscathed, and the impressive-looking Boris, whose elegant clothes were still in good condition, acted as our spokesmen and told a great tale about how we were all topnotch, irreplaceable specialists who had been summoned to Vorkuta to get a manufacturing plant under way. They pointed to one as an example of our treatment at the hands of the thugs, and swore that we would not let matters rest there. The head of the prison, clearly furious, called for the prisoner who was the *starosta*[7] of the cell. An unusually picturesque criminal was now led in. His ugly mug was of a brick-red hue and covered with scars. His shirt front was open, and

6. The insignia of Chekist prison wardens.
7. *Starosta:* literally "elder"—someone appointed by members of a group of prisoners, etc., to be their spokesman vis-à-vis the authorities. (Tr.)

around his neck hung a cross, set with rubies, which he must have stolen. The expression on his face was one of total servility. The prison head bellowed at him like a bull: ". . . I will have you all shot without trial. Do you people think you can get away with robbery right under my nose?"

The crook stared at him obsequiously, and the moment the prison head stopped for a breath, the crook began shouting back: "Citizen Warden, it all happened without my knowledge. I was in the baths at the time— I'll give them hell for this . . ."

He was lying in his teeth, of course. He and his crew had started in on us as soon as they came back from the baths. However, the head of the prison softened his tone: "It was a *bytovik* who started it?"

"Of course," answered the *starosta* respectfully.

"Get everybody out of that cell and have it searched!"

We tried to get back the items of clothing that the criminals had already put on, and all the other little things they had pocketed. When we were let back into the cell, we were able to collect everything that was ours, except for a small bag of peas belonging to Boris, which had been spilled over the floor; when they saw what was happening, the criminals had done this deliberately, so that later on they could gather the peas up one by one and eat them. Otherwise, our victory was complete. We were led away to a cell that was really peaceful—its population consisted mainly of war invalids: men with canes and crutches. It seemed like paradise—no more thievery, no more brawls or din. We got ourselves settled and then dropped off to sleep.

Our remaining days at the transit prison were brightened by Lev's stories. As if under a magic spell, we listened for hours at a time to his magnificent professorial voice. His presentation of Alexandre Dumas gave depth and Christian meaning to his work; his dissolute brawlers were shown to be shining heroes doing battle with the dark forces of evil. With his legs crossed and the inevitable blanket thrown over his shoulders, Lev always sat on the upper tier of bunks. While he talked, he remained frozen in one position. Later, I came to understand that this "lotus pose" was as necessary to him as to the yogis, for it enabled him to compose his thoughts.[8]

The ubiquitous Ruchkin learned from the cell guard that it was owing to "Red Sava" that we had originally been put in a cell, "where they were forever drinking and dancing"—these were the romantic terms in which the criminals had described their way of life there. During the long wait we had in the corridor upon arriving at the transit prison, "Red Sava"

8. In chapter ten I have already told of his yogi-like bathing in the snow during the winter of '43–'44, while he was in the cells at Vyatlag.

had tipped off a guard whom he knew that Boris was a "beaver"—which in slang meant that he was the possessor of a precious wardrobe—both what he was wearing and what he had stashed away in the bag where he kept his belongings. At this news Boris, the poet and philosopher, became unrecognizable as vindictiveness and hatred took complete hold of him. We thought we might have a chance of getting even with Sava on the day of our departure from Kirov. But Sava lay low and we could not immediately locate him. Obviously he had no desire to share the journey to Vorkuta with us. Boris found him in the very cell where we had had our first battle. He was called out and attached to our transport.

A general fanfare of laughter and jeers heralded the reception of the two *bytoviks* who, after their stay in the cell with Sava and his friends, were now stripped of their warm clothing and other belongings.

Some prisoners who were being returned from Vorkuta told us just before our departure that the railroad was finished as far as the city itself. So it was now obvious to us that we should not be put to work on it. Our small transport was installed in an ordinary passenger coach instead of the usual cattle car. In view of our wretched clothing which gave us so little protection this was indeed a good piece of luck. And something deep inside me was saying that the worst horrors were over, that nothing in the future could hold much terror for me. In contrast with what I had already lived through, what was yet to come could hardly be worse.

A New Year's Toast

It was warm in the Stolypin coach. That same winter whole contingents of prisoners had been transported to Vorkuta in cold freight cars because of the shortage of fuel. Men who were poorly dressed froze to death. By the end of the trip the corpses were piled in stacks. It was a long time before many of the survivors could bury the terrible memory of that extreme cold.

We, on the other hand, enjoyed comforts that were practically unheard of in those years. The upper berths of our compartment were already taken by the time we came in, but the lower bunks were not the usual overcrowded hell—there were no more than eight people in them, so that in the daytime we sat on the benches, and during the night lay in a huddle on them and on our baggage. The guards were relatively tolerant, though because of some oversight of theirs, we had to travel a couple of days without any bread. Although it was the darkest season of the year, some light reached us from the corridor. In general the atmosphere disposed us to storytelling, discussions, and quiet reflection. The journey lasted two weeks altogether.

Lev was silent these days; so Boris now held the center of the stage. For three days in a row, we listened with bated breath to a marvelous adventure tale about a girl named Susie, who under the most unlikely circumstances managed to hold onto her innocence. I am sure that the author of the novel, Cecil Bart, was not responsible for all the details with which Boris adorned his own version. Taking account of the tastes of his audience, he added some very spicy details. Whenever Susie got into a scrape, he always made the same comment: "Susie realized that the path of virtue is like a tightrope: once you fall off, there's no getting back on it." This we repeated after him in chorus, even imitating his intonation.

In the intervals between listening to Boris or taking part in discussions, I made an effort to sum up mentally my experiences at Vyatlag. Most of all I thought about the friends I had left behind. The man who did so much to help us adapt to the hardships of camp life, Georgi Leimer, had died at the end of 1942 from pneumonia which he caught while riding in a railroad engine. At least that is what we were told. It is my belief, however, that he virtually committed suicide. I myself had had to make two such journeys. Most of the time I stood on the footplate of the locomotive. Only when my face grew stiff from the cold did I step into the cab and thaw out. Georgi had a fairly balanced diet, high in caloric content. He also wore felt boots and a short coat with a warm fur lining. It seems to me that he could have gotten sick no other way than by throwing open his coat and exposing himself to the wind until he was frozen stiff. After the rest of us were transferred to the fifth section of the camp, Georgi felt that he was cut off from everyone. On the rare occasions that we ran into him, he talked a great deal about his loneliness. His intuition being more acute than ours, he saw that arrest was threatening us and it was plain to us all that the interrogators would attempt to make him out as our ringleader. And the horrible conditions of the camp prison were better known to him than to us. Our general disillusionment with the Germans he suffered with particular intensity. For him the future presented quite a hopeless picture. In addition to all this, he was deeply upset by a quarrel with Yuri; he complained about it, and with good reason. Along with his many positive gifts, Yuri has one terrible quality: he was incapable of gratitude and could forget or misrepresent what others had done for him. He, of all people, should have been especially grateful to Georgi, without whom he might not have survived his first winter at Vyatlag. Yuri was a first-class designer, but he was ambitious and vain. He wanted to play a central role in the machine shop, and yet at the same time he wanted to stay out of all discussions that might prove dangerous. In an effort to respect his wishes, we usually kept silent in his presence. But this was not enough for him: he even expected us to refrain from conversing among ourselves, as he did not care to run the slightest risk of any bad consequences to himself. Naturally, it was impossible to satisfy this whim of his, so eventually he vented his outraged feelings on us all. His quarrel with Georgi had been of a similar kind. It is sad to have to recall all this, but to me the question of relationships among people who may eventually become fighters for the same just cause is extremely important.

The Zionist Boris had stuck in my memory as a tall fair-haired man with Mephistophelean facial features. Less prone to error than the rest of us, he also had an astonishing ability to concentrate on problems. Already at Butyrki, even before Hitler had started the war, he was sure that Germany would be crushed. He had argued his case by pointing to comparative statistics that showed the economic superiority of the grand coalition then about to come into being. The initial successes of the German army in no way disconcerted him—and, as it turned out, he was wrong by only one year in the date he predicted for Germany's defeat. Burning with a fanatical hatred of Hitler, he was convinced that the Nazi dictator's atrocities against the Jews would lead directly to the swift formation of a viable Jewish state, and he ventured to say that it would start taking shape the moment the war ended. With calm assurance he awaited that time; then he would act. As for escapes and uprisings, he did not want even to hear about them. In jest he used to express his gratitude to "Comrade" Stalin for putting him behind bars, even complaining that he had been given only three years instead of five, for with five he would get out just in time to celebrate victory over Germany.

The fourth fellow prisoner in Vyatlag of whom I now thought was my favorite of all, Vasili. Politics held absolutely no interest for him. By nature he was a man of action. He would have been ideal as a soldier of fortune, an adventurer, a gold prospector, a hunter, or a conquistador. As a Zaporozhian Cossack by origin, he considered home as merely a place to rest. To him a settled routine meant doing jobs of the most tedious sort. But under the Soviet system this free-soaring eagle was doomed. Not only had he been condemned to spend a total of fifteen years in prisons, labor camps and exile; even when he was finally released, he would still be forced, under the regulations on residence passports,[9] to live only in one specific town, never leaving for any length of time except to go on vacation. Vasili, of course, was not alone in all this. This has been the tragedy of all Russians for the past half century. Scientists and engineers were to some extent able to maintain a little independence even in these conditions. But people who still had any yearning for personal initiative and private enterprise, anybody who was vigorous and energetic, was automatically suspect and subject to annihilation. Those who by some miracle stayed alive were transformed into slaves and confined to one place. Activity that for them was the very breath of life was replaced by irksome labor in the service of the state, by television and vodka. The enormous spread of alcoholism under our dictatorship can be explained by the enslavement of men created for independent activity.

Suddenly my reflections were interrupted. Earlier we had decreed that everyone should take his turn at telling something amusing. It had to be something from his own experience. So far, the laurels had gone not to our minstrels, Lev and Boris, but to some likable fellows of working-class origin. Back in the transit prison they had been able to observe the gestures and mannerisms of the criminals and reproduced them for us in some hilarious skits. Now came my turn—nobody was exempt from making his contribution.

Although one should beware of generalizations, it is safe to say that in those days the more thoughtful among us often perceived life through a prism of tragedy. I, therefore, told the story of the chief of the supply depot at Vyatlag, a well-dressed man of fifty, who had once been head of an important prison and who used to stand in front of his house just about nightfall. He was scared to death of unlighted buildings and would wait outside for hours until someone came along, went in, and made light. My story was greeted by dead silence, and then my listeners asked me to dig into my memory and come up with something of a comic nature. So I told them about the time when the camp authorities had attached a renegade criminal as a tutor to the engineers' barracks in Vyatlag—he was seconded to us from the camp's "cultural" section, and though he

9. In Soviet usage, the word "passport" means an identity card valid only within the country. One's place of residence (city, village, region) is shown in it and no change of residence can take place without the permission of the authorities, which is only rarely given. Workers on a kolkhoz (forty-eight percent of the population) have no passport and need a special permission from the kolkhoz president for any travel. Thus, in the twentieth century, they are the only serfs on earth. A passport for foreign travel is available only to the privileged and requires a long and complicated procedure.

had finished only two grades of school while we all had higher education, he now took charge of our political indoctrination. I fully expected that everyone would burst out laughing. But the reaction was the same as before. My stories proved to be so unsuccessful that my audience finally left me in peace, and once more I plunged into thoughts of Vyatlag.

Now I want to tell my readers about two of the most extraordinary *zeks* I met there. In the summer of 1942, a young man of thirty-five or so, Max Borodyanski, showed up in our machine shop. He was a cheerful and convivial Odessan. As a supply officer, he held a pass that allowed him free movement within the whole of Vyatlag. As a *bytovik,* he should have given us a wide berth, but he was drawn to our discussions as if by a magnet. There was no one else he could talk with so freely. His duties required him to travel all over the place and he came in contact with a wide range of people. From his travels, he reported on the realities of Soviet life, both sad and ridiculous. As a *bytovik* it was awkward for him to comment too directly on what he told us—he left that to us, confining himself to one invariable remark at the end of every story: "All perfectly normal!" The venomous sarcasm in his tone often made any additional comment on what he had been telling us seem superfluous. Good-natured laughter was response enough.

He was also a financial genius. I am sure that if he had been in the West, he would have become a leading banker. Before his arrest he had handled terrific amounts of money, always keeping within the law in some way or other—or so he told us—and amassed a secret fortune. Perhaps he would have gotten away with it indefinitely if he had behaved with a bit more modesty. He spent money like crazy. Every day he and his family dined in one of Moscow's best restaurants, where everybody knew him. The headwaiter always took Max's little daughter by the hand and led her up to a large bowl filled with fruit or candy. Such restaurants always swarmed with undercover agents. So the question was bound to be asked: How did he come by all that money, and wasn't he perhaps a spy? He was tried and sentenced for embezzlement—in the Soviet Union any kind of private enterprise is illegal. In December of 1942, when Max was found to be seriously ill, he was certified unfit to work.

The second memorable *zek* was a top-notch instrument designer called Leonid Lindberg. He was either a German or a Swede by origin. Because he was a namesake of the American flier, he was immediately dubbed "Charles." He was a member of the party and had been director of a large plant that produced artillery shells. Attesting to his extraordinary ability was the fact that in an isolated region like the taiga and without any specialized manuals, Lindberg set up the process for manufacturing any type of machine tool that we needed. In a series of lectures that he gave at that time, one session dealt with a highly technical problem concerning lathes. It was a tribute to his great knowledge and spectacular memory. To engineers in the free world it must be obvious that a specialist of Lindberg's accomplishments should have made a brilliant career and been assured of prosperity and security throughout his life. But under Stalin he fell a victim to the departmental intrigues that no one in his position could entirely avoid. He was sentenced to eight years under the decree of 1940 which laid down penalties for "impairment of the nation's productive quality." He might well have received a heavier sentence had it not been for his outstanding professional knowledge which had enabled him to refute some of the false charges against him and to turn to his own advantage the mistakes that he caught in the testimony of the witnesses and "experts" called by the prosecution. Otherwise, he might have been convicted of sabotage and given the maximum sentence—death—or a twenty-year term.

In his dealings with us Lindberg showed himself to be an excellent comrade. This fact makes it all the more regrettable that in my own eyes he always stood out as a perfect specimen of the collaborationist. Each day, with the conscientiousness typical of a German, he put his talents and even his personality at the service of the dictatorship in return for his party card. It is a sad fact that the entire Soviet system is kept going by men like Lindberg. Where truly vital matters are concerned, such people are singularly lacking in a proper sense of their own worth. In compliance with party directives, and pushed by the fierce exhortations of the press, they responded to any demand or order within the sphere of their activity with utmost application and care.

Vorkuta at last. The camp to which we were assigned was of tremendous size—seven to eight thousand prisoners, all of whom were employed in one capacity or another at the Capital Coal Mine. We were in luck. Apart from coal mines, however, Vorkuta had a modern engineering plant and two extensive machine shops. There was also a great deal of building, both industrial and residential. This meant that engineers occupied a predominant position in most of the camps of the area. We realized this straightaway, and all of us—both engineers and workers —were very pleased: wherever things are good for engineers, they are good for the workers as well.

The best camp at Vyatlag seemed very inferior to what we found in our new location. At least that is what we thought upon arriving. In spite of being quarantined in the barracks for new arrivals, we were adequately fed. After moving in, we piled our belongings on the bunks and left Lev to guard them while we went outside again. Only Boris had a private food supply and he had promised to put on a feast that evening in celebration of fast-approaching 1945. When we returned a little later, Lev looked very upset. It turned out that he had been tricked by some criminals. They had sat down a short distance off and started smoking. Lev began casting envious glances toward them, and one of yelled out, "Hey, do you want the butt?" Lev fell for it and rushed over to them. But they kept him waiting until the last of the gang had had his puff at the cigarette. While Lev sat there with his back toward our belongings, one of them sneaked away, crawled under the bottom bunks, and pulled out Boris's bag. In the same stealthy manner he got to the door and made off. Drunk from just a few drags on the butt,[10] Lev went back to our things and started checking to see whether they were all still intact. By this time, of course, the criminals had disappeared without a trace. Lev was so distraught that we hastened to do everything we could to console him.

That evening we took a stroll around the zone. Midnight was not far off, but we hadn't a thing to greet the New Year with. We dropped into another barracks, where an acquaintance of the ubiquitous Ruchkin was quartered, but he had already gone off to some friends to welcome in the New Year. Then we sat down near the doorway and Rushkin explained to the barracks orderly that we would stick around until his acquaintance got back. Everyone else in the barracks was asleep. We filled up some jugs with a brew made from pine needles, and when the hands on the clock pointed at twelve, Lev proposed a toast: "Let us drink to our becoming makers of history rather than its objects."

10. I still fail to understand how he managed to combine smoking with being a yogi—that he was one, I have no doubt.

13

VORKUTA

Which Camps Were Worse

The logging camps were considered to be the deadliest of all, but even worse were the gold fields of Kolyma, where the frosts were really vicious. During the war years at Vyatlag, only twice did the temperature drop as low as minus fifty-four degrees,[1] and in a three-year period at Vorkuta it once went down to minus forty-five degrees. But at Kolyma such extreme cold was a daily feature throughout the winter. And yet the prisoners were forced outside to work—even at minus sixty degrees. As a man from a northern clime, I had been used to freezing winters ever since childhood and am still fond of them. After leaving prison, I was a real Moscow "walrus." But I cannot imagine how men in inadequate camp clothing were able to work all day in the cold of Kolyma, especially with a wind blowing. It was outright murder. Every man who worked outdoors aboveground perished; I never met anybody in this category who had come through alive. Most people from there who survived and whom I met had held soft jobs as medical orderlies, etc.

The railroad and highway construction camps took the highest toll of human lives during the years of peace, and probably in wartime as well. In such notorious camps as those which supplied labor for the northern railroads, the Baikal-Amur Line, the Salekhard-Ob Line, and all the new highways, the prisoners were made to lay rails and road surfaces in particularly harsh conditions—their camp zones moved as the construction progressed, so they had no permanent living quarters. They spent night after night in tents with no heat whatsoever, especially when they were

1. Temperatures are given according to centigrade scale, not fahrenheit. (Tr.)

working in treeless areas. Even though the prisoners were eaten alive by lice, they were terrified of taking baths on the rare occasions when it was possible. Icy winds blew through all the chinks in the makeshift bathhouses and there was just no place where they could dry themselves properly. When they came into their quarters thoroughly soaked after working twelve hours in the rain, they would go to sleep on the duck boards rather than on the bunks. In this way their clothes, which they did not remove, had a better chance of drying out. The death rate among them was unimaginably high because of the terrible incidence of disease, particularly of endemic dysentery, since there were no facilities for boiling water. It was very difficult to get anyone to serve as guards in these temporary camp zones except the worst brutes whose cruelty knew no bounds and who loved to take it out of the already unhappy prisoners. Delivery of food supplies was erratic in these places and the bread ration was frequently issued a few days late. We used to say that every railroad tie rested on the dead bodies of several prisoners—and it was the truth.

It had been Kurbatov's intention to have us sent to that sort of camp, which in wartime would have been even worse. But we were lucky: the railroad had already been completed. Instead, we ended up in a long-established camp, where the prisoners were employed on industrial projects. It was the kind which was expected to show results and reach its targets. This meant that competent engineers and technicians were valued to some extent and consequently were kept in relatively good health which made it possible for a man to do his job and sustain life at the same time. In the mining and construction zones, however, unspecialized workers were subjected to relentless exploitation and soon "wore out"—after which they were shipped off to the invalid camps in the Karaganda region. This happened to Lev K., our beloved history professor, after six months in Vorkuta.

At Vorkuta the mines were the equivalent to Vyatlag's logging camps. But although a miner's job was no less fatiguing than a lumberjack's, the food at Vorkuta was adequate, thanks to American aid and to the vital importance of the coal produced in Vorkuta during the winter of 1945–1946. Thus a man in good physical condition could do his work without overtaxing himself.

Most of the new arrivals urgently needed rest and an increased diet over a period of two or three months. Any sensible employer would have seen to this, and it is possible that General Maltsev, the head of the whole Vorkuta combine, would have done so—he had a keen business sense, even if he was a martinet—but the camp system simply did not allow for such things. But at least Maltsev regularly sent large transports of worn-out prisoners to the invalid camps. They were amply made up for by replacements—and the mortality rate there, even in that comparatively good year, could not have fallen much below the average for all Soviet camps. In other words, people were exterminated at Vorkuta during those years on the same scale as in all the other camps.

Our quarantine period lasted about a week. Afterward, we were hustled past the medical commission. In spite of the fact that at Vyatlag I had been classified as an invalid, the commission now stamped my documents, along with everyone else's, with the letters *TT*—meaning "fit for hard labor." Nobody in my group—neither the engineers nor the skilled workmen—really gave a damn, because we knew that our professional skills would save us. But for some who had arrived with us, this classification spelled tragedy, particularly for the Ukrainians and for the middle-aged and elderly, who were already painfully exhausted from the interrogations at Vyatlag and had no familiarity with any kind of factory work.

We did not have to wait long for our job assignments. Boris was sent to the "know-how combine"—this was our nickname for the division where men with an inventive turn of mind and clever hands repaired burned-out electric bulbs of high voltage, manufactured paper, pencils, and other objects. Boris was his own master there. He was given a private room in the barracks, soon found a woman to live with him, and enjoyed the select company of the most educated prisoners in the camp.

Ruchkin landed up in the planning section, Lev in the kitchen, and I in the design department of the engineering plant. Being very proficient at their jobs, Misha Dyachkov and Mishutkin also got jobs in the plant. Salmin was first put on a building site—new wings were being added to the plant. This meant that he had no choice but to live in our barracks. However, we made it clear to him at the outset that the sooner he found himself a berth elsewhere, the better. Three weeks later, he was shipped off to the so-called "Northern District," where a good deal of construction was under way and engineers were much in demand. We never heard anything of him again.

The plant operated in three shifts of eight hours each. Counting the time we spent getting there and back, we put in nearly a nine-hour day. Our position was a privileged one. The diet was sufficient and clothing was appropriate to the season.

The unskilled workers employed to build the new wings—ninety percent of them were women—ordinarily spent twelve hours a day on the job. But not infrequently they were held up an extra two or three hours, because their brigade leader was unable to convince the head foreman that their production quota, excessive as it was, had been more than met. We felt sorry for them, but there was no way we could help them. Theirs was another world. Yet the line dividing it from ours was thin enough, and you could easily find yourself crossing it.

The Communists had started out by promising equal rights to all. But it was not long before equal rights gave way to the most shocking inequalities. We had become so used to the whole scheme of things that the difference, for example, between our situation and that of the other prisoners was generally regarded as a quite natural one and thus was not even worth discussing.

After my first two months in the design department, a former professor at the artillery academy, N. Beresnev, appeared on the scene. He was quite exhausted, but thanks to his warm winter clothes, he had at least escaped frostbite during a very trying journey to Vorkuta—he had been transported in a cattle car. Since our drawing boards were side by side, we quickly became friends.

The next transport brought a Russified Dutchman called Heinrich van Bibe. He was also in very poor shape, and after putting in a few days at our office, he fell ill and went into the camp infirmary. As soon as he had put on a bit of weight, he returned to work in his capacity as a metallurgical engineer and got a new foundry ready for production.

Within a very short time Beresnev, van Bibe, and I became inseparable, and during our first year in Vorkuta, before we were issued passes to move freely about the whole camp area, the three of us whiled away the long arctic nights very agreeably in each other's company. Petrovich, as we called the professor, was a marvelous storyteller, in no way inferior to either Lev or Boris. My trading operations in tobacco, which I still received on occasion, were taken over by Heinrich; so on top of it all, we could smoke at no cost. Total bliss.

"A Trite and Bourgeois Mind"

Petrovich was a native of Vyatka—now called Kirov—the chief city of the region where Vyatlag was set up back in the thirties. Until 1917 Petrovich and his family had lived in modest comfort. His father was employed by a steamship line and late in life became a junior partner in the firm. His mother looked after the house, and his brother and sister went to the local high school. Every Sunday the mother baked pies, and the entire

216

family went to both matins and vespers in the cathedral, where the boys sang in the choir. They kept geraniums on the window ledges of the house. Life for this industrious family flowed along serenely. They did their best to be good citizens; during the First World War they made donations for the benefit of wounded servicemen; Petrovich's father bought war bonds; mother and sister knitted warm articles of clothing for the soldiers. His father saw the overthrow of the tsar as the end of Russia.

Shortly after the October Revolution, a detachment of fifteen sailors arrived in town. They kicked out the elected representatives to the city council and introduced the new Bolshevik "order." Two reserve regiments of the old Imperial Army were stationed in Vyatka but they offered not even a show of resistance. The only people to put up a fight were the members of a hunting club—old men with smoothbore rifles. Most of them had fought in the Balkan War way back in 1877 and they were not frightened of bullets. They tried to storm the city council building but were met by machine-gun fire. Nearly all of them were mowed down on the spot: the Cheka mopped up the survivors. The dregs of society were now absolute masters over the citizens of Vyatka. Soon there were searches, arrests, executions of hostages, requisitioning of private property, and compulsory labor service of all kinds. People began denouncing each other and mutual mistrust was deliberately fostered among them. They had never been so humiliated and degraded before. Petrovich, however, seldom talked about the end of the idyllic days in Vyatka. Most of the time he chose to recall all that was good in the lives of ordinary Russian families in the pre-Revolutionary era. Regrettably, he referred to people of his class as *meshchanye*.[2] Petrovich, obviously trying to get a rise from us, would puff out his cheeks a little and then proclaim "I belong to the *meshchanye!* I am a *poshlyak*[3] and proud of it!" Although we took it as a joke, it actually made immeasurably more sense for us than any so-called revolutionary doctrine with its chimerical promises of a happy future for everyone—which had to be paid for by millions of lives and led to the enslavement of the nation.

Before his arrest Petrovich had lectured at his academy on machine components. He apparently was so preoccupied with the subject that, to our regret, he did not find the time to write down and expand on what he had observed in his early years—not even in the diary which he kept

2. This word can designate either townsmen belonging to the middle class, usually on the lower rungs of it, or people with commonplace interests and narrow views.
3. Petrovich is saying in effect that he is just a plain, ordinary citizen—a common man; *poshlyak,* however, is usually employed in a derogatory sense, meaning a vulgarian, a Babbit. (Tr.)

faithfully while in camp. All he managed to put down were a few generalizations which showed how attached he had been to the simple comforts of the old days. He also noted down that the happiness of ordinary humans has its basis in hearth and home—symbolized by those red geraniums, for example, which testified to the beginnings of material well-being. This truth was a new revelation for us Russians, whereas the West had recognized it for ages.

Petrovich's expressions of respect and love for the "trite and bourgeois mind" amounted to saying that every man should be the owner of a private residence for himself and his family, and earn a wage substantial enough to provide the necessities of life. Furthermore, he should enjoy civil liberties, have the capacity to defend both himself and his peers in the face of danger, bring up his children in a religious faith, and have access to truthful information.

The Secret Millionaire

Throughout that winter at Vorkuta, the three of us worked as ordinary designers. At 4:30 P.M. we returned to the barracks. After a leisurely hour at dinner, we had the whole evening to ourselves. Petrovich would tell us his stories, and the rest of us were appreciative listeners, while taking our ease and restoring our strength. Now and then we got into fierce discussions.

Most of Petrovich's tales offered vivid scenes from everyday life in a Russian provincial town. It was like a beautiful dream. But in my own mind, all his stories blended into a single picture of the wholesome, happy, busy life of a people who rejoiced in their strength and knew that they counted for something. It was all doomed to destruction. But throughout that winter we avoided talking about the catastrophe which had overtaken it.

On one occasion Petrovich told in great detail, as only he could do, about a secret millionaire with whom he had shared a cell for quite a long period in a transit prison. It seems that he was an unusually intelligent man, apparently with an outlook much like Petrovich's and mine. At the time Petrovich knew him, the man was about forty. During the time of one of the purges in the 'twenties, he was thrown out of the Plekhanov Institute of National Economics while in his second year. He had in any case already realized that he was wasting his time there and had been meaning to leave of his own free will. He had been required to attend endless classes in political indoctrination, and he was sick to death of all the absurd meetings students were forced to go to, not to mention various kinds of "voluntary" work. The trial in 1928 of the engineers who were guilty of absolutely nothing, the campaign against "wreckers" that went on for three years, and the general policy of harassing specialists convinced him that his decision to get himself kicked out of the institute had been the right one. In those days, the starvation rates of pay were the same for everybody, whether you were an accountant, a teacher, a skilled workman, an engineer, or a physician. Furthermore, a diploma exposed you to increased surveillance on the part of the secret police and the danger of being held responsible for anything that went wrong. After making a cold-blooded appraisal of the whole situation, Petrovich's acquaintance decided that he could do much better for himself by exploiting the shortcomings of the Soviet accounting system. But first he had to make a careful study of it, so he got himself hired as a bookkeeper. Soon afterward, he went into another office as a junior accountant. This place was a division of the Central Cooperative Society and dealt in dairy products. He soon understood that a great deal of public money was being embezzled. This was exactly what he needed. He watched everything that went on, but was careful not to get involved himself. Then one day the inevitable happened: as a result of some departmental intrigue or a denunciation from a stool pigeon, all the employees were arrested. An investigation and trial followed. Since it was not a political case our hero was allowed to examine the record taken during the preliminary investigation and the court proceedings. Armed with all this technical knowledge and experience, he then got a job with a state organization involved with meat products. His tactics were the same as before. When this organization also ran afoul of the law (in a big way and with a hint of sabotage), he was called in to give expert testimony. He was paid a miserable salary. During this whole period, 1929–1934, when food and consumer goods were rationed in the cities, his income just sufficed for purchasing the minimum allowed.

By the end of the second trial, he concluded that his apprenticeship had lasted long enough and that the time had come to start lining his pocket. During his "training" period he had been able to make some useful contacts; he now got a new job which offered the right opportunities. He carefully chose associates of proven reliability, and in the course of nearly ten years, he brought off a number of brilliant schemes. He enriched not only himself but his protégés as well to the tune of several million rubles, at state expense. Bearing in mind all the mistakes of his predecessors, he never once set foot in a restaurant. And he did not wear expensive clothes. As for owning a car, he didn't even dream of it. The small private apartment he had been lucky enough to get was furnished according to the prevailing standards of poverty and wretchedness. He acquired a dozen or so apartments and country dachas, but always under the names of relatives or middlemen. In the same way, he bought antique furniture and invested large sums in jewelry and foreign currency. When he really wanted to enjoy life, he headed for one of his dachas—after bribing doctors to give him a medical certificate enabling him to take sick leave for a certain number of days. As soon as the war began, he purchased exemptions from military service for both himself and his closest accomplices.

His arrest in 1944 came to him as no surprise. As a matter of fact, he was fully prepared for it. Even before the event, he had hired an eminent lawyer and set aside money for bribing the interrogator, the prosecutor, and other members of the tribunal. While in prison, he received a weekly package containing the choicest American food stuffs, although other prisoners were allowed to receive packages much less frequently. The guards even used to make cocoa for him. According to the letter of the law, he was sentenced to ten years. In addition, the authorities confiscated his personal property, which was represented as being two wornout suits and the wretched furniture in his "legal" apartment (though in fact they took away only about a third of the furniture). All his wealth, of course, remained beyond their reach. The lawyer and the court officials, out of gratitude for the handsome fees he had paid them, and hoping to receive more in the future, began thinking of ways to win his release as soon as possible. At first they considered trying to arrange for his escape in some foolproof manner, but on hearing that a general amnesty would be declared after the war, they decided it would be better to wait for this. The millionaire was quite cheerful—even rather smug—about the whole thing and liked to lecture Petrovich about the difference between them. Talking of the amnesty which might be granted, he put up a mock-defense of the Soviet government's policy. His argument was roughly as follows:

"For example, let's take you, Professor," he would say. "You've lost everything—position, personal belongings, even your clothes. You and your family are labeled enemies of the people. Your apartment in Moscow is occupied by other people now. And the one you had in Samarkand, where you were evacuated, was taken away the moment they arrested you there. No doubt, you feel they've done you a great wrong, especially when you stop to consider that you didn't commit any real crimes. But since you're now embittered to the depth of your soul, you really do represent a potential danger to Soviet society. The leader of our people, Comrade Stalin, takes this into account. So he will hardly extend his pardon to include political prisoners like you. But it's a different story with me. I'm very well off and have no reason to harbor a grudge against the Soviet authorities. Once they turn me loose, they'll be getting a trust-worthy member of society—one not given to thoughts of subversion, one who will support the actions of both the party and the government. . . . Have a cigarette, Professor. And sample the smoked fish. It's pretty good. . . ."

Petrovich told me that the millionaire's ironic tone, together with the expression in his eyes, made it quite clear that in his mind he was really saying something else: "You and your kind are damned fools! And yet you think you're so clever. All you do is it and talk about nothing. You're incapable of action. You should take a lesson from me: I robbed them of tens of millions of rubles and got off very lightly. I hate this regime as much as you do. But I fought it with figures, using the methods of the ordinary people. You intellectuals can never change your ways. Well, you can just rot here till you die—no one is going to be very sorry for you."

14

VORKUTA
(Continued)

The Jugglers

I first heard the well-known medieval legend, *The Juggler of the Mother of God,* from a young fellow who, as a displaced person, had worked in Germany during the war and was later convicted by the Soviets of collaborating with the Nazis. Some time long ago, in the south of Italy, there was a wandering juggler with a son who had fallen gravely ill. His condition appeared hopeless. The juggler sent up a fervent prayer to the Madonna. Though his words were rough and simple, there could be no doubt about the strength of his sincerity and faith. A miracle took place: help was granted and the boy recovered. The grateful father stepped inside the first roadside chapel that he came to and stood awe-stricken before the image of the Madonna. Unhappy about the illiterate prayer that he had addressed to her earlier, he went down on his knees and started tossing his clubs into the air. The Mother of God nodded her head and smiled.

I was reminded of the juggler that spring when Petrovich, now fully recovered from the ordeal of his journey to Korkuta, lovingly described to us during our evening conversations the work on cam gears which he had first begun in evacuation at Samarkand. If it had not been of direct interest to the military, one would only have rejoiced that he still had the strength of mind to carry on his scientific research even in these conditions, but in this case I could not refrain from giving him the benefit of my experience in such matters.

"Petrovich, exactly whose favor do you hope to win with your juggling act? You may be a professor specializing in tool-making, but I also am a specialist—a specialist in living under prison conditions. Now listen to me for a while. Your hopes are all in vain. At best, your work will simply get lost and never see the light of day. At worst, it will be stolen by somebody else and be published under his name. It's not going to bring you either an early release or a reduced sentence. You won't get anything out of it except humiliation. Be more conscious of your personal dignity. Learn from my mistakes: remember my work on the land mines. You must agree with me that we should not participate in any project that serves a military purpose or directly strengthens the regime. As long as you and I are engaged at the Vorkuta engineering works in repairing coal-mining machinery, we can take comfort in the fact that it is being restored for peaceful purposes. But your cam gears would go inside range finders or similar complex and murderous artillery instruments. You know more about all this than I do. Wake up and have done with it! What you're doing now is juggling before the Devil."

Petrovich belonged to that punctilious, overzealous breed of people who in the camps earned only ridicule, condemnation, and sometimes hatred from the other prisoners. The fate that had befallen all the prisoners had made of them one giant clan, and much of the effort of the Chekists, needless to say, went into trying to destroy this unity. And this unfortunate circumstance made it even more important that not one of us should behave in a way detrimental to his fellow prisoners. I often had to have a word with Petrovich on this score—especially after he was named head of the technical department—and remind him of the conditions in which we all found ourselves. Regrettably, the merciless environment had taught us ruthless egoism. Most engineers with an inventive turn of mind were seduced into collaborating at one time or another and the creation of the special prison research establishments for work on secret projects was the result of such proneness to temptation, rather than of any long-range scheme elaborated by the Chekists. At Vyatlag I had myself helped in the production of land mines. Back in 1941, Georgi had succeeded in ousting the stool pigeons from the machine shop not simply by guaranteeing more efficient production but also by suggesting a new military device, which, with Yuri's help, he had submitted to the authorities. At the time, this had seemed to us a reasonable price to pay for strengthening the position of our group in the machine shop, but how do we know that this very useful idea suggested by these two talented engineers might not later find practical application in strengthening the war machine?

Georgi's suggested invention, however, was nothing—a mere escapade in the spirit of Gil Blas—in contrast to the case of another engineer, Makhotin. This man had come out in our transport from Moscow, and then, together with other engineers from the Putilov Works, was sent to a logging camp. All his colleagues had either perished there in 1942 or ended life in the barracks for the dying. Georgi discovered that Makhotin, on arriving at Vyatlag, had boasted of his loyalty to the party, his exceptional qualifications, excellent connections, and great projects, which he proposed to put into effect right under the eyes of the Chekists, virtually without leaving his office. Early in 1942, he again showed up in our midst, wearing a peaked winter cap and a heavy brown coat of excellent quality. Several times a day he went to the kitchen to fill his unusually large mess can. His work was top secret, and he was doing it in the office of the security officer, at his own suggestion. About the same time we became aware that two ex-Putilov engineers had been thrown into the cells and that Makhotin had played a suspicious part in this. We all gave him a wide berth, convinced that he had stolen his invention from another engineer of extraordinary ability. About two months later, he was shipped out of the camp on a special assignment, very likely to a *sharshka,* where the military engine he had been working on would be readied for production.

A Test of My Professional Ability

Petrovich advanced rapidly in his new job. The rest of us learned a great deal from him. With his help, I not only got a better understanding of how to adjust cogwheels, but was also able to solve such problems as deducing from an examination of its cogs what specifications had been used in the manufacture of a broken crankshaft. All this was interesting and useful to me. These little matters sustained my lifelong love of engineering, even though they gave me no real opportunity to test my professional ability in practice.

The engineering-design unit and the forge were located in the same building. Since each day I frequently had to go past the hammer presses, I was able to take a close look at the work being done there. What struck me in particular was the great variety of forging operations. On lathes and other cutting equipment, the so-called machine time for processing a piece is usually estimated according to the number of turns that the spindle has to make, the original dimensions of the piece, the depth to which it must be cut, etc. To put it briefly, the minimum time for processing an item can be calculated in advance of the operation by referring to very reliable technical specifications which were worked out years ago and have been incorporated into standard manufacturing procedure.

In respect to forging operations, however, the processing time is reckoned differently. As a matter of fact, it has been worked out systematically to a very limited degree, in spite of the fact that the blacksmith's trade has been practiced almost from days immemorial. In the manuals, only timings for separate phases of a forging operation are indicated. From these the production engineer attempts to derive standard measures for determining the whole amount of time required for processing an article from start to finish in a forging operation. Only a first-class engineer could cope with a task like this, and then only in a forge engaged in mass production where the same item was being turned out on a large scale; but where it was mainly a question of differing individual orders—as in our forge—fixed timings were both difficult and unreliable.

However, watching as a piece that was being processed changed its dimensions under the blows of the hammer, I suddenly thought: why not solve this time problem by estimating how much labor is spent on deformation of the piece and by determining the efficiency rate of the forging operations for both the entire processing period and the separate phases of it. Using the original size of the piece as a basis, it would not be difficult to calculate the amount of labor that goes into deformation. And by time keeping, the efficiency rate of the forging operations could be determined.

Petrovich, along with the other engineers, believed that, because of the great diversity of forging operations, a single method of the kind I proposed was not feasible. Thus they saw no practical value in my idea and predicted that it was doomed to failure. They said that three lifetimes would be needed to work out a problem of such magnitude. But I nevertheless wanted to try it out as a test of my abilities, to find out whether I had the qualities of mind needed for carrying out a much higher mission: that of delivering people of the world from the threat of a further spread of Communism. I felt that, if my efforts at resolving the time problem proved successful, I would be capable of providing constructive answers in dealing with this other—and more important—question.

Despite my friends' attempts to dissuade me, I got myself transferred as production engineer to the forge shop and took on the responsibility for fixing production quotas there. My first step was to appoint two timekeepers; within six months I added three more. Together we compiled a manual for setting quotas on a technically sound basis. The production schedule could not, of course, be held up while I was making my theoretical calculations; so we had to make educated guesses as to how some of it would work out in practice. My head was functioning pretty well in spite of the mediocre quality of the daily diet. The current work ran smoothly. During this initial, and most difficult, period I let only five serious mistakes get by, whereas there had been one after another before the introduction of my method—conclusive evidence that my idea was basically a sound one. My work was of purely engineering interest and had no connection with war production. It appealed to the camp administration inasmuch as it promised to bring some order into an extremely neglected aspect of production, and I was assigned to the technical division of the Vorkuta Coal Combine. For a prisoner this was a position of some consequence: I was given a permit to travel without a guard within a thirty-kilometer radius beyond the barbed-wire zone, and my rations were considerably improved.

My day began at four in the morning, when, at my request, the barracks orderly awoke me. Until seven I remained in the barracks to work on my calculations. From eight to five, except for an hour at mess, I was at the plant. Shortly after five I would lie down fully clothed on my bunk and cover my head in order to drown out the din and chatter of my friends just returning from work. I slept until seven or seven-thirty. After supper, from half-past eight until midnight I poured over books that were necessary for my project. This extra sleep enabled me to have two good working periods each day. For over two years I held strictly to this schedule. For the most part the problem I had set out to solve proved to be unusually complex. At Vorkuta I did about ninety percent of the work on it and finished it off completely during the next twelve years. But it was not until 1959, in Moscow, that I was finally able to have published a brief summary of my study. It shows that forging technology can be transformed from an uncoordinated set of operations into a streamlined system by clearly defining the time factor for all the separate phases, which are thus combined into a single whole.

After my release, I could undoubtedly have defended a dissertation on my Vorkuta research project. But I had no time to prepare myself for the various examinations involved, and apart from that, I had no desire to make myself any more conspicuous than I could help.

226

"His Lowness"

At the end of 1946 our food took a turn for the worse. American supplies were no longer coming in, and in many regions of the country yet another famine was beginning. Some of us received parcels from home, and those who were able managed to get by on these. The workers in the factory made lighters, cigarette holders, and cases which were then sold outside the camp by prisoners with passes to move around freely. I had to make do with the camp ration.

Many of us were in charge of key areas of production. Heinrich was named head of the foundry. An old Vorkuta hand, Kostya Mitin, became chief technician for the plant as a whole, and Dima Shchapov was made responsible for installing new machinery and equipment. A number of other shops were also put under the direction of prisoners. At that time the machinery was all American-made—we were quite dazzled by the names of the firms—and several of us who knew English were put to work translating the operating instructions which came with it.

Our plant was given important jobs to do. Under Kostya's direction a group of engineers assembled a frame for a railroad bridge that was to span the Vorkuta River. Another group oversaw the construction and installation of equipment for a cement factory. In view of the essential nature of our work, the camp commandant was greatly dependent on the plant director and often made concessions to him. As a result, the most responsible of the engineers—twelve in all—were allowed to share a separate room in one of the smaller barracks, with each man having a bunk that bore some resemblance to a real bed. Our trio—Petrovich, Heinrich, and myself—were among the lucky dozen.

Our cozy evening chats came to an end. Now that they had passes, Petrovich and Heinrich seemed to spend most of their time at the plant. But once a week the appeal rang out, "Everybody fork over thirty rubles!"[1] and, after collecting the donations, someone would go out and buy liquor. In view of our special position the guards looked the other way when the "field marshals," as they called us, were having a party. We would have our drinks while still at the plant, and then go back to the barbed-wire zone for the real fun.

We needed to let off steam, to laugh and joke a little. And although there was not much reason to celebrate, with a bit of alcohol and much ingenuity we managed to get into the right mood. The highlight was al-

---

1. These are rubles of the Stalin period (see note, p. 165). In Vorkutlag I received, as a specialist, two hundred rubles monthly.

ways a mock jousting tournament. Those of lighter build mounted the shoulders of their larger comrades and, flourishing pillows, endeavored to topple an opponent from his "horse." The rules of the game did not permit the "horse" to use his hands in order to hold on to his rider. We roared with laughter until our sides were sore. Our intoxication quickly wore off, and the "jousters" fell into a sleep worthy of the knights of old.

In our earlier days at Vorkuta, during our evening discussions we had often talked about the human affinity for titles and status. I was of the opinion that aspiration toward so-called equality—especially with one's betters—is a manifestation of envy. As soon as the average revolutionary receives a title and an income, he will calm down, and the revolution can go to hell as far as he is concerned—though this, of course, does not apply to the small minority of fanatics. Petrovich would argue heatedly that ordinary people had no hankering whatsoever after titles—all they needed were the comforts of hearth and home and they didn't care a damn about anything else. Petrovich's eloquence prevailed, and for the time being, we had to agree with him. Now, under more favorable circumstances and with no informers in our midst, we set up an experiment involving us twelve prisoners, all of whom were Soviet citizens, including four ex-party members. Our origins lay in either the peasantry, the working class, or, like Petrovich's, in the old lower middle class, the *meshchanye*. During one of our "thirty-ruble" binges, Petrovich proposed that everybody have conferred upon him a title to his liking. Kostya, the noisiest and cocksurest of all our crowd, wanted to be a prince and to be addressed as "Your Highness"; Valyera also insisted on the same. Petrovich and I became "counts," and Heinrich a "baron." As I had expected, the game thoroughly delighted everyone. There was much joking and laughter, and instead of its ending with that one night's spree, the game continued for days.

My life now became much easier and more agreeable. Previously I had been forced to waste a tremendous amount of time and go through endless bureaucratic procedures just to secure the most basic tools for my men who were working on the time-keeping problem in the forge shop, or to lay my hands on an optical pyrometer or a stop watch. But now everything changed. I could walk into Valyera's department, for example, and say in a low voice to someone who knew about our game, "Announce to your prince that Count Panin humbly beseeches a brief audience of him." Within a few minutes the door to the office would be opened halfway in a ceremonious gesture, and I would be told, "Your presence is requested." Approaching the desk at which Valyera was seated, I would address him as "Your Highness," and his broad mouth would stretch in a grin from ear to ear, and the green-flecked eyes in his pockmarked face shine with rapture.

"Have a seat, Count. I am at your service."

"Most worthy Prince, forgive me for intruding. You are engaged in solving a problem of the greatest urgency, while my request is of so paltry a nature that I find it embarrassing even to bring it to your attention."

"What are you talking about, Count! I am always glad to see you. What's on your mind?"

Valyera spoke with warmth and sincerity. There had been times, however, when we were considerably less friendly toward each other. I now indulged in outright flattery and I addressed him by his "title" twice more as I stated my request. Everything was settled quickly and amicably.

Petrovich, by his own definition a *meshchanin,* a trite and bourgeois mind, had one fault: he talked too much and was fond of gossip. On two occasions he was admonished on that score, and on the third he was threatened with a beating—despite the fact that he was a professor. The first two instances I managed to smooth over, but this was before the introduction of "titles" and the whole business was tricky and unpleasant. The third time, after a much more flagrant breach of conduct, I went to the injured party who happened to be the other "prince," Kostya. Because his ways were those of a hardened camp veteran and he was fond of the same sort of tricks as the criminals, his "title" was soon to be converted into "His Lowness"—a nickname that no doubt stuck to him forever. But at that moment he was still "His Highness," and I set out on my unpleasant mission to his official "residence," taking "Baron" Heinrich along as the other "second." We adopted the reserved tone appropriate to "seconds."

"Has Your Highness had a good night's sleep?" Heinrich inquired.

I stopped him. "Baron! You are going too far. You are much younger and inferior in rank. You will speak only when His Highness addresses you first."

"His Highness" was quite pleased with all this pomp and ceremony. As we talked, I translated his camp-style threat "to beat the daylight out of Petrovich" into language more in the tone of the gentlemen's dueling code and insisted on a peaceful settlement between two such high-ranking personages. We soon succeeded in smoothing over feelings quickly and painlessly. After moving to new quarters we gave up our game of "titles."

They say that in Old Russia the boyars kept professional buffoons in their retinues. Very probably they did, for we ourselves saw such types in the camps. In a neighboring barracks, for instance, the duty officer kept a crazed Trotskyite called Ruvim who sang in a hoarse voice—or, to be more precise, caterwauled—the Nazi anthem *Horst Wessel,* his eyes bulging and twitching. It was for this performance that the duty officer prized him.

Ruvim had gone mad during one of the executions at Vorkuta. These were always carried out by shooting in one of the abandoned stone quarries just outside the city as punishment for alleged offenses in the camps. At the end of the war, the firing squad was made up of towheaded, puny youngsters, hardly more than fledglings. Prisoners who were returned to our camp after undergoing interrogations and receiving an additional sentence told how those kids, almost in tears, pounced on one strapping bandit. They had a struggle tying him up and leading him out to be shot. Rumors went around that they were the sons of Chekists who had managed to fix them up with safe jobs as executioners to save them from service at the front.

Besides these everyday shootings there were also two mass executions at Vorkuta. The first went down in the memory of eyewitnesses as the work of the so-called "Grigorovich Commission." In 1938 the famous strike of the Trotskyites broke out. At dozens of camps, scattered over a vast area, everyone refused to go out to work. Official reaction was swift and vigorous. Reprisals were taken against the strikers by a detachment of Chekists led by Grigorovich. The Trotskyites were then transported to a camp where a brick factory was located and each day some of them were shot to death. Not many survived—only a few very young and unimportant ones, including Ruvim, and several stool pigeons who had particularly distinguished themselves in their role. Naturally, everyone subsequently avoided them as if they were infected with some loathsome disease.

The second mass executions under the supervision of a Chekist called Kashketin mainly affected the criminal element. I never met any eyewitnesses to it because of the terrible toll taken by the war years of camp prisoners from that period. But there were stories according to which Kashketin had picked mostly on bandits and any one else who might be considered a potentially dangerous troublemaker. The criminals got scared and began to turn out for work, and put their backs into it—but only until Kashketin and his colleagues returned to Moscow.

Kashketin would begin his daily program by having the prisoners lined up in formation for inspection. While making the rounds, he would stop suddenly and fix his eyes on a likely prospect. Then came the order: "Step out of ranks." This meant certain death before the firing squad. Whenever he came up to one of the thugs, who were easily distinguishable from the other prisoners, he would question him about his nicknames and aliases and make him list all of them. After that he was led off.

In our fashionable "field marshals' " quarters we managed well enough, but the cruel facts of life all around us were much in evidence. In the coal mines, and especially in the zones where the criminal element held sway, things were done that would have made anyone's hair stand on end, even ours—and we had seen just about everything. One gang leader, for instance, found out that his girl friend had been cozy with a *frayer*. The gang put her on trial in their own court and passed sentence: they undressed her, cut off her breasts, disfigured her to a hideous degree, and threw her bodily out of the barracks. At the camp headquarters she refused to name her tormenters because she did not want to lose her standing with the criminals and preferred to die as one of them.

On another occasion, some criminals brought liquor into the barbed-wire zone. After getting drunk, they went on a rampage. They broke into the kitchen, wolfed down the choicest provisions, and then urinated into all the cooking pots.

At the mines life was especially hard on the Balts, whom the criminals had dubbed "lamps" because of their slight mispronunciation of the Russian word for this item of a miner's equipment. The crooks, of course, landed the best jobs for themselves and their buddies, lording it over the Balts, whom they robbed and beat mercilessly. It was the Balts who did the heaviest and most dangerous work.

At one of the mines, Lithuanians and Bendera Ukrainians, ex-partisans who had fought in the forests against the Stalinists, formed a solid alliance, overthrew the reigning thugs, and themselves took control of things, including the food distribution. Life in their zone now became bearable.

In our zone the chief of the planning division was a handsome fellow with dark blue eyes. He was by no means a great intellect, but as one who abided by the simple, clear-cut principles of Christian ethics, he skillfully adapted them to the conditions within our zone. His strong-mindedness not only kept the flunkies in control, but also had a substantial effect on the civilian overseers who worked there. He demanded that the official food ration be distributed with absolute fairness to everyone, and in particular that the best foodstuffs should be given directly to the prisoners instead of coming to them only via the mess. The consequence was that thievery in the kitchen, hitherto unbridled, decreased considerably. He did all this unobtrusively, and we only learned about it later because he occupied a bunk next to Petrovich for about a year.

Someone in our own highly privileged community had been sent a book on ancient Egypt. Upon reading it, one could not help drawing analogies. The slaves who erected the pyramids were fortunate men by comparison with the slaves who supported the structure of Stalinist tyranny. The Egyptians were quite well fed. They even got a clove of garlic in their daily allotment. And there was no freezing cold in the desert. Since a slave had market value, he warranted some care and attention, instead of being regarded as an enemy who had to be quickly destroyed.

Many times it came home to us that men of good will only had to unite and become aware of their duty and strength for evil to give way and retreat, eventually ceasing to be effective even within its own stronghold.

On the Wings of Love

Some of the Decembrists' wives set out for the Siberian prisons where their husbands were serving penal terms. They went out in closed carriages and under all the protection that money, titled positions, and loyal servants could provide. Naturally, they aroused the admiration of society and the sympathy of local officials, and to some extent, their hard road was made somewhat smoother.

Under the Stalinist regime the wives of men convicted under Article 58 were forbidden to visit their husbands. The extremely rare exceptions were liable to entail grave consequences. In return for our compilation of the manual on production quotas, I and another prisoner by the name of Bulgakov received from the camp administration, with the approval of the Ministry of Internal Affairs, permission for our wives to visit us.

Insofar as I could do anything about it, I did not want to contribute further to my wife's distress, but since she was herself very anxious to come and see me, I hadn't the heart to discourage her. At that time, she still loved me very much. Somehow the darker aspects of life had bypassed her, not affecting her purity of spirit. She had very little understanding of the world we lived in. I had never shared my own thoughts and ideas about it with her. It seemed to me that between the male and the female realms there was a sharp dividing line that one had to observe: it was for the man to resolve life's more serious problems; it was for the woman to look after the home and children, to involve herself in art and religion. Now that I am in my declining years, I can see that my view still holds true: women are designed expressly for motherhood and caring for the family.

At Vorkuta there were a great many Russianized Germans. Among them were some excellent men. In the camps they were made to suffer nearly as much as our own people. During the first year of the war all Germans who were capable of working—and who were guilty of nothing at all—were packed off to the camps as so-called "labor conscripts" (this term was invented to distinguish them from the other prisoners). They had worked in the logging camps of the Vyatlag district under the very same conditions as our people. Their women and children had been shipped to places of exile. By the time I am now describing, fewer than half of the Russianized German prisoners were still alive. Nearly all those in the prime of life or older had perished.

There was one detail that smacked of Swiftian grotesqueness: the Germans had been allowed to keep their party and trade-union cards. Thus it was that these live skeletons behind barbed wire had to organize and attend party and trade-union meetings, where they were expected to praise Comrade Stalin to the skies for the happy life he had granted them, and to sanction every action of the Soviet state, including their own imprisonment.

I was now able to make arrangements with some German engineers, good acquaintances of mine, to receive my wife in a room in a little snow-covered house where there was a supply of coal which had been laid in the previous autumn. It was a lucky thing for me that the bachelor who normally lived there had gone off on a lengthy assignment. I had a pass that allowed me to leave the camp, but as a convict I was forbidden to set foot inside the railroad station. Therefore, I sent two young colleagues, Misha and Petya, to meet my wife. Although they were also living in prisoners' barracks inside the barbed-wire zone, by some irony peculiar to the Stalinist system they were considered free men, for as yet they had been neither indicted nor sentenced. In theory, since they had served as Vlasovites, the two were simply being held pending an examination of their case. Late in 1946, Vlasov men, as well other former Soviet war prisoners, began receiving terms of twenty-five years—in rare instances, ten.

I should explain that new categories of prisoners began to arrive in the camps in the years right after war. There were huge contingents of Vlasovites, war prisoners, displaced persons, legionnaires, soldiers from "national" Nazi SS divisions, Germans who were regarded as war criminals, followers of the Ukrainian nationalist, Bendera, White émigrés, including many who had fought as Vlasovites. As far as we in the camp were concerned, these new groups may be defined as follows.

The Vlasovites: Russian troops who had fought against Stalin's forces, either as members of German Wehrmacht units or of the purely Russian divisions organized by the Nazis under the command of the ex-Soviet general, A. A. Vlasov. Their numbers exceeded one million.

Prisoners of war: Red Army officers and men who ended up in Germany either in POW camps or at slave labor. The first five million who were captured in 1941 had looked on Hitler as a liberator and had no desire to offer resistance against his armies. In the years that ensued, the vast majority of those who fell captive to the Nazis did not surrender willingly. The Vlasovites were recruited from both kinds of POW's.

Displaced persons: Soviet civilians whom the Germans had forcibly transported to Germany where they were put to work. A good many of these people, however, had gone there voluntarily.

The legionnaires: special military units that the Germans had formed from various Soviet, but non-Russian nationalities: Kazakhs, Kalmyks, Caucasians, Georgians, and others.

The SS: Elite Nazi troops, including divisions made up of Baltic nationals (Latvians, Lithuanians, Estonians).

Bendera's followers: Ukrainian nationalists, mainly from the western Ukraine, under the leadership of Stepan Bendera. They waged guerilla warfare against both Hitler's and Stalin's forces.

There was hardly a better place for learning about a man than prison, transport, or camp. Out in civilian life you might work alongside people for ten years and not know them as well as you would after spending two days with them in a transit jail. Since in a camp situation you had contact with a man every single day, you could not help finding out what he was really like. If a fellow prisoner was honest and aboveboard with you, then you repaid him in kind. Your enslaved condition was mitigated by a sense of inner freedom. The prospect that you might die tomorrow disposed you to pour out your soul. At Vyatlag I closely observed those who had been war prisoners in Germany, and at Vorkuta those who had served in the Vlasov forces. At the forging shop, among my work crew of five men, two were Vlasovites.

Vlasovites should not be compared with conscripted Soviet soldiers, but rather with those who volunteered for service in the Red Army and stayed in it for patriotic and idealist reasons. Either individually or in accord with their comrades, the men who joined the Vlasov Army had decided that there was no alternative except to fight the most terrible kind of war—one on both sides of the front and against two opposing despots. While the idealist Red Army men supported the Stalinist tyranny, the Vlasovites were resolved that it had to be destroyed. Naturally, back home the families of the Vlasovites were treated as hostages by the Soviet state, whereas the families of "patriotic" officers received financial assistance from it. In the eyes of the world as well as in our own, we would have appeared as a nation of abject slaves if, after all that we had endured over twenty-five years, the Vlasov Army had not come into existence. But venal Soviet journalists have taken great pains to slander and denigrate these heroes from among the ordinary people. One cannot avoid noting that whenever people of high position commit a gross blunder, our journalists make excuses for it or simply overlook it. When they pass judgment on ordinary people, these same journalists forget that those who created their disastrous situation are the truly guilty ones.

Our work in the forging shop had been going along very smoothly, so much so that I was able to let my men off for a three-day rest; and for the remaining time that I would be absent from the shop, I gave them their working instructions in advance. I had no intention of showing up at the plant for one whole week. I assumed that permission to visit with my wife gave me this right. The question of lodgings—even with heat—had been settled with the aid of kind people. As for food, we would have to get around that problem with the resourcefulness which by now was second nature to Soviet citizens. There was famine in parts of the country, and everywhere severe shortages, as well as the inevitable ration cards. Moscow was no better off than any other place, and my wife was unable to bring much with her. Heinrich brought my camp ration to us in a special lunch pail of three compartments, and she somehow managed to add touches of her own, thus changing it into a home-cooked dinner. Since bread was then rather cheap in the camp, I had no trouble providing us with a second ration of it for a little money.

In the evenings friends dropped in—Petrovich, Heinrich, and several other men in our circle who had passes. My wife treated us to homemade delicacies and brewed a beverage which bore some resemblance to coffee. Everyone was more than content. I placed a very strict injunction against political discussions, and we got along quite well without them. Petrovich in particular filled the gap. His tales of day-to-day life in another era were both relaxing and interesting—and to my wife, even romantic. She promised him that on the return trip she would stop off in Kirov (as Vyatka was now called) to pay his mother a visit. She and

Petrovich spent considerable time thinking over what she should tell the old lady about her son.

One evening Heinrich embarked on his pet historical thesis, namely: that during the time of Bismarck, Germany and Russia could have united into a single nation. He set forth the advantages, prospects, opportunities, as well as the power, that would have resulted from such a union. His little blue eyes shining and his face all aflush, "Cast-Iron Heinrich," as we used to call him, overwhelmed us with reasons and proofs. Actually, all of what he said had much merit. Petrovich sometimes took issue with him, but Heinrich would refute all his arguments. Meanwhile, I simply lay back and listened, thinking that reason and logic do not always rule human society. More frequently the high and mighty of this world gladden their peoples' hearts with devastating wars and, in the twentieth century, with organized cannibalism.

My wife would steal an occasional yawn, for none of this talk held any interest for her. When Heinrich finally ran out of steam, I asked Petrovich, in order to amuse her a bit, to relate how on September 12, 1946, we made a wager that we would give up smoking. We were still in very real danger of a relapse, of course, because not more than six months had passed since that day. Made wise by my own unsuccessful attempts, I had proposed written terms, any violation of which would require handing over for three months the bonus that we received as specialists—this monthly award had a value equivalent to six and a half pounds of sugar. Furthermore, the violator would have to make a public confession of his failure. To reinforce the weight of this written agreement, two witnesses added their signatures to ours. Since that time neither of us had had as much as a single drag. Petrovich embellished the story with a series of fictitious details.

It was all great fun. Heinrich was at the top of his form. He went on from Bismarck to our practical joke involving an Estonian who worked in our shop as a draftsman. This Estonian spoke Russian fairly well, and with a youthful love of mischief we decided to pass him off as a famous palm reader. The first to fall victim was one of our plant workers, Vera, the camp mistress of the head doctor at our infirmary. One day she blurted out to Petrovich that her doctor was impotent. Petrovich soon transmitted this secret to us, and, binding our soothsayer to an oath of silence, we furnished him with this piece of gossip. Without trying very hard, we aroused Vera's interest in him. It all ended with our arranging a meeting between the "palm reader" and the couple. The Estonian made a big impression with his "readings," but they soon got suspicious. We had a big laugh over it. Vera's feelings, of course, were hurt, but it wasn't long before everything was back to normal.

But however much we tried to amuse ourselves, our laughter was never very far from tears. The next day disaster struck. Although we had tried hard to keep my wife's visit a secret, the word got out among the other prisoners; and someone went blabbing to the authorities. Such a long visit was generally not permitted and therefore was considered absolutely illicit. The next morning, to make my absence from work less conspicuous, I set off for the barbed-wire zone at the time when the bread ration was being handed out. I came back to an empty house. The fire had gone out in the stove. My bright-eyed angel had vanished. I learned from neighbors that two soldiers had taken her away. It was a good thing that they hadn't found us both at home. I then rushed off to the plant where I sent Misha and Petya over to my technical department, asking them to explain the whole story there and make themselves available to my captive wife. Within forty minutes two Chekist officers came to escort me to the headquarters of the camp armed guard.

It was only for very serious offenses that people were ever taken there. Afterward they were shipped off for six months to a lime factory in a penal camp. It was not as bad as "Captain Borisov's dacha" and the sentence was not intolerably long, but even so, by the time people returned from these camps they were in pretty poor shape. At headquarters I was not immediately brought before the commanding officer. That was a good omen. My armed escort even offered me a smoke. Apparently someone had phoned in from my department and explained the situation in a persuasive manner. Since the most important thing for headquarters was to save face, they had decided to do nothing more than revoke my pass. I quietly pointed out that permission for my wife's visit had come from Moscow, that everything had been done through official channels. They then told me I was at fault because I had not informed headquarters in advance: "As an educated man you should know these things. Hand over your pass!" All this was obviously said as a matter of form. There was no screaming or shouting. Then the order was given to my escort: "Take him back to his department!" My heart grew lighter and my spirit rejoiced. If I had been so stupid as to tell them beforehand about the arrival of my wife, headquarters would have allowed us only a two-hour visit—in the presence of a Chekist officer. But we had been able to steal eight days of happiness. The gamble had paid off. We were people who had been tempered by fire and inured to adversity. Meanwhile, my wife had kept up her head and told her side of the story calmly. She demanded official permission to ring up the technical department and told me she had been ordered to leave the camp as soon as possible. Petya and Misha got a train ticket for her. But since her train would not come through until two days later, she had to spend the remaining time in the company of my two friends. She and I arranged to say good-by at the plant on the day of her departure. At ten in the morning Heinrich brought her over, having provided her with a pass through one of his workers. The atmosphere was charged. We met in a laboratory attached to the foundry. Our farewells were tense and hurried. Then Heinrich led her away. Sadly I walked behind them as far as the guardhouse at the entry to the plant. As I walked back slowly in the direction of the forging shop, deep in thought, three Chekists ran past me toward the plant. Evidently, after Heinrich had presented the pass bearing her name, the sentry, acting on previous instructions, had immediately phoned headquarters. There a decision was made to punish me right away for a flagrant (to their official minds) violation. But, thank God, the whole matter was disposed of without any grave consequences. Shortly afterward, Petya and Misha got my wife settled on the train. Two weeks later, my pass was returned to me; however, my range of movement was considerably reduced. Often I walked past the little house where she and I had spent those few days. Each time my heart was wrung with sadness.

Robin Hoods

Among the prisoners who arrived in the camp during the two years right after the war were partisans—Lithuanians and Bendera's Ukrainians, who had fought in their home territories against the occupying Communists. They were fond of relating tales about their life in the forests —daring raids, hand-to-hand skirmishes, terrorist assaults against the Chekists. During the two weeks I was deprived of a pass, I spent the evenings by myself, pondering the techniques of this type of warfare. My own early recollections helped me to arrive at a judgment about it.

As children, we listened with delight, but without worrying our heads over the fine points, to eyewitness accounts of the guerrilla war waged by Makhno in the Ukraine; of Antonov's peasant uprising in the Tambov district; of the "Green" partisans who hid out in the forests. Our young hearts were completely on the side of these unfortunates, who were forced to defend the lives of their loved ones against constant repressions,

238

religious persecutions, and attacks from bandits, all things that were familiar to us also in the cities.

Much depends on one's home training. I had the good fortune to read books that glorified chivalry, valor, loyalty, heroic deeds. And at a much later period in my life, this helped me to see the degree to which I had strayed from the ideal and to find the right path again. From childhood we had had instilled in us the rules of fair play—never to resort to inadmissible methods or to hit a man when he was down. Until 1917 normal Russian families had brought up their children in this spirit.

The activities of Russian partisans against Napoleon during the Patriotic War of 1812 had seemed disgraceful to me—just as sickening as the savage warfare carried on in that same period by the Spanish guerrillas against the French army. Here we had the heroic armies of Christian nations coming together on the field of battle; then, without warning and under cover of darkness, men not brought up in the spirit of military glory and thus capable of all sorts of cruelty and villainy infiltrated into the open struggle between units of well-trained regulars and perpetrated what amounted to cutthroat banditry.

Now, in my later year, life was forcing me to recognize that terrorist acts and partisan warfare are legitimate,—but only insofar as these activities offer people the sole means of resistance against a state that engages in the systematic annihilation of its citizens; in undermining religion; in economic enslavement (the confiscation of private property and the suppression of individual initiative and enterprise); in depriving men of their right to fight honestly and openly for their own interests as well as for civil rights.

In the event of an army's absolute defeat, its government has no choice but to sign a peace treaty—and observe it. Once it regains strength, it may, if necessary, initiate a new war, but it should do so openly. Terrorism and partisan warfare against a "conventional" conquering enemy, on the other hand, are certainly not admissible and should be subject to international condemnation and proscription, for such activities lead to repressions against entirely innocent people and make life into a hell on earth for them. Since they have no real justification, they must be regarded as criminal.

But the guerrilla warfare conducted by Makhno, Antonov, or the "Greens" against the Bolshevik regime was completely justifiable. It was the peasant's response to Red terrorism, systematic looting, loss of basic human rights, mockery at religious faith.

The partisan activities of Poles, Yugoslavs, Frenchmen, and others against the Nazis were also perfectly legitimate, as were also the guerrilla warfare and terrorism of Bendera's Ukrainians against Hitler and Stalin —not to mention the Balts' struggle for independence against the occupying Soviet forces.

The Prisoner's Code

Our professor, Petrovich, though he excelled at his work, was frequently at odds with other prisoners. As head of the plant's technological division, he was too demanding for the good of the camp. According to him, jobs were not completed as fast as he wanted them to be. On one occasion Heinrich and I succeeded at the last moment in restraining his desire to have some erring prisoner put into the punishment cells for a couple of days. At first we threatened to break off our friendship with him; then we attempted to point out that for him to resort to such a measure would be absolutely unfair since the offender was just a greenhorn in the camp. During the course of our talk, it struck me that Petrovich, partly owing to the pressures of day-to-day living under the Soviet system, had developed a cruel, callous attitude toward the average man that conflicted sharply with his ideals. Finally, he was forced to accept our arguments.

This was the only serious run-in we ever had. Still, I was convinced that the standards of behavior that I expected of anyone living in imprisonment—standards which took shape in the terrible conditions of the war years—had value not only for newcomers to camp life, but also for old hands as a means of countering the corrupting influence that the morals and manners of the criminal element and the Chekists were constantly exerting. After thoroughly reviewing my own experiences, I drew up a set of rules which had guided my behavior for a long time past. My code can be summarized in ten precepts:

1. Wipe out the stool pigeons.
2. Repay a blow with a blow.
3. Help the deserving.
4. Keep your nose out of your neighbor's business.
5. Don't look for trouble.
6. Remember that your bread ration belongs to you alone.
7. A slave morality is for Chekists to live by.
8. Your friends are like your family.
9. Be a slave without but a warrior within.
10. Save your soul, and you'll save your body too.

240

By observing these commandments a prisoner can hold firmly to his human dignity, no matter what the conditions of the camp may be.

Petrovich's desire to have the new prisoner thrown into jail violated several articles of my code: by his rude interference in the man's business, he was resorting to Chekist methods and thus behaving in a most intolerable fashion. It was a breach of the fourth commandment. During the day's work we sometimes had to remind a prisoner what his duties were. Whenever such a need arose, there was nothing wrong in taking him aside and dressing him down privately. This was quite enough. Under the conditions that prevailed in our plant, stronger methods were not necessary. Every man there valued his job too much to jeopardize it. And because Petrovich wished to take action that accorded not with our code, but with the slave ethics of the Chekists, he was in violation of the seventh commandment.

Petrovich broke the fifth rule by turning his back on our appeal for solidarity among prisoners, and thus earned our scorn and condemnation. It was a veiled implication of this rule that you might one day be called to account for your behavior at a transit prison, where other prisoners might kill you for having infringed it.

15

ON THE WAY TO MOSCOW

Execution of Criminals

In early September, 1947, it was announced to me that I was being transferred from Vorkuta. A change of camp was a big event in the life of any *zek*. Naturally I wasted no time in learning where the transport would be heading. Since I was working in a managerial capacity, I had no trouble in finding out that it was bound for Moscow, evidently on orders from Fourth Administrative Headquarters, Ministry of Internal Affairs, which had charge of special engineering projects at research-and-design centers (*sharashkas*) inside the prisons. I was not particularly eager to go, and even made some attempt to stay behind. But I decided there was no choice but to submit to fate.

The transport from Vorkuta was always assembled inside a special transit zone, where I arrived early in the morning with two other prisoners. There, on the night before, five common criminals had been executed, despite the fact that in May of this same year Stalin had issued a decree replacing the death sentence with a twenty-five-year term in either a prison or a corrective labor camp. The news of the executions, which were not preceded by trials, gave us all cause for alarm. We learned that the victims were "regular" criminals. For offenses committed inside the camp, they had been sentenced to a stint at the lime works in the penal camp, which was under the control of their implacable enemies, the "bitches." The regular thieves knew in advance that death by torture would be all they could expect there. Naturally they refused to go, especially since the death penalty had just been abolished. They took over an empty barracks, where they ripped apart a brick stove. When the security people discovered the hideout and tried to recapture them, the crooks started heaving bricks at them; and one or two of the guards got bruised. The security force then locked up the barracks, with the gang still inside. The commander of the guard turned for help to the Vorkuta headquarters, which had radio contact with the Ministry of Internal Affairs in Moscow. From there came the order to shoot all the mutinous criminals. This was not an official death sentence; it simply was an emergency measure for suppressing armed resistance against the authority of the state. To the victims it hardly made much difference whether they were shot before a firing squad or just mowed down. A squad with automatic weapons was brought over from the camp's Chekist detachment. In the face of such firepower how much can a man do with a brick? The criminals, of course, were gunned down—all of them. We had the opportunity of looking over the barracks before it was put back in order. The stove was in shambles, and there were blood stains. But the corpses had already been hauled away.

Most of us saw nothing out of the ordinary in this bloody incident, nor can it be said that we were especially upset by it—by this time we were pretty hardened. Brutal behavior was commonplace for us; life was cheap. We merely gave a wry smile at this latest demonstration of the regime's regard for its own laws, well aware that those in charge did just as they pleased. In the Soviet Union, the vague and contradictory laws—and the decrees that countermand them—are considered as "guides to action"[1] only, and offer every possible scope for tyranny and malpractice.

A Forerunner of the Dissidents
of the Sixties

In the transit prison there were a lot of young women from the Ukraine, where at that time—as so often before—there was famine. To our question, "What are you in for?" we received the stock reply, "For grain." Anyone caught stealing ears of grain on a collective farm got a ten-year sentence. It was a foregone conclusion that as soon as those girls reached the coal mines, they would fall into the clutches of the criminals and run the whole painful gamut of shame and humiliation.

At this same transit point I met a prisoner from Georgia. I was

1. From Marx's famous phrase, which Stalin frequently quoted: "Marxism is not dogma; it is a guide to action."

astonished at how freely he talked. Yet it was highly doubtful that he was either a provocateur or an informer. I especially recall two things he said. First, he argued that a man should try to be both a Christian and a democrat. Second, he believed that Stalin had been created by us Russians despite the dictator's Georgian origin. According to my new acquaintance, the Georgians did not recognize Stalin as one of their own, whereas the Russians had elevated him to the status of an idol. In those days, to make frank statements of that sort amounted to signing your own death warrant: the Chekists would conclude that a man like this must surely be the ringleader of a terrorist organization—which would have meant death for quite a number of other innocent people and most probably for his family as well.

By this time I had undergone a considerable, if gradual, change. Although by nature I was a man who loved truth and liberty, my constant struggle to stay alive under the most difficult conditions had made me rather like an inhabitant of the jungle where the faintest rustle in the undergrowth may be a portent of ambush and sudden death. In the camp you had to be constantly on your guard against talking too much: you had to be watchful of every suspicious movement—even the slightest. After seven years in the camps, I regarded the outspokenness of the Georgian professor as well nigh incredible, quite beyond my imagination.

Our conversation was interrupted in a rather unusual manner. Another prisoner (a "flunky" who acted as a work supervisor) walked over to him and said, "That's enough! If you keep up that kind of talk, we'll put you in solitary." The prospect of landing in the punishment cell obviously did not appeal to the Georgian; he made off to his own barracks, and I never saw him again. As to what became of him in the future, I had no way of finding out. So many people passed through the transit prison and were then sent on in so many different directions that you seldom encountered anyone again. Now and then, after a lapse of many, many years, you might pick up a bit of news about this one or that. But despite the fact that no word about that Georgian was ever to reach my ears, our meeting remains fixed in my mind.

Our tendency to adapt to a horrible system of somebody else's making produces a slave complex in us. Why did we worry so much about what we said under these conditions? Wouldn't it have been better to come right out and state publicly what we thought and believed, as the Georgian did, not caring about the consequences?

Georgians who ran afoul of Stalin or Beria were destroyed wholesale just like anybody else. During the war, at Vyatlag, there was a small group of them. Its nucleus consisted of men who had belonged to the

Georgian branch of the Mensheviks.[2] Among them was Vashekidze, the foreman in charge of supplies at the machine shop, who had been in the camps ever since 1924. Once he said, "My honor is all that I have left." There was a chivalrous strain among those men from Georgia. To this day they live in my memory as reliable, staunch, and courageous people.

Gradually our minds were groping toward ways of fighting the Soviet system, even though the conditions we lived under would seem to have made struggle of any sort utterly impossible: logging camps, deep mine shafts, the construction of useless roads, building sites buried in Arctic ice and snow, brooding Northern Lights, unbearable cold. Yet only four years later the whole system of slavery was to be shaken to the core—to the extent that the regime had to abandon much of it, or at least drastically reduce its scale.

The Georgian was ahead of his time by almost fifteen years. In that transit jail I heard the voice of a free man, and he remains in my mind as a forerunner of the open champions of democracy who emerged in the sixties to proclaim the need for liberty and elementary legal forms.

In the 1960's, when the regime's most highly placed figure himself condemned Stalin (though the traditions of Stalinism have continued to live, even to the present day), a half-century of silence was abruptly ended. Among the first to raise his voice was Aleksandr Solzhenitsyn. It is a wonderful thing that we have such people as he, but under a system of party dictatorship such dissident voices cannot by themselves suffice: they must be seen as complementary to the intense struggle being waged at the deeper levels of society.

Kirov Transit Prison Revisited

En route to Vorkuta I had passed through the transit prison at Kirov. And now I found myself there again. Recently, some attempts had been made to separate the prisoners by categories. Our members were growing by leaps and bounds and the end of the war saw a large influx of prisoners who had served in the army. Many had gone on reconnaissance missions into enemy territory, or fought at the front, often in hand-to-hand combat with the enemy. Quite a few Soviet soldiers were violently bitter over Stalin's infamous amnesty of 1945: at the end of the war all the deserters were let off scot-free, while those who had fallen captive

2. The Russian Social-Democratic Workers' Party (RSDRP), until the October Revolution of 1917, was composed of the Bolsheviks (those who were in the majority) and the Mensheviks (the minority). This division occurred at the Second Congress of the RSDRP in 1903; after the October Revolution the Mensheviks were proscribed.

or been cut off from their units by the enemy were packed off to the camps. Until the decree abolishing the death penalty was issued, war veterans had been receiving ten-year terms. But afterward, they started getting twenty-five. On the transports out to the camps, they were thrown indiscriminately among the criminals and the *bytoviki*. They soon started playing a trick to improve their situation: a war veteran with a twenty-five-year sentence would find out on the sly which prisoners in the transit prison had only the tail end of their sentences to serve, and he would then strike up a conversation with one of these "short-termers," eliciting all his "vital statistics": surname, first name, year of birth, charge, length of sentence. Or else he would memorize these details as they were reeled off by his prospective victim at roll call. After that he would keep a careful watch on the door of the cell, and as soon as a warden came in to read out the names of prisoners assigned to the next transport, he could rapidly recite all the details of the man whose identity he had decided to appropriate. He would then be taken off for the transport instead of his gullible victim. This kind of thing eventually assumed epic proportions, and it was not for several months that a stop was put to it, during which time scores—possibly hundreds—of ex-soldiers managed to take a short cut to freedom. Even I, with six years to go, had to keep my wits about me.

It was because of this trouble with the ex-soldiers that the authorities decided to separate the flood of new prisoners by categories. Since the *kontriki* (the "political" offenders) were far more numerous than any other group, we now found ourselves packed inside our cells like sardines. During the day everyone sat either on the floor or on his bundle of belongings. At night, simply because there was nothing else we could do, we virtually lay on top of one another with our feet in our neighbors' faces. It was impossible to get to the slop bucket without stepping on bodies. The heat was terrible. Everyone sat unclothed and bathed in sweat. We were brought only boiling water, and we felt even hotter after drinking. I remember that when we were taken out to the toilets, we thought only of drinking as much cold water as we could from the washbasins.

In the cells a kind of seniority was observed in respect to the place you occupied—a newcomer moved by gradual degrees from a position on the floor near the slop bucket to the window and the bunks, where he was able at last to lie down properly and get some sleep. Naturally, the first night for a newcomer was pretty hard to bear. I remember mine: the stench from the bucket, and the men who kept treading over me on the way to it.

246

Before I was sent off on the transport, my more or less respectable-looking camp attire was taken away. To replace it, I was handed clothing that must have served twenty people before me: a quilted jacket which had been patched over and over again, an old pair of quilted trousers, a peaked cap which must many times, during searches, have yielded up its hoard of treasures—matches, bits of razor blades, and knives sewn inside it by a whole generation of criminals. There were numbers on both the front and back of my shirt to enable me to identify it in the bathhouse—such numbers were also worn by prisoners doing hard labor at some of the Vorkuta camps. Apart from all this, I wore a cross around my neck on a piece of string. Some newcomers imagined that I must be a dreadful cutthroat, of the type who adorn their breasts with crucifixes—not in the name of religion, but out of a heathenish desire to decorate themselves or to mark themselves off from everybody else. To heighten the illusion, I was at that particular time in good physical shape. I had even gotten a tan under the meager sun of the far north. Altogether, my appearance bespoke an old hand from the hard-labor gangs, one who had gone through hell and high water—and then some. And I now bore myself in keeping with my appearance.

A young Latvian from a different transport had been put in with our group from Vorkuta. But on the first night in the cell, instead of taking a place alongside me on the floor, he disappeared. Suddenly I looked up and spotted him lying on a bunk among the Latvians. And there I was, a veteran of the camps, spending a hard night on the floor. I have always willingly submitted to rules that applied equally to everybody. But I considered it unjust that a healthy youngster should be enjoying privileges that were denied the rest of us. I therefore addressed myself in a rather high and mighty manner to the *zek* in charge.

"Chief, how can you allow things like this?" I asked, throwing in the customary swear words.

The cell leader readily agreed with me: "Some other fellow has left. You can have his place."

Very likely, I would have left it at that—I do not much like picking quarrels. But not quite certain about what to do, I continued talking with the cell leader.

"Why don't you see to it that the rules here are observed?" I insisted.

"If the *muzhiks*[3] choose to sit on the floor, let them."

"Maybe the *muzhiks* like to cower in the corner or sleep on the floor. But I don't. That youngster and I came here the same day. And there

3. Literally, "peasants"—prisoners who out of fear or indifference refused to stand up against the criminal element.

he is, lying on a bunk. If you have no set rules in your cell, then I think I have every right to that place."

The cell leader's response was brief: "O.K. I'm not standing in your way. Go ahead. Take it, if you can."

I was now in a belligerent mood. I shouted to the *muzhiks:* "You don't mind putting up with this? You don't want to lie down? You prefer to sit on the floor?" They gave no reply. Then, with an air of bravado, I forced my way through the crowd and up to the bunk where the Latvian was lying. "Come on now, get down! This is my place."

The other men occupying the bunks had belonged to an SS division that the Germans had formed solely of Latvians. They were strapping, fair-haired fellows covered in scars. No wonder the legitimate claimants to the bunks were afraid to act.

I repeated to the youth: "Clear out of here! You arrived here the same time I did and you don't even know the taste of *balanda* yet." Then I laid claim to the bunk by putting my belongings on it. The other Latvians were sitting up and taking notice. Everyone of them was probably stronger than I. They hadn't been worn out yet because their ordeal in the prisons and camps was just beginning. I could see that a fight was inevitable. Since I had nothing to lose, I swung around and let two of them have it in quick succession. I thought they would now beat me to a pulp. But nothing of the sort—they were scared to hit back. So now I really let them have it. There was no question of further resistance. The youth climbed down and I took his place on the bunk. I had won with very little trouble and no bloodshed.

This incident is worth relating only because of what followed it. I should explain why I had achieved such an easy victory. For one thing: there had been too many SS men in the neighboring bunks. Being so closely packed together, they could barely get to their knees and it was impossible for them to maneuver around and take a swing at me. Furthermore, the fight took place right after most of the other inmates of the cell had just returned from the toilets but had still not settled back into their places on the floor. This meant that I had plenty of room to maneuver in front of the bunks. If a couple of the Latvian SS had taken it into their heads to jump down to the floor, they would certainly have got the better of me. Possibly they feared that some of my cellmates would pitch in and help me. They might also have thought that I had a knife concealed inside my shoe, that I was a master of the underworld in-fighting techniques that inspired terror in everyone. The criminals had a habit of smashing someone's jaw or face into a bloody mess by butting it hard with the crown of the skull.

I now lay on the bunk, going over the incident in my mind and wondering whether my conduct had been entirely blameless from the standpoint of camp ethics. Suddenly I remembered the German cellmate whom I had earlier noticed sitting next to the hotwater tub. I raised myself up and took a good look at the fine, but wasted, features of his handsome seventy-year-old face. He seemed only half-alive, his strength gone and his days numbered. "Go over there," I told myself, "and offer him your place. You'll be doing a kindness and making up for your bad behavior—you started out to stand up for justice but in fact you end up as an old *zek*, a dog that fights for a slightly better place." I gave some thought to the feasibility of obeying this impulse, but soon realized how impractical it was. First of all, the old German was among the latest arrivals since he was sitting by the cell door and then, although our attitude toward the Germans had considerably softened by now, they were still thought of as the wartime "Fritzes." And finally, there were other men just as exhausted as he who might loudly protest that he had arrived in the cell after they had.

My thoughts were suddenly interrupted. I could feel myself being pressed from both sides. Apparently my neighbors had decided to stage a come-back. Upon a signal they set to and started heaving at me. I did not wait for the end of this performance. Without saying a word, I began to shove my boots hard against my neighbors' bare shins. Since my newly won position was not yet secure, I had purposely kept the boots on. The Latvians shouted to each other in their own language and then moved back to their own places. They did not try to molest me again.

If I had turned my place over to the German, he would soon have been only too glad to get back to his old place by the door. It was clear enough why nobody tried to claim his rightful place in the bunks. Though it was not very wise of them, the Latvian SS men were obviously taking their hatred for the Soviet system out on the other prisoners.

Prince Sviatopolk-Mirski

It was no later than the following day that there arose an opportunity to make amends for my misconduct. That evening five more prisoners were shoved in among us, though the cell was already jam-packed. A transport en route from Moscow had just pulled in. Despite the growing darkness we still had no lights. Obviously there was a power breakdown somewhere. All of a sudden a voice rang out in the dark—a fine clear Russian voice—asking if we would like to listen to a story. All *zeks*, from the lowest criminal to the most highly educated among them, are fond of a yarn. When a man is in prison, nobody is more welcome to him than a good storyteller. So we immediately made room for the new prisoner in the middle of the cell and began to listen to his fascinating tales.

We were a hard, brutalized lot, and our speech was uncouth and brazen. We were always bragging loudly in front of one another; with old *zeks* like myself this habit might have seemed almost second nature. But the newcomer spoke in a totally different way. Prince Sviatopolk-Mirski was a man from another world. His appearance was that of a prince directly from the books of my childhood. He was rather tall, about thirty-five years of age. His face, by nature quite pale, had become ashen, worn, and emaciated. His hair, a very light shade of brown, was closely cropped. His large blue eyes were splendid. Evidently something was wrong with his leg, for he had a slight limp. He seemed like an angel to me. Much later, after coming to the West, I was to meet similar people in Rome. The prince had never made any secret of his identity. He was picked up by the Soviet police somewhere in Poland. For White émigrés, punishment was swift and arbitrary. In spite of the fact that he had been a mere boy during the Civil War and could not have taken any part in it, his social origin alone was reason enough for his being shipped off to Vorkuta.

The prince turned out to be a most interesting man. We sat as if bewitched, listening to him for half the night. I especially liked his account of America, where he had gone in the twenties while still a young man. There he had been warmly received. If we were to take his word for it, of five American women one was beguiling, one ravishing, and at least one of the remaining three a beauty. He had nothing but praise for them. America, according to him, was a dream country, sparkling with life. He went on to relate his many adventures there. To me this occasion was nothing less than a feast of the spirit.

He also gave some description of Poland and of the Nazis' campaign to exterminate the Jews there. He had been able to hide and protect one of them. Later, when the Red arrived on the scene, he in turn was kept under cover by Jews who had managed to survive. To sum him up in a word, this man was a genuine aristocrat of the spirit, an aristocrat not by virtue of his title but of his inherent worth.

I regarded the prince with considerable compassion; but I could not understand why he seemed to regard me in a similar vein. Eventually, I saw the reason: he, as well as the other prisoners, had mistaken me for someone sentenced to hard labor because of the numbers on my clothes.

250

I was rather amused by the prince's pity for me. In this packed cell, I was the last person to be pitied. I was, as they say, "riding high": I had a vast experience of camps, professional skills of the necessary kind, an ability to get along in the most killing conditions, and, most important, a firm belief in God that enabled my spirit to endure. Furthermore, I could now look forward to a little respite. It was with some sadness that I looked at the others, who, I felt sure could not last in the deadly places they would probably land in. My heart ached most of all when I thought of the prince.

Shortly after the prince had finished his story, I and a few other prisoners were called out for the transport. While I was getting dressed, it occurred to me that it would be entirely possible to give up my place on the bunk to the prince: first of all, he was a storyteller; secondly, he had a bad leg. I put my proposal to the others in such a way as to allow for no rebuttal. Nobody voiced any objection. I helped the prince to climb up to the bunk and then wished him good-by.

Grigori Gryaznoi

We were driven in a Black Maria from the Kirov Transit Prison to a train, where we were installed in a Stolypin coach. In those days prisoners were being moved in vast numbers to camps in the northern and eastern regions of the country. If anyone was sent in the opposite direction, toward Moscow, it meant that his case was being reviewed, that he was going to be used for his professional skills, or that he was being put in a prison instead of a camp. This explains why there were only ten of us in one compartment. It was luxury indeed to travel without sitting on top of each other's heads. Also, the company was good, as it had been in the transit prison we had just left, and there was plenty of interesting conversation.

One of our number, however—a Kuban Cossack, who recounted endless tales of his hunting and military exploits—continuously sang the praises of the regime. With some aid from my other traveling companions, I tried to discover how he came to have such an attitude. Whenever I pinned him down, he would say he didn't mean it. But after a couple of hours he would be back on his previous tack. It wasn't long before the reason behind his odd character became clear to me. He belonged to an element bred in an atheistic environment; he was one of those people who thought only about themselves and never gave a damn for anybody else. Egotism and materialism come naturally to men like him. His Cossack family had supported the Soviet regime during the Civil War. Because of that, they were allowed to stay on in the Kuban. His father had been chairman of a model collective farm. In the interests of propaganda, the district party authorities did not strip the farm bare, leaving its members enough for their subsistence. As the spoilt son of the chairman, our friend did not have to work and in consequence was able to enjoy all the natural bounties of the rich Kuban region: he hunted for wild boar, shot pheasants, and went fishing. By comparison with other families, his lived fairly well for quite some time. But the dispossession of the kulaks, along with other repressions, eventually hit them, too. Nearly all his family perished. But all that mattered to him was the fact of his own survival.

When I saw what sort of person he was, I felt sickened: "You live on these happy memories because you haven't yet had a good dose of the camp," I told him, "and because you still get parcels from home, with lumps of fatback as thick as your fist. But you're not going to worm your way out of this situation so easily. Just wait until you've had a taste of some other camps. Then remember my words. You hope that by singing the praises of the regime you'll somehow get your case reviewed. But it won't help you. They've given you twenty-five years, and you'll serve every one of theim, in spite of your pro-Soviet attitudes. Maybe you should be grateful to the tribunal: you might learn some sense now."

I was never in the least surprised by acts of lawlessness and oppression on the part of the regime. For this reason, I never got into an argument with either the camp authorities or our guards—except in cases of really exceptional highhandedness. As a rule, my friends and I simply laughed to ourselves, repeating what Max Borodyanski used to say: "Nothing out of the ordinary!" But those who still regarded themselves as loyal Soviet citizens were constantly kicking up a fuss over something or other. Not long after my talk with him, our friend from the Kuban had a set-to with one of the guards during an evening visit to the toilets. He was so insolent that the guards threw him into a punishment cell. There, after putting him in special handcuffs, they beat the daylights out of him. The handcuffs tightened at the slightest movement, thus impeding the blood circulation and causing such pain that the Cossack screamed his head off. This sort of punishment was just the right medicine for him. It helped him see things as they really were.

During the journey I felt extremely sure of myself and even militant, because I well knew that transports and transit prisons were places where viewpoints could be exchanged fearlessly. The risk of being given away by a stool pigeon was slight; for under the circumstances peculiar to a transport or a transit prison he had no one to protect him and thus did everything possible to avoid suspicion.

At one point during our denunciations of the regime a pale, consumptive-looking Armenian, who hitherto had kept silent, suddenly broke into speech. With the Southerner's characteristic excitability, he let forth a spate of words, all to the effect that some remarkable men were to be found among the Chekists.

"After I was put away for good, my wife's brother, a high-ranking Chekist, took both her and my two children in. He even made it possible for her to send me parcels now and then." A thing like that was still possible in Armenia and Georgia; their peoples had traditions that bound them closely to one another.

"But surely you are aware that your case is an exception. I cannot recall any other like it," I countered. "We all have the same objective: the establishment of justice. Oppression, brute force, and terror are essential only to those who go against truth, reason, and the laws fundamental to human life. We are not out to take revenge on anyone, nor will we ever. I am a man with religious faith; I firmly believe that one's deeds in this world will be judged only in the other world. Do the kind acts of your brother-in-law outweight all the evil he did while 'at work?' That's something that we here on earth don't know. But in drawing up any balance sheet of your own, you must take into account both sides of a man's actions."

Another companion who sticks in my memory of that trip was a strapping, broad-faced fellow, a native of the Smolensk region. He had fought two years at the front. After returning home, he failed to invite his neighbor, the district prosecutor, to a drinking party. Shortly afterward, he committed some petty offense; and out of pure malice, just for the sake of settling personal scores, a criminal charge was brought against him. But before he could be brought to trial, he went off to Vorkuta, to visit his brother who commanded the camp security guard there. The brother's history, in its own way, was typical of that of thousands with his kind of background. He had served through the whole war, earned his officer's shoulder boards, received decorations, and spent a year and a half in Germany, with all the rights and privileges enjoyed by a member of an army of occupation. He tasted the delights of real cigars, whiskey, and French champagne. In accordance with his means and rank, he shipped home articles that had been stolen from German civilians. Unfortunately, there came a day when he had to be demobilized. Back in the homeland he found famine, the same old *kolkhozes*,[4] people dressed in rags and often living in wretched lean-tos. . . . He had lost the capacity for regular daily work, and he had not had time to acquire a profession before the war. And so he was forced to accept an offer to go out to Khanovei, a small, isolated railway stop—the gateway to the Vorkuta coalfields. The only thing there was the camp, unless you counted the ever-blowing winds, for which this region was famous. In the long, dark season all that he had left was liquor. With simplehearted honesty our traveling companion told how his brother, blind drunk, would dash out of his small house into the blowing snow and the fierce cold and begin blazing away at the Northern Lights with a carbine rifle. He blasphemed and shouted obscene oaths at the accursed slave existence he was leading. Back inside the house he would rampage about, smashing anything within reach of his fists, until, finally exhausted, he toppled over and went into a heavy drunken sleep.

When our traveling companion was located two months after leaving for Vorkuta, an order was sent out for his arrest. It was his own brother who had him put into the isolation cell. From there the brother delivered him over to the convoy for conduct to the prison in his home town, where he would be tried for his crime.

The un-Russian face of a tall, broad-shouldered Swede in our company had a magnetic quality and looked as if it were sculpted from a block of granite. He had served as a volunteer in the Finnish army. After the conclusion of the Second World War, Soviet agents in Helsinki had arrested him on the street. For some reason or other, the Finnish police had not intervened. He was now on his way to Vladimir Prison from the camp at Inta, situated to the south of Vorkuta. From relatives in Sweden he received care packages. Consequently, he made a smart appearance in his foreign attire of military cut. He undid his duffle bag and took out some tasty things to eat which he proceeded to chew complacently after he had eaten his ordinary ration along with the rest of us. All this rubbed us the wrong way. Even though there were no firm rules on this score, any one of us in his place would have passed out a rusk apiece to the others or divided a hard biscuit into three shares. And not one of us there ever had enough, despite the fact that we were not going hungry at that time. A gesture of generosity from the Swede would have been accepted with warm gratitude, and his prestige would have risen. But, instead, a good many oblique glances were cast in his direction. It hurt to watch a hero, a volunteer, a man of strength and courage, a model of valor for any of us to emulate, making such a bad impression. Some time later, as I

4. Collective farms.

marched alongside him through the streets en route to a transit jail, I explained in Russian, which he understood very well, that it was foolish of him to offend his brother travelers.

"If there had been only criminals in the compartment with you, they would have stripped you of your fine clothing and emptied your duffle bag. You didn't have it bad in our company. So why did you stray from your ideals? Why didn't it occur to you to share with your less fortunate companions just a few of your sweetmeats?"

As I thought further on this subject, I thought of the following simple truths which clearly flow from the Gospel:

— You may be exceedingly virtuous; but if you bear no love for other men, your virtues have no real value.

— If out of a sense of sacred duty you have gone to the aid of others and thereby attained glory, then all honor and praise to you.

— But if you have done your utmost for those in extreme misfortune, from motives of love and compassion, then your sacrifices, in the eyes of the Lord, are thrice blessed; for indeed you have helped lay the foundation for a world brotherhood. Out of your deeds will spring the shoots of love. In the beginning, your love may not be returned; but as time goes on, the chances are it will become reciprocal.

We were unloaded from the coach near a railroad bridge. You could not imagine a worse place from the point of view of our armed escort: there was an endless flow of gaping passersby. One old lady in a shawl and a moth-eaten coat stopped on the path just above our heads and let out a lament: "Where are they taking the poor dears to? My, they're all skin and bones!"

As was prescribed in such cases, we sat on our meager piles of belongings. The Swede who remained alongside me attracted particular attention from the passing onlookers. The escort commander, a lieutenant, seemed rather nervous and ashamed about his work. In accents from the Volga region, he lit into the old woman: "Move on, move on! You can't stand here. They're not serving time for nothing. People don't end up like this because they've been good. These fellows are bandits."

We chuckled to ourselves. From somewhere at the rear of our formation, we heard a voice saying: "Watch out—you may be joining us tomorrow, so be careful what you say!"

The lieutenant went off somewhere, and we soon got bored waiting. Finally, a voice rang out: "Form a column of fives! One step to the right or left will be treated as attempted escape. The guards will shoot without warning." More threats followed. Then came the command, "March!" It was the busiest time of day; the streets were crowded. Most people continued walking by, but some stopped and looked compassionately at our procession. The guards, all Kirgiz or Uzbeks, led us along the main thoroughfare. They carried their carbines at the ready, with bayonets fixed; and they were in a nasty mood.

Among the civilians passing close by us, I caught sight of a young fellow, about twenty-five, with light brown hair and a candid handsome face. His blue eyes were full of sympathy and pity. I thought of a line from Rimsky-Korsakov's opera: "I do not recognize Grigori Gryaznoi, I do not recognize myself."[5] The alert, bold youngster, now plainly in my view, was an archetypal Russian daredevil. Walking but a few steps over toward the Swede and me, he threw a pack of cigarettes into the midst of our column. One of the armed escort shouted and cursed at him, brandishing a bayonet in the direction of his stomach. But he didn't bat an eye. The prisoners picked up the pack of cigarettes. "Grigori's" tall figure practically concealed the lovely young woman standing behind him. But I could see that she had the same light brown hair and blue eyes as he. From behind her brother—or husband—she pitched a bread roll over to a fourteen-year-old boy in our ranks. Again there was alarm and confusion as the youngster scurried to pick up the roll. Those two youths out there were right after my own heart. They belonged to a breed of people which in these nightmare years had been virtually exterminated.

The congestion in the admissions cells at Gorky Transit Prison was frightful. Two other transports had also just arrived. In addition there were boys, aged twelve to sixteen, who had been collected from jails all over the Gorky region to be sent to a detention colony for juvenile offenders. Most of those kids had a canny, utterly fearless look. Obviously, prison was nothing new to them. But there were a few boys completely bewildered by what had happened to them.

Fairly close by me lay a little fellow not more than ten, his face white as parchment. After a bout of vomiting, he moaned quietly. Now and then he would cry for his mother. I shouted over to the prisoners near the cell door: "Call for the doctor!" From the other side somebody could be heard muttering, but nobody showed up. Through the mass of sitting and pros-

5. It was not by accident that I thought of this line from the *Tsar's Bride*. Grigori Gryaznoi was a member of Tsar Ivan the Terrible's personal bodyguard. In doing the tsar's dirty work, Gryaznoi showed extreme daring. People living under the Soviets were, with rare exceptions, just like him, inasmuch as they were involved, by force, in the dark deeds of our era. The epigraph to my book also alludes to this.

trate bodies I threaded my way to the door and started banging on it. The warder, a woman past fifty, retorted that it was already late, that the doctor had gone.

"Take the boy to the dispensary," I begged, "they can do at least something for him there. If he stays here, he'll die."

But for response I got only silence, as though she had walked away. Since my appearance already suggested that I was a criminal, I began to shout in a voice that fitted the part: "Listen, Auntie! Do you know what you're up to? If you want to kill us grown-ups, that's okay. But now you're killing children. Where do they find animals like you? You think you can get away with this?"

A couple of minutes passed. Then someone outside cried, "Give us the patient!" We carried the youngster into the corridor. The children and women in Stalin's camps seemed to me like something out of the Apocalypse.

When I woke up the next morning, I glanced around and saw that we had all been put in the same cell. It was one usually reserved for prisoners awaiting trial. Below the window were five professional criminals: youngsters with quite ordinary faces belonging to the category known as "Stalin's thieves."[6] They were children of liquidated kulaks, orphans whose parents had been imprisoned, homeless waifs from the war years. Next to them was a man of about thirty whom I hardly noticed at first, although he looked very familiar to me. Finally our eyes met, and he waved to me: "Hey, chief!" This was the way the criminals addressed you, and it sounded a little ominous. At the transit prisons, it was an accepted practice to hold kangaroo courts for the settling of personal grudges. But I was not aware of ever having done anything underhanded against any of the criminals. Whenever I had clashed with them, I always fought in the open and not behind their backs. But if they wanted to pay off a score with me, it was better to face up to the "charges" straightaway and find out exactly what they were all about. Pushing my way closer toward the window, I recognized the man as someone who had worked as a toolmaker and metal craftsman in Lindberg's shop at Vyatlag. He was a first-class thief-recidivist. We began chatting amiably. I recalled how he had been given his release together with an order drafting him into the army. At first he had hidden under his bunk, but there was no escape, and he ended up with Rokossovski.[7] He related how he had

6. The name we in the camps gave to those whom the conditions of the Stalinist regime had driven to thievery.

7. A Soviet field marshal during the Second World War.

deserted, but was then lucky enough to fall under Stalin's amnesty. Soon afterward, he committed another robbery, which got him back into prison. He had escaped, but now he was behind bars again.

Other criminals standing round him were all set to act as "judges" in a violent showdown, but they lost interest when they saw that the two of us were not about to grab each other by the throat. One of them asked my old acquaintance whether I had ever done any harm to the thieves. But as soon as the erstwhile toolmaker put his mind at ease on that score, there was no question of any "proceedings." However, if the "court" had consisted of sadists and malevolent degenerates, this whole situation could have led to a serious jailhouse brawl—even to my death.

My Meeting with Lev Kopelev

Eventually I arrived in Moscow—in Butyrki Prison, to be precise. I found myself jammed into a cell with other newcomers who were being assigned to prison research centers (*sharashkas*). We made up a congenial company—in the main, mechanical engineers, electricians, radio technicians. There were also a few chemists. Apart from us, there were men who had been recently sentenced and soon would be bound for a camp. Because of the rapid turnover of personnel in our cell, I managed to graduate to a bunk near the window only ten days after my arrival.

Once in the middle of the night, I was suddenly awakened by a noisy commotion. I looked up and saw[8] in the center of the passageway a handsome man in the prime of life, with black eyes and hair. He had the build of a guardsman. He kept up the racket, talking as he went along, obviously in a state of great agitation. From what I could make out, he had very recently been convicted and given ten years. Seething with anger, he refused to admit guilt to any crime and loudly proclaimed that he would regain his freedom. Since he was only a novice at prison life, his excitement was understandable. I went off to sleep again, but he continued in his rage for quite some time. Just before daylight I was aroused once more. Someone was climbing onto the bunks near where I was sleeping. Being an inveterate fresh-air fiend, and thinking he might be going to shut the window, I told the culprit off in plain camp language: "What the—do you want up here? Why are you closing the window?"

"I don't want to close it. I simply wanted to try and get a nap up here," he replied.

"All right," I said "that's different. Climb up and lie down. You've sounded off more than enough for one night."

8. In the prisons and camps the lights were never turned off at night.

258

In the morning, as soon as I woke up, we introduced ourselves. His name was Lev Kopelev. This was the beginning of our friendship, constantly interrupted by little "skirmishes" and extensive "engagements," all of which resulted from Lev's loyalty to the regime. He passionately defended everything that was being done in the country. His general position could be boiled down to a single formula: "If something is still wrong, then it is just a matter of putting it right." In those years, both in the jail and the *sharashka,* he seldom ever made concessions. He believed that everything was moving along just splendidly. At a much later period our debates at the *sharashka* were described by Aleksandr Solzhenitsyn in *The First Circle,* where Lev Kopelev appears as the character Rubin.

There seems to be a permanent alliance between the Soviet state and hunger. Either the regime cannot or will not feed the population. With the war at an end, what real necessity was there for continuing to starve our people? It was always the same old story: "bottlenecks" or "growing pains."[9]

As for us in the jail cell that morning, the usual meager bread ration and something resembling tea were being distributed. I saw Lev going over to his knapsack, from which he extracted a loaf of genuine white bread—moreover, it was fresh. He broke it apart and handed me half. After seven years I had forgotten not only how white bread tasted, but even how it looked. If Lev had given me only a tiny bit of it, I would have been rapturously happy. But here was *all* of a half-loaf! His grand gesture affected me in the same way as had the outspokenness of the Georgian and Prince Mirsky's marvelous tales. A generous nature and a nobility of spirit distinguished Lev from ordinary men. I am deeply fond of people of his kind. Yet his views were in total opposition to mine. He looked on me as a fossil because of my faith in God, my view of the February and October Revolutions, and my sharp criticism of what was happening in the life of our country. And when he tried to persuade me that, contrary to what I thought, all was going remarkably well, he seemed like some prehistoric monster to me. According to him, we who had been so long in the camps and prisons knew nothing of what had been taking place on the outside. Therefore, we simply could not understand how splendid everything now was. It was, of course, true that I had been seven years behind barbed wire, but during that period I had constantly met other prisoners who were just fresh from the outside. I always enjoy a lively exchange of ideas, and so I was now glad to meet in Lev an opponent who was similarly fond of debate. As a matter of fact, I had by

9. Over the post-war years these clichés were always cropping up in the pages of Soviet newspapers. They are in use even today.

this time almost forgotten that such people still existed. Whenever any had chanced to come my way, it immediately became apparent that they were stool pigeons in disguise. Now I was confronted by this misguided fanatic, yet for some reason I did not find him objectionable, probably because he not only stood up for his convictions but also tried to find convincing arguments in support of them.

By and large, I looked on his approach to things as a sort of harmless eccentricity; but he might end up paying for it with his head under present conditions. The general attitude in the camps and prisons was now very different from what it had been in 1940, when the majority of the prisoners had been loyalists who groveled before the Chekists and the camp authorities. Those were the days when we were entirely at the mercy of the informers. But now we had an entirely different breed: Red Army veterans and Vlasovites. Their mood was militant and they refused to think of themselves as beaten. The sort of thing Lev was saying could get him into serious trouble with them. But Lev was a reckless young man who never worried about what other people thought. At the end of his first day in the cell, he offered to entertain us by reciting two poems by Pushkin, "The Slanderers of Russia" and "On the Anniversary of Borodino."[10] It was an unfortunate, not to say inappropriate, choice and his performance could not have met with a more frigid response.

However, nothing could obscure for me the fact that he was a very splendid person, in spite of his avowed devotion to the regime. He was an exceptionally learned philologist and German scholar with a knowledge of many languages, and he was always the life of the party.

Since I had already been interviewed by representatives of the Fourth Directorate of the MVD,[11] I knew that I was going to be assigned to one of the *sharashkas,* and I told Lev that I would make every effort to get him into the same place, possibly as a translator or a librarian—he had no technical background whatsoever. Upon arriving at the *sharashka,* I lost no time in calling on the commandant and offering good reasons why he should arrange to have Lev Kopelev transferred there. Aleksandr Solzhenitsyn, already an inmate of the *sharashka,* wholeheartedly backed my proposal, even though he ran some risk of losing his librarian's job should Lev arrive.

10. The two poems are written in a declamatory patriotic tone unusual for Pushkin. (Tr.)

11. At that time the secret police had two separate departments: the MVD (the Ministry of Internal Affairs) and the MGB (the Ministry of State Security).

The Sailor from Auschwitz

In the cell at Butyrki Prison my attention was caught by a young man around thirty with a rather unprepossessing exterior: button-nosed, sickly pale, stockily built. On the left side of his chest, just above the nipple, was tattooed a six-digit number which I couldn't help noticing while we were at the baths. In explaining how he had come by it, he gave me a detailed account of his adventures. His name was Viktor Trushlyakov. At the beginning of the war a marine unit had been formed of sailors from ships that had been sunk. It was an elite corps. By this time Hitler's stupidity and barbarism had revealed themselves in full measure and the marines had fought like tigers, either at Sevastopol or Kerch—I don't remember which. After being wounded, he was captured by the Germans while unconscious. Twice he tried to escape, but finally he landed in Auschwitz, where he had been branded with this mark on his chest. On the whole he had gone through hardships comparable with what we had suffered during the war years in Soviet camps and prisons. Viktor was also assigned to our *sharashka*. His head was filled with inventions. One was a device for maneuvering tanks by remote radio-control, through gear boxes for high speed transmissions. I had assisted him in the selection and calculations of a variable speed reductor. He also had certain general scientific ideas which, it seems, had been suggested to him by a Catholic monk who died at Auschwitz.

16

AT THE SHARASHKA:
1947–1950

On Meeting Solzhenitsyn

The *sharashka* to which Trushlyakov and I were taken late one evening of October 1947 was situated next to Ostankino Park on the outskirts of Moscow in premises that formerly had belonged to a theological seminary. The *sharashka,* like others of its kind, was an engineering-design and scientific research unit that made use of the professional training and experience of prisoners. It was the same one that Solzhenitsyn later used as the setting for his novel *The First Circle,* in which the immates are brilliantly described. At the time we came there, it was still being organized and no serious work had as yet begun. As a result, our daily routine was relatively lax. Reveille was at seven in the morning and lights out at ten in the evening. We could walk around in the grounds whenever we wished.

The morning after my arrival, as I was drying my face on a government-issued towel, an impressive figure of a man in an officer's greatcoat came down the stairs. I took an immediate liking to the candid face, the bold blue eyes, the splendid light brown hair, the aquiline nose. It was Aleksandr Solzhenitsyn. After the transport and the month spent in Butyrki, I was starved for fresh air; so within moments I followed him outside. There was nobody around except for several prisoners conversing under the old linden trees on the lawn. Since I was still wearing the camp outfit that gave me such a cutthroat appearance, the other prisoners at once came up to me—except for Solzhenitsyn who strolled by himself some way off; but as soon as the others had satisfied their curiosity about me, he came over and suggested we take a short walk together. I shall never forget the first thing he said to me: "As I was coming down the stairs, what should I see in the darkness of the lobby but an image of the Savior Not-Made-by-Hand." Now that books are being written about Solzhenitsyn, I should like to mention that in Gleb Nerzhin, the main character of *The First Circle,* he gives an extraordinarily truthful and accurate picture of himself.

The Prisoner's Eighth Commandment

By the time that Lev Kopelev arrived at the *sharashka,* Sanya Solzhenitsyn and I had already established friendly relations. Lev himself very soon fell in with Sanya, since they had much in common. They had fought on the same front and had studied at the same institute; both had remarkable talents in the use of words. Lev, a fount of literary scholarship, was also unusually well informed on historical and political matters. Their friendship was hence perfectly understandable and natural. More difficult to explain is how I found myself in the same company, especially since Lev and I were poles apart on all basic questions concerning both past and present. I believe that at the beginning it was because I served as an antithesis to the two of them and hence as a kind of stimulant. Without intending any reproach to the author of *The First Circle,* who was in no way obliged to provide a photographic reproduction of life at the *sharashka,* it must be said for the record that, in describing the disputes between Rubin and Sologdin, he gives only a faint reflection of what these exchanges were actually like. As the one who was on the attack, I had no choice but to call things by their right names and to go at the Stalinist dictatorship hammer and tongs. And that, of course, infuriated Lev, provoking him to violent objections in support of a system which it is impossible to defend. For every such argument that we had, one of us could have received a twenty-five-year term for "slander" and the other ten for "failure to report." I doubt that our disputes would have been acceptable material for a novel that was intended to appear in the Moscow magazine *Novy Mir*[1] and they are consequently much toned-down in *The First Circle.*

Lev's lack of self-restraint was also due to the fact that, by comparison

1. Solzhenitsyn's first work, *One Day in the Life of Ivan Denisovich,* was published in *Novy Mir,* and he evidently hoped that both *Cancer Ward* and *First Circle* might appear there, too; but both were banned from publication in the Soviet Union. (Tr.)

with me, he had very little experience in debating. For the first time in his life, here at the *sharashka,* he was finding out what it was like when inwardly free people exchanged views. Until now he had always lived in an environment where people either assented to everything he said or else kept their mouths shut, knowing how terribly risky it was to engage in frank, open discussion wherever party members might be present. I realized that he had never thought of an open clash of opinion as a way of getting at the truth and standing up for it. He was content just to score debating points and so, feeling the ground give way under him, he would lose his temper and start shouting, or even become abusive. At times he seemed ready to kill me, but within a day or two things would calm down again. Very soon some opportunity for a new argument would arise, and we would be at it again. Usually these encounters were strictly between the two of us, though now and then we would turn to Solzhenitsyn for arbitration.

During those first six months, when the work at the *sharashka* was still only being organized, we spent many wonderful evenings in the library. Lev related his combat experiences, giving us his observations on the Germans, with whom he had contact as an interpreter. To this day I regret that we devoted only very few evenings to poetry readings. Both Lev and Solzhenitsyn recited beautifully. On one occasion I prevailed upon them to read something from Mayakovski's early works. Lev chose a passage from the poem "A Cloud in Trousers," and Sanya read "The Vertebrate Flute." Neither liked the poet very much; nonetheless, they recited him with great understanding. In my opinion the laurel wreath went to Sanya. With his dramatic talent, he enhanced the sound and sense of the lines by acting them out.

In the 1920's, I had not shared the enthusiasm of other people for Yesenin, Mayakovski, and Pasternak. The first of these had seemed to me simple-minded and confused; the second I found odious because of his ardent pro-Soviet attitude; the third bored me stiff. Pasternak had to stew in the Soviet cauldron another thirty years before he was capable of writing *Dr. Zhivago.* It was in the camp, actually, that I first had a proper look at Mayakovski's work, and in that phase of my life he touched a responsive chord with his brashness and crude strength, which harmonized with the brutality of camp life. At a later period, while in exile,[2] I made a special study of his art and of the poet himself—his personality was an integral part of his creative work. But at the *sharashka* we read his early Futuristic poems primarily for amusement.

2. I.e., after being released from the camp, but still compelled to live in a particular part of the country. (Tr.)

Solzhenitsyn is a man of exceptional vitality who is so constituted that he never seemed to get tired. He often put up with our society simply out of courtesy, regretting the hours he was wasting on our idle pastimes. On the other hand, when he was in good form or allowed himself some time for a little amusement, we got enormous pleasure from his jokes, witticisms, and yarns. On such occasions the flush on Sanya's cheeks deepened; his nose whitened, as if carved from alabaster. It was not often that one saw this side of him—his sense of humor. He had the ability to catch the subtlest mannerisms, gestures, and intonations—things that usually escape the rest of us—and then to reproduce them with such artistry that his audience literally rocked with laughter. Unfortunately, he only indulged himself in this fashion very occasionally among his close friends—and only if it was not at the expense of his work.

After leaving the *sharashka,* we were kept for thirty-five days at Butyrki while awaiting transfer to a "special camp."[3] Most of that time Sanya and I spent together. In the evenings he would always come up with some skit or other, imitating people he had been talking with, or, most often of all, acting out dialogues between prisoners and representatives of the authorities. The best was a telephone conversation between the director of the acoustics laboratory in the *sharashka* and the Chekist Shikin. I often asked him to repeat this for me.

In his writings, now a part of world literature, Solzhenitsyn shows how well he is able to inject subtle humor in generous quantities. *The First Circle* is permeated with it. Good-natured humor (as opposed to satire) is almost totally absent from Russian literature, and Solzhenitsyn, at least in my eyes, is better at it than any other Russian writer.

It was Lev who organized most of our evening entertainments, and for the first few months we were very much under his domination in this respect. One day I told my two literary friends that Russian verse held very little appeal for me because I failed to find in it any call to nobility, chivalry, or high deeds. And I quoted some lines from the scout's anthem: "Flinch not from work and danger. Remember that you are young and strong." "That's not poetry!" they exclaimed both together. I then asked them to tell me of any poet who reflected similar sentiments in a genuinely poetic form. The eighteenth century was too much of a bygone era, and in the nineteenth century the best-known poets did not sing of the ideals of chivalry but only made fun of them or deplored them. The ballads translated by Zhukovski lacked vigor and seemed insipid, and the other

3. "Special camps" were for political prisoners. Both Solzhenitsyn and the author were sent to one in central Asia, after being removed from the *sharashka.*

poets of that era were generally uninterested in the theme of chivalry. As for the twentieth century, Lev came up with one poet whose spirit was in close harmony with my own, even though he was not exactly what I had in mind. From memory Lev began reciting Gumilev, whom he loved and revered. Executed on orders from Lenin in 1921, Gumilev has not only gone unpublished throughout the era of Soviet rule, but every effort has also been made to consign his memory to oblivion; thus his poetry was for us a real discovery.

Sanya was then enamoured of Yesenin, several of whose better poems he read to us. But he was unable to win us over to him. With the passing years, however, my view of Yesenin has changed. I came to understand how a well-chosen collection of his verses might rekindle a love for the soil and the normal pattern of peasant life, especially among those in whom such feelings have been deliberately crushed by decades of collective farming.

Lev attempted to interest us in Bagritski,[4] but without success; neither his form nor content made any appeal to us. On the other hand we were captivated by Lev's renditions of the romantic songs of Vertinski.[5] He not only conveyed the melody and the lyrics with the right feeling, but he also reproduced Vertinski's characteristic gestures. As I watched, I couldn't help forgiving all his enthusiasm for Marxism-Leninism-Stalinism.

"Your friends are like your family." This eighth rule in the prisoner's code proved very well founded in the *sharashka*.

"The Language of Maximum Clarity"

I always referred to the Russian we spoke as "bird language," since it contained a great many borrowed foreign words, little or not at all understood by those who used them. I advocated a "language of maximum clarity" which I demonstrated in practice, causing much hilarity, amusement, and lively debate in our small circle. Lev was a first-rate philologist. Sanya was inferior to him in his knowledge of foreign languages, but when it came to a subtle understanding of Russian he had no equal, already in those days. In such brilliant company my arguments did not go unchallenged. The main lines of my thesis were as follows:

— A vast number of words in the contemporary Russian language are

4. A Soviet poet who died not long before World War II.
5. Russian singer who returned to the Soviet Union from emigration after World War II. (Tr.)

of foreign origin. They are alien bodies quite unconnected with the Slavic roots of the language. By using them we sacrifice precision in conveying our own ideas, as well as in understanding other people's, and create the illusion that we are lending clarity to our expression. As a result, we flounder in inaccuracy, ambiguity, and mumbo-jumbo. Our thinking and our speech remind one of a telegraph signal which converts words into dots and dashes but in the process constantly garbles them. In our ordinary everybody conversation we take even less trouble to be precise about our terms, spewing them out without proper regard for their aptness or lack of it in expressing the real sense of what is in our minds. All this is a fruitful source of confusion, facilitating distortion and deliberate deceit.

— A "language of maximum clarity," according to my idea, should consist of not more than a few hundred basic words, of which we have had a clear understanding ever since childhood. Several thousand concepts of a more complex nature should then be formed from these roots as compound words or expressions. At first the use of dictionaries might be required; but inasmuch as these elaborate compounds consist of familiar native roots, they will be easily memorized.

— In the sciences a "language of maximum clarity" would be unsurpassable for the accurate definition of concepts, though for practical purposes of international communication some foreign words would be permitted or even recommended.

— It is possible to create such a language. Though I am not a linguist, with no help from anyone I have fashioned a primitive, but workable model of what I mean. It is, of course, only a poor approximation. A proper "language of maximum clarity" would have to be worked out by experts and specialists in the field.

Many times I suggested to Lev that he take on this task. But he always turned it down—to my mind, for no good reason. With his vast knowledge, marvelous memory, capacity for work, and vigorous mind, he would have been able to do a rough outline or the whole thing while in prison and then put it into final shape when he was out. A great many people would have been grateful to him. Using the principles I have set forth here, painstakingly working out my terminology and refining it, I have succeeded in throwing some light on those mysterious concepts of the physical world, time and space—matters I have dealt with in works which I hope to publish very shortly in the West.

Lev rejected my proposition because it came from a man with an ideology alien to his own. In that respect he reminded me of the Communists in the first years after they had seized power—benighted, stunted people who had nothing to operate with except "class consciousness."[6] They divided the population into those who were to be stood against the wall and shot and those whom they would merely rob. Naturally, they totally distrusted people not of their own kind, and anything these had to say or suggest was regarded as coming from the "class enemy." Thus life became perfectly simple: no one was any longer required to think. Lev also could not swallow the fact that this scheme for designing a language of maximum clarity came not from a learned doctor, but from an obscure man with no scholarly degree or title. Then there was the fact that all his life Lev had been hopelessly mired in a system of pretended clarity, so that to undertake a task which by its very nature was concerned with absolute precision, he would first have had to break himself of bad habits of many years' standing. This would have been of enormous benefit to him, but in the process he would also have had to sacrifice some of his egotism, and—most important of all—shed his illusions about Communism and the methods by which its goals are attained. But Lev was so imbued with a fanatical faith in the postulates of Marxism that he could not conceive of his future work unless it was based on ideas derived from this source.

In all likelihood Lev's attitude was also influenced by the violent attack of the Michurinists[7] on "bourgeois" genetics, the "findings" of Lepeshinskaya[8] (for example, that living cells can be created from animal hydra after they have been pulverized in a mortar), Oparin's[9] explanation of the earth's origin, etc. These Marxist "discoveries," all inspired by quotations from Engels, elicited nothing but ridicule and contempt from intelligent people, and, as was only to be expected, they were denounced after the death of Stalin as illiterate charlatanism and sheer eyewash. But at the time I am speaking of this had not been so much as hinted at, and Lev, with his usual enthusiasm, was wholly engaged in studying the ideas of Engels—which are so noteworthy for their superficiality, as, for example, his contention that man's descent from the monkey goes back to the moment when the latter began to perform purposeful labor with its paws. In connection with this particular passage Lev assured us that all the

6. Soviet propaganda was constantly persuading the ordinary citizen that he was obliged to have "class consciousness" in order to expose the enemy.

7. Followers of the Soviet plant breeder and horticulturist, Michurin.

8. Lepeshinskaya belonged to the Bolshevik Old Guard. Her "theories" on genetics further contributed to stultification of Soviet biology initiated by T. Lysendo. Under Stalin's patronage she was awarded numerous honors, despite her crass ignorance.

9. Oparin, a chemist, was another of Stalin's "scientific" galaxy.

languages in the world had developed out of a word meaning "hand." His researches and discoveries caused a great deal of laughter. His pockets bulged with a wide variety of foreign dictionaries, and in all of them he found support for Engels's brilliant notion, which by now he was laying down as if it were his own. But suddenly all these theories of his were dealt a cruel blow by fate. In *The First Circle* Solzhenitsyn correctly notes that Lev (Rubin) experienced kindness only at the hands of his ideological opponents; from those who shared his intellectual attitudes he got nothing but the shabbiest treatment. This is just what happened now. The Father of all the Sciences, Comrade Stalin, as a result of his "brilliant" labors in the field of linguistics, suddenly denounced Marr's[10] theories on the class nature of languages. Thus Lev's hypothesis fell apart, since Marr also had been sustained by similar pronouncements from Engels and had attempted to prove their validity.

We were grateful to Lev for the amusing moments that his "discoveries" afforded us. My "language of maximum clarity" provided us with entertainment for even longer, since I went on giving demonstrations of it during the whole of our two and a half years at the *sharashka*. It even found a certain practical application in the work that Lev[11] was doing in line of duty on sound patterns—in his researches he invented some new terms by forming compounds from native Russian roots.

While we were carrying on our debates in the *sharashka* and I was doing everything I could to impress on people the importance of a "language of maximum clarity," Vyacheslav Ivanov, an extraordinary poet and thinker, was dying in Rome. After coming to the West, I read his tale about Prince Svetomir. I was enchanted not only by the profundity and strength of the piece but most of all by its language. For me it was the archetype of the "language of maximum clarity"; it was founded on wisdom and an all-encompassing view of life. My own attempts to do something similar can only be regarded as a single ray emanating from the brilliant sun of Ivanov's language.

The Rehabilitation of Sologdin

My first job at the *sharashka* was to set up and inspect mechanical equipment, most of which had been seized as reparations from plants belonging to the German firm of Lorentz. I was left pretty much to my own devices and consequently had plenty of free time. At first I spent it

10. An eminent Soviet linguist of Marxist orientation.
11. In connection with the work on "voice prints" described in *The First Circle*. (Tr.)

269

trying to recondition my memory by learning thoroughly the rules of German grammar. After that, I took up translating articles in German and French technical journals. I soon discovered that my ability to memorize purely factual data was irretrievably lost. I found it necessary to repeat a word a hundred times in order to fix it in my mind. Even so, it slipped away from me within a very short while. But anything in the life around me that struck me forcibly—even though I may not have been very aware of it at the time—became firmly fixed in my mind, which is the reason why I am now able to write these *Notebooks*. I consoled myself with the thought that, if the sense of touch becomes more acute among blind people, then it follows that my intuitiveness must grow keener to compensate for lack of memory. By this time I was wholly preoccupied with my chief purpose in life: to defend mankind—in particular, the ordinary working people—from evil that exists in the world. It was my desire to make at least a modest contribution to the common cause of men of good will[12] everywhere.

As an engineer I was quite at home when it came to applying the laws of mechanics and physics. But upon entering the hazardous realms of history, sociology, and philosophy, I realized that I would be unable to achieve anything of value without the guidance of the universal laws which operate not only in the physical world but also in human spirit and, hence, which determine the development of society. I spent ten years of my life, from 1948 to 1958, in pursuance of this task—though I must admit that I was sometimes forced to interrupt my work for long periods.

Early in 1948 I started seriously pondering a question that had intrigued me for a long time. Ever since my student days I had been of two minds in respect to Hegel's laws of dialectics, which Marx, as he himself expressed it, "turned upside down."[13] It was quite clear to me that everything in technology and science must be governed by universal laws of nature, and I therefore began to study the application of Hegel's three laws of dialectics to the processes of thermodynamics.

The principal value of the laws of development, as I called them in my "language of maximum clarity," is their application in areas where the action of the universal laws of nature has not yet been adequately studied: in sociology, biology, theology.

12. The term "men of good will" is subject to many different interpretations. But I am referring to those people who, in the struggle against evildoers, are capable of taking the initiative in establishing justice for all men on this earth.

13. Lenin, as well as his successor Stalin, also maintained that Marx had turned Hegel's dialectics upside down (see *History of the Communist Party of the Soviet Union; Bolsheviks: A Short Course,* chapter 4). This phrase was drummed into the heads of all Soviet citizens.

During my arguments with Lev, I resorted to examples from everyday life, such as washing pots and pans, constructing a table, staining a floor. To my way of thinking, whenever a man simply lifts his hand, all the universal laws come into play and affect the action in a way which may even be described. Lev raged in protest and scorned my lowly examples, shouting that all this was blasphemy, that the laws of dialectics may be applied only to the central aspects of being. Because of his attitude—or better to say, his total inability to approach these laws as an engineer does—Lev was not able to benefit from our debates in such a way as to reexamine his own system of ideas.

In *The First Circle,* my efforts at mastering the laws of development are reflected in the conversations between Nerzhin and Sologdin and in the disputes between the latter and Rubin.

In the spring of 1948 the *sharashka* was put under the control of the Ministry of State Security (MGB). I landed in the engineering-design office, while Sanya and Lev wound up in the acoustics laboratory. I tried to get a job that would give me the highest possible degree of independence and the least amount of work. My researches demanded free time and calm. I was able to assure myself of the first by strictly applying the Seventh Rule in the prisoner's code: "Let the Chekists live by slave's ethics"; calm I obtained from prayer and, later on, to some extent from yoga.

Our office had been asked to prepare drawings for control panels and also a design for the panels' mechanical coders. The second was not at all to my liking since it was of direct benefit to the Stalinist regime. At the outset it had appeared a purely civilian project, and I therefore did not object when I was assigned to develop one particular version. I put together a crude device simply to get the project off my back. A professor of mathematics approached me several times during working hours and questioned me about my effort. To an experienced cryptologist[14] the defects in my work would have been readily apparent, but he gave no such indication and did not warn me as any decent fellow-prisoner should have done. During the "inquest" on my work, the treacherous mathematician quickly pointed out its cardinal deficiencies. I was absolutely crushed. For a failure of this kind I could have been shipped off posthaste to a camp, but evidently the administration at the *sharashka* had by now recognized the impossibility of expecting rapid and brilliant results unless those on the project had sufficient time to prepare their work. I decided to take the bull by the horns and declared my unwillingness to work with coding devices until I could come up with a design that

14. A doctor of mathematical sciences.

would do away with gears. After thinking the matter over, the authorities consented, and thus I gained the opportunity I needed for putting my plan into effect. Engineers are men of a special breed. The fact that an engineer has no wish to do a certain job does not free him of the sense of humiliation he feels at having bungled it. For this reason I kept turning over in my mind a new scheme for a mechanical coder—with the sole aim of restoring confidence in me, but with the firm resolution that the regime would not profit from it.

Within a year I had found a theoretical solution which satisfied not only myself but also the highest authority in the field of cryptology, Professor Timofeyev, whom Solzhenitsyn marvelously portrays under the name of Chelnov. It was, of course, impossible to dispense completely with gears, but I had designed a mechanism that drew a vastly superior array of interconnected curves. An extremely complex graphical curve that was drawn by three rods linked together could not repeat itself in ten thousand years of operation. This mechanism did not draw random curves but represented the state-of-the-art that would require several years to decode. I persuaded "Chelnov" to give his expert opinion on my proposed design in complete secrecy, and the authorities thus never got any inkling of what I had done. The professor was very anxious that we submit the idea as a joint project, considering that it might earn us a remission of our sentences, since my coder could at last solve the problem of creating the telephone scrambler on which our *sharashka* was working on Stalin's personal orders. I gave "Chelnov" my view on the inadmissibility of strengthening the dictatorship; and on one of those days when the periodic destruction of rough drafts and other scrap paper took place, I burned all the material connected with the coder.

I now quietly and successfully continued to work at the *sharashka* quite unaffected by all the hustle and bustle typical of Soviet institutions. Reveille was at seven. After the morning exercises I sawed and split wood under the open sky. From nine till one and from two until eight, I worked mainly on things of no direct interest to the Ministry of State Security. From nine until ten-thirty in the evening, I regularly devoted my time to the problem which most concerned me. For the sake of better health I always slept by an open window. On Sundays, except for woodcutting, I did no work at all. I received rations of the lowest category. However, each month we were paid what would today be the equivalent of three rubles. The *sharashka* authorities were not at all happy about me, but at least I managed to arrange my time in such a way that I could read several books a month and talk with friends.

Suddenly, on the fourth of November, this pattern of life was abruptly upset: twenty *zeks,* including Professor Timofeyev, Lev, and myself, were taken away to Butyrki, where we were kept for an entire week. Frankly speaking, we had no particular reason to complain. By comparison with people in the camps, we had a fairly easy time of it—there was really nothing so terrible about spending a few days in this kind of jail. The only thing that bothered me was the stool pigeons whose numbers had increased enormously and who had become quite brazen. In such conditions of continuously increasing vigilance (now a real psychosis), it became clear to me that there was little point in trying to stay on at the *sharashka,* especially in view of my constant arguments with Lev in the presence of others and also in view of the fact that after my ten years in the camps the authorities kept a very close watch on me. Furthermore, I thought I would like to complete my camp "education" with a stay in one of the special camps about which we already had some idea from the accounts of eyewitnesses—but I would only be able to check these if I went to one myself.

For a few months I kept aloof from my friends during our daily walks while I weighed the pros and cons, prayed, and asked God for his counsel. Life was certainly not easy in the special camp where I eventually landed, but I never once regretted leaving the *sharashka.* The special camp gave me an experience of life which the *sharashka* could never have given me. Moreover, it offered me an opportunity to share with the brotherhood of camp prisoners the knowledge and reflections I had accumulated over many years. An opportunity of that sort could never have arisen under the conditions of the *sharashka.*

Upon reaching this decision, I set out that March to make it a reality. I openly showed my lack of interest in the work and dragged my feet in every way, handing in completed assignments only after I had been reminded several times. I often "talked back" at the authorities and some evenings I did not report for work. In springtime men willing to do chores outside were picked at roll call. Naturally, only the manual workers at the *sharashka* were usually considered for this kind of thing. But I boldly expressed my desire to join them. For days on end I soaked up the spring sunshine. None of the other engineers would ever have dared to do such a thing for fear of losing their jobs.

Solzhenitsyn also had his reasons for wanting to leave, and he joined me a couple of times in volunteering for work in the fresh air. On May 19 we were chatting amiably as we raked up the leaves, when suddenly a junior officer from the Security Section came up and said, "Panin and

Solzhenitsyn, get your things together and be ready to move out!" That same day we were sent to Butyrki. From there, after thirty-five days, we were put on a transport for Ekibastuz in Kazakhstan.

Before leaving, however, I went to turn in a precision instrument I had borrowed and met the secretary of the party organization, a design engineer who knew me well. He suggested that I write an official request to be kept on at the *sharashka*. I thanked him and said I did not want to stay on. Most likely, this was simply a trap set by the Chekists disguised as engineers—my overly independent behavior had irritated them and they calculated that I would grab at this straw to save my skin, after which they would simply laugh in my face when my hopes were dashed. It was also possible that the lady who appears in *The First Circle* as Emina had made an effort on my behalf. She and I had a jokingly flirtatious but absolutely platonic relationship.

The portrayal of Sologdin's eccentricities in *The First Circle* needs a word of explanation. Chopping wood was a thoroughly sensible activity and essential for good health. The same can be said of sleeping at night with a window slightly opened to allow a flow of fresh air into the cell. And there are certain sentences attributed to Sologdin which I can only have intended at the time in a strictly jocular sense.

In an interview given to an American correspondent in 1972, Solzhenitsyn revealed that there is another version—the original one—of *The First Circle*. I hope that when it is published, Sologdin will be rehabilitated by the author himself and transformed from a lady's man and careerist into something more worthy of—and nearer to—his living prototype.

17

AT THE SHARASHKA
(Continued)

The Pure in Heart

Blessed are the pure in heart, for they shall see God.
—Matthew 5 : 8

I long ago ceased attaching importance to a person's external attributes. "For there is no distinction between Jew and Greek: the same Lord is Lord of all and bestows his riches upon all who call upon him." (Rom. 10 : 12) For that reason, I never spurned a man simply because of his membership in the Communist party, and I learned to regard atheists as my brethren in urgent need of help. I always try to look beyond the externals to what is really important, judging a man in accordance with the extent to which he lives up to the following principles:

— It is deeds, not words that matter.

— Stand up for your convictions, but know when to admit defeat rather than persist in error: this is the price of progress.

— Love your neighbor and help him now instead of thinking only of future generations. Find out what he needs, and do not urge on him what you *think* he needs.

— Refrain from inciting malice and envy. Do not be vindictive. Remember that all men are brothers and that many matters can be resolved by peaceful means. Whenever it becomes necessary, intercede on behalf of the oppressed and arm yourself with a weapon of the same caliber as that of the aggressor.

Some people need to have only one attribute to exert a stronger hold on you than if they possessed many other qualities. In my native land there are very few individuals of mature years who belong to the marvelous breed of the pure in heart. A repressive regime has put their firmness of spirit to the supreme test.

Lev Kopelev was one such person. During one period of relative peace between us, we were sitting on our bunks one evening after supper. His lips spread slowly into a thoughtful smile; throwing off his party armor, he recited from memory and with deep feeling from the Apostle Paul:

" 'Even though I speak in the tongues of men and angels, but have not love, I am as sounding brass or clashing cymbals. Even though I have the gift of prophecy, know all mysteries, possess all knowledge, and have all faith, enough even to move mountains, but have not love, then I am as nothing. And even though I give away all my estate and offer up my body for burning but have not love, I will not profit thereby.' How well said. I would be a staunch defender of all that if Marxism hadn't come along."

"Lev," I replied, "at this moment you are your true self. Stop being so obstinate: you can't go on defending something that is rubbish. It only demeans you. If you take up the weapons of truth, there'll be few to equal you. Even though the old Slav god Perun still dwells in my heart, my abode of salvation is Christianity, the wellspring of pure goodness and noble precepts. Unfortunately, like most people, I have strayed far from the commandments of the Saviour. I expend a lot of effort to overcoming temptation, making up for my shortcomings, showing sympathy for others, curbing my own arrogance and sharp tongue—I feel it my duty to correct my faults. But you do everything you can to make yourself worse, even though all the good in you is crying out to be given its head. In your soul you are really a Christian—and we can only envy you." Ten minutes of relaxation before the bell rang for the evening shift had banished his fatigue, and Lev was once more every inch the Communist as he returned to his work.

Another person of the same type is the woman dearest to me in this late period of my life. She was born in 1922 and was brought up by her idealist mother as a loyal supporter of the regime. She studied at the well-known Twenty-fifth Model School in Moscow, which was attended by children of highly-placed Kremlin officials. Among them were Svetlana and Vasili Stalin. As a student, caught up in patriotic fervor, she went off as a volunteer to the front, where she served in army intelligence and was even wounded in action. According to the custom then prevalent, she joined the party while serving at the front and remained in it for thirty years.[1] Through those long years she sat through countless party meetings,

1. It is impossible to leave the Communist party of the U.S.S.R. of one's own volition.

but she evaded involvement in any of its dirty assignments. It was clear to everyone that she had too much courage and pride to take part in such things. In 1943 she was hauled in for interrogation in connection with the Arkadi Belinkov case,[2] but the Chekists could get nothing out of her. During the years when the dictatorship was steadily growing in strength—before the death of Stalin—she fearlessly declared herself of the side of a man who had been publicly denounced as an enemy of the people. As a consequence, she began to be harassed and was dismissed from her job. In 1971, after two heart attacks, this gentle and frail woman fought singlehandedly against a whole pack of party bureaucrats in order to get permission to leave the U.S.S.R. The home of this woman was a haven for the oppressed and the persecuted. Her free time was at their disposal, and her assistance was available to those in need. Her purity of heart always preserved her from wrong-doing, and her kind deeds strengthened her soul.

The Potapovs

While at the *sharashka* I doubt that a single word ever passed between the engineer known in *The First Circle* as Potapov and myself. I felt a deep antipathy toward him, even though he did no direct harm either to me or to his other associates. I only have to call him to mind to become instantly charged with contempt, as if a current from an inductor were passing through me. My recollection of this character is different from Solzhenitsyn's.

For me Potapov was a prime example of those people of good will who forget their duty, their higher obligations to other human beings. Instead, they crawl on their bellies in order to serve and prop up a regime based on terror and oppression. Potapov understood everything as well as we did, but he would never reveal his private thoughts. He talked only on neutral topics and then only with cautious persons like himself. He was always in mortal fear of displeasing the authorities, of attracting the attention of the Chekists. He was a man of uncommon ability, a fine engineer. He knocked himself out in trying to prove to everybody that he was an indispensable specialist. And in that he succeeded, holding on at the *sharashka* longer than anyone else, although he was no specialist on telephonics. Solzhenitsyn described him as a "bewildered robot." He indeed

2. A highly talented journalist, writer, and critic. During his student days he was sentenced to ten years in the camps because of the manuscript of a novel he was writing. He died in the United States in 1971.

played the robot's role, but as for bewilderment—any doubt or hesitation arising from a lack of understanding of what he had to do—he didn't have a bit of it. Hard-working by nature, he had no trouble being a robot, a distinction that gave him many advantages: security, good relations with the authorities, better food, the maximum that a prisoner could receive in pay, and meetings with his wife. The majority of the convicts were favorably disposed to him, probably because he satisfied the two chief requirements of a prisoner: he was neither a stool pigeon nor a thief. In general he went down well with people—he was always ready with a smile and was forever quoting from Pushkin's *Yevgeni Onegin*. But I could see what he was really like underneath and his double dealing—for that's essentially what it was—disgusted me. When a man who has been fed on propaganda since childhood and is thereby corrupted thinks only about himself and cares nothing for everybody else, it is understandable. I have met many such people along my way and often experienced a mixed feeling of aversion and pity when I saw how hideous they had become. With Potapov it was an entirely different matter. Raised in a Christian family, he had been able to finish elementary school before 1917 where he had been given religious instruction. He was aware that a great many of his relatives and friends had been jailed, executed, or shipped to remote parts of the country. But he had chosen to withdraw into his cozy shell and to masquerade as a mechanical robot. Before the war he had been the chief engineer at the Dnepropetrovsk Electric Power Station, in which capacity he was lucky to escape arrest in 1937. During the war, after his capture by the enemy, he thought only of how he might survive and, upon returning home, keep up his good relationship with the Stalinist regime. But he miscalculated. All war prisoners were treated in the same way and no exceptions were made for anyone. The Chekists sent him off to do ten years. In prison he surpassed everybody in his industriousness and servility. After his release he rose rapidly: he obtained an apartment, a position, a car, and a dacha. He was quite indifferent to the struggles, unhappiness, and ordeals of others. As long as he was comfortable, he didn't care a damn about anything else. There are many people like him, and he soon found himself accepted among them. As for men who acted out of conscience, he wrote them off as failures and eccentrics who just weren't in touch with practical realities. Sometime in the mid-1960's I met him by accident in the home of a mutual acquaintance. He was smug and arrogant. And as in the old days, he kept his mouth shut whenever the conversation turned to politics. It all made a very disagreeable impression.

It was the Potapovs of the world—but of a somewhat older generation

—who were responsible for the catastrophe that began in October 1917. There were Potapovs serving as officers in Petrograd and Moscow. But they sat out those short October days in their quarters, playing cards and drinking coffee. As they liked to put it themselves, they wanted to stay neutral and not involve themselves in the great world events then taking place. But even if they did not understand the significance of what was happening, at least they might have shown a little concern over their own fate. Some were prevented from doing so by the intellectual nonsense with which their heads were stuffed, others by doubt and timidity, but the majority were simply reluctant to sacrifice themselves—an attitude that led to the fall of the Provisional Government, the crushing defeat of the cadet officers in Moscow, the breakup of the Constituent Assembly. The Potapovs kept hoping that someone else would deal with the mere handful of revolutionary sailors and soldiers from the reserve regiments that had never even seen any action. But nothing of the sort was to happen and soon the Potapovs were being hauled off to the Cheka, where they were either stood against the wall and shot or conscripted into the Red Army. And so it was that these officers, even though filled with loathing and revulsion toward their new masters, fought conscientiously on the side of the Reds. In this new situation (where they would be shot by a commissar or sent to the Cheka for refusing to cooperate) they forgot about their "neutrality" in a hurry. The general staff of the Russian Imperial Army had consisted almost entirely of Potapovs who now simply moved over to the general staff of the Red Army.

The Potapov element was just as huge in the world of business, among bank clerks and similar functionaries. If they had refused to serve the new regime, it would have been paralyzed and overthrown within a few months.

In the years that followed, when the Soviet Union began to arm itself to the teeth, it was the special engineering-design departments set up in the prisons[3] that produced the best rifles, artillery, tanks, and aircraft. The inventors who worked on them eagerly overcame all the inertia of the bureaucracy in order to push ahead as rapidly as possible with their bombers, fighter planes, rockets, poisonous gasses, and bacteria for germ warfare. Before the war they justified the armaments drive because it was necessary to save the country from invasion by Hitler, and after the war, because it was the only way of countering "capitalist encirclement and American imperialism." But just who are they, these servants of the regime? By and large they are the Potapovs, who have now proliferated in vast numbers. They fill the top-secret institutes that are referred to

3. These were the forerunners of the *sharashkas*.

only by a number; they jam the special military experimental plants. To win a meager bonus they propose new technological advances, or make discoveries of military significance. Their minds are constantly on doctoral theses and scholarly degrees, as well as the material blessings that flow from them. For the sake of all this, they are prepared to sell their souls to the devil.

All those who furnish modern despots with atomic and hydrogen bombs, ballistic missiles, and other weapons of mass destruction we haven't yet heard of should realize that if they play a part in the development of such devices, they are either cannibals or Potapovs. The first are quite unconcerned by the prospect of innocent people being wiped out, and the second know full well that they are engaged, purely out of self-interest, in preparations for mass murder.

The Old and the Young

We had among us a twenty-two-year-old American mulatto, born of a marriage between a Jewish father and a Negro mother. He had worked in some capacity or other at the American embassy in Moscow. After getting married in the Soviet Union, he apparently took steps to change his citizenship. But just at that time he ran afoul of the Soviet authorities and was given twenty-five years. He had no specialized background, so he was assigned to the filing department. Maurice's face was rather dark, his hair curly and black. His fingernails were of a bluish hue underneath. We had merely read about this peculiarity of Negroes previous to his arrival, so it was interesting for us to see it with our own eyes.

Back in the twenties it had been hammered into our heads that American Negroes existed only for the purpose of being lynched. Later on, we heard that this practice was restricted to the Southern states. In the camp, incidentally, we came across some statistics of the "trials" rigged up by the criminal element in Soviet prisons, along with figures on the murders of prisoners who had been "lost at cards."[4] In the course of one month the victims of such practices outnumbered those lynched by the Ku Klux Klan over a ten-year period. But the fact was that the Blacks were still not enjoying all the rights and liberties of American citizenship, and for this reason Maurice was assured of our sympathy, though he rather stood out from the rest of us by his behavior—to our minds his manner was too free and easy, and he behaved rather noisily at the table during mealtime.

4. The thugs used to stake some man's life on the outcome of a card game, and the loser was obligated to kill him.

He gained fame and glory throughout the *sharashka* the time he delivered to the prison director a formal request—written in verse, with the help of Lev Kopelev—for a new pair of boots. In a mocking tone Maurice wrote that he didn't want just ordinary boots, but a pair which would hold up through his piddling twenty-five-year term. He expressed the hope that his sons—and his grandsons—would also be able to wear these remarkable shoes. Even in so relatively privileged a place as the *sharashka* a pair of boots lasted hardly a year—and if you were doing hard labor in a camp they had a life span that measured not in months but in weeks—the absurdity of this situation was all too obvious. The poem ended with the line: "Sadly yours, Maurice Gershman, the *zek*." For a couple of weeks Maurice was the *sharashka*'s hero and won a lot of smiles; somehow he got away with this piece of mischief.

The next time, his freedom-loving nature expressed itself in an absolutely incredible fashion. Once at supper we were given kasha that had got burned a little while it was cooking. I myself paid no attention to this and simply ate up the portion. The more privileged prisoners[5] pushed the stuff aside without saying a word. But Maurice seized his plate and shot it across the floor along the aisle between the tables, right in the direction of an approaching security officer. At an American college such behavior might have been in the natural order of things, but at the First Camp of the MGB (as our *sharashka* was officially designated), this sort of trick was tantamount to throwing a bomb. The astounded officer tried to say something, but Maurice got in first and started shouting that he was not a pig who could eat any old garbage, that he had no desire to live in this country, and that he wanted to be sent back to the United States. The effect was extraordinary. The officer simply tried to get him to calm down and stop shouting. If it had been one of us, he would have found himself in no time in the commandant's office and then on his way to Butyrki—which was not so bad if it only meant a spell in the punishment cell there, but if they decided to bring a new case against you, it was quite another story. Maurice, however, fared differently: he was summoned by the authorities and told he would be sent to a real camp. Once again he got cheeky. When finally he was taken away, some of us concluded that the authorities had reconsidered his case and were sending him back to America. If this was in fact so, then as his old fellow-prisoner, I send him belated but heartfelt greetings.

On three different occasions I met Professor Svetnitsky, once a colleague of Rutherford. In 1941 he spent two weeks in Butyrki in the cell where we were waiting for a transport. At that time he was a strong,

5. Those who received a diet higher in calories than ours—more butter, sugar, etc.

healthy man of about sixty. I believe that this first-rate scientist would have made a considerable name for himself if he had not been so rash as to return "home" to the U.S.S.R. in 1937. Besides being a physicist and chemist, he had a splendid knowledge of the Persian poets. Upon our request he would recite from memory Saadi, Firdousi, and others. He was also fond of telling about his travels in the West and about life there. We had previously heard so many scintillating accounts that we were by now somewhat spoiled. Nonetheless, we listened to the professor's stories with great interest and were never in the least bit bored.

In 1948 the professor turned up at the *sharashka,* working as a civilian in one of the secret-project laboratories. He had grown fat and flabby, his facial features had changed out of all recognition, and he had lost his teeth. He did not recognize me and, in order not to cause him embarrassment, I gave no sign of ever having known him. But one day I went up and asked him for his opinion on the principle of Le Chetelieu, about which I had read in an organic chemistry textbook back in 1935. His response was immediate: "The rule is now considered obsolete, and I don't advise you to apply it."

Several months later, the professor was again arrested. His photograph was removed from the honor board,[6] where an empty space now stared at us. Solzhenitsyn tells of this in *The First Circle.* The news spread rapidly among us, and curses were heaped on the torturers who were now subjecting this venerable scientist of seventy years to fresh ordeals.

My third encounter with the professor was at second hand. A good acquaintance of mine, formerly a prisoner at Kolyma, had been with the professor in the same cell sometime in the fifties, at the time that their cases were being reviewed. And now at the end of the sixties he paid Svetnitsky a visit in Moscow. Now ninety years old, the professor had preserved his liveliness of mind and recited for our acquaintance a little verse: "Hunger and cold—I have lived through it all. And I am still young because I thumbed my nose at them."

Afanasyev was neither a youth nor an old man, but in the prime of life. He was a naturally gifted person possessing a wealth of skills in many different areas, but he had not completed his higher education. There was nothing he couldn't do well, and he achieved professional standards in anything he undertook. At the *sharashka* he was engaged in television research, and in 1949 he built a set having, at that time, the largest screen in the U.S.S.R. (60×60 cm.). Afanasyev also had an extraordinary gift

6. In the U.S.S.R., photographs of men and women who have distinguished themselves in their work are posted on honor boards in factories and other enterprises.

for music and played the violin. He was a good Christian, but being a man of proud and independent disposition and having a great sense of his own worth, he tended not to take account of the fifth rule of the prisoner's code, "Don't get above yourself," and consequently ran into a great deal of trouble during his imprisonment. At his interrogation he also behaved with fierce defiance, refusing to give testimony, denying everything, and accusing the interrogators of organizing a frame-up. The Chekists forced his "accomplices" to denounce him for all they were worth. In those days refusal to admit one's guilt had no substantial bearing on the outcome of his case. The interrogators simply overwhelmed Afanasyev with piles of damning testimony, and the court handed him the maximum penalty. He did not take the trouble of writing a letter of appeal. But since executions were not then in fashion with the authorities because of the great need for manpower, a lawyer at the prison wrote an appeal for him. When the hour for his execution arrived, he was brought from the death cell with his belongings. The "death commandant"—the name we used to give to executioners in political prisons—ordered Afanasyev to put his hands behind his back and, covering him with a pistol from the rear, steered him along the corridors, hallways, and staircases of the vast underground dungeon. The march came to a halt by the main entrance, where Afanasyev was told that his death sentence was being commuted to ten years in prison. This whole performance illustrates with what malevolence the Chekists were capable of taking it out on someone if they had been thwarted in their desire to execute him— there was an established rule in Soviet prisons that a condemned man must be given his pardon the very instant he stepped out of his cell. The mock "execution" left two small bald patches the size of bullet holes on the back of Afanasyev's head. During those moments of waiting for death, neural processes in his mind had engraved an indelible picture of the two seemingly inevitable Chekist bullets being fired into the back of his head. These marks were very conspicuous when he once returned to the *sharashka* after five days and nights in the punishment cell, where his head had been shaved bare. He had landed there because he had been insolent to the *sharashka* authorities. If someone else had done it, he would have been put on the next transport to an ordinary camp; but since Afanasyev was extremely good at his job, they put him in the punishment cells instead.

I felt the keenest sympathy for him. Twice we celebrated Christmas and Easter together, although by nature he was a loner and had no friends. On the day of my departure I dropped into his lab to say good-by. Thankfully, it was not a secret lab, and I spent several minutes with him and a pretty young woman, one of the free workers employed by the *sharashka,* who happened to be there, too. I thought to myself that this forbidden liaison would soon earn him another spell in the punishment cells—it was obvious that, without intending to, this magnificent fellow had aroused strong feelings in her.

A Twentieth-Century Faust

Nearly all the characters in Solzhenitsyn's *First Circle* had living prototypes. Nerzhin, Rubin, Kondrashov, Pryanchikov, and Spiridon were taken directly from life. Agniya, Bobynin, Ruska, and Innokenti were composites of various people. Yakonov, Roitman, Shikin, Gerasimovich, Abakumov, Stalin, and others have undergone a literary reworking at the author's hands. The prototype for the painter Kondrashov I often met again when I lived in Moscow, between 1957 and 1967 until the moment when we quarreled.

Kondrashov was quite unconcerned with politics. He was in love only with his art. Trained as a mathematician, he knew all about literature and was interested in Ancient and European philosophy. He did not deny the existence of God, though he regarded Him as a kind of supreme being who did not require him to belong to any of the established religions. Because so many books were unobtainable in Moscow, one had to depend on serious conversation to a much greater degree than is the case in the West: without such exchanges life would lose its meaning for me. In Kondrashov I saw not only a painter—as much as painters had always attracted me—but also a very worthwhile man to debate with. As a rule, I refrained from comment on his painting, but once I found it necessary to express an opinion about it. Insofar as he belonged to any school, it was to the Realist painters of the nineteenth century: his people looked like people, a cup of tea was three-dimensional and appeared to be the real thing, his tree was a solid tree, not a diagram of one. But sometimes he would make an ear disproportionate to the length of a man's face when he worked with clay. His work was remarkable for its brilliant colors, which he applied with the skill of a master. His paintings should have been taken out of his hands the moment he completed them, because he was never satisfied with them and spoiled most of them by endless retouchings and refinements. He worked ten years on his painting *Othello, Desdemona, and Iago.* As always, he started with the subjects' heads. In 1959, after two years at it, the picture was finished—to my eyes, at least. Desdemona was leaning against the balustrade of a stairway. She appeared to sense that death was imminent. Her face was ashen white, her eyes downcast. Standing on the step above was Othello, his massive head bent toward her. His large features, twisted by hate and torment, were splendidly conveyed. His hair looked as if it had been sculpted from stone. It was plain to see that he was torn between wrath and love, suspicion and hope. The colors of his garments were in keeping with the turbulent state of his mind; the crimson cloak suggested the folded wing of some large bird. The only change I thought necessary was the removal of Iago from the foreground. In all other respects the painting looked finished. But Kondrashov was of another mind. He considered the work to be only at an intermediate stage.

He worked on it for a further eight years, jealously concealing his creation from the eyes of others. He had decided to let me see it only after he had put the final touches to it. At last, in the summer of 1967, the day came. Before my astonished gaze was something quite monstrous. Othello's neck was so elongated that it suggested the body of a huge python. By contrast, the head was so reduced in size as to be reptilian, and the eylids were like an alligator's scales. Desdemona had been transformed into a she-devil who looked rather pleased with herself as she cast a sly glance in Iago's direction from beneath lowered eyelids, happy that she was so capable of arousing Othello's jealousy. In the first painting Iago had been a clever schemer, but in this one he was a cunning and vindictive demon, an agent of death and decay. I was struck speechless: it was like some kind of bad dream.

Then I exploded: "You have given your soul over to the Devil. You are a twentieth-century Faust. But the old Faust was at least perfectly aware of what he was doing and made certain conditions. But you have fallen into the Devil's clutches without even knowing it."

On leaving I begged him not to destroy either version, but to preserve them both—for the sake of his contemporaries and posterity. Kondrashev was offended, and after that our relations were never the same again.

In 1959 Solzhenitsyn and I had together seen the first version of the painting. He stood looking at it thoughtfully for quite a long time and found it to his liking. He also considered it a finished work. Suddenly, with the vigor characteristic of him, he rapped out: "I quite understand why great artists have always drawn on the eternal subjects in Holy Scripture, and I can see why they also find inspiration in Shakespeare's art. But I cannot understand why an artist should be so firmly attached to the subject matter of ages so remote from ours after he has been witness to the sufferings of people close by him. Fidelity, jealousy, and treachery as they exist in our own day are right in front of him and all around him."

18

AT THE HARD LABOR CAMP: 1950–1953

Stalin's Brand of Hard Labor

In 1943 Stalin switched to the offensive on all fronts. The shift was marked by two innovations:

— the introduction of the death sentence by hanging for particularly bad offenders (the rest were executed by shooting, as before);

— the discovery of penal servitude.

The same line of thought that prompted Generalissimo Stalin to fasten the insignia of the old Imperial Army on the shoulders of his officers also led our great "military genius" to look at the tsarist archives and see how forced labor convicts had been treated in the old days. Tsarist hard labor was a bed of roses compared with the Soviet system of prisons and camps: there had, of course, been no production quotas, and during the 1900's prisoners were not required to do hard labor at all. There had been plenty to eat: bread in abundance and buckwheat kasha with fried pork cracklings. Aside from this regular ration, a pound of meat—right to the ounce —was issued to each man.

With his universal genius Stalin introduced his own unchallengeable modifications into the idea he had borrowed. Hard-labor convicts were put to work of the most backbreaking kind. They were put in separate camp sections, where the barracks were kept locked throughout the night. Four numbers were sewn on their camp clothing—on their caps, on both the back and front of their shirts, and on one trouser knee. The foremen, especially in the early days, ruthlessly eliminated *tufta*[1] from work-

1. *Tufta:* See note on page 50. (Tr.)

286

assignment sheets. The convicts were marched into the mess hall in brigade formation and for the slightest infraction they were thrown into punishment cells. Throughout the camps and prisons the Chekists put rumors into circulation that the hard-labor convicts consisted mainly of the most incorrigible traitors, Gestapo men, and cutthroats.

While I was working at the plant in Vorkuta, I was once sent over to one of the hard-labor barracks, which existed side by side with the regular camp zones. I had gone to see Bobrov, a brilliant engineer, whom the plant, contrary to regulations, used as a consultant whenever extremely complex problems arose. He had been given a special office away from the other prisoners and worked there together with a number of free employees of the camp. He was a quiet, tall man with a regular, but roughly hewn, profile. His great powers of mind and will impressed me immediately. He had worked for the Germans as chief engineer at a Messerschmidt aircraft plant. He told me how he had emerged as the victor from a little clash with Field Marshal Goering.

When I asked him what sort of people the other hard-labor prisoners were, he smiled ironically and said that for the most part they were harmless Ukrainian peasants who had been jailed as a result of informers' denunciations. In later days, at the special camps, we found that what Bobrov had told me was entirely accurate: the major military offenders picked up in the territories recaptured from the Germans were hanged or shot, and only the small fry were sent off to penal servitude.

In *The First Circle* the engineer Bobynin had no real-life counterpart in the *sharashka*. Solzhenitsyn created this figure, to some extent, on the basis of my recollections of the engineer Bobrov to which he listened with great interest.

Encounters Along the Way

Sometime during the final days as we were waiting for our transport at Butyrki, Ruska[2] was brought over from the *sharashka* and placed in our cell. Anyone who has read *The First Circle* will doubtless recall this enterprising, resourceful, and bold youth—the one who falls in love with Klara. He was being shipped out to Vorkuta. Sanya and I regretted that he was not going along with us.

The transit jail at Kuybyshev, the first stop on our journey, was a rest home by comparison with others we stayed in. In no other transit jail

2. The inspiration for Solzhenitsyn's creation of this character came mainly from P. Gertsenberg, who today is living in Israel.

were we ever fed so well. We were quartered in what had formerly been stables. Although there were a great many of us, we had plenty of open space in the aisles between the bunks and could move back and forth with no difficulty.

One day about dusk, some men from a transport fresh out of Moscow were marched into our ward. Among those at the head of the column was a tall Viking in a foreign uniform from which the insignia had been stripped. He had a candid face, ash-blond curly hair, and bold blue eyes. He looked around at his new surroundings with considerable interest. After making his acquaintance, I learned that Arvid Andersen was a Swedish count and the son of a millionaire. As a volunteer he had joined the British army during England's difficult hour and fought until the end of the war. Among other things, he had engaged in hand-to-hand combat with a German division at Ardennes. After the war he graduated from the General Staff Academy in Stockholm and then served on a military mission in West Berlin. During the post-war years he fell under the influence of Marxist ideology and, in that connection, wrote a couple of articles, using all the standard phrases. In 1947 he came to Moscow with a delegation from the Swedish General Staff. A great fuss was made of him and he was even driven out to a luxury government estate on the outskirts of the capital where he was given everything the heart could desire. Later, in East Berlin, while on his way to visit a woman singer of his acquaintance, he was trailed by Soviet Chekists, seized and carried off to Moscow. There he was held under arrest in an out-of-the-way country house, well covered by guards armed with submachine guns. Teachers were sent out to give him lessons in the Russian language and Communist political doctrine. The Soviets demanded that he write an article damning capitalism and praising the Stalinist regime. In return, they offered him a job on the Soviet General Staff and all the material privileges that went with it. With indignation and scorn he turned down the whole proposition. It was one thing to indulge in a casual flirtation with Marxism on the pages of a magazine, but quite another to play false to his own principles. He believed that the European nobility would never forgive General von Paulus for his act of betrayal and had no wish to incur similar opprobrium.

After numerous attempts at persuasion had failed, his captors resorted to threats. Finally they transferred him to the Lubyanka in Moscow, to the inner prison, where he was put in a special cell, smartly furnished, on the top floor. Vyshinski, the minister of Foreign Affairs, and Abakumov, the head of State Security (MGB), came to talk with him. Arvid became menacing, demanded his freedom, and shouted so loudly that the foreign minister turned white as a sheet. But Abakumov, in a quiet, cold-blooded manner, summed up his situation in few words: "Since you've rejected our proposals, you'll have to stay in prison." He said that Arvid would be sentenced to twenty years, but that in view of his special position, certain privileges would be granted to him: they would not shave his head, and they would give him ten rubles a month (according to present-day rates of exchange). Since he had not, however, been given any money for the journey, Sanya and I shared in brotherly fashion the little money which we still had left over from the *sharashka*. He was being transported in a separate compartment—this despite the overcrowding in all the other "cages" on the train. At the transit prison the arrangements for his isolation had broken down: either they had no solitary cells or the documents accompanying him omitted to mention that he was to be kept separate in transit jails. In any case, Arvid ended up spending two weeks among the rest of us just like any other prisoner.

Prior to that time, I had run across a great many aristocrats, both Russian and foreign; but for princely dignity and complete self-confidence, Arvid was quite outstanding. Not long before my departure for the West, a professor's son told me that his father had spent some time with Arvid in Krasnouralsk Prison back in 1956, and that Arvid was still unbroken. After coming to the West, I tried to get some information about him from the Swedish embassy in Rome, but there I was told that they had no information about a missing person of this name. I should tell the Swedes one further detail that has stuck in my mind and which will be enough to enable them to continue the search from him: his mother was an Englishwoman and a close relative—perhaps a sister—of General Robertson, who was in command of the British Zone of Occupation in Germany after the war. In the U.S.S.R. there are scores of men who were personally acquainted with Arvid, and there are hundreds who have at least heard of him. The Swedes have the right to know about the heroic conduct of one of their sons.[3]

At the same transit prison Solzhenitsyn and I became friendly with a Ukrainian called Pavlik. He had landed in prison as a follower of Bendera. In appearance he reminded me of an ancient Roman legionary. His chest and thighs looked as if they had been cast in bronze; his well-proportioned arms and legs were bound in muscles of iron strength; his shoulders were unusually broad. But the oval face, the aquiline nose, and the strong chin were reminiscent rather of ancient Greek sculptures. And

3. After being in the West a while, I realized that the Soviets may have forbidden him to reveal his true identity. Solzhenitsyn also makes this supposition in Volume I of *The Gulag Archipelago*.

these features were set in the framework of his smooth black hair. With his liveliness and inborn vitality, he resembled the musketeer from Gascogny immortalized by Dumas. There were many courageous people among my friends, but Pavlik was like a lion. I saw him in action for the first time when some of the criminals called Volodya Gershuni[4] "Mr. Fascist." Frail and thin, the boy began to shake with anger and went for the men who had insulted him. He had not yet learned the *zek*'s fifth commandment: "Don't look for trouble." He didn't yet know that it was not essential to react to the verbal abuse which was a normal part of prison life. The word "insult" had no meaning for us; only acts of physical violence were thought worthy of a response in kind. Intervening just in the nick of time, Pavlik rushed to Volodya's aid and with no trouble at all drove off his persecutors. The criminals then drew knives. Pavlik seized the nearest of them by the wrist and gave his hand a sharp wrench. The knife dropped from his hand, and Pavlik picked it up. Now that he was armed, he was itching for more combat. But the cutthroats had no stomach for tackling a man with a knife, so Pavlik had won the day. This incident only reinforced our reputation as "vicious *frayers*."[5]

Pavlik was very easily influenced. When in the company of Bendera men, he was a Benderist. When with Solzhenitsyn and other former army officers, he was an ex-lieutenant of the Soviet Army. In my presence he conducted himself like a true son of a trooper who had served in the "Wolf Squadrons"[6] under the White general, Shkuro. But no matter what role he played, he put himself into it body and soul.

Later, in a subterranean cell of the famous prison in Omsk, we arranged an evening of comic entertainment in order to cheer up the newcomers from the western Ukraine who were put in among us at the Kuybyshev and Chelyabinsk transit jails. Solzhenitsyn started it off for us, but then he left. He had no desire to fritter away his time on such idle pursuits. Even in those days he was already busily gathering and pondering material for his future books. We had others who could put on comic turns and tell funny stories, and they kept things moving along. Among them was Volodya Gershuni. Without a trace of a smile, in the deadpan manner of Buster Keaton, he kept us in stitches with short stories by Zoschenko and Shklovski.[7] This firmly established his reputation as very good company indeed.

Volodya was the nephew of the socialist-revolutionary terrorist Ger-

4. A Soviet dissident who is again serving a term of imprisonment.
5. See page 35. (Tr.)
6. His father actually had been a cavalryman in the "Wolf Squadron" during the Civil War.
7. Soviet writers.

shuni. He was constantly telling us that all Jews are brave, and he considered it his duty to prove it by his own personal example. Since he now belonged to our group, we several times had to take the rap for the various scrapes he got into. No sooner had we arrived at the special camp than, true to form, he lost his temper with the officer in charge of the guard at morning roll call, calling him a Fascist swine. With one punch the officer knocked Volodya off his feet and then kicked him again and again while he was on the ground. He was then given ten days in the punishment cells. All this happened even before we had a chance to settle in, and we learned of the incident from eyewitnesses. Not long after, Volodya was written off as mentally ill and shipped off to Karaganda with a party of invalids.

After Pavlik and I had become close friends, I initiated him into my "prisoner's code." I lost no time preparing the younger people traveling with us for what they would have to face, and thus, by virtue of the first, ninth, and tenth commandments, making them into fighters who would stick together and never yield to provocations from the Chekists. I continued this work during my term in the special camp. Thanks to my course of instruction many of them were later able to participate in the series of awesome events which were eventually to involve all of us. Our morale was high in those days. How satisfying it was to find myself among seasoned warriors—men who had been jailed not for invented crimes but for tangible acts of resistance against the regime. When the time was ripe, they would deliver blows with weapons of their own forging.

Even in the pre-war years, most *zeks* had been of the right kind—given the proper conditions they, too, would have been ready for action, but they would inevitably have been betrayed by the spineless party members who joined them after the great purge of 1937. Under such circumstances only a war could spark off effective action among them.

The Blessing

One day, while en route to the special camp, the front car—the one our group was in—stopped squarely on a crossing near a whistle stop. Solzhenitsyn and I had been lying on the top bunks and talking. When the train came to a halt, we looked out of the window. At the crossing gate stood a small woman of about forty. The wrinkled, high-cheekboned face, with the peculiar slanting set of her eyes, indicated that she was either a Mordovian or a Chuvash. Her dark clothing was shabby and patched all over. She was wearing broken, worn-down boots and thick stockings of coarse homespun. An old, faded kerchief was tied peasant-fashion under her chin. In short, everything was of the usual standard of poverty found among the general populace. For a long time now, squalor had failed to rouse our notice because it had become so commonplace. Suddenly we both sat up to attention: large tears were streaming from the woman's eyes. Having made out our silhouettes inside the detention car, she lifted a small, work-calloused hand and blessed us with the sign of the cross, again and again. Her diminutive face was wet with tears. We kept staring at her; we simply could not tear our eyes away. The train started to move again; still she continued making the sign of the cross, no doubt in the hope that her blessings would travel with us. After a few seconds she vanished from sight, for we were separated from the windows by the corridor.

Who was that poor woman? How many of her family and friends had the Chekists destroyed? How much anguish had fallen to her lot? A suffering woman had blessed us on our hard journey, and Sanya and I carried away in our hearts that beautiful image in ragged clothing.

Many times in my life I have received blessings from priests. But the blessings of the tiny, heart-weary woman at that nameless whistle stop affected me just as deeply as the Pope's benediction during my stay in the Eternal City years later.

Peschanlag-Steplag

In preparing for World War III, Stalin operated under his favorite catch-phrase of "strengthening of the home front." More and more people on the old blacklists were arrested or rearrested, and their numbers were swollen by a mass round-up of Jews, carried out as part of the struggle against "rootless cosmopolitanism." Other victims included biologists denounced as "Weismanist-Morganists," and anyone who had even the remotest connection with the "Oppositionists."[8] People regarded as potentially dangerous—particularly war veterans—were henceforth to be put in special camps (*osoblags*)[9] organized in 1948 and given code names on the orders of the Great Paranoiac, who was afraid by now of his own shadow. In these new camps the same system established in the hard-labor camps back in 1943 was put into force and the inmates of these

8. I.e., the oppositionists in the Communist party. Show trials of these people were held in 1936–1938. (See also chapter 8.)

9. Among them were Rechlag at Vorkuta, Berlag at Kolyma, Ozerlag in Taishchet, Dubrovlag in Mordovia, Peschanlag and Steplag in Kazakhstan.

were now transferred to the *osoblags*. Once again, the regime displayed its blatant contempt for its own laws by unceremoniously transferring prisoners originally sentenced to ordinary "corrective" labor to the new special camps where they were made to do *hard* labor. Our contingent, for instance, was bound for Ekibastuz in Kazakhstan which was at first part of Peschanlag and later of Steplag.

At the end of August, 1950, our transport was handed over at Pavlo-darsk Prison to the armed escort that would convoy us to Peschanlag. I had seen many such escorts in my time, but the sort of cutthroats who made up the present one I had only heard about. Though it must be said we were a pretty tough lot as well and were never behindhand in express-ing our sentiments. Among the "Westerners," as we used to call the Ukrainians from the western provinces of their land, a good many wore crosses around their necks. During a body search a guard laid his paw on the cord attached to my crucifix, but he didn't pull it off. (I had fashioned the cross from a toothbrush handle.) The guard looked at me question-ingly, no doubt wondering whether I belonged to the Ukrainians. More than the other prisoners in our group, I was at his mercy, since I had notebooks that he might decide to confiscate. Without resorting to shouts or curses, I announced quite firmly that I would not take a step any-where without my crucifix. Having learned his lesson from militant prisoners on previous transports, he didn't dare afford himself the pleasure of snatching away the cross; so he left it—and my notebooks—in peace.

We were loaded onto three-ton trucks, twenty-five men and their baggage to each vehicle. The forward part of the van was separated from us by metal caging and reserved for three or four guards with carbines. The trucks raced over the roadless steppe. Through the twilight hours and the night, the guards shot off one flare after another into the sky. When they let us off along the way to relieve ourselves, we had a perfect opportunity to disarm them and drive back as far as the edge of town. But those of us who were recognized as the leaders of our group were not ready to gamble on an escape attempt just then.

Before the night was over, we reached Ekibastuz. In spite of what we had been told in advance, many still hoped right up to the last minute that we were not being taken to a hard-labor camp. But they realized their mistake as soon as they saw work-supervisors and other "flunkies," all with numbers sewn onto their clothes in the prescribed places. In answer to our questions, we learned that the food was sufficient, that there were no "goners"[10] here, that parcels from home were allowed,

10. See note on p. 52. (Tr.)

that the discipline was very strict, that the daily guaranteed ration was seven hundred grams of bread on non-work days as well as on work days. We also found out there were almost no criminals here, nor any women. We were further told that it was no easy matter to get off hard labor on the strength of one's special skills. Besides the guardhouse—a stone structure with damp, unheated punishment cells—the camp also had a barracks with barred windows which was surrounded by watchdogs and barbed wire. This was the so-called BUR, a special punishment block. All the other barracks also had barred windows and the doors were kept locked throughout the night. None of this was exactly news, since back at the *sharashka* former inmates of the special camps had given us much advance information.

Two days after arrival, we were issued with the standard camp garb and an artist from among the prisoners traced our numbers on with paint. Then we were split up into brigades (work gangs) and taken out to do our first job—digging foundations for Finnish pre-fabricated houses. Two weeks later, we began to work as bricklayers. Since I was not getting packages from home, I had to husband my strength. It was therefore essential to reduce the amount of time I spent at hard labor, especially since the tenth commandment in my code forbade me to become a burden on others. I tried to help the brigade leader to write up the work sheets, and the first few times I added incidental tasks (which we had actually performed), such as hauling sections of the prefabs from one site to another, I also put in all the time we had to stand around doing nothing because of inefficient management. But the foreman—a free employee—simply crossed out all these items, and it became clear to me that his attitude made it impossible for me to be of use. In these conditions, I advised the brigade leader to get the prisoners to do only as much as was required to earn the "guaranteed" minimum bread ration—you only needed to do thirty percent of a day's work quota to qualify for it. Most of the "Westerners" were already getting parcels from home, so the prospect of a short ration didn't worry them all that much.

It wasn't long before another engineer and I had a stroke of luck: we landed jobs in a woodworking factory and were assigned to a small machine shop there. We were asked to handle the problem of repairing a device for making liquid oxygen. It stood in a half-ruined state in a temporary building that had been hastily put up around it. The machine had been kept outside under a tarpaulin for a whole year and as a result the inner surfaces of the cylinders in the compressors had rusted. Fittings had been pilfered and the documentation on it had been used for making cigarettes. Armed with the seventh commandment in the prisoner's code and recalling how Till Eulenspiegel[11] had painted portraits of the grand-seigneurs, I announced with unshakable aplomb that I would undertake to repair the device and get it into working order. But I was quite clear about what I was doing: knowing how the Soviet system of supply worked, especially at the level of the camps, I was sure that before the needed materials could be obtained, my term of imprisonment would be over.

Where there is a will there is a way. After about three months I had figured out exactly how the whole thing worked and made drawings for the necessary new parts. I wrote an application to the supply department for everything needed to bring the device back into operation. At the Irtysh Coal Trust[12] they could see very well that it would be much simpler to get a new machine than to obtain even a tenth part of what I had specified in my order and they dropped the idea altogether. During this time, I got to know the engineers in charge of the main machine shop. In "special camps" transfers to other units were not encouraged, nor was the utilization of engineers in their special fields. But my new friends came up with a plan whereby I would fill the post of a brigade leader who had been transferred elsewhere. I couldn't refuse it, so for a two-month period I took the brigade out to the work area—which meant that I had nothing to do all day long. On my own initiative I therefore did some engineering-design work and soon won recognition from the head of the machine shop who was a free employee. He was now able to arrange for me to work with him as an engineer, and I then handed over my job as brigade leader to Solzhenitsyn, who through the autumn and winter had been doing ordinary hard labor. I felt it my duty to provide my friend with a breathing space that would allow him to devote time to his creative work.

With the advent of the warm weather, Solzhenitsyn began reciting to us from his first work, a long poem called *The Road*. Toward evening we would gather outdoors, sitting on our quilted jackets that we spread out on the drying ground, and would listen with rapture. Solzhenitsyn has a fantastic memory and knew by heart the whole of his poem with its

11. The chief character in Charles de Coster's novel. For six months Till gave the appearance of painting the portraits of illustrious men. Finally he invited in his subjects and showed them a plain white canvas, declaring that only men of true noble blood would be able to see their portraits on the canvas.
12. Mines in Kazakhstan.

thirteen hundred lines. In order not to omit anything, he checked off each stanza on a rosary which one of the Ukrainians had given him.

Seven years later, with exile already behind us, I once asked Sanya when he happened to be in Moscow for a brief stay about the fate of that first work. He replied that he had come a long way since then and that the poem had a number of weaknesses—he felt it was long-winded and repetitious—but that he would set about revising it. I strongly urged him to leave it exactly as he had recited it to us in Ekibastuz. If he felt the need to write a poem in accord with the formal literary canons of the fifties, then he could go ahead and compose another one. I would be extremely disappointed if he has ignored my advice and destroyed the original of that unique, inimitable memorial to those years in the hard-labor camp. For me it overflowed with youth, strength, and purity of spirit.

A monument should be erected to Solzhenitsyn while he is still alive and it should represent him in a dark quilted jacket and a fur hat with ear flaps, as a bricklayer taking a rest from his work on a new wall (which should be done in black marble), his neck wrapped in a towel, his eyes gazing into the distance, his lips whispering lines of verse, and in his hands the prayer beads. This is how we saw him as each week he recited for us new stanzas from his steadily growing poem.

It was extraordinary how he composed new lines in his head the moment the images and ideas came to him. He almost never committed anything to paper. That would have been too risky. One evening he was unable to find a sheet of paper on which, by way of an exception, he had written something down. It failed to show up anywhere in the barracks. All night he tossed and turned on the hard bunk. When the call for reveille sounded, he was already by the door, ready to take off the second it was unlocked. He carefully retraced his steps of the previous day and—wonder of wonders!—found the piece of paper, written in his inimitable hand, just where it had dropped into a crevice between a couple of stones on the roadway. Sanya had to do his creative work while being constantly spied upon; if that scrap of paper had fallen into the hands of the camp Chekists, they would have rigged up a case against him. At that time he was still going to his bricklayer's job every day. We were proud that a writer of the highest caliber was developing in our midst. His quality was already obvious in those days.

The transfer of an entire brigade from one job to another was far more easily effected than the reassignment of an individual prisoner from brigade to brigade. I was therefore able to get three brigades assigned to the machine shop. All three were made up of people of the right kind—and among them was Pavlik.

At that time Stalin's fear and distrust of people had reached its peak, as can be seen from a brief description of his extraordinarily swollen system of surveillance in the camps. First there were the camp guards; then the Chekists representing the Ministry of Internal Affairs (MVD) and those from the Ministry of State Security (MGB); above these was the mysterious representative of a section known as "K" or "M" who, according to rumor, reported directly to high-ranking members of Stalin's palace guard. Special quarters were allotted to each of these various groups of security officers in the camp.

The camp and another zone around it were both surrounded by barbed wire. Man-traps consisting of sharp-pointed stakes were set into the ground and tilted at forty-five degree angles in the direction of the prisoner's living quarters. Between the two barbed-wire fences there was a wire with leashes for specially trained shepherd dogs. A strip of earth just outside the fences was always kept plowed so that anyone trying to escape would leave clear prints on the freshly upturned earth.

The jailhouse with its punishment cells, the "special regime" barracks (BUR), the prisoners' quarters with barred windows, the rows of barbed wire that surrounded the zone, the watchdogs—all this had a permanently depressing effect on the weaker spirits among us.

The BUR

For the lightest infraction a prisoner could be put in the BUR. Inmates consisted mainly of people who had attempted to escape or refused to work, as well as religious believers who spent all their time saying their prayers. Before going to the BUR you first had to do a spell in the punishment cells. One of the regular inhabitants of this cheerless place was a Hero of the Soviet Union,[13] Major Vorobyev, who set the standard for everybody else who contemplated escape while doing hard labor. There were ten others like him, and they also spent most of their time in the punishment cells and the BUR. The tactics of these "escapers" were always the same: when they were made to do particularly back-breaking jobs, they would haul the driver out of a dump truck that had come to pick up a load of stone and three of them would climb into the cab, and anybody else wanting to could jump on behind. Then they

13. The highest award in the U.S.S.R.

would take off, ramming through the gates and tearing down the road as fast as the vehicle would go. From the sentry towers ringing the quarry, the guards would open up with machine-gun fire at the wheels of the truck. The escort guards who had brought the prisoners there would aim at the tires with their automatic rifles and puncture them. From the camp headquarters jeeps would rush in carrying reinforcements armed with submachine guns. The prisoners would be pulled down off the dump truck and then beaten, but not severely, since it had not been necessary to go out and look for them—the whole business would have been enacted in full sight of everybody, and without any resistance from the prisoners who knew they could not possibly succeed. As a matter of fact, the guards rather enjoyed it all: it offered an easy way of earning praise from their superiors without over-exerting themselves. Once more the "escape artists" would be put in the punishment cells and then in the BUR, and the whole cycle would be ready to start over again. I tried to learn from Vorobyev what motivated them to resort to such a futile technique. He explained that his own idea was to get away to Moscow and tell the Supreme Soviet about what was going on in this camp. I could only smile at this. I, too, had once made an unsuccessful attempt to escape, so it was easy for me to see the mistakes in other men's attempts. Any man who takes it upon himself to make a break for freedom has to be prepared for everything, including resistance to his pursuers; otherwise, he is merely deluding himself and playing games with the camp authorities. Escapees without weapons who offer no resistance are bound to be caught. But if they obtain weapons, they thereby make it plain that they are prepared to sell their lives dearly, and for this reason the Chekists may even allow them to get away altogether. Many looked on the "escape artists" from the stone quarry as heroes. Certainly they had to have plenty of guts to try to make a break in broad daylight under a hail of bullets. In order to lift the morale of the other prisoners, we used to stress that aspect of these escapades. As for my own opinion about them, I expressed it only among my intimates and asked that they keep it to themselves.

As the BUR filled up with men who took a more practical approach to things, methods of escape changed, becoming more rational and less desperate. Soon after our arrival the giant Estonian sailor Tenno and his diminutive companion ducked under the barbed wire one night after lights-out and, thanks to the fact that there were no dogs around, successfully escaped from the camp area. They managed to get across the Irtysh River and beyond Omsk, where they fell victim to their own spinelessness and were recaptured.

Sensible attempts at escape took the form of tunnel-digging which started beneath the BUR itself and continued out beyond the zone. Once, almost every inmate in the BUR made his escape along this underground passage.

But the most clever and successful breakout was carried off by two prisoners during a fierce blizzard. Throughout the night snow had swept into heavy drifts against the barbed wire, completely covering it over, and the prisoners crossed over the packed snow as if it were a bridge. Since they had the wind at their backs, they unfastened their quilted jackets and made sails of them by spreading them wide open and holding them out with their arms and hands. The wet snow[14] had formed a hard crust that wouldn't give way under foot. While the blizzard lasted, they were able to cover nearly two hundred miles and arrived at a small inhabited place. There they got rid of their rags with the numbers on them and merged with the local inhabitants, who gave them refuge. They were lucky to have landed among the Chechens.

The Chechens and the Ingush are closely related Moslem peoples of the Caucasian region. Most of them are determined and courageous. They had at first believed that Hitler would free them from the shackles of Stalinism, and when the Germans were finally driven from the Causasus, Stalin ordered their resettlement, along with other minorities, in Kazakhstan and other parts of Central Asia. Many of their children, as well as the sick and the elderly, perished. But the Chechens were very tenacious of life and liberty and were thus able to survive this barbarous deportation. Their chief strength lay in their religious faith. They settled down in closely knit communities and in each village the most educated man among them took upon himself the duties of the mullah.[15] They tried to resolve their differences and quarrels by themselves, without resorting to the Soviet courts. Despite government-imposed fines, Chechen girls were not sent to school at all, while the boys went only for a year or two, long enough to master the rudiments of reading and writing. Thus a protest of the simplest kind, made in a direct, palpable manner, enabled the Chechens to win a victory for their nation. Their children were brought up to have some idea of their religion, if no more than the most basic one. They were trained to respect their parents, their nation, and its customs. They were taught to hate atheism, and would not be tempted to boil in this particular cauldron, no matter what inducements were held out to them. There was constant friction with the authorities: Stalin's

14. The temperature was hardly below the freezing point.
15. A Moslem priest. (Tr.)

minions played their usual dirty game, and many Chechens ended up behind barbed wire. They were reliable, brave and strong-minded people. You didn't find stool pigeons among their kind. If one did crop up, he was doomed to a short life.

In later years after my release, I very often held up the Chechens as an example to my acquaintances, suggesting that they should learn from them the right way of standing up for their children, of protecting them against a pernicious, unprincipled regime.

One person who was permanently confined to the BUR was the religious ascetic, Tverdokhlebov, one of those members of the Orthodox Church who had gone underground, belonging to what would be called in the West the "Catacomb" church. He had arrived in the camp together with several other members of his secret brotherhood, which had a long name that I don't remember and which flatly rejected the official Soviet church headed by the Patriarch Aleksi. They were well informed about the vile misdeeds of the venal princes of the church, and denounced them as representatives of the anti-Christ. They considered themselves the true Orthodox Christians, who recognized no innovations, and resisted the temptations of our era. The brotherhood was led by a woman and her two sons; they had all been given twenty-five-year sentences. They came from the working class—mechanics, metal workers, miners, truck drivers. Before their arrest, they had lived in the Donets Basin, famous for its coal mines. At the transit prison in Kuybyshev, there had been fifteen or so of these people, and I got to know them while we were all there together. Only three of them wound up with me in the camp. Tverdokhlebov was a highly qualified mechanic and fitter for compressors, diesel engines, and pumps. From his replies to a series of technical questions that interested me, I could see that he was a real expert at his job.

Upon arriving at the camp, he categorically refused to have the numbers put on his clothing, regarding them as the brand of Satan and thus offensive to a Christian. To avoid serving this same Satan, he refused to do any work whatsoever; he would not take any food from the kitchen because it might have contained animal fats, which he did not eat on principle. He consented to take only bread and sugar. However, on Wednesdays and Fridays he gave the bread away to his barracks mates. He spent all day and part of the night in prayer and in meditations on spiritual subjects. He had almost no religious education, but the clarity of his understanding and interpretation of the truths of Christian doctrine was absolutely amazing.

He endured countless days and nights in the punishment cell, enough to kill an ox. Each time he came out, he was more lean than ever. There was no point adding anything to his sentence, for he already had twenty-five years to serve. After trying out every means of coercion at their disposal, and having utterly failed to break his indomitable will, the authorities finally gave up and allowed him to satisfy his modest demands. After this the Latvian orderly in the BUR, probably at the instigation of the authorities, began to make fun of him and several other men who were always at prayer. We set the orderly straight, advising him to get out altogether if he valued his neck; so he asked to be transferred to the camp jail. It was becoming fashionable to ask to be locked up at one's own request!

At the transit jail in Kuybyshev I had got acquainted with still another ascetic who now spent much of his time in the BUR. He had been dressed in the cassock of a novice monk and thus stood out conspicuously from the others. He settled himself near the slop bucket by the cell entrance. We immediately offered him a nice spot on the bunks, but it wasn't long before he went back to his original place. For a few hours in the daytime he would lie curled up on his meager pile of belongings; the rest of the day and nearly all night he prayed. Seeing his devotion to prayer, one or two of the warders, as a token of respect, offered to take him to the toilet separately from the rest of us—an incredible thing, yet I heard it with my own ears. Evidently he belonged to a different branch of the underground church; although his views coincided with Tverdokhlebov's, he was not recognized by Tverdokhlebov's followers because they felt he had no right to style himself a "novice monk." This thin, frail man was also now undergoing the ordeal of hard labor, but he bore it all and emerged triumphant. Many sturdy young prisoners came down with tuberculosis after ten days in the punishment cell, but it seemed that nothing could wear down the religious believers who devoted themselves to prayer.

A good many prisoners were thrown into the punishment cells and the BUR as a result of informers' denunciations. Our good friend Yuri Karbe spent the whole autumn there because of someone's baseless slander to the effect that he had been planning an escape.

People had told us that in the special camps the Chekists had tried to rig up phony cases just as everywhere else, but nothing came of them for the simple reason the majority of the inmates already had twenty-five year sentences, so there was no point in giving them more. Apart from this, the new generation of prisoners, with their militant spirit made life very difficult for their interrogators. These rigged cases also proved useless as a way of intimidating the rest of the prisoners, and might even have led to an explosion of open unrest. It was then that the Chekists thought up the idea of the BUR and began relying on it as a way of punishing the prisoners. But a man in the prime of his years and strength, with front-line experience (of which the Chekists, holed up in the rear, knew nothing), quickly recovered after leaving the BUR, particularly since the food there was adequate. To resort to the old means of wearing prisoners down through overwork and starvation, dear as it was to Chekist hearts, was now becoming impossible: output would have declined sharply and the production schedule of the Ekibastuz coalfield would have suffered accordingly. This had happened in the case of my brigade: in response to the foreman's rejection of the items of *tufta* I had added to the work sheets, we had agreed among ourselves on what amounted to a "go-slow" strike. The work supervisor became alarmed because of lagging output, and when we complained to him about the foreman, he gave instructions to give us higher rations for our work, so that the *zeks* now received top rations for less output. I could see that the prisoners in this hard-labor camp, which was so frightening at first sight, had great bargaining power.

Until the spring of 1951 the situation did not change. The Chekists put great pressure on the informers, but these reported only matters of minor importance and never came up with any major denunciations for fear of reprisals at the hands of the prisoners. All the same, they caused us a good deal of trouble, and many of those whom they had sent to the BUR dreamed of getting even with them the moment they got out. The pressure in the boiler was steadily rising. Conditions were clearly becoming intolerable. We knew for certain that there would be outbreaks of violent protest, though we could not foresee exactly what form they would take. One could feel an approaching storm in the air.

Ekibastuz as it was in our time is described by Solzhenitsyn in his short novel, *One Day in the Life of Ivan Denisovich,* through the prism of a fictitious *rabotyaga.* Of course, in order to describe our hard-labor camp completely one would have to write a dozen such stories. Later on, in the West, Solzhenitsyn indeed published such a book. *The Gulag Archipelago* tells in detail of life in all the prisons and camps from the very beginning of the Soviet regime.

19

AT THE HARD LABOR CAMP
(Continued)

A Setback for the Chekist Terrorists

In the autumn of 1950 I had again begun to work as an engineer when I was asked to repair the device for making oxygen. At the same time, I continued my private researches, which involved quantum physics. To do this, I kept the same hours as in Vorkuta: I got up at four in the morning and worked until seven. During the working day, which began at ten, I contrived to squeeze out another two hours for my studies. After the evening meal, I slept until taps; then I carried on until midnight. I was so immersed in my researches that I took only Saturday evenings and Sundays off for my friends. I did not isolate myself from people altogether, but I now strictly limited my activities on behalf of my fellow prisoners. During the transport and the first two months at hard labor, I had tried to pass on to my intimates the benefit of my experience, along with the commandments I had formulated at Vorkuta, especially emphasizing those which called for the determination to overcome great odds. I came to an understanding with my comrades that in the event of emergencies I would try to help, but I begged them not to involve me in routine matters. At the same time, we agreed that we should leave Solzhenitsyn pretty much alone and not distract him from his literary work.

Reports came to us of a fire that had broken out in Dolinka,[1] where

1. A settlement in Kazakhstan, approximately three hundred miles from Ekibastuz.

sections of our Peschanlag camp were located. Most likely it was a case of arson and mutiny. Shortly afterward, a transport of prisoners arrived in our zone from Dolinka. They made it known around that there were no stool pigeons among them, that they were able to talk aloud about things we would confide in low undertones only to our closest associates. On the job they all behaved rather out of the ordinary: they took sunbaths, sat around talking, and smoked. They told a supervisor who was supposed to come and inspect them once a day to mind his own business and not interfere in the work of the brigade. When the supervisor threatened to write down the number of the prisoner who had answered him back, the latter announced gently, but firmly, that he spoke on behalf of them all, so the supervisor must write down everybody's name. Then they demanded that the free employees in charge of the building site should write out the work orders beforehand and pass them on directly to the brigade. They spoke their minds about the work quotas in the camp, pointing out how preposterous they were, and said they must have been dreamed up by an idiot or a juggler. They recommended that the man responsible should demonstrate himself how he thought they could be achieved in practice while they just watched and smoked. They then proceeded to haggle over the work quotas with much ribaldry and leg-pulling, eventually settling for a most favorable arrangement which enabled them to count in all their incidental jobs and always assured them of the guaranteed minimum bread ration. In the evening, whenever a guard called someone out for the punishment cell or the BUR, the prisoners made it clear to him in a courteous way that Mykola or Stasik had come down with a bellyache that day and couldn't therefore be allowed to go off by himself, so they would all go with him to the BUR together. If the jailer tried to lay a hand on Stasik, a solid phalanx of his brigade mates would form around him. At the same time they would smile and talk amiably to the guard, even offering him a cigarette. The authorities realized they were no longer capable of handling these men. Without stool pigeons it was impossible to know what they were saying among themselves or what their mood was or who their ringleaders were. They hence decided it would be best to split up the prisoners from Dolinka and disperse them among the other brigades. The Dolinka men were by and large Ukrainian Benderists, Vlasovites, and Lithuanian Robin Hoods. They knew how to use carbines and machine guns; but since they never had a chance to acquire any civilian skills, none of them was qualified for work in our machine shop.

There were now some ominous events. In the loft of a neighboring barracks the body of someone who had hanged himself was found. From my thirteen years in the camps I remember only a handful of suicides—except, of course, for people driven to despair while under interrogation. My comrades had the same suspicion as I, and soon afterward we learned that the suicide had been an exposed informer. Two weeks later, on separate building sites, two stoolies were murdered in one day.

Adjacent to the camp hospital was a barracks filled with young men suffering from tuberculosis. They had contracted the disease while in the punishment cells, usually in the wintertime. They had all been victims of informers, on whose account the BUR and the punishment cells were never empty. Vengeance and hatred against the informers were mounting and awaiting release. The Dolinka prisoners, now scattered among various brigades, gladly passed on their methods of dealing with informers.

In the unceasing battle against the informers the methods varied according to changing circumstances. In wartime the forces of nature, as well as the conditions of hard labor, which some stoolies also did, made it unnecessary to take any special measures against them. At Vorkuta the authorities themselves despised informers and sent them down to the mines, where criminals soon finished them off. At the *sharashka,* resistance in any tangible form against squealers was not possible because, for one thing, security was far too tight there. But at the hard labor camp—something quite new—informers were done away with in broad daylight by their own victims. This naturally provoked the liveliest discussion among us.

All my life I had been opposed to terrorism in any form and had always supported the struggle against it. But in conditions of unabated Chekist terrorism against prisoners in the camps, informers became instruments of terror, and were, in effect, terrorists themselves. Under those circumstances the elimination of a notorious informant who had caused the death of several prisoners and undermined the health of many others was an act of self-defense and self-preservation in the face of terrorism. One had to cut off the tentacles of an octopus. The fact was, the informer always chose to let himself be used in this way. He wormed himself into the trust of others, sounded out their views, provoked them into giving themselves away, wrote denunciations against them, lied about them, and slandered them.[2]

2. The informers may be likened to Leninist agents, whose activity was aided by money from the German general staff in 1916–1918. The agents appealed to our troops to abandon their positions and stop the war that we were so close to winning. Those turncoats should have been court-martialed in the field. The cowardice and apathy of the Provisional Government led the nation to ruin.

The informers carried on an endless secret war against the prisoners. At our hard labor camp both the stool pigeons and their masters were too zealous in their harassment of the prisoners, despite the fact that they were doing their jobs well and, in general, behaved well, even though they had been unlawfully transferred to the status of hard labor prisoners. It was, therefore, only a matter of time before the informants received their just deserts.

Retribution was carried out systematically. During the course of eight months forty-five informers were done away with. Operations against them were directed from a clandestine center, evidently composed of several prisoners from the Dolinka transport. We saw how a number of stoolie prisoners, unable to stand the threat of liquidation that hung over them, sought to escape their fate by getting themselves put in the camp jail—the only place they could hide from certain retaliation. They were all kept in the same cell, which was dubbed the "funk hole." This merciless action against the informers severely hampered the work of the Chekists—without their secret collaborators they could neither see nor hear what was going on.

Hoping to reduce tension in the camp, the Chekists tried to bluff us into believing that they were going to reduce our sentences. They would summon one of us and ask what town he'd like to settle in after his release, and when he replied that he still had twenty-three years to go, they would say:

"No, you won't have to stay in that long. Your case is being reviewed."

It was all too obvious, and before long we began laughing in their faces at this nonsense.

Next they made clumsy attempts to provoke bloodshed among prisoners of different nationalities. For instance, they tried to stir up trouble between the Ukrainian Benderists and the Moslems (Chechens, Ingush, Tatars, Azerbaijanians). But we saw through their plan and brought it to nothing. The man in charge of all the camp guards, Lientenant Mochekhovski, a Chekist who had served with Kovpak's[3] Red Partisans, worked especially hard to arrange a St. Bartholomew's Night. We often saw him nosing around in the camp. But for the time being at least, the prisoners were out only for the blood of the informers in their own ranks.

3. Kovpak was a famous Bolshevik guerrilla leader during the Civil War. (Tr.)

Strength of Spirit

Since coming to the West, I have read Krasnov's book *The Unforgettable*. The author was at Ozerlag in the years I have reported on. He describes things which, thanks to our solidarity, would have been out of the question among us. The difference is staggering. At Ozerlag they were terror-ridden, meek, unprotesting, and went in fear and trembling of the guards. They were shot, tortured, and made to do work that no human was designed for.

Not all camps were the same. We know that in Hitler's concentration camps they made prisoners stand up and yell, "I am a Marxist swine who sold out Germany!" But nothing came of an attempt to introduce a similar practice at the Spasski Camp, which was populated with invalids, with people dying of tuberculosis or silicosis contracted in the mines at Dzhezkazgan. The camp authorities at Ekibastuz were no more successful when they tried to get us to say "Good morning" to our guards and doff our caps respectfully as they walked by.

In the spring of 1951 occurred what we were later to call the "proud suicide." In one of the construction brigades there was an austere, aloof man of about thirty, a former German or Hungarian officer. He kept himself apart from everybody else, but he was very much respected by everybody else in the brigade. As they were being led out to their work site one day, this man, for no apparent reason, stepped out of the last rank without saying a word and headed straight toward the guards who were bringing up the rear of the column. He had his hands in the pockets of his quilted jacket. When the guards shouted a warning, he did not respond. He was cut down by a hail of bullets from an automatic rifle. No one in the marching column was hit because he deliberately walked toward a guard whose gun was not trained on the men in front. No one ever learned the motive behind his action, but it had a profound effect on us all. It made us aware that there were some truly proud men in our midst. It seemed that by his magnificent way of dying he had fanned our smoldering rebellion into flame. No doubt, he had relatives and friends somewhere, but for the sake of his cold, premeditated gesture of protest he sacrificed everything. Only heroes are capable of such acts.

Up to this time—evidently in accordance with their standing orders— the escort guards had always kept their distance and behaved "correctly." But now, after the "proud suicide," their attitude toward us changed sharply and relations became tense. While they were lining up the prisoners to take them out to work, they called them "fascists," "counterrevolutionaries," *"benderas"*[4]—it was clear that the guards were receiving stronger doses of indoctrination at their political classes. One day, after we had already entered the machine shop, one of our men could not be accounted for; so the guards ordered us back outside and beyond the sentry post. But the prisoners had by now all gone to their various departments, and the brigade leaders refused to comply with the guards' instruction, suggesting instead that they re-count the men at their work locations. This incident was typical of the kind of resistance we put up in those days. The brigade leader who protested loudest of all was our Pavlik. The guard commander invited him to go out as the prisoners' representative to the guardroom and make his explanations there. The trap was too obvious for words. None of the prisoners' leaders happened to be there at the moment, and Pavlik, guided less by prudence than by reckless bravery and a desire to distinguish himself as a hero, did exactly what the guards themselves had never seriously thought he would do. Resolutely he stepped out from the group of brigadiers and headed directly for the sentry post. Knowing how dangerous this might prove, the brigade leaders rushed off in different directions to call their prisoners together. Within a few minutes, as if in response to a military command, almost two hundred of them had assembled in front of the sentry post, and more came running up after them. Somebody let out a yell: "Release the brigade leader!" and the cry was immediately taken up by a hundred other voices. A couple of minutes passed, and then the door to the guardroom swung wide open, as if it had been kicked. Standing at the threshold was Pavlik, red as a lobster. He made a dash for it over the first ten yards of critical ground, anywhere along which the guards could have gunned him down from behind without any risk of hitting other prisoners. He walked briskly and confidently over the rest of the way to where everybody was standing by the entrance to the shop. In a few words he related what had gone on behind the closed door. He had stood unafraid in the center of the guardroom and was soon involved in a slanging match with the guards, who accused him of "counterrevolutionary sabotage." Although seething with rage, Pavlik showed no sign of it and said, in effect, the following:

"We are the revolutionaries, not you. We're fighting against your jailhouse fascism. For thirty-four years you've been calling yourselves revolutionaries. But it is *you* who are against *us*. It is *you* who are the real counterrevolutionaries. Stuff that in your pipe and smoke it."

His words had a staggering effect on the soldiers. They had never

4. A contemptuous reference to a Ukrainian who had served under Bendera.

heard such a view expressed before. The commandant, who had been momentarily dumbfounded, pulled himself together and ordered his men to seize the firebrand. But it was not so simple—evidently these peasant youths had never been trained in either boxing or judo, and in any case they were just no match for Pavlik. He tossed them aside like kittens and leaped out of the door.

The evident determination of the other prisoners to stand and fight made it impossible for the butchers to act as they would normally have done. As long as he was surrounded by his fellow prisoners both inside and outside the shop, Pavlik was safe. Only through the use of armed force could he be taken. With the atmosphere so heavily charged, it would have been very risky to bring submachine squads into the zone: they could easily have had their weapons seized from them. It was one thing to fire into a crowd from a secure position, and quite another to move into the midst of an enemy who, although unarmed, was firm in his resolve.

The Storming of the Prison

The authorities were now in something of a quandary. In an earlier day the prisoners had gone out to work and meekly submitted to the system, but now the network of informers had been put out of action. The flunkies (*pridurki*) suddenly grew polite and no longer cursed and swore at us. They became wholly receptive to the demands of the brigade leaders. The rate-setter began to call into question the production quotas fixed by the Irtysh Coal Trust. All the brigades were now getting the maximum bread ration. No one was starving, and there was not one single "goner" (*dokhodyaga*) among us. And what was more, every two or three days the prisoners, with no hardship to themselves, donated a portion of their food to those in the punishment cells and the BUR—but not, of course, to those in the "funk hole," where the stoolies had taken refuge. The camp authorities were afraid to make complaints to the central administration: that could lead to their being charged with incompetence. The Chekist sections responsible for gathering intelligence also feared for their hides: they must have dreaded the prospect of an investigation and evidently kept quiet—though it is possible that any reports they may have compiled were simply not forwarded to Moscow by other Chekist sections in Peschanlag, or were salted away in the depths of the Ministries, since nobody wanted to hear about the failures of the Chekists, only about their successes.

. . .

More than five thousand prisoners were concentrated in our camp. The authorities now decided to divide it into two zones so that the Bendera men would be separated from the rest of us. By doing this, they hoped to break our united front and make it easier to track down the ringleaders.

The prisoners suspected of having killed the stool pigeons were languishing in the isolation cells. But their interrogators could get nothing out of them, and in the prevailing atmosphere the authorities had no choice but to start releasing them one by one. Then Lieutenant Mochekhovski, probably with the Chekists' permission, threw certain of the suspects into the cell where the surviving informers had gone for their own safety—he knew that the stoolies would interrogate the suspects under torture. But terrorism bears within itself the seeds of its own destruction and it now worked against the Chekists: by that move they unwittingly destroyed the very foundation of the hard labor camp.

The screams and groans of the suspects could be heard inside the other cells of the isolation jail. After a couple of days, reports of these tortures reached our ears. On January 21, 1952, the machine-shop brigades, as always, returned last to their barracks—those working under shelter of a roof had to put in a longer day. As I was coming out of the mess hall and tucking my spoon inside my felt boot, I caught the unmistakable sound of palings being ripped out of a fence. Klekshin, a model for a character in Solzhenitsyn's *One Day in the Life of Ivan Denisovich* and once a prisoner at Buchenwald, was hard of hearing; nevertheless, he too was startled by the noise. We exchanged glances. Near the main roadway that divided the camp in half, we spotted some dark figures, running and yelling. We could not make out exactly what they were shouting. The isolation jail was adjacent to the guardhouse box, just off to the right of it, and I ran over in that direction. My companion failed to keep up with me and dropped back, evidently turning off to the left, toward our barracks. Some prisoners were tearing stakes out of the fence that ran around the brick-built jail and, using them as battering rams, were trying to knock the bars from the windows of the stoolies' cell. But the bars would not give way. Then they rolled up a barrel of fuel oil, the kind we used for kindling the ovens in the bakery.[5] Three bucketsfull were splashed into the cell, but before they had time to ignite it the machine guns in the watchtowers went to work; the camp guards, called out from their barracks, started firing their carbines from the roadway. Most of the prisoners participating in the operation had

5. The Ekibastuz coal contained up to sixty percent ash and did not burn well at all.

seen service in the war and they immediately scattered, zigzagging and keeping their heads down, just as they must have done during an attack at the front. A minute later, there was nobody in sight. Getting back to our own barracks would have been especially dangerous, because to reach it, we would have had to cut across the road along which the carbines were laying down fire. Making short dashes, we headed for the entrance to the nearest barracks,[6] the one adjacent to the isolation jail, and stood in the doorway there.

I now learned from some of the incensed participants that it had all started on the spur of the moment: a man who delivered bread from the bakery had told the prisoners, just after they had come in tired from the day's work, of the anguished screams from the suspects. They had simply seen red and gone on the rampage without any plan whatsoever, so that the operation had produced no tangible benefits. It would have been better if they had earlier followed the man delivering bread through the door of the jail, tied up the guards, released the prisoners, and then finished off the informers in the heat of the moment. I weighed the possibilities of such a plan while the shooting was still going on.

Suddenly the gunfire stopped, and I made a dash for my own barracks. "Stop, or I'll shoot!" someone shouted. To be caught outdoors at a time like this could mean death. My only hope was that the door to the barracks would not be locked from the inside—I completely forgot that in the hard labor camp the door was always shut from the outside after lights-out. A pair of bullets slammed into the lintel just above my head. I jerked open the door and flung myself into the barracks. Huddled together on the floor in the corridor were some other men who had taken refuge here from the shooting. Within a few minutes Volodya Timofeyev, along with Bogdan and several other youngsters, came running in—it was quite evident that they had taken part in the storming of the jail. There were still a few stoolies left in our brigades, and naturally they made a mental note of us. The shooting was now more by way of warning and hit none of the live targets who had reached the safety of the barracks. Only a few prisoners had been killed, but the guards finished off some of the wounded by beating them with iron bars. The total number of dead did not exceed a dozen.

These events had caught us quite unprepared, and the next day the machine-shop brigades, the most loyal in the camp, just went off to work as usual, as though nothing had happened. We soon realized our mistake. There was no question of completing our production quota that day.

6. This barracks was nicknamed the "Karabas," after a notorious transit jail in Kazakhstan.

Free employees with passes to the shop dropped by constantly and tried to squeeze out of us some details of the event, which somebody dubbed "The Lenin Massacre," since it had occurred on the anniversary of Lenin's death.

That evening we learned to our shame that we had been the only ones to turn out for work. As a token of protest, all the other brigades had refused to do so that day. Justifiably, they damned us as a bunch of scabs. But there had been no effort to coordinate the protest effort— nobody had told us anything about it in advance, and it had not occurred to us to act on our own.

On the following days it was decided to declare a work stoppage and also a hunger strike. It was clear that this time everything was in the hands of reliable leaders. In the barracks the prisoners approved a series of demands to be presented to the camp administration: the calling-in of the prosecutor general of the republic,[7] a halt to repressions, the punishment of the people guilty of administering torture in the isolation jail. Three thousand prisoners stayed inside the barracks, refusing to go to the mess hall or to collect their bread ration. They refused flatly to work. The guards practically went down on bended knees, begging the rebels to change their minds, but people shouted out from the rear ranks, called them butchers and murderers, and asked whether they weren't tired of beating wounded men to death. The guards retreated in confusion. Men who had been receiving parcels from home now brought out the remains of their supplies and pooled them in common; each brigade then organized what amounted to a very nominal meal, since these food parcels had to be kept in the camp storeroom and their recipients were given only enough from them to last a few days at a time. On the first day of the strike, the cooks and bakers went to work, but then they had to carry the food in buckets from the kitchen to the garbage dump. The various barracks kept in touch with each other through the men who delivered coal, and these were told to relay instructions to the cooks not to prepare any more food. The chimneys in the mess-hall area stopped smoking. The camp zone now made an eerie impression. The days were windless and freezing cold. The smoke from the rows of barracks looked like long grey candles. There was not a soul to be seen outdoors; a deathly quiet lay over everything.

On the second and third days of the strike the guards started coming into the barracks again. The prisoners repeated their demands and categorically announced that until the arrival of the prosecutor general there

7. Each republic (in this case, Kazakhstan) in the U.S.S.R. has its own prosecutor general.

could be no talk of ending the strike. From outside contacts we learned some grim news: the Bendera men in the adjacent zone had not joined the strike. We realized that the rebellious prisoners from Dolinka had been split up between the two camp zones, thus making it impossible for them to maintain contact. Toward the end of the third day, from the "Karabas," where the invalids[8] lived, we got an alarming report that they were nearing the end of their strength and wanted the hunger strike to be halted. Somehow we persuaded them not to give up yet. On the fourth day the prosecutor general, along with the top camp administrators, flew in. They walked in and out of the barracks, listened to our demands, but made no concessions. They warned that if we didn't work the next day, we would be tried on a charge of "counterrevolutionary sabotage." From the back rows came shouts: "The hell with that! You've sucked enough of our blood! Let's hear from the prosecutor!" (The prisoners did not believe that this official really was the prosecutor.) Someone yelled: "The prosecutor must punish the guilty, but all you people can do is make threats!"

The prosecutor and his retinue then left the scene, but apparently they had succeeded in intimidating quite a few of the men, and there was talk about ending the hunger strike the next day. The young Ukrainians, including Volodya and Bogdan, argued desperately against it. Finally, it was decided to hold a general meeting to discuss the situation. What else could these youngsters, fine and honest as they were, really do? Stalin had only to lift his finger and they would all be shot in no time. It proved very simple to undermine their shaky, naïve proposals with the usual arguments. It was clear to me that unless I intervened they might very easily give up and make a shameful offer of surrender. During those few days, I began to see distinctly that my own fate had already been decided long ago and that whether I got involved in further actions would make no difference one way or the other. I had been seen running inside the barracks when the shots were fired at me, so that I could in any case expect to receive an additional sentence for my supposed part in setting off a mutiny. This, then, seemed the right time to show that such an accusation against me would be perfectly justifiable.

With no qualms at all I took the floor and began urging a continuation of the strike. I could not produce any very strong arguments in favor of the proposal, for it was obvious that the Chekists were bound to make good their threat of reprisals. But everything inside me said that we must

8. Prisoners who had just returned from the hospital but were not yet going out to work. Nonetheless, they received the guaranteed minimum daily bread ration of seven hundred grams.

not knuckle under—give us another day or two, and we would win an important moral victory. I spoke in vague generalities—something not characteristic of me—and with neither lucidity nor logic. But in front of this particular gathering I had intuitively chosen the surest approach: it was not so much my arguments—though, of course, these were not lacking in weight—as my earnestness that won them over. What I said may be summarized as follows:

— The prisoners in the "Karabas" will quit the hunger strike, but we must not disgrace ourselves by beating them to it: we have already "distinguished" ourselves enough by going out to work the day after the massacre. If anyone here can show good cause why well-fed, healthy men, who get a substantial number of food parcels, should abandon the hunger strike before anybody else, let him speak up. Anyone who betrays the memory of those who were killed will be looked on as traitor to the prisoners' struggle against the tyranny and lawlessness of the camp administration.

— We will end the hunger protest only after forcing the prosecutor and the camp administration to agree to our demands. Later on, of course, they will break their promises. Still, victory will ultimately be ours. We must think not only of tomorrow, but of the day after tomorrow as well. We all have long prison terms, but victory will at least improve the conditions of our existence and the inevitable repressions will be much less severe than in the past.

— For us it will be a trifle to go hungry for a couple more days, but for the authorities it can have a decisive impact on their careers, which are more important to them than anything else.

Solzhenitsyn told me afterward, "Your voice rang out like pure silver. Your whole manner expressed conviction and faith in the rightness of our cause. This was the finest day in your life." Be that as it may, the proposal to halt the strike was voted down. To achieve this I had, of course, compromised myself even further in the eyes of the authorities.

The next day the prosecutor and the camp administrators completely changed their tune. They consented to discuss things with us and promised to make all the reforms we had asked for, to forego repressive measures, to punish the guilty parties within the camp administration. We could clearly see that it was all bluff and that they would most surely have their revenge. But we nevertheless reveled in the joyful awareness that we had carried off a victory. The work stoppage and the hunger strike had lasted five whole days. The authorities now gave us the full bread ration to which we had been entitled for this period—indeed, for the next few

314

days they even doubled it. In addition, we were allowed to watch movies and were given clean bedding. Before long the authorities started inviting the brigade leaders for "consultations," during which they gave them all kinds of assurances. But at the same time they tried to inveigle them into telling what they knew. All this was in preparation for the coming reprisals. The stool pigeons in the "funk hole" were transferred somewhere else, and the prisoners they had tortured were returned to the barracks—only to be removed from the scene as soon as the reprisals started.

Reprisals

Two weeks passed before the reprisals got under way. Then a team of interrogators arrived from Karaganda, and the questioning began. At first, no arrests were made. We had put the wind up the authorities, and they feared that arrests within the camp might lead to renewed outbursts on the part of the prisoners. The first arrest took place outside. While on the way to work, our column was stopped and surrounded by a squad of soldiers armed with carbines and submachine guns. They ordered us to sit down on the ground. An officer whom we had never seen announced that upon any violation of his order they would open fire without giving any warning. The Chekists were obviously enjoying their triumph. The officer then shouted out the surnames of several youngsters who had served as contact men during the hunger strike and who, for that reason, had been noted by the guards. We had all known that reprisals were inevitable, but thought that we might have been able to continue our resistance for another week or two. It would have been better not to let them take our five comrades away—we should just have gone on sitting there for another couple of hours and shouted at them until they got scared and decided to take us on to our work. Moral right was on our side: after all, we had been promised that there would be no repressions. But the leaders of the strike decided otherwise: since there was no way of avoiding the reprisals, they felt that for the present we had no choice but to yield some of our ground and then carry the torch of our common struggle to other places. There was something to be said for this decision, since the Stalinist dictatorship was at its zenith. The boys who had been named got to their feet. They didn't want us to go on sitting around and freezing on their account. They walked over to the guards, who immediately handcuffed them.

After this incident the prisoners in our zone began receiving summonses to interrogations. Most of them returned. The watchword now passed on to everybody was: Try to survive this difficult period and spread the flames of resistance everywhere. It was clear enough that the Chekists would not keep us all here together—one way or another they would fix us and would break us up and disperse us among the other camps.

When our camp area was divided in two, the isolation prison had remained in our half, and the hospital in the Ukrainian part. Doctors were brought over under guard escort to examine the sick, who were then transferred to the Ukrainian zone, if treatment was required. For several months now, Solzhenitsyn had been plagued with a tumor. Before all these ominous events, the doctors had wavered in making their diagnosis, but now, at long last, Sanya managed to get moved into the hospital. So early in February he left us, and the four years we had spent in close contact with each other came to an end; henceforth we would be traveling separate roads.

Much later on, after we had both been released, we met only at infrequent intervals.

On the thirteenth of February I was told not to report for work, and at ten A.M. I was led away for questioning. I knew I would not be coming back, so I said good-by to my friends and asked them to take good care of my belongings, which included my notes on the laws of dialectics, as well as my research on forging operations and other technical subjects. Several interrogators, half of whom were Kazakhs, were waiting for me. They kept exchanging remarks in their own language. To all questions I gave the same reply: "I don't know, I didn't see anything, I didn't hear anything. . . ." Then they tried to blackmail me by theatening to add time to my sentence. But I cut them short: "One more year or ten more years in the camp is nothing compared with eternal life." I had long ago understood how one must talk with people like them, and I now spoke with the utmost independence, even with contempt. Sometime earlier, during the meetings between the camp administration and the brigade leaders, we had been pleased to see that the authorities were not putting an anti-Soviet construction on the recent events and had decided instead to treat them as a refusal to work or a mass outbreak of hooliganism.[9] The authorities were now trying to save their own skins:

9. Five *zeks* were tried on charges of inciting to disobedience and about the same number for killing informers. Two hundred men were shipped off to other camps. Thirty of them were first given six months in the punishment cells and then in the BUR. There were no executions. The Benderists had not been involved in the "refusal to work"; but for their defiant behavior, their protests, and their undoubted

they knew that for failing to put down a political uprising they could all be shot. To the interrogators' questions about my role in the events, I answered that I didn't engage in hooliganism nor keep company with hooligans, and that my only concern was with science (even though—through no fault of my own—I had so far little to show for it!). But, I went on, if they wanted to implicate me in some political case of their own concoction, they should bear in mind that I understood very well why they had chosen to present the whole affair as a matter of "refusal to work" and that, in giving evidence, I would reveal their motive. By this time, however, they were no longer taken aback by such impudence —in this respect I was no different from my fellow prisoners. After a brief exchange in Kazakh, they took me off to the camp jail.

The jail had been erected a year earlier. The brick walls had not properly dried out and there was hoarfrost in the corners, since the stoves were almost never lighted. The window panes, broken during the attack on the jail, had not yet been replaced. The *zeks* tried to block up the holes with rags. Whatever heat there was came from our bodies. The days dragged by and I was not once called back for further interrogation. I was left there for six weeks.

While in jail I made friends with Yusup, a Tatar. Born in Azerbaijan, he was the son of prominent party workers. In 1937 Stalin's satrap, Bagirov,[10] put all of his party colleagues into prison on the grounds that they wanted to split off Azerbaijan from the U.S.S.R. Bagirov himself conducted the interrogations of the principals in the case. With unspeakable Eastern refinement he inflicted the most terrible tortures on his recent colleagues and intimates. At that time Yusup was hardly more than a boy. His nose was broken, and several times he was put in a strait jacket. He became so weak that he got tuberculosis. In his parents' home religion had been completely banned, so as a child he heard nothing at all about the Moslem faith; but under the influence of what he learned from friends and of all that he had lived through, he eventually returned to the traditions of his forefathers. He was a magnificent person, a pure soul that one could always rely on.

Among my other cellmates was a big, strapping fellow, a criminal by

participation in the killing of informers, they underwent severer punishment than any one else. Seven hundred of them were sent to Dzhezkazgan, where for a long time they were taken out to work in chain gangs. But the punishment had little effect—before long they again started causing trouble.

10. Secretary of the Central Committee of the Party in Azerbaijan during the thirties.

profession, who claimed to have served in the Vlasov army. From the tales he told he must have continued to steal and rob while in Germany. Since criminals were not much liked in the hard labor camps, he may well have invented the part about having been a Vlasovite in order to find favor with his fellow prisoners.

Sometime during my first week in the jail, the news went around that the woodworking *kombinat* had caught on fire. Nearly all its buildings were of wood. With Kazakhstan's scorching sun and winds, wood soon turned tinder-dry and would explode into flame like gunpowder. By evening nothing was left but smoldering ashes. The men who were erecting the *kombinat* had all belonged to brigades from the Benderist zone. It was not hard for us to guess whose hand was behind this incident. And I rejoiced that our struggle was being carried forward.[11]

While in the jail I met many different types of men—colorful and brilliant, strong and unbreakable. And life there was very eventful. One night we were awakened and taken to another cell where we assembled for a transport. Before we were sent off, food parcels were distributed to those men from whom they had been withheld while they were in jail. They now began greedily filling their bellies, and there was precious little left over for those of us who had received no packages. Yussup and I were passed by altogether. But we didn't hold it against them—these men had all been in other cells and didn't know us from Adam. I could consider myself very lucky that Lieutenant Mochekhovski, who had conducted the search of our belongings before returning them to us, had overlooked my notebooks. During my harrowing journey as a *shtrafnik,*[12] these manuscripts escaped the vigilance of jailers and convoy guards. All they seized from me was a small book of passages from the Gospels. Far less suspicious-looking articles were taken from men all around me; I succeeded in holding on to my treasures through eleven searches—all conducted very strictly, since we were regarded as a pack of dangerous mutineers.

Our transport made stopovers at Pavlodar, Omsk, and Karaganda. Finally it reached Spassk, which had been dubbed "The Camp of Death" because of the many executions that had taken place there, not to mention the thousands of incurably sick and disabled who were dying there. We

11. I referred to this operation as "The Funeral Pyre of the Vikings,"—a book of this title by Percival Wren was tremendously popular among us. To my mind, all who laid down their lives in the fight against terror were like Vikings.

12. A prisoner sentenced to be transferred to a place of special punishment. It derives from the word *shtraf*—"punishment," or "penalty."

were received and led away as befitted *shtrafniki,* and they kept us under the most oppressive conditions, usually in dungeon-like cells or punishment barracks. But it gave our hearts a lift to read on the walls of all the toilets, "Greetings to the heroes of Ekibastuz!" or similar inscriptions. Strictly speaking, we had done nothing really heroic. We had simply demonstrated things which had been clear to me for a long, long time and which I had constantly been concerned to pass on to others:

— Even under the most trying camp situations it is possible—and necessary—to fight Stalinism.

— On the whole, reprisals for daring, well-coordinated acts are much less severe than for minor infringements of the rules.

— When a man shows his fear of them, the Chekists are brazen, ruthless, and downright bloodthirsty. But they become far less so as soon as a prisoner can discern a weakness, even the slightest, inside their ranks and in their relations with each other. The main thing is always to stand up to them: under a steady attack from men of good will, evil always retreats.

Our strike of three thousand men had shown for the first time that it was possible to wage an open struggle against the tyranny practiced in Stalin's camps, and this at a time when his system of repression and terror had reached its apogee. We had defeated the Chekists and thus destroyed the myth about Stalin's special hard labor camps. And our action had been followed by a whole series of concessions on the part of the authorities. We had pointed the way for all who wished to make a stand against tyranny, against human debasement. The echo of what we had done quickly resounded throughout the Empire of Gulag, eventually making possible the uprisings at Dzhezkazgan, Vorkuta, and elsewhere. All this made great inroads in the slave-holding system in our country.

In telling my story, I have endeavored to be as accurate as possible, taking pains to discard anything that might be dubious or ill-founded. In each new camp I came to I always endeavored to alert people to the terrible dangers threatening us all.

My six-month journey as a *shtrafnik,* my stay in the punishment cells at Spassk, and further run-ins with interrogators, my encounters with ordinary working people, and my eventual transfer to a "peaceful" camp at Karaganda; my release from camp and banishment for life in northern Kazakhstan (which fortunately turned out to be only three years, owing to Stalin's death[13]), all will be described in a second volume of the *Notebooks,* provided that I am granted the strength and the time.

After all the mistakes that have marked man's course through history, it would be desirable not to have them repeated—in either the present or the future.

13. The "Organs" waited eleven years, until 1955, before giving me a certificate of rehabilitation which stated that an order dated August 19, 1944, had been rescinded and all charges against me dropped for lack of evidence.